CW01023526

1642 : LITERATURE AND POWER IN THE SEVENTEENTH CENTURY

Proceedings of the Essex conference
on the Sociology of Literature
July 1980

edited by

Francis Barker
Jay Bernstein
John Coombes
Peter Hulme
Jennifer Stone
Jon Stratton

University of Essex 1981

British Library Cataloguing in Publication Data

1642: literature and power in the seventeenth
century.
1. English literature - History and criticism
- Congresses
I. Barker, Francis
820'.9 PR434

ISBN 0-901726-18-4

BSD CS7

CONTENTS

PREFACE

Following the successful conference on 'Literature, Society and the Sociology of Literature' held at Essex in 1976 it was thought that much might be gained by concentrating future conferences on a particular theme or topic. Accordingly, it was decided to plan a series of conferences that would focus successively on a number of critical historical moments such as '1848', '1936', '1642', '1789', etc. The ambition is that such a series of conferences and their resultant proceedings will bring together historical and literary theory and research with the effect of making a concentrated and significant impact on the areas they address.

Most of the papers appear here as given at the conference. Terry Eagleton's conference paper will appear as part of his book on Walter Benjamin (forthcoming from NLB) and is replaced here by a different piece. Roger Pooley was unable to give his paper at the conference: we are pleased to include it here.

For their help with organizing the conference and/or producing and distributing this volume we'd like to thank Moira Collett, Eilen Roberts, Margaret Iversen, Diana Loxley and Jean Poynter. We are grateful to the Department of Literature at Essex for financial assistance.

The Editors

University of Essex
March 1981

THE TREMULOUS PRIVATE BODY

Francis Barker

'February 9th (Lord's day). Up, and at my chamber all the morning and the office doing business, and also reading a little of *L'escholle des filles*, which is a mighty lewd book, but yet not amiss for a sober man once to read over to inform himself in the villainy of the world. At noon home to dinner, where by appointment Mr. Pelling come and with him three friends, Wallington, that sings the good base, and one Rogers, and a gentleman, a young man, his name Tempest, who sings very well indeed, and understands anything in the world at first sight. After dinner we into our dining-room, and there to singing all the afternoon. (By the way, I must remember that Pegg Pen was brought to bed yesterday of a girl; and, among other things, if I have not already set it down, that hardly ever was remembered such a season for the smallpox as these last two months have been, people being seen all up and down the streets, newly come out after the smallpox). But though they sang fine things, yet I must confess that I did take no pleasure in it, or very little, because I understood not the words, and with the rests that the words are set, there is no sense nor understanding in them though they be English, which makes me weary of singing in that manner, it being but a worse sort of instrumental musick. We sang until almost night, and drank mighty good store of wine, and then they parted, and I to my chamber, where I did read through *L'escholle des filles*, a lewd book, but what do no wrong once to read for information sake. And after I had done it I burned it, that it might not be among my books to my shame, and so at night to supper and to bed.'

from *The Diary of Samuel Pepys*, entry for 9th February 1668

The scene of writing, and of reading, is, like the grave, a private place. We must explore the contents of this privacy, in relation to what is publicly speakable, and draw the diagram of the structure of confessions and denials of desire that gives this passage its peculiar numinosity, and, in principle, as a representative, a special place in the history of the bourgeois soul.

In Pepys' chamber, unlike the quiet tomb in which the dismembered but visible body of Marvell's beloved was recently interred, if not echoing songs, at least ghostly mutterings can indeed be heard, rustling among the feints and side-steps of the text's involuted speech. Where in Marvell's poem sex was the objective, publicly invoked and celebrated, and death the price of its refusal, here we have entered a different, secluded domain to which sex has been banished; a silent bedroom, traversed by whispers which intimate - of necessity, obliquely - a sexuality which cannot any longer be frankly avowed.

The discourse of the Navy Office clerk is, no doubt, attenuated. That is part of its charm and is certainly the stylistic register which has characterised its reproduction and transmission in the history of writing. Not too verbose, barely literary; after all that rhetoric that preceded it, a breath of fresh air. With the verbal excess of the Renaissance behind us, not to say _sotto voce_ those other excesses of the recent revolution, we emerge at last into a clear, known world of facts and events, of business and leisure, and into a discourse appropriate to that world. A discourse shorn of its ornaments; a plain style for our bourgeois times. At least, this is how we have been taught to read Pepys' text by those commentators who have identified its significances for us in a way characterised by nothing so much as a plainness, an obviousness given in the image of a mind writing down mundane events according to the clear order of their unfolding, providing a text whose regularities, it is said, are determined only by the pattern of the empirical, whose transcription it is. 'Up, and at my chamber all the morning and at the office doing business'. This is the discourse we have learned to read, which in its unalterable presence leaves us strictly nothing to say. Nothing further can be said. Everything is here and now, perceived and written down. What is beyond perception is never paused over. The text is not a fiction and cannot thus be criticised. We have been trained to read in silence, fixed by its light, taut factuality - by a small technique of sensibility rather than a grand gesture of power - into the inexorable domain of the quotidian real.

And we have acceded in this discourse to a social reality which is, whatever dangers it may hold, essentially simple. It is here, there, given, waiting to be written down. Clarified already in its commonsense existence, life needs only the perceiving mind and the writing hand to become text, tracing and recording its contours. The apparency of the bourgeois world and its texts is born.

There is probably a good deal to be said about what might be called the conservative value of discovering and promulgating this description of the discourse of the clerk. Especially important would be the way in which this text, or at least the assumptions governing the reading of it here cited, might come to stand in for discourse itself, for all discourse, and would then function to abolish not only the history of style that precedes it, but all history, the aura of its relative antiquity enticing us to become knowing enough to smile at its little proprieties and to appreciate in the world it reflects those picturesque differences that momentarily block, and thus freshen, our recognition of how like our own world it really is. Doesn't plainness of style, and the epistemological naivety it suggests, thus function as a guarantee of profound identity, allowing us across a gulf which we call history but which by the very nature of this particular claim to intelligibility is nothing more than the deployment of sameness along a chronological axis, to glimpse and embrace in Pepys, the 'man' rather than the text, the duration and durability of the affections, pleasures, discontents and even - let us not be too superior even in our admissions of equality - the petty vanities which are truly our own? Textual good sense would come to dominate not only the rightness of the world's appearances, but also the inexorability of the domain of time itself, the sign, in other words, of a radical incapacity for essential change.

Yet, for all that, the plain style works as a mask, or at best a detour, for both Pepys, the 'I' that writes and is written, and for the commentators who have reconstructed what turns out to be so little of him. The material history of the text ought to provide a converse image of this mystificatory clarity. A text ciphered and partly coded, hidden in a difficult early seventeenth century short hand, written in secret and kept locked away during Pepys' lifetime (and him driven blind by it), bequeathed, lost for so long a period to the _public_ domain; against what odds of obscurity has all this imputed transparency been achieved. And at what risk, or perhaps promise, of truncation of the bourgeois soul it has come to represent.

It is most signally in the practice of writing advanced by the text itself that this foreshortening is achieved. The passage deploys two recensions of the same alibi on either side of an interpolation which is, in part, parenthesised. Perhaps this is the typical structure of all bourgeois discourse? At any rate, the a-libi-dinous justification of reading 'for information sake' belongs properly to what has been called hitherto the discourse of the clerk, and no doubt also provides, in general if not actually by the local authority of these particular lines, the basis for the informational mode of reading that has characterised the reception of Pepys' text.

But what is remarkable here is not the relative lack of opacity of the self-deception (to and for whom is Pepys writing this secret text?) but the indirect, although nonetheless urgent, manner of its self-exposure in another discourse within and around that of the clerk. Unspeakable in their 'proper' place, the pleasures of the lewd text, _L'escholle des filles_, surface, and are in turn denied, elsewhere; in confessions and disavowals apparently disconnected from their real source, the guilty reading, yet forever connected back to it by the sign of their very excess over the textual motivations which only apparently justify their actual disposition in the passage.

So, the proposition that Pepys reads the lewd text over 'to inform himself in the villainy of the world' (the grammatical third person is significant, as if, which is the case, he is trying to speak of someone else, another self, although 'in' speaks eloquently if ambiguously of where Pepys already thinks he is in relation to the sin of the world) barely succeeds in even containing another discourse, one concerning desire, disease, the mess of the body and its passions, that disrupts and intrudes upon the calm order of plain speech. In spite of the steps the discourse of the clerk takes to forestall these others, and of the fact that, arguably, this is its principle _raison d'être_, it nevertheless ruses with itself, and becomes self-treacherous.

In this way we can begin to understand the precision of verbal usage which otherwise looks erroneous. The item 'yet _I must confess_ that I did take no pleasure in it', which purports to refer to a certain kind of singing that Pepys despises, provides an efficient instance. The whole passage is dominated by its initial 'Lord's day', which functions doubly: from an 'informational' point of view it is a temporal mark - all the Diary's Sundays are identified in this way - but discursively it is an admonition whose minatory value must be contained within the punctuational cordon sanitaire of the bracket within which it has been confined. But the insulation that separates the 'Lord's day' from the rest of the passage is not impervious to every kind of charge. While it serves effectively to permit the efficient pursuit of 'business', which is mentioned, unproblematically, in passing, it otherwise merely redoubles the anxiety associated with the lewd reading. So that when we come to Pepys' comment on his lack of enjoyment of the singing, a religious idiom is incited. Singing is perhaps bodily enough a practice to have given the right clues without such an overt confession of the need to confess. In any case, only truly Pepysian efforts of common sense, or informational reading, could avert the recognition that what is at stake here is the simultaneous admission and denial of the furtive pleasures of the French text, displaced onto an apparently innocuous, and, significantly, public and social pastime. By the same token it is not perhaps too frivolous to suggest that the tongue loosened by alcohol has its part to play here. The 'sober man' of informational reading, the bourgeois citizen grave in the dignity of his public demeanour, is, we can now see, almost inevitably not just one who has drunk 'a mighty good store of wine', but one who must blurtingly confess himself to have done so.

The text employs massive means - not of repression, for everything is said, eventually; even if it is not acknowledged as having been said - but of diversion: we are asked to look 'by the way' at 'other things'. But just as no amount of raucous singing by Pepys and his friends will ever drown out the loquaciousness of the half-silence in which the forbidden book is enjoyed, so, the more the text denies interest, diverts attention, only the more clearly does it identify its unacknowledged drives. No doubt, as the empiricist would have it, the parenthesis of smallpox and childbirth at the centre of the passage is simply part of the 'day's residue', faithfully noted by the honest recorder. But why these sentences, just here, deployed in quite this relation to the others? Can it be with total fortuitousness that Pepys speaks 'by the way' of a young woman 'brought to bed' in an idiom not only of child-birth but of sexuality (as if the connotative, and indeed material connections were not explicit enough)? And to speak in the same breath of disease, dis-ease, an affliction punishing the body so loathed by Pepys, as by any sober man on the Lord's day, and moreover, a privatised affliction after which people are 'newly come out' to be 'seen all up and down the streets'. The connotative relations established here are clear: from the bedroom to the public scene; from sickness to health; from private, sick sexuality to sexless public health.

It is the same 'fortuitousness', which is uncanny but far from arbitrary, that governs what we are told of the quasi-mythical Mr. Tempest. Envied for his youth, and his sexuality (we now know what the metaphor 'sings very well indeed' means), he is also feared for his perspicacity. Truly a tempest come to disturb the calm order of the bourgeois *domus*, a man who 'understands everything in the world at first sight', as if, a good sight-reader of music, his ability will flow over, to penetrate the concealments and immediately see through to the hidden text with which Pepys pleasured himself that morning and which he will surely take to bed with him that night. It is because of the threat represented by Tempest that Pepys finally burns *L'escholle des filles*, to finally make sure. In the presence of such a seer it is not enough to hide the text, like the *Diary* itself, in layers of cipher and, at the moments the language of prurience calls most 'frank' in a garble of foreign languages (see how Pepys *tells* his desire that the truth of his own text should not be read - 'I understood not the words ... there is no sense or understanding in them though they be English'), but all that guilt must be absolutely consumed by a cleansing, purifying fire. The smallpox of sexuality is to be cauterised by a sacred flame, just as London itself, visited for its sins by plague a few years earlier, is then purified by fire.

So. An image of a man. A typical man. A bourgeois man. Riven by guilt, silence and textuality. Forbidden to speak and yet incited to discourse, and therefore speaking obliquely in another place. Who says sing when he means fuck, who fears sex and calls it smallpox, who enjoys sex and calls it reading, who is fascinated and terrified by texts and so reads them once, but only for information's sake, who is sober and drunk. Who would rather burn his body, who would rather go blind, but who, as in the storm of rage with which he tears, elsewhere in the Diary, his wife's pathetic love-letters, obliterates the texts instead. A representation of a representation, moreover. Behind it all, not even an adulterous act, but an act of reading. A lewd book.

In all this we can now see the fate of that citizen for whose civil liberty in the context of opposition to pre-publication censorship of writing Milton had argued in Areopagitica. For one thing he is classically mad. The structure of Pepys' discourse conforms precisely to - using one example among many possible - R. D. Laing's semi-theoretical diagram of the schizoid subject: a public persona and an intermediate self which are not 'really' the subject's own (that part of Pepys which consumes the pleasures of the French text is not really Pepys, the Diary tries to say), and within both of these a disembodied 'inner self', in the case of Pepys, the 'I' that writes the text itself. And as the transactions of this passage show, the bourgeois citizen, constituted in his area of private freedom, has been made to work, as Althusser said, 'all by itself'. No longer a matter for licensing by the state, in any of the senses possible here, the bourgeois subject becomes self-censoring. The I that writes deletes from its own text the unacceptable, or at least allots it to a marginal or parenthetical status, but from which it nonetheless threatens to return.

This is now, finally, the precise status of the body and its passions. Descartes probably started it, as we can see in that famous passage from the Discourse on Method (which might also have served as an epigraph for the present paper) where he affects to deny a certain kind of responsibility for what he is about to do to philosophy:

> 'So my intention is not to teach here the method which everyone must follow if he is to conduct his reason correctly, but only to demonstrate how I have tried to conduct my own. Those who take the responsibility of giving precepts must think themselves more knowledgeable than those to whom they give them, and, if they make a mistake, they are blameworthy. But, putting forward this essay as nothing more than an historical account, or, if you prefer, a fable in which, among certain examples one

> may follow, one will find also many others which it would be right not to copy, I hope it will be useful to some without being harmful to any, and that my frankness will be well received by all.'

We have encountered 'frankness' before, and this is, of course, the last thing Descartes is being here. There are at least two ulterior strategies at work in this text. The easy, reasonable tone which is given throughout to the conversational _persona_ who utters the _Discourse_ is essentially a device of seduction, designed to lure the putative non-philosophical reader on along the path towards the quite outrageous proposition Descartes will advance. But this passage is also one among many in the _Discourse_ where Descartes seeks to evade the conditions of censorship, and of less direct but no less dangerous ideological censure that he anticipates - rightly - that the text will encounter. Indeed, it has been argued that the _Discourse_ as a whole is a kind of Trojan Horse intended to smuggle through the scientific work which was for Descartes the proper centre of his discursive activity, although we remember him, of course, more for the _cogito_ and those famous dualisms.

But at any rate, the disclaimer is there. For whatever reasons, Descartes, while no doubt committed to his text, does not make the strongest of claims for its Truth. On the contrary, what he offers is a particular kind of exemplary narrative, a fable,which, among other things, implies an already-constituted reader equipped with the critical techniques that will enable him or her to sort out in the _Discourse_ the valid from the false. The important point here is that the modern subject which is to dominate bourgeois thought, that lonely _ego_ which, at the crucial step in the argument, the moment of _cogito_, doubts the existence of everything except its own thinkingness, even including, significantly enough, the existence of its own body, emerges within an implicitly censored narration.

But it usually comes as a surprise to first-time readers to find, eventually, after the absolute erasure of the body and all other objects 'of a corporeal nature' in the instant of the _cogito_, that when Descartes has established the existence of God and reconstructs the external world, the outcome is that long exposition in the fifth part of the *Discourse* of the structure of the heart and the circulation of the blood. In a similar way, the entirety of the sixth (and last) of the *Meditations on the First Philosophy in Which the Existence of God and the Real Relation Between the Soul and the Body of Man is Demonstrated* is devoted to describing and accounting for the body. For all the *cogito*, it turns out that the health of the body is the highest good and the end of philosophy.

In Descartes' text, and even more clearly in that of Pepys, the body is consigned to what can be described, borrowing a term from Derrida, as a supplementary status. Neither wholly present, nor wholly absent, the body is confined, ignored, exscribed from discourse, and yet remains at the edge of visibility, troubling the space from which it has been banished.

This passage from the *Diary* and this situation is a destination for the seventeenth century, and a beginning for ourselves. But this should be said carefully. Neither should be conceived teleologically. Just as not every beginning is an Origin, so not every outcome is a teleological goal. It is not as if everything that went before had to lead to this text, to this settlement, still less can it function in respect of ourselves as a once and for all determination of unalterable consequences. But rather a cardinal point of self-understanding which can only be identified by virtue of that hindsight which is no more than the capacity to fashion here a genesis for some of our own conditions and dilemmas. A topical key to structure, not a magical cause.

Enough of the past is lost, and looks in any case so different from different points of vantage, for history itself to be regarded as no more (and indeed, *no less*) than a present fiction which must be constructed obliquely or directly according to the often only half-apprehended order of contemporary needs and struggles. Not everything in the seventeenth century led inexorably to Pepys (who knows or can *now* care what other possibilities were lost?): it is enough that the seventeenth century now leads to this text-man, alone in his chamber with his discourse and his sex; raging, solitary, productive.

[This paper is part of a larger project which will eventually trace a path from the spectacular publicity of the Elizabethan and early Jacobean stage, across the revolutionary struggles of the 1640's, to the private conditions of Pepys' secret journal. In the version delivered at the Essex conference, elements of the larger design were sketched in by reference to texts by Descartes, Marvell and Milton. Here, apart from the opening allusion to Marvell's lyric 'To his Coy Mistress', and some discussion of Descartes, these analyses have been largely set aside to undergo a more thorough development elsewhere; the present version concentrates on the *terminus ad quem* of this local history, in Pepys.

F.B. 6th October 1980
Hirsholmene, Danmark]

SEVENTEENTH CENTURY WOMEN'S AUTOBIOGRAPHY

Sandra Findley and Elaine Hobby

We decided to write about women's autobiography because of our political commitment as feminists to reclaiming and rereading forgotten women writers. The exclusion of women's writing from the literary curriculum is a part of the wide-ranging subordination of women in our society today. This exclusion is justified by the use of aesthetic criteria which are gender, as well as race and class based. We are not asking for these texts to be added to a list of recommended 'minor writers'. We want to challenge the ideological assumptions which have led to the dismissal of women's writing and of women's experience. This does not mean to say that we expect to find women's experience represented untransformed in the texts we examine, as we hope this paper itself will demonstrate.

All of the autobiographers we are looking at were born between 1620 and 1625, reaching womanhood in the 1640's. They belonged to the first generation of women who grew up with the shift in the meaning of marriage which was to constitute the foundations for the bourgeois love marriage of a later generation. This shift, beginning early in the seventeenth century, saw the importance of the financial situation of a future wife start to give way to a re-strengthened emphasis on the need for female moral worth.

This 'moral worth' was not a nebulous concept, but absolutely specific. It referred to a woman's sexual chastity, known variously as her 'honour', 'honesty' or 'reputation'. Lawrence Stone(1) has pointed out the difference in the meaning of the word 'honour' when applied to a man or a woman in this period:

> 'A man's honour depended on the reliability of his spoken word; a woman's honour on her reputation for chastity.'

Female sexual chastity has virtually always been considered important in the constitution of femininity. In tracing the history of female protest in these seventeenth century women autobiographers, we are claiming that whilst certain demands and threats have been made to women throughout history and across cultural barriers, both the forms of the subjection, and the forms of protest have their own specificity.

In 1621, the first Lord Montagu advised his son, 'In marriage looke after goodnes rather than goodes'.(2) Stone notes, however, that this sort of advice was most widespread amongst the gentry, and that apart from Lord Montagu the only peers to express themselves in these terms were Archibald Marquis of Argyle and Dudley Lord North, both writing in the 1660s. Since we could add to these Sir James Halkett and Charles Rich, this attitude may not have been as simply class-specific as Stone suggests.

In a broader context, the shift in the meaning of marriage was part of what Michel Foucault charts as the move from a society of blood to a society of sexuality,(3) where the mechanisms of power came to be addressed to the body. The address to the body took different forms for women and men; the recurrent metaphor describing the relationship between husband and wife in this period was that of the head and the body:(4)

> 'The man is as the Head, and the woman as the body ... And as it is against the order of nature that the body should rule the head: so it is no lesse against the course of all good order, that the woman should usurpe authoritie to her selfe over her husband, her head.'

By 1650 the need to maintain the bodily chastity of married women had reached such an extreme that adultery by a woman became for the first and only time in this century a capital offence.

The love marriage was a way of containing women's bodies which asked women to submit voluntarily to sexual monogamy in ways which might appeal to them. Significantly, the love-match placed an enormous burden of conflict on the woman: what was important was where and how she loved, not simply the loving itself. In law, though, a woman was wholly dominated by her husband. The virtual obliteration of the married woman is graphically described by a writer known only as T. E., the author of The

Lawes Resolution of Womens Rights which appeared in 1632:(5)

> 'In this consolidation which we call wedlock is a locking together. It is true, that man and wife are one person; but understand in what manner. When a small brooke or little river incorporateth with Rhodanus, Humber, or Thames, the poor rivulet looseth her name; it is carried and recarried with the new associate; it beareth no sway; it possesseth nothing coverture. A woman as soon as she is married, is called covert; in Latine nupta, that is, "veiled"; as it were clouded and over-shadowed; she hath lost her streame. I may more truly, farre away, say to a married woman, Her new self is her superior; her companion, her master ... All (women) are understood either married, or to be married, and their desires are to their husbands, I know no remedy, yet some can shift it well enough. The common laws here shaketh hands with divinitye.'

It is because women were almost entirely circumscribed by their husbands that these autobiographers write predominantly about their relationships with the men in their lives. Men set the limits within which women could struggle for their female version of bourgeois individuality. This leads to the curious fact that our paper, whilst wanting to deal with these women as interesting in themselves, can only talk about them in relation to their husbands.

The seventeenth century is marked by the development of a sharp division between two separate spheres - the private, where the woman belonged, and the public, which belonged to the man. The writings of Hobbes and Locke nowhere consider the possibility of the inclusion of women in the States they describe. Margaret George has suggested that the fundamental 'bourgeois personality' was male, that individual man was both subject and object of the new society.

We see these autobiographies as different attempts to negotiate the boundaries of femininity. None of the autobiographers can be called feminist, if that involves having a conscious political ideology. All of them, though, articulate the problems they experience as women, and/or offer various forms of protest.

It should become clear that these women come from different classes, though all of them are bourgeois or aristocratic. They also have varying degrees of commitment to opposing sides in the Civil War. We do not wish to deny these differences or to suggest that a detailed class analysis might not shed further light on how they came to write as they did. We are, however, uneasy about any attempt to fit women into a class theory which has been developed in ignorance of the existence of women, and which pays no regard to women's different relation to the mode of production. In this paper, our primary interest centres on these women's exploration and challenge of their femininity.

Because of the marginalisation of women's writing and women's experience by both literary ideology and by male bourgeois and marxist historians, we have to explain who these writers were. Naming the women itself presents a problem, since they all change their names during the course of their stories, when they change their father's name for their husband's; that is, when they cease to belong to their fathers, and become their husbands' property. To avoid confusion, we have referred to the women by the name they use themselves, that is, by their husbands' names.

Anne Halkett was born in London on 4th January 1623. Her father, Thomas Murray, was tutor to Charles I. Her mother, Jane Drummond Murray, was later governess to the Duke of Gloucester and Princess Elizabeth. Both of Anne Halkett's parents were, she tells us, at different times provost of Eton College:(7)

> 'For all recompence to my father's care in discharging his duty, hee was made Provost of Eton College, where hee (li)ved nott long butt died when I was butt three months old; yett itt seemes the short time hee lived amongst these prebends, they were so well sattisfied both with him and my mother that affter my father's death they pettitioned to have his place continued to my mother a yeare, which was never before granted to any woman. And during her time they all renued there leases as a testimony of there respect and desire to give her that advantage.'

She did not marry Sir James Halkett until 1656, when she was 33. She lived for 28 years after his death, and during this time wrote the majority of the twenty-one volumes, or eight thousand manuscript pages, which make up her works. Her interest to the male historian lies in the fact that she helped in the escape of the Duke of York, later James II.

During her exploits in the Royalist cause Anne Halkett met and fell in love with Colonel Joseph Bampfield, a Royalist spy. Bampfield had been separated from his wife during the Civil War because they took opposing sides in the conflict. The Colonel maintained to Halkett that his wife was dead, and claimed to be in love with Anne herself. However, from time to time news reached Halkett that the Colonel's wife was in fact still alive. On each of these occasions she fell ill:

> 'I began to have great debates with myselfe, and the conflict betwixt love and honour was so great and prevalent that neither would yield to the other, and betwixt both I was brought into so great a distemper that I expected now to end all misfortune.' (p.57)

The conflict between love and honour which brings Halkett to the brink of death arises from social demands for her sexual chastity in an above all monogamous marriage. She had entered into an engagement for a future marriage with Bampfield. This placed her in an uneasy position because the kind of engagement she had made would not be clear to other people, and anyway the nature of the contract she had made was itself the subject of legal controversy. In this period there were two types of spousal: either a commitment to marry spoken in the present tense, which made a marriage with or without the presence of a priest; or a spousal *de futuro*, by which two people promised that they intended to marry. Both forms of spousal became a marriage once the relationship had been consummated, but the spousal *de futuro* did not itself constitute a marriage, and either person could marry someone else. Legal cases concerning whether or not the spousal *de futuro* was binding continued to be fought into the eighteenth century.[8] Halkett's engagement was probably a spousal *de futuro*:

> 'I did consentt to his proposall and resolved to marry him as soone as itt appeared convenientt; but we delayed itt till wee saw how itt pleased God to determine of the King's affaires.' (p.28)

She went on to write:

'I confese I did justly suffer the scourge of the toung for exposing myselfe upon any consideration to what might make mee liable to itt, for which I condmen myselfe as much as my sevearest enemy.' (p.28)

Later, when Sir James Halkett proposes marriage to her, she refuses because 'I had that tye upon mee to another that I could nott dispose of my selfe to any other if I expected a blessing' (p.76). Halkett endeavours to persuade her that her engagement to Bampfield was not legally binding, but it is not until she has seen a lawyer that she will allow herself to consider marriage.

Anne Halkett evinced neither passionate love nor a willingness to marry Sir James for the status and financial security he could offer her. His attraction for her is that he is 'honourable' and he recognises her 'honour':

'I acknowledged his respect had been such to me that were I owner of what I had just right to, and had never had the least blemish in my reputation (which I could not but suffer in considering my late misfortune), I thought he deserved me with all the advantages was possible for me to bring him; but it would be an ill requital of his civilitys not only to bring him nothing but many inconveniences by my being greatly in debt ... Yet all this did not in the least discourage him, for he would have been content at that time to have married me with all the disadvantages I lay under; for he said he looked upon me as a vertuous person, and in that proposed more happiness to himself by injoying me than in all the riches of the world. Certainly none can thinke but I had reason to have more than an ordinary esteem of such a person, whose eyes were so perceptable as to see and love injured virtue under so darke a cloud as incompassed me about.' (p.77)

Halkett arrived at this criterion for the choice of a marriage partner after failing on two separate occasions to form a love alliance. In an early love affair Halkett's mother had forbidden her to allow the address of her suitor because a marriage with him would put the marriage chances of his brothers and sisters in financial jeopardy. Halkett continued to see Mr. Howard in secret, and it was only when he broke his word to her by falling in love with another woman, that she broke off the connection:

> 'Since he hath made himselfe unworthy my love, hee is unworthy my anger or concerne.' (p.22)

The manuscript of the autobiography breaks off soon after Halkett's marriage to Sir James. The contradictions which she experiences about virtue and marriage are resolved at a social level once she is married. These contradictions show themselves in several ways: in the form of stress-related illnesses; in an effort to find a resolution in religious confession and meditation, and in a deep uneasiness with the power of language to signify her meanings.

The ability of words to convey 'truthful' meanings is constantly called into question by the text. Despite her uneasiness with the signifying power of language, Halkett made use of the ambiguity of words to disobey her mother. When her mother forbade her to <u>see</u> Mr. Howard, Halkett meets him wearing a blindfold.

Halkett's preoccupation with the equivocal nature of words was a contemporary concern of grammarians and philosophers. Locke explained:(9)

> 'But when having passed over the original and composition of our ideas, I began to examine the extent and certainty of our knowledge, I found it had so near a connection with words, that unless their force and manner of signification were first well-observed, there could be very little said clearly or pertinently concerning knowledge.'

The autobiography is Halkett's attempt to justify herself and her actions, where there is a proliferation of possible meanings. It is written out of the twin motives of confession and vindication. Ritual Christian confession is not enough, as it allows the hearer to form her/his own interpretation. This can prevent a confessing woman from protecting her reputation. The centre of the text is Anne's abortive confession to Mr. Nicolls the chaplain, of her spousal <u>de futuro</u> with Colonel Bampfield, who was already married. The immediate effect of the confession to him had been to release tension:

> 'I immediately left trembling and found a great security both of mind and body.' (p.35)

However, Mr. Nicolls uses this confession to bring her reputation for chastity into doubt, and to divide her from her woman friend. The autobiography is written to redress this and to win the reader over to a belief in her virtue. It is for this reason that she says little about a two-year span which, though eventful, contained nothing which might bring her chastity into doubt. She also skates over the events of her childhood, simply saying

> 'What my childish actions were I thinke I need nott give account of here, for I hope none will thinke they could bee either vicious or scandalous.' (p.11)

Although Halkett apparently made no attempt to have her autobiography published, it is constantly addressed to an assumed reader - a reader who is constructed as judge, and therefore given powers of absolution:

> 'Itt is not to bee imagined by any pious, vertuous person (whose charity leads them to judge of others by themselves) butt that I looked upon itt as an unparaleld misfortune (how inocentt so ever I was) to have such an odium cast upon mee as that I designed to marry a man that had a wife.' (p.35)

The pattern of confession and forgiveness belong to traditional Christian practice and ideology.(10) Her need to vindicate herself comes from the specific oppression of women. This produces her apparently contradictory remark about Mr. Nicolls:

> 'though hee had injured mee beyond a possibility of forgiven by any as a woman, yett as a Christian I forgave him' (p.47)

The reader is offered the constant example that her confession should lead to our judging in her favour. For example, during her early involvement with Mr. Howard, her mother sends a woman to reprimand her. Halkett explains the situation, however, and

> 'when shee heard, shee sadly wept and beged my pardon and promised to doe mee all the service shee could.' (p.19)

A woman's honest reputation is exceedingly insecure, and can be lost through what others may say about her. She does not have recourse to fighting anyone who asperses her, as a man does. She can, however, try to take control of the situation through words - explaining, vindicating, confessing.

Mary Rich, the Countess of Warwick, was the youngest surviving daughter of Richard Boyle, the Earl of Cork, one of the richest and most powerful men in Ireland. He successfully arranged the marriages of all Mary's older sisters - two of them being only twelve years old at the time.(11) Mary's intended husband was introduced to her when she was fourteen. Her autobiography deals with the consequences of her refusing to marry him. In addition to her autobiography and her diary, she wrote nearly two hundred meditations.

Mary Rich's writings have been taken up as religious tracts, and so depoliticised, or rather put to a new political use. Extracts from her diaries were printed by the Religious Tract Society in the middle of the nineteenth century.(12) The preface to this edition reads:

> 'On the whole, Lady Warwick stands before us as an eminently devout and excellent character. Her life and writings present to our fellow country women - especially those in the higher classes - a noble picture of true piety, dignity and grace, which the daughters, wives and mothers of England should seek to cultivate and display.'

This account of Rich's activities disguises the fact that women could and did take up religion to some extent on their own terms, giving it their own meanings and uses. There are obvious examples of Rich's contemporaries creating some kind of independence for themselves through religious activities. Keith Thomas, Ellen MacArthur and Ethyn Williams have drawn attention to the existence of women preachers and prophets, and to the practice in some of the radical sects of women leaving their husbands if they did not agree with their own new religious convictions. Particularly interesting in this respect are Quaker women, who argued in favour of women's spiritual and practical equality with men. Several of them wrote their own autobiographies.

There are innumerable places in Rich's diary where an escape into meditation or prayer or reading a 'good book' clearly marks a respite from servicing her husband. These activities were not simply 'liberating' of course. Such passages in her diary are often accompanied by an appeal to God to help her accept more completely her subjection. But within the narrow confines of what was possible, she is staking out some territory of her own. The diary entry for 22nd September 1667 reads:

> 'In the afternoon, was hindered by my Lord's commands from going to church, for which I was much troubled, seeing him so passionate about it; but after my Lady Jane Clifford was gone, I retired, read, and meditated; and after I had earnestly prayed to God to give me patience, and a contented mind in my condition, I was composed.' (p.128)

The fact that her husband experienced her religion as a threat to his control over her, is demonstrated by his cutting down the trees in the Wilderness, the place where she went to meditate. Before he had done this, her diary more than once contains the comment:

> 'In the morning, as soon as my Lord, who that day went to London, was gone, I retired into the wilderness to meditate; my meditation was sweet.'

There is little reference in the autobiography to these experiences which fill the diary. They are merely shadowed in the fact that her first trip to the solitude of Lees is made despite her husband's attempts to dissuade her, and that her autobiography ends with her delighting in being 'a widow indeed'. The absent centre of this text is her disobedience of her father in marrying against his wishes. It is this disobedience which explains for her the great unhappiness of her marriage. Once again it is the diary which reveals this:

> 'The sin that in an especial manner God was pleased to break my heart for was, my disobedience to my father; this sin I did bemoan with plenty of tears, and confessed God was righteous in letting me read my sin in my punishment.' (p.247)

In the autobiography her actual unhappiness in her marriage is guarded by a compulsory celebration that it was her marriage that brought her to her religion:(13)

> 'Here let me admire at the goodness of God, that by His good providence to me, when I by my marriage thought of nothing but having a person for whom I had a great passion, and never sought God in it, but by my marrying my husband flatly disobeyed His command, which was given me in His sacred oracles, of obeying my father; yet was pleased by his unmerited goodness to me to bring me, by my marriage, into a noble and, which is much more, a religious family ...'

Rich's first proposal of marriage had come from a Mr. Hambletone, introduced to her by her father as a possible husband. Her rejection of this proposal suggests that she was hoping to make a love match. In retrospect, Rich justifies her disobedience of her father as a 'good providence of God' since Mr. Hambletone lost his estate in the Irish rebellion the following year. This she comments, she 'should have liked very ill', for if she had married him it would have been for the sake of his estate.

Further offers of marriage followed this one, but Rich declined them all, despite her father's pressure:

> '... the report that he would give me a very great portion made him have for me many great and considerable offers, both of persons of great birth and fortune; but I still continued to have an aversion to marriage, living so much at my ease that I was unwilling to change my condition, and never could bring myself to close with any offered match, but still begged my father to refuse all the most advantageous profers, though I was by him much pressed.' (p.4)

Finally she fell in love with Charles Rich, a younger son of the Earl of Warwick. The decision to marry him was fraught with conflict between her desire to both follow the inclinations of her passion, and to do her duty to her father. The love match did not prove to be a happy choice. Rich's diary details numerous occasions when she was made miserable by her husband's passion. By this time passion no longer signified love, but instead had come to mean anger.

It is the unhappiness of her married life which produced the first half of the autobiography which reads like the romances that Rich recalls enjoying at that time. She delights in his courting her, and in the (only too illusory) power that being the desired lady gives her:

> 'By his more than ordinary humble behaviour to me, he did insensibly steal away my heart, and got a greater possession of it than I knew he had.' (p.7)

He promises to be a kind husband to her to make amends for his lack of wealth, in true romantic style. The autobiography is an attempt to explain and justify the marriage, and reconcile herself to it. She could not write it, however, until Charles Rich was dead.

Rich's story demonstrates that the move to marrying for personal affection, far from being a liberation for women in recognising their individuality, is merely an exchanging of one kind of oppression for another.

Ann Fanshawe was born in London in 1625. Her father, Sir John Harrison, was knighted for his financial support of the Crown. She married Sir Richard Fanshawe in 1644, and over the following twenty years, she tells us[(14)]

> 'had six sons and eight daughters borne and christned, and I mis-carryed of six more, three at severall times and once of three sons when I was about half gone my time.'

After the Restoration, she accompanied her husband on his trips as Ambassador to Spain and Portugal. Her autobiography appears to be the only thing she wrote.

Whereas Anne Halkett's story traces her independent development up to the time of her marriage, and ends there, Ann Fanshawe's autobiography effectively begins with her marriage, and ends with her husband's death. It is addressed to her son as

> 'the most remarkable actions and accidents of your family as well as those of more eminent ones of your father and my life.' (p.102)

Throughout the text she explicitly points things out to him. In this respect it is different from Hutchinson's biography of her husband which, though it opens by addressing her children, rapidly shifts to addressing a far wider audience.

If it is true that Fanshawe has written solely for her son's eyes, this autobiography is the most 'private' of those we have read. This is interesting since its subject matter is the most 'public', dealing almost entirely, as it does, with her accompanying her husband on State business.

The apparent paradox of such 'public' writing being addressed to a 'private' audience directs us to the real contradiction that has produced this text in the form it takes. This becomes clear if we trace her path to contented wifehood. Fanshawe shows us how, in her youth, she had to cease being a 'hoyting girl' and take over the feminine duties of running first her father's, and then her husband's house. Her description of the distribution of power in her husband's household could have been taken straight from the conduct books of the day:

> 'Though he would say I managed his domesticks wholy, yet I ever governed them and myself by his commands, in the managing of which I thank God I found his approbation and content.' (p.103)

She had not yet fully learnt, though, that her preservation was to come from her willingly confining herself to feminine concerns. She describes being tempted by women friends into trying to find out from her husband about State matters. He firmly reproves her, reminding her that though his heart is hers, she has no right to know about the public affairs in which his honour rests. She meekly accepts his direction, and regrets her 'folly ... so vile' (p.116).

Fanshawe immerses herself into her husband, rejoicing in their union:

> 'Glory be to God we never had but one mind throughout our lives, our soules were wrapped up in each other, our aims and designs one, our loves one, and our resentments one.' (p.103)

The absorption of the wife into her husband is interestingly demonstrated in an anecdote which Fanshawe narrates. Trying to acquire a pass for her husband and herself to leave England during the Civil War, when she knows that no such permission will be given to a noted Royalist like her husband, she hits upon the scheme of disguising herself and asking for one in the name of 'Harrison' - her maiden name. The pass is sold her for a crown.

> 'I thanked him kindly, and so immediatly went to my lodging, and with a penne I made the great H of Harrisson 2ff, and the 2rr's an n, and the i an s, and the s an h, and the o an a, and the n a w, so compleatly that none could find out the change.' (p.138)

A woman had to change her name on marriage, changing herself, as Fanshawe says, 'so compleatly that none could find out the change'. Fanshawe here, though, is turning this necessity to her own use. She presumably already knew about the orthgraphic similarities of her two surnames, having had to cease writing the one and begin signing herself with the other. She is uneasy about using her maiden name here, though - a name she no longer has a right to - and makes a point of saying that her husband was amused and delighted when she told him what she had done (p.103).

By accepting the wifely role, Fanshawe gains the reflected glory of being associated with such a man. The passage we quote above about her husband and herself being of one mind continues with the realisation that

> 'to commend my better half (which I want sufficient expression for) methinks is to commend myself.' (p.103)

She also gains an interesting and varied life, as she accompanies him on his trips abroad. She points out more than once that her status as the English Ambassador's wife was such that she was allowed to visit places usually off-limits to women, and given respectful attendance by the aristocrats in the Spanish and Portuguese Courts.

The considerable role that Fanshawe played in her husband's career was far from unusual for an upper class woman during the Civil War years. Alice Clark mentions a large number of women who managed and defended estates during their husbands' absences. She records Dr. Denton's reply to his friend the exiled Sir Ralph Verney who proposed to send his wife to England to attend to his business there. He urged him[15]

> 'not to touch upon inconveniences of your cominge, women were never soe usefull as now, and though you should be my agent and solicitor of all the men I knowe (and therefore much to be prefered in your own cause) yet I am confident if you were here, you would doe as our sages doe, instruct your wife, and leave her to act it with committees, their sexe entitles them to many privileges and we find the comfort of them now more than ever.'

Both Margaret Cavendish and Ann Fanshawe played this part for their exiled husbands. Anne Halkett was instrumental in helping the Duke of York escape from the Palace of Westminster, as well as defending Brampton Castle from the Roundheads, organising aid for wounded soldiers, and managing her own lawsuits and financial problems. Fanshawe helped to secure her husband's release from prison, and she outwitted the customs authorities so that she and her children could join Sir Richard in exile.

That the active lives of Fanshawe, Halkett and to a lesser extent Cavendish should be worthy of comment owes something at least to the subsequent constriction of women's social roles. The marriage of Ann and Richard Fanshawe is a love match, and this love offers a protection where otherwise Lady Fanshawe's behaviour might have been considered unfeminine. When the ship on which the Fanshawes are travelling is attacked by pirates, Lady Fanshawe is sent below-deck so that the pirates, seeing no women, will believe that the ship is a man-of-war and not board it. Lady Fanshawe bribes a cabin boy to give her his clothes so that she can go on deck:

> 'I crept up softly and stood upon the deck by my husband's side as free from sickness and fear, as I confess, from discretion; but it was the effect of that passion which I could never master ... But when your father saw it convenient to retreat, looking upon me he blessed himself and snatched me up in his arms saying "Good God, that love can make this change". And though he seemingly chid me, he would laugh at it as often as he remembered that voyage.' (p.128)

It is because Ann Fanshawe is absorbed so fully into her husband's life that this text is both her autobiography, and the biography of her husband. It trails off rapidly after his death, and is apparently 'unfinished'. Since she achieved what she did through becoming truly feminine, it is not surprising that the autobiography is not addressed to the public world. Such an act would be in direct opposition to the way in which she had lived her life.

Lucy Hutchinson is known as the author of a biography of her husband, Memoirs of the Life of Colonel Hutchinson. The notebook in which the fragment of her autobiography appears also contains some poems. In addition, she wrote two books of religious instruction, addressed to her daughters, and made a translation of Lucretius. In contrast to the other women we are considering, she was a Parliamentarian. The Memoirs trace the involvement of herself and her husband in the events of the Civil War. Whereas Ann Fanshawe's autobiography is also the biography of her husband, Lucy Hutchinson attempted to write two separate accounts of her own and Colonel Hutchinson's lives.

Her autobiography is a brief fragment which is broken off mid-sentence, with subsequent pages of the manuscript torn out. It is not unlikely that following Hutchinson's 'failure' to write her own life, she turned to writing the biography of her husband. Here her reputation is safe, as she constructs an image of herself as a dutiful loving wife, who lives in and through her husband. This wife appears in the Memoirs as 'she', whilst the author is 'I' who can stand outside marriage and is not threatened by the disappearance of the femme covert. However, like Rich, she was only able to write once her husband was safely dead. Cavendish, unlike Hutchinson or Fanshawe, was able to achieve a separation of her own and her husband's biographies. Her Life of the Duke of Newcastle appeared in 1668, some twelve years after Cavendish's autobiography. After publishing the Life of the Duke, she wrote nothing new, and when Natures Pictures was reprinted in 1671 the autobiography was omitted and the title-page altered to hide the omission.

Lucy Hutchinson's early education was unconventional. She could read English perfectly by the age of four, she claims, and by the age of seven she had eight tutors. She notes the subjects they taught her - languages, music, dancing, writing and needlework - and goes on to say[(16)]

> 'but my genius was quite averse from all but my book, and that I was so eager of, that my mother thinking it prejudiced my health

> would moderate me in it; yet this rather animated me than kept me back, and every moment I could steal from play I would employ in any book I could find, when my own were locked up from me.'

Furthermore, her father allowed her to learn Latin. This she learnt so well that she soon knew more than her brothers at school, despite the fact that she was only taught by her father's chaplain who she thought 'a pitiful dull fellow'.

Hutchinson was encouraged by her father in these unfeminine accomplishments which led her into competition with her brothers. However, her mother was not so happy. Hutchinson explained:

> 'My mother would have been contented if I had not so wholly addicted myself to that as to neglect my other qualities. As for music and dancing I profited very little in them, and would never practice my lute or harpsichords but when my masters were with me; and for my needle I absolutely hated it.' (p.17)

Lucy Hutchinson was clearly not the kind of daughter her mother envisaged when after having three sons she 'was very desirous of a daughter'. Hutchinson's transgression of the boundaries of femininity by her attitude to her studies is made clear through the agency of her mother. She was nevertheless able to describe this in her autobiography since, as she makes clear in the Memoirs, it was her learning which first attracted Colonel Hutchinson to her.

The break in the manuscript comes soon after this explanation of her early education. There are in fact two breaks in the manuscript: the final one follows a surviving paragraph which describes her mother's rejection of her when a second daughter is born who becomes Lady Apsley's favourite.

The first break, which like the second happens mid-sentence, occurs when she is about to recount an early love affair with a man who she subsequently realised was unsuitable for her. The sentence which mentions this affair is omitted from the 1905 edition of the autobiography and memoirs.[17]

Whether Hutchinson herself destroyed these parts of the manuscript, or whether this was done later by someone else, can only be a matter for speculation. What is certain is that this destruction tries to ensure that the Lucy Hutchinson who is remembered is she who was the honourable wife and good mother constructed in the Memoirs.

Similar kinds of censorship have been practised on Halkett's and Fanshawe's autobiographies. Passages from Fanshawe's have been deleted, and writings covering the two-year span after the death of Halkett's mother and before her affair with Bampfield have been torn out of the text. Halkett's autobiography also breaks off soon after her marriage to Sir James, where pages have obviously been destroyed. Again, we cannot say whether this was self-censorship or a subsequent interference. Some clear examples of self-censorship are in Rich's autobiography. For example, when Charles Rich was forced to keep away from her for fear that anyone might guess about their relationship, Mary Rich's sister-in-law would plead his cause with her. Originally Rich wrote that her sister 'would so plead for him, that it worked too much upon me'. Left like this, it is clear that Mary Rich regretted having let herself be persuaded to marry him. Later she altered the manuscript, so that her unhappiness in her marriage appeared better disguised. The addition of a comma and the word 'very' changed the meaning of the sentence entirely, so that now it read that her sister would so plead for him 'that it worked, too, very much upon me'.

Margaret Cavendish, the Duchess of Newcastle, was born into the largest land-owning family in Colchester. Two of her brothers fought on the King's side in the Civil War. She joined the Court at Oxford as a lady-in-waiting, and accompanied the Queen to France. There she met William Cavendish, the Duke of Newcastle, who had fled from England after the defeat of the Royalist troops which he had been commanding. When she returned to England briefly in 1653, she arranged for the publication of her first two books, Poems and Fancies and Philosophical Fancies. Between then and 1668 she published in all twelve separate works, some of which went through more than one edition, ranging from natural philosophy, to plays, poems, stories, her autobiography, a biography of her husband, and a collection of semi-fictional letters.

She is known to bourgeois literary criticism as the biographer of her husband. Wherever her name appears, the 'merits' and 'failings' of the Life of the Duke of Newcastle are seriously discussed. It is the only one of her works which has been reprinted several times, and in various editions, this century. Most of these more modern editions also include her autobiography.[18]

Long before the Life of the Duke of Newcastle appeared in 1668, however, Cavendish had written her autobiography. It appeared in 1656 as 'the true story at the latter end' of a book of stories entitled Natures Pictures Drawn by Fancies Pencil to the Life. What distinguishes this autobiography from the others we discuss, therefore, is the fact that it was written explicitly for publication, and was published during the life-time of its author. More than once she explicitly addresses her readers.

In writing for publication, Cavendish goes further than any of these women in breaking into the male, public world. Her work is indeed both produced by this male/female, public/private divide, and extraordinarily self-conscious about its existence. She does not want to be confined and defined wholly by female 'honour', or sexual chastity, but desires the 'fame' which can only come from the male, public world. All of the books open with a series of Epistles to her readers. One of those prefacing Natures Pictures, the book which includes her autobiography, reads:[19]

> 'I confess my Ambition is restless, and not ordinary; because it would have an extraordinary fame: And since all heroick Actions, publick Imployments, powerfull Governments, and eloquent Pleadings are denyed our Sex in this age, or at least would be condemned for want of custome, is the cause I write so much.'

The final paragraph of Cavendish's autobiography explains that she has written it to establish - or, we might say, to construct - her individuality and identity separately from the husband whose name she bears. This passage is also delightfully typical of her writings, as she compares herself aggressively to Caesar and Ovid:[20]

> 'But I hope my readers will not think me vain for writing my life, since there have been many that have done the like, as Cesar, Ovid, and many more, both men and women, and I know no reason I may not do it as well as they: but I verily believe some censuring Readers will scornfully say, why hath this Lady writ her own Life? since none cares to know whose daughter she was, or whose wife she is, or how she was bred, or what fortunes she had, or how she lived, or what humour or disposition she was of? I answer that it is true, that 'tis of no purpose to the Readers, but it is to the Authoress, because I write it for my own sake, not theirs; neither did I intend this piece to delight, but to divulge; not to please the fancy, but to tell the truth, lest after-ages should mistake, in not knowing I was daughter to one Master Lucas of St Johns, near Colchester, in Essex, second wife to the Lord Marquis of Newcastle; for my Lord having had two Wives, I might easily have been mistaken, especially if I should dye and my Lord Marry again.'

There is an irony in the fact that when Cavendish comes to define explicitly who she is, the only criteria she has available to use are the names of her father and her husband. Her actual practice, however, both in her writing and in her day-to-day life, serve to distinguish her from others. She appears in Pepys' Diary as an eccentrically-dressed woman. Her own explanation of her choice of clothes is made in her autobiography:

> 'I took great delight in attiring, fine dressing, and fashions, especially such as I did invent myself, not taking that pleasure in such fashions as was invented by others: also I did dislike any should follow my Fashions, for I always took a delight in a singularity, even in accoutrements of habits.' (p.304)

Although in law Cavendish may have 'lost her streame' by marrying, in her practice she can still distinguish herself from her husband. At one level she may have been subsumed by him; but Natures Pictures includes some passages identified as written by the Duke; they are incorporated into the text, however, as part of the body of Cavendish's work.

Making a bid for fame in the public world could cause Cavendish's reputation for feminine chastity to come into doubt. The conflicting demands of 'fame' and 'honour' combine to produce the autobiography. This is why, although it deals with the publication of her early works, it is overwhelmingly concerned with constructing a picture of her as a virtuous, truly feminine woman. She says:

> 'But whatsoever I was addicted to, either in fashion of Cloths, contemplation of Thoughts, actions of Life, they were Lawful, Honest, Honourable, and Modest, of which I can avouch to the world with a great confidence, because it is a pure Truth.' (p.304)

She says twice of her childhood 'we were bred Virtuously, Modestly, Civilly, Honourably, and on honest principles' (pp.268 and 271). Her modern biographer, Douglas Grant, has accepted at face value her depiction of herself as blushing and retiring when at the Queen's Court.(21)

The fact that the autobiography is written in part to defend her against being thought unfeminine comes out as well in her description of her behaviour during her visit to London in 1653:

> 'Nor seldom did I dress my self, since he I onely desired to please was absent, although report did dress me in a hundred severall fashions.' (p.294)

If we compare this remark with that quoted earlier, where she proclaims her delight in using fashion to make herself 'a singularity', the directly contradictory demands of 'fame' and 'honour' are made manifest.

Cavendish's depiction of her inferiority and obedience to her husband could be taken straight from the conduct books of the day - books which were written to direct women how to behave. She says that her husband married her because she was so shy that he could mould her to his desire. This prolific writer also claims to be silent in his company, hanging on his every word:

> 'Not that I speak much, because I am addicted to contemplation, unless I am with my Lord, yet then I rather attentively listen to what he sayes, than impertinently speak.' (p.297)

We are not questioning whether Cavendish actually <u>was</u> subservient to her husband. The point is that she should repeatedly assert her subservience in her autobiography. It is in keeping with this highly repressive image of her own femininity that she should attack other women who might dare to speak publicly, entering the male sphere, and counsel them to attend to their reputations:[22]

> 'The truth is, our Sex doth nothing but justle for the Prehemi-nence of words, I mean not for speaking well, but speaking much, as they do for the preheminence of place ... but if our Sex would but well consider, and rationally ponder, they will perceive and finde, that it is neither words nor place that can advance them, but worth and merit: nor can words or place disgrace them, but inconstancy and boldness: for an honest Heart, a noble Soule, a chaste Life, and a true speaking Tongue, is the Throne, Crown, and Footstoole, that advances them to an honourable renown.' (pp.290-91)

We mentioned earlier that the bulk of Cavendish's writing has been ignored by literary criticism, which is mainly interested in her biography of her husband. Interestingly enough, she actually wrote nothing new after her presentation of herself in the _Life of the Duke of Newcastle_ as an entirely submissive wife. In this book, she is not present as the controlling author figure in the same way that she is in her other works. When she narrates her journey to England to plead for some of Newcastle's estate, she does not mention her writing and publishing whilst there, which she does describe in the parallel account in her autobiography. She also presents herself as writing not for fame, and from her own inspiration and genius, but firmly directed by Newcastle. He has dictated what should be included and what excluded, she says in the Preface, describing her

> 'submission to his Lordship's desire, from whom I have learned patience to overcome my passion, and discretion to yield to his prudence.' (p.xli)

The contradictions between fame and honour have become so great that silence results, and she is absorbed into the non-identity of the _femme covert_.

This is particularly ironic since she, like Rich, depicts herself as having married for love, although she would rationally have preferred to remain single:

> 'Though I did dread Marriage, and shunn'd mens companies as much

> as I could, yet I could not, nor had the power to refuse him, by reason my Affections were fix'd on him, and he was the onely Person I ever was in love with.' (p.280)

Both Fanshawe's and Halkett's autobiographies have features which were later seen as characteristic of the novel. Halkett's techniques include irony, in her account of her relationship with Mr. Howard, as well as a sustained and sophisticated use of suspense. Margaret Bottrall[(23)] suggests that Halkett's autobiography could be a novel, 'packed from cover to with romance, excitement and suspense'. Bottrall comments further on the novelistic skill with which Halkett handles her retrospective account. Conversations from over twenty years before are recorded as though they are written down verbatim, although in fact they have all been shaped to follow the narrative logic.

John Loftis, the Oxford editor of the autobiographies of Halkett and Fanshawe, comments in his introduction that we are more accustomed to encounter Halkett's style of writing in prose fiction than in seventeenth century biography. He complains, on the other hand, that Fanshawe's text reads at times like the transcription of household lists. Certainly Fanshawe makes a wide use of detailed description which could be considered typically female. However, this description of the Fanshawe's room in Spain is of the quality later used by Defoe in Robinson Crusoe or Moll Flanders:

> 'We were lodged in a silver bedstead, quilt and the curtains and vallances and counterpanes of crimson damask, embroidered richly with flowers of gold; the tables of precious stones and the looking-glasses bordered with the same, the chairs the same, with the bed and the floor covered with rich Persia carpets, and a great brasero of silver filled full of delicate flowers, which was replenished everyday so long as we stayed.' (p.160)

Male writers such as Defoe, Fielding and Richardson used typical features from seventeenth century women's writing. They expropriated female forms of writing and with their privileged access to the public sphere gained recognition and distinction as pioneers of the literary form which dominates the teaching of literature today. It was not until the widespread re-emergence of female protest in the latter half of the eighteenth century that women could reclaim the novel as their inheritance, and find a public voice for their work. Significantly, many of the concerns which emerge as typical in the novel in this period had appeared before in Aphra Behn's novel of 1688, Oroonoko.

These autobiographies were written out of a developing division between public and private life. Whilst men had access to both public and private spheres, middle and upper class women were restricted to the private sphere. Eli Zaretsky(24) has developed Clark's insights into the beginnings of the private/public divide to demonstrate how central this juxtaposition is in the workings of capitalism. The family becomes a 'private sphere', where the individual personality is supposed to find freedom to develop and be itself, away from the competitive workings of the State. Zaretsky's analysis shows that the development of the private sphere was accompanied by a growth in self-consciousness:

> 'One indication of the expansion of self-consciousness was the proliferation of diaries in the seventeenth century. More broadly, the same period saw the invention of silvered mirrors, the spread of autobiography, the building of chairs instead of benches, the spread of private lodgings, and the rise of self-portraits.'

Only twelve known autobiographies were written in Britain before 1600. Over two hundred survive written between then and 1700. The 'sudden' development of autobiography as a form of writing can be situated in a female world of the private and self-conscious. As we said, men also had an access to this realm, but it was one which was determined by their privileged access to the other sphere. In this way they were able to take out into the public sphere what they had relegated to the private.

Of all the writers we have talked about, Cavendish comes closest to breaking through these divisions. She arranges her own entry into the public world through the publication of her texts. It is significant in the context of the future development of the novel that her autobiography was published by her as part of a book of stories. In the second edition of Natures Pictures, though, the stories were reprinted without the autobiography. She is finally silenced by the threat to her femininity involved in this essentially aggressive attempt on the public world.

Footnotes

1. Lawrence Stone, The Family, Sex and Marriage in England 1500-1800 (Weidenfeld and Nicolson, 1977), p.503.

2. Lawrence Stone, The Crisis of the Aristocracy 1558-1641 (Oxford, 1965).

3. Michel Foucault, The History of Sexuality, volume one (Random House Inc., 1978), p.147.

4. Thomas Gataker, Marriage Duties Briefly Couch'd Together [London, 1620], quoted in Margaret George, 'From Goodwife to Mistress: the Transformation of the Female in Bourgeois Culture', Science and Society, 1973.

5. Quoted in Roger Thompson, Women in Stuart England and America. A Comparative Study (Routledge and Kegan Paul, 1974), p.162.

6. George, op cit, p.155. George's argument is stimulating, but its concern to show the evils of capitalism results in a picture of the changes taking place in the seventeenth century which is far too linear.

7. John Loftis, ed., The Memoirs of Anne, Lady Halkett and Ann, Lady Fanshawe (Clarendon Press, 1979), p.10.

8. Gellert Spencer Alleman, Matrimonial Law and the Materials of Restoration Comedy (Wallingford, Penn., 1942).

9. John Locke, An Essay Concerning Human Understanding [1690], ch.9, section 21.

10. For further elaboration of this, see Foucault, op cit, passim and pp.62-4.

11. Charlotte Fell Smith, Mary Rich, Countess of Warwick (1625-1978): Her Family and Friends (Longmans, Green, 1901).

12. Mary Rich, The Countess of Warwick, Diary (the portion from 1666-1672, The Religious Tract Society, 1847), p.xiii.

13. Mary Rich, Autobiography, ed. T. C. Croker (London, 1848), p.15.

14. Loftis, op cit, p.106.

15. Alice Clark, Working Life of Women in the Seventeenth Century (Frank Cass, 1968), p.20.

16. Lucy Hutchinson, Memoirs of the Life of Colonel Hutchinson ... To which is prefixed The Life of Mrs. Hutchinson (Bell & Sons, 1905), p.17.

17. The omitted sentence reads: 'anyone mentioned him to me I told them

I had forgotten those extravagancies of my infancy, and knew now that he and I were not equall; but I could not, for many yeares heare his name, without several inward emotions ...'.

18. Facsimile reprints of Sociable Letters and Poems and Fancies were published by the Scolar Press in 1969 and 1972 respectively.

19. Natures Pictures Drawn by Fancies Pencil to the Life. Written by the thrice Noble, Illustrious, and Excellent Princess, the Lady Marchioness of Newcastle ... Printed for J. Martin and J. Allestrye, at the Bell in Saint Paul's Churchyard, London, 1656. An Epistle to my Readers.

20. The Lives of William Cavendish and of his wife Margaret Duchess of Newcastle, written by the thrice noble and illustrious Princess, Margaret Duchess of Newcastle, edited by Mark Antony Lower (John Russell Smith, London, 1872), p.310.

21. Douglas Grant, Margaret the First. A Biography of Margaret Cavendish Duchess of Newcastle 1623-1673 (Rupert Hart-Davis, London, 1957).

22. The women Cavendish is referring to are, no doubt, those of the radical sects. This remark, therefore, also has origins in her class position and her Royalism.

23. Margaret Bottrall, Every Man a Phoenix (1958), p.149.

24. Eli Zaretsky, Capitalism, the Family and Personal Life (Pluto Press, 1976), p.43.

[The argument about Margaret, Duchess of Newcastle is developed further in Elaine Hobby, The Fame of the Honest Margaret Cavendish, unpublished M.A. thesis, University of Essex, 1979. The argument about Anne, Lady Halkett is developed further in a University of Essex (1979) M.A. essay, Sandra Findley, The Autobiography of Anne, Lady Halkett.]

'SPIRITUAL WHOREDOM': AN ESSAY ON FEMALE PROPHETS IN THE SEVENTEENTH CENTURY

Christine Berg and Philippa Berry

A few years ago, the debate among Marxist feminists over the problem of gendered subjectivity in literature was an extremely heated one. Women who were trying to elaborate a rigorous critical practice which could encompass - and transform - the problematics of both Marxist and feminist critical theory in relation to literature seemed on the brink of a major breakthrough theoretically. Sadly, this breakthrough never quite materialised. Today, feminist theoreticians are doing excellent work in a wide variety of different spheres; but this thorniest of theoretical questions - that of the relationship of gender to literary practice - has yet to be adequately tackled. Our paper certainly does not claim to provide any definitive solutions to this problem. But we hope that it will at least serve to re-open what we consider to be a critical area of debate for feminists and Marxists of both sexes. And perhaps some of the questions which we will be raising within the narrow scope of this paper may help to resituate the controversy on rather firmer ground.

The prophetic texts or fragments of texts which we will consider today cannot be situated within the context of any precise literary function or genre. But in the apocalyptic frenzy of the revolutionary period, when many conventional forms of imaginative literary practice had either completely disappeared or temporarily gone underground, the prophetic medium afforded several women a vehicle for imaginative self-expression which was considerably less restricted than those media of verse and prose formerly available to them. Women writing in England before the revolution, unlike many of their European counterparts, had invariably chosen the most conventional of current literary formulae for their nervous - and usually very brief - excursions into the treacherous domain of a male-dominated literary practice. But however derivative and stale these spasmodic attempts at literary production by women may have been, they were certainly symptomatic of a growing anxiety over the relations between the sexes which eventually came to a head in the explosive events of the 1640's and 1650's. While the anxiety extended well beyond the sphere of literary activity, to society as a whole, it received eloquent expression in several of the best literary works that both open and close this period - that is, the long century which runs from the death of Elizabeth to the Restoration of Charles II. It is within this context - of a near revolution in literary perceptions of the relation between sexuality and language, as well as within the context of a temporary social and sexual revolution - that we have chosen to situate the female prophesyings of the mid-seventeenth century.

Viewed from such a perspective, the irruption of female speech into the once tabooed domain of public activity - both in the religious and political spheres - may be seen as a watershed in a process whose beginning and ending can be traced in specific literary works. Yet sadly, in the last analysis, this process enacted a purely circular movement. Thus the literature of the seventeenth century might most accurately be described as tracing a progression through three distinct stages. In the first of these, which can be distinguished in the Jacobean tragedies of dramatists like Shakespeare and Webster, in the Holy Sonnets of Donne, and in an anomalous play like Middleton's The Roaring Girl, the highly fixed representational procedures of the early Renaissance, wherein men were writing about and representing female sexuality, are visibly under strain. The inscription of the feminine is becoming increasingly problematic. Indeed some of Donne's Meditations and Holy Sonnets break decisively with old representational techniques in their elaboration of a literary process wherein the signifying centre associated with the poet has become explicitly feminine (as opposed to female). What followed this crisis, as the second stage in this literary progression, was a brief moment - that of the 1640's and 1650's - wherein a small handful of prophetesses actually represented their own sexuality within a discussive medium where an explicit political content was subsumed within a highly personalised mode of expression. Finally, this representational cycle might be described as closing in a work like Milton's Paradise Lost, where a highly sensitive exploration of the possibilities of social and sexual revolution is ultimately contained by Milton's reinscription of the erring Eve as a kind of Restoration courtesan. By this means her provocative sexuality, together with all the possibilities which it had opened up within the text of the poem (as well as within the historical juncture of the Revolution), is finally placed - not so much condemned as recognised to represent a tragically lost opportunity, the fading hope of millenarian transformation and release.

The phenomenon of prophecy was of course not restricted to this historical time and place. Nor was prophesying during the revolutionary period the exclusive prerogative of women. Yet it is notable that prophecy in its most exaggerated form - that is, in the form in which it most clearly distinguishes itself from a rational discourse - has much in common with that phenomenon described by Luce Irigaray as 'the language of the feminine', and by Julia Kristeva as the semiotic; while its evident affinities with the discourse of hysteria have frequently been commented upon. We would stress that to confuse such a discourse with a female language, and to see it as articulated merely by women would be a mistake. Freud recognised early on in his career that the phenomenon of hysteria was not restricted exclusively to women. Likewise, a feminine language is one which both sexes may possess. But it does seem clear that the availability of this non-rationalist discursive mode made entry into the domain of politico-religious debate easier for a number of women, whether their contributions to public speech were made within the comparatively narrow confines of a single church or meeting house, or were available and proclaimed within a wider social spectrum. The prophetesses Eleanor Davies, Mary Cary and Anna Trapuel not only published or had their prophesies published by others, they also delivered oracular speeches in various places of public eminence like Parliament or Whitehall. The rough treatment received by many of the prophets of this period (both female and male) as the Revolution progressed - or sought to become more stable - is particularly striking. What emerges, in fact, is an enormous anxiety over the unique phenomenon of prophetic speech, and its refusal satisfactorily to be assimilated into a fixed symbolic order. Yet in what respect exactly did this kind of discourse constitute a threat? We believe that its threat lay precisely in its feminine character. By the sustaining of a multiplicity of various levels of speech and meaning, as well as by relinquishing the 'I' as the subjective centre of speech, the extremist forms of prophetic discourse constitutes an extremely dangerous challenge to conventional modes of expression and control within seventeenth century patriarchal society.

Luce Irigaray's description of a 'feminine' language suffers from a tendency to collapse this notion of a feminine mode of speech into the physical body of the woman, and so revert to a crude biologism. Yet in spite of this deficiency, her remarks are of some interest in the context of this paper, for her description of this language associates with it many of the characteristics of prophetic speech:

> 'First of all I would say it has nothing to do with the syntax which we have used for centuries, namely, that constructed according to the following organisation: subject, predicate, or; subject, verb, object ... There will always ... be a plurality in feminine language. For a feminine language would undo the unique meaning, the proper meaning of words, of nouns, which still regulates all discourse. In order for there to be a proper meaning, there must indeed be a unity somewhere. But if feminine language cannot be brought back to any unity, it cannot be simply described or defined, there is no feminine metalanguage. The masculine can partly look at itself, speculate about itself, represent itself and describes itself for what it is, whilst the feminine can try to speak for itself through new language, but cannot describe itself from outside or in formal terms, except by identifying itself with the masculine, thus by losing itself.' (1)

Irigaray's rather generalised description becomes much more useful and comprehensible, however, when it is related to Julia Kristeva's more sophisticated distinction between the semiotic and symbolic orders. For Kristeva, the semiotic is the site of articulation of the drives prior to entry to the symbolic, a rhythmic and essentially synchronic world into which the categories of time and space have not yet been admitted. Nonetheless it is also the place from which the infant child must emerge on its way to becoming a gendered subject. Kristeva has described the process as follows:

> 'Discontinuous quantities of energy traverse the body of what will later be a subject, and, on the verge of its becoming, they dispose themselves according to the constraints imposed on this body - always already semioticised - by the familial and social structure. Energetic changes at the same time as "psychic" marks, the drives thereby articulate what we call a *chora*: a non-expressive totality constituted by the drives and their stases in a mobility which is dynamic as well as regulated.

> ... The place of the engendering of the subject, the semiotic chora is also the site of its (the subject's) negation, where its unity gives way before the process of charges and stases that are producing it. We will call this process of semiotic engenderment a <u>negativity</u>, in distinguishing it from that negation which <u>is the act</u> of a judging subject.' (2)

As we shall demonstrate below, it was precisely this quality of 'negativity', this process of semiotic engendering, that rendered the prophetic utterances of the revolutionary period so devastating in their socio-sexual implications.

In spite of its avowed hostility to magic and popular superstition, the Protestant Reformation was clearly a key factor in the popular revival of the spirit of prophecy during the latter part of the sixteenth and the early seventeenth century. By virtually abolishing the church's long-established function of mediation between men and God - most clearly symbolised by the mechanisms of the confessional - Protestantism placed enormous stress on the individual conscience and the individual's relationship with God. In other words, it left God speaking directly to his elect. It was therefore incumbent on each separate soul to negotiate their relationship with the deity alone, and given the terrible contemporary fear of damnation and hell-fire, the pressure to achieve divine illumination was immense. Hence prophecy might be described as appearing first of all as a proclamation of one individual's secured salvation and election. This election is subsequently interpreted as an injunction to the prophetic individual to accept responsibility for the public articulation of the divine <u>logos</u>, as part of a missionary or revolutionary programme.

Viewed from the perspective of rationalist epistemology and an increasingly centralised state machinery, this prophetic explosion evidently constituted a severe challenge and its threat was already beginning to be dimly perceived by the end of the sixteenth century. In 1558, John Harvey published <u>A Discursive Probleme Concerning Prophecies, how far they are to be valued, or credited, according to the surest rules, and direction in Divinitie, Philosophie, Astrologie and other Learning</u>. Harvey's aim in this tract was to dismiss the contemporary explosion of prophesying by separating the rational man out from the irrational and mystical man or prophet. His emphasis on the different temperaments and physical conditions of these two 'types' is particularly interesting:

> 'Misticall men pretend divers, and sundry misticall causes; but you must be faire to pardon many sensible and reasonable personages, of good reckoning, and sharp conceit, accompanied with direct consideration and judgement, that will not easily be induced to believe more, than either humane reason shall probably persuade or divine authoritie canonically inforce. I see not any naturall, or supernaturall excellencies: neither am I so melancholique, or furious, as to attribute much unto melancholy, or furie, howsoever some against Morall and Naturall reason account of these moodie, and raving passions, as Delphicall, or Sybilline prophets proceeding in truth of very bad and distempered constitutions, both of bodie and minde.' (3)

It seems not insignificant in this respect that the irruption of a melancholic or irrational passion should become a characteristic feature of early Jacobean drama - an irrationalism which, incidentally, is perceived as most damaging and subversive when associated with women. Jacobean tragedy returns obsessively to the problematic image of the female, and the dark enigma of female sexuality. Indeed, the unstable or indecipherable nature of this element is frequently presented as the direct or indirect cause of tragic catastrophe. This intuition is eloquently articulated by John Webster in The White Devil and The Duchess of Malfi, where the irruption of female desire instigates tidal waves of violence and revenge amidst the masculine communities of the plays. In a comedy like Middleton's The Roaring Girl, although tragedy is avoided, the same essential threat is recognised. The final refusal of Moll, Middleton's androgynous heroine, to discard her masculine attire and be reassimilated into conventional society, is uniquely disturbing.

An atmosphere of sexual disturbance and imbalanced relationships between the sexes is as characteristic of Shakespeare's tragedies as sexual harmony and equilibrium had been of his comedies. Only in Macbeth, however, are these themes explicitly connected with the phenomenon of prophecy. Indeed Macbeth might almost be described as dramatic prelude to the historical drama of the 1640's and 1650's. The eerie opening of Shakespeare's Macbeth presents the audience with a strange encounter -

the meeting between Macbeth and Banquo and the three weird sisters on a deserted heath. Yet this episode might almost be designated the literary prelude to the epistomological uncertainties of the middle of the century. The various critical attempts to explain the function of the witches in a drama of political conflict have had only partial success. But this dramatic interlude has two features which are of particular interest in the context of this paper. Firstly, Shakespeare lays considerable emphasis on the conflict between these two groups, a conflict which he presents as primarily a linguistic one - between two languages and two corresponding modes of perception which might broadly be characterised as a rationalist versus a prophetic semiotic discourse. Between these two discursive modes, Shakespeare suggests, there can be no satisfactory point of contact. Banquo's opening address to the weird sisters immediately acknowledges that the nature of the dilemma facing the two men is essentially one of interpretation. The men lack any adequate system of knowledge within which to place either the witches or their disjointed speech:

> 'What are these,
> So wither'd and so wilde in their attyre,
> That looke not like th'inhabitants o'th'earth,
> And yet are on't? Live you, or are you aught
> That man may question? you seeme to understand,
> By each at once her chappie finger laying
> Upon her skinnie lips: you should be women,
> And yet your beards forbid me to interprete
> That you are so.' (4)

Both Macbeth and Banquo recognise the marginal status of these women to civilised society - a marginality typified as much by their repellent androgyny (now a distorted version of an early Renaissance ideal) as by their 'imperfect speech'. And Banquo recognises the essential incompatibility of prophecy with rationalism as soon as the women have vanished:

> 'Were such things here, as we doe speake about?
> Or have we eaten on the insane Root,
> That takes the Reason Prisoner?' (5)

Macbeth's personal tragedy, however, which ultimately extends to a whole society, derives essentially from his desire to adopt this alien and fragmented communication to serve his own political ends. Thereby he unwittingly unleashes a torrent of fantasies and subconscious desires which transform a rational man into a monster, a demented tyrant who has become wholly prey to his imaginings, of his unconscious mind. Hence Macbeth raises a second extremely important question - how can a prophetic or symbolic discourse safely be assimilated into a rationalist framework? To this dilemma the play finds no satisfactory solution. Yet its central theme - that of the political appropriation of prophecy and its attendant dangers - would become a great political concern some thirty-odd years later.

Amid a dozen or so women recorded as prophesying during the revolutionary period, there are only three of whose prophetic utterances any substantive evidence now remains. These were the Lady Eleanor Davies, Anna Trapuel and Mary Cary. While the Lady Eleanor might be regarded as in some sense inaugurating the political prophesyings of the mid century (she predicted the death of Charles some twenty years before it actually happened), Anna Trapuel and Mary Cary surfaced at a time of extremist revolutionary fervour, and were closely associated with the aims and objectives of the millenarian Fifth Monarchist group. The careers of these women were all characterised to various degrees by enormous fluctuations in their public reputation - fluctuations which can invariably be related to the extent to which their prophesyings were felt to be acceptable or useful by the ruling clique or by any other of the revolutionary groups. The public images of Eleanor Davies(6) and Anna Trapuel in particular oscillated between popularity and notoriety, as periods of public adulation and acclaim alternated with spells in Bridewell or Bedlam. Thus their ecstatic behaviour, together with the alien communications which this engendered would temporarily be validated and assimilated whenever these utterances coincided with the particular political strategy of any revolutionary group or groups; only to be marginalised again, and labelled socially unacceptable, as the flood of their prophesyings proceeded to overrun these short-term political aims and objectives in its apocalyptic fervour. Yet in each of these women, the outpourings of the prophetic spirit takes on a slightly different character, as different relations between the semiotic and the symbolic, between the discourses of prophecy and the status quo, are established in each case.

Lady Eleanor Davies, sometimes called Douglas, married the poet Sir John Davies in 1609. She seems to have led a relatively quiet married life until, in 1625, she suddenly received the spirit of God, and developed a prophetic ability overnight, abruptly appropriating a mode of imaginative inspiration which had formerly been restricted to her spouse. The flood of prophesying which succeeded the spiritual awakening continued for over twenty years, relatively unabated. Lady Eleanor is reputed to have heard a voice from heaven proclaiming, 'There is nineteen and a half years to the Judgement Day, and be you as the Meeke Virgin'. Thereafter she considered herself clothed with the Spirit of the prophet Daniel, calling herself 'elect Lady', 'the Lord, His handmaid', and 'the prophetess of the Most High'. Some of her later prophesies are published with this subscription: 'from the Lady Eleanor: the Word of God'. This summary assumption of divine election was defended quite simply:

> 'As showed in the Scriptures, there is nothing so secret, That shall not bee discovered: And the Clearnesse now of these future things, being come to passe, with the rest shortly to be accomplished; Begets and creates this Boldresse in Mee, to dissolve or breake this precious Ivory-Box of Times and Seasons Mistery: Sharing of the lost day at hand, the happie time of the end.' (7)

Although the Lady Eleanor showed a remarkable degree of self-consciousness (and a shrewd business acumen) in consistently transmitting her prophecies to publication in the handsomely bound and printed volumes, the remark I have just quoted is actually one of very few references to herself as an active and conscious subject in a huge body of prophetic work where subjectivity almost completely disappears, and where conventional subject-object relations are utterly abandoned within an extraordinary fragmented syntactic structure. In a prophecy delivered to Cromwell by Lady Eleanor in 1657, this quality of syntactic chaos is still very much in evidence:

> 'For the Armies General, his Excellency.
> My Lord,
> Your interest in the National unparaleld Troublesome Times:

> The Flaming Sword for expelling the Man in your hand, which crams with no inferior Honor that Name of youre. Hereof by her Hand a touch presented. Derived from his own, namely, A α O. Letters of no mean Latitude: Armed beside with his Sword: Sun and Moon when as stood in Admiration, witness sun moon their golden characters, stiled eyes and Horns of the Lamb, etc. Their voice gone out into all lans Psal (Revs), like their here, every one when the fifty days at an end, heard in his proper language, αc (Acts 2) The Prophet Joel as foresaw and others. By whom Decyphr'd his Thundring Donative of the Crown and Bended Bare (Rev.6) as much to say, O: Cromwell, Renamed be victorious so long as Sun Moon continues or livever.
> Anagram, Hail Rome: And thus with one voice, come and see, O. C. Conquering and to conquer vent forth.' (8)

In spite of this chaotic and overwhelming jumble of biblical and personal imagery, Lady Eleanor seems to have achieved a certain amount of reputability during the Cromwellian administration. This was partly due to her enthusiastic support for Cromwell as the agent of apocalypse in her prophesyings, but certainly also due to the fact that her prophesy of the death of Charles had proved extremely convenient for the Cromwellian faction at the difficult time of the King's execution. Lady Eleanor's career before the revolution, however, had been far from easy.

In 1633 her prophesy of the King's death elicited a charge of blasphemy which resulted in an astronomical fine of £3,000 and imprisonment in the Tower. The Lady Eleanor's crime was succinctly described by her judges:

> 'forasmuch as she took upon her (<u>which much unbeseemed her sex</u>) not only to interpret the Scriptures, and withal the most intricate and herd places of the Prophet Daniel, but also to be a Prophetess, falsely pretending to have receiv'd certain Revelations from God, and had compil'd certain Books of such her fictions and false Prophesies or Revelations ... for these her said bold attempts and impostures, tending to the dishonour of God, and scandal of Religion, whereof she was found and adjudged guilty by the Court, she was thought well worthy to be severely punished.' (9)

The Prophetess' crime was therefore threefold: one - she had boldly interpreted the scriptures, and so usurping a function long since restricted to men; two - she had <u>pretended</u> to be a prophetess, and to be the recipient of the word of God; three - she had actually published and disseminated these false prophesies, thereby continuing to public political and religious dissent. The question which the Lady Eleanor's trial raised most acutely, however, was the difficulty of distinguishing false prophecies from true ones; and this was to be a recurrent dilemma of the revolutionary period. The decision of the judges in this case seems to have been reached as much on the basis of her femaleness (and so of the inconceivable possibility of her reception of the word of God as much as because of the treasonable matter that she prophesied). The fulfilment of the Lady Eleanor's prophecy in January 1649 therefore must have given a number of judicious men considerable food for thought.

The pre-revolutionary career of Lady Eleanor Davies which was characterised by frequent internments in Bedlam or the Tower, was paralleled after the Revolution by that of Anna Trapuel, whose brand of fifth monarchist prophesyings soon became distinctly distasteful to the Cromwellian Protectorate. She in fact had a much stormier career than did the other prophetess of the fifth monarchy, Mary Cary, or Mary Rande, as she was sometimes known, who seems far more practical in her application of the prophetic gift than either Eleanor Davies or Anna Trapuel. Her prophesyings are generally placed within the context of reasoned political polemics which make specific material requests, such as for the propagation of the gospel, the new modelling of the universities, the Reformation of the Laws, and the supplying of necessities to the poor. She is constantly commenting upon and interpreting her symbolic discourse thereby reforming it to the more acceptable discursive domain of political debate. Even her announcement of the coming apocalypse is astonishingly mild compared to the unstructured outpourings of the other two women:

> 'Now as it most clearly appears to me from the divine oracles of the Scriptures, having compared the works of God, and his Word together, I have in the ensuing discourse held it forth ... that the time is already come, wherein the appointed time of the prevailing power of the Beast over the Saints, is come to a period; and accordingly Jesus Christ hath begunne to bringe downe the poer of the Beast, and to lift up his saints ...'. (10)

The career of Anna Trapuel was compared by William Tyndall to that of John Bunyan, but his description of her prophetic career also makes clear the extent to which her prophetic delirium went beyond the more controlled and regulated divine inspiration of Bunyan:

> 'Fleeing as a child from sin to legal rectitude, she attended cautionary sermons which failed to remove the burden of the law or to provide the grace which periods of terror and the indignation of the Almighty appeared to recommend. Intermittent ravishings of the spirit were followed by the discouragements peculiar to the chief of sinners, as she called herself, and, after the reception of grace by a relapse and the knowledge that she alone had sinned, the sin against the Holy Ghost. When the wrath of God had somewhat abated, however, she enjoyed the sensations of the disciple, beheld symbolic visions, communed with a variety of angels, and by her openings and trances, became the object of pious interest. Up to this point her story resembles that of Bunyan, but the account of her ministry is marked by a difference which must be ascribed to her conditions as to the strangeness of her gift. The sickness which fell upon her as upon Bunyan was more sociable than his; for she admitted the public to the infirmary of her body and soul, and displayed her curious motions, delirium and fits of ravishment and palsy to the fascinated and devout. The pouring forth of the spirit was such that she prophesied incessantly both day and night with no appearance of fatigue and uttered in bed great quantities of verse, which the faithful recorded. She also exercised her gift of song, continuing without pause for nourishment or repose, until at last, as her autobiography relates, "In the afternoon, while I was singing, they sent the Constable for me."' (11)

Anna Trapuel appears to have inhabited a world very similar to the mythic dimensions of the semiotic as these have been defined by Kristeva. Song appears to have figured very largely in her prophetic career. The famous ecstasy at Whitehall, which occurred in 1654, consisted largely of songs or fragments of songs whose content evidently appeared to many to go beyond the bounds of decent female behaviour. At any rate, Anna's utterances had to be anxiously defended by her friends and political allies who published and commented upon the particular ecstatic outburst:

> 'If any be offended at her songs; of such it is demanded, if they know what it is to be filled with the spirit ... then may they judge her ...
> There be various reports gone abroad concerning this Maid, too many being such as were not according to truth; whereby

> it come to pass that the things she spake do not appear to men as they came from her, but as deformed and disguised with the pervertings and depracings of the Reporters; therefore it was upon the heart of some that heard her ... to present to publick view a true and faithfull Relation of so much as for some 7 or 8 dayes could be taken from her, by a very slow and unready hand.' (12)

Anna's earnest prophesyings had been relatively acceptable to the Cromwellian faction for like those of Eleanor Davies, her first utterances appeared to present Cromwell as a triumphant agent of the apocalypse, a new Gideon. Yet this original unqualified support was steadily modified as she appears to have moved closer to the ideas and beliefs of fifth monarchy and as it became increasingly evident that Cromwell's revolutionary zeal had clearly defined limits. Trapuel's later prophesies were increasingly critical of the Protectorate's timidity and of Cromwell's backsliding:

> 'Let not him say, as they said of old, who put the day far from them, that the vision was for many days, for a time yet afar off; But let them accept of the day and time that thou hast put into their hand.' (13)

This change of attitude culminated in the Whitehall outburst, where the former association of the Protectorate with Gideon was decisively rejected:

> 'If he were not the backsliden, he would be ashamed of his great pomp and revenue, whiles the poare are ready to starve, and art thou providing great palaces? oh this was not Gideon of old ...' (14)

After the scandal of her Whitehall trance, Anna Trapuel was arrested and thrown in Bridewell for spreading subversion. She herself commented sadly on the fall from popularity to notoriety that followed:

> 'England's Rulers and Clergie do judge the Lord's handmaid to be mad, and under the administration of evil angels, and witch, and Many other evil terms they raise up to make me odious and abhorr'd in the hearts of good and bad, that do not know me.' (15)

Her later prophesyings convey more acutely than ever before a sense of despair and lost hopes, the gradual fading of millenarian dreams:

> 'Who can forbear taling up a lamentation concerning poor England - whose prophets prophesise falsely, and the Priests been rule by their means, and the people love to have it so, but what will they do in the end thereof?' (16)

The prophecies of Eleanor Davies, Anna Trapuel and Mary Cary represent only a fraction of the enormous prophetic activity which the English revolution generated - prophesying which ranged from pro-Royalist propaganda to the most radical of millenarian sentiments. Many of the women prophesying during this period left little or no trace other than their names - Mary Gadbury, a Ranter who called herself the Spouse of Christ (and also eventually landed up in Bridewell); Elizabeth Poole, whose prophesyings were briefly used by Cromwell and Ireton during the 1640's; Elizabeth Joceline, Sarah Wight and others.(17) Almost all those who prophesied at this time, both male and female, experienced difficulties of some kind or another - by the end of the revolutionary decade of the 1640's there were already signs that the Cromwellian administration was trying to restrict prophetic activity - attempts which prompted Jeremy Taylor's tract on The Liberty of Prophesying as early as 1647, and a sermon given by Thomas Case before the House of Commons in the same year, in which he extolled the virtues of prophesy. Yet it seems clear that the female prophets of the period represented a threat that was in some respects more severe than that of any male prophetic figures of the day. This may in some respects be attributed to the more chaotic nature of many of their prophesyings; but we believe that the anxiety which these women promoted had rather deeper causes which related to the unique nature of the prophetic phenomenon, and to the scarcely admissible possibility that a woman could possess and transmit the word of God. The verbal transmission of the logos appears to have been threatening enough - the possibility of a physical logos being produced, in the shape of a new Messiah, induced even greater traumas. A number of women in this period proclaimed at different times that they were pregnant with the Christ, announcements which usually prompted rapid precautionary measures by the State. Probably the best known of these, a woman called Mary Adams, was immediately thrown into prison upon making the announcement. It was then proclaimed in a public statement (which suggests that popular interest in the matter had run high) that she had given birth to a monster and committed suicide. What really happened is anybody's guess, but the incident was certainly symptomatic of a deep anxiety about the possession of meaning.

The years between 1640 and 1660 might therefore be described as a period which opens with an excess of revolutionary activity on both the physical and verbal planes, a period characterised not only by Civil War but also by a fierce and bitter debate over the possession of meaning, of the logos. By 1660, however, the revolutionary struggle had failed on both these fronts. It is this tragic failure of course which constitutes the theme of Milton's Paradise Lost. In Milton's handling of the figures of Eve and Satan moreover, especially in the scene of temptation in the garden, the possibilities which the revolutionary period had opened up are quite explicitly surveyed. The enormous complexity of this scene seems symptomatic of Milton's own divided attitude to the revolution and its eventual failure. It has often been pointed out that Milton feels a great deal of sympathy for Satan as the failed revolutionary hero par excellence. We would argue that a fairly similar attitude can be traced in his treatment of the character of Eve, who is a figure of tremendous ambiguity within the poem.

Ultimately, however, Milton seems to have been unable to admit women to possession of the logos, and so to a specific relation with God. The Knowledge which the fruit of the tree offers Eve is the Knowledge of her body, of her own desire, but the speech which this produces is in the language of the court courtesan. The relationship of Adam and Eve at the end of the poem is hence fundamentally unchanged from that with which it began, as the female is returned to the control of her spouse:

> 'He for God only, she for God in him'.

What we have been trying to argue in relation to speech of the female prophets, therefore, is that these women and their prophetic activity represented a significant site of resistance in the revolutionary period - resistance against the acceptance of sexual difference and all that implied in the seventeenth century, this refusal of gender hinged upon the vital contemporary question of the possession of meaning or the logos. This challenge had of course been posed before, by various women writers and poets, but the threat which it represented became much more acute when the contest was over not only the actual word of God but over the public.

In these utterances, the assumption of gender and of sexual difference is implicitly refused, to be replaced by a peculiarly androgynous mode of speech which is tremendously threatening. When God delivers his word through or across the body of a woman, his masculine integrity and purity is evidently in danger of pollution. At best, the oracles of these women reinstate the feminine within these spheres of religious inspiration and political debate which had long since excluded it. At worst, their prophesying raises the awful, scarcely conceivable possibility that God might actually be a woman. This problem of sexual identity is precisely the dilemma which psychoanalysis has faced in its confrontation with hysteria. In a recent article on sexual 'difference' in Screen, Stephen Heath remarked:

> 'The success of Freud and psychoanalysis with female hysteria was an understanding of it as a problem of sexual identity in phallic terms: the hysteric is unsure as to being woman or man, "the hysterical position - having or not having the phallus"; hers is a body in trouble with language, that forcing of the signifying matter, resisting and accepting simultaneously the given signs, the given order. Listening to the woman as hysteric, psychoanalysis opens and closes the other scene, with the point of closure exactly "sexual identity", "sexual difference"; hence, symptomatically, the curious lag of psychoanalysis felt by Freud with regard to femininity, women still the great enigma, the "dark continent" ...'. (18)

In conclusion, perhaps Freud and Breuer's early studies in hysteria are worthy of some reconsideration. Not only was his interest in hysteria the beginning of Freud's departure in the direction of psychoanalysis; it was also a phenomenon whose uniqueness and beauty he never failed to acknowledge, unlike many of his successors. Ultimately, however, he too saw it as essentially futile and unproductive:

'I cannot accept Janet's view that the disposition of hysteria

> is based on innate physical weakness. The medical practitioner who, in his capacity as family doctor, observes the members of hysterical families at all ages will certainly be inclined to regard this disposition as lying in an excess rather than in a defect. Adolescents who are later to become hysterical are for the most part lively, gifted and full of intellectual interests before they fall ill. Their energy of will is often remarkable. They include girls who get out of bed at night so as secretly to carry on some study that their parents have forbidden from fear of their overworking. The capacity for forming sound judgments is certainly not more abundant in them than in other people; but it is rare to find in them simple, dull intellectual inertia and stupidity. The overflowing productivity of their minds has led one of my friends to assert that hysterics are the flower of mankind, as sterile, no doubt, but as beautiful as double flowers.' (19)

Footnotes

1. Interview with Luce Irigaray, Ideology and Consciousness, No.1, May 1977, p.65.

2. La Revolution du Langage Poetique, pp.27-28. Julia Kristeva Semil, Paris 1974 (author's translation).

3. A Discoursive Probleme Concerning Prophecies, John Harvey, London, 1588, p.4.

4. Macbeth, W. Shakespeare, I, iii, lines 38-46.

5. Macbeth, I, iii, lines 83-85.

6. Eleanor Davies was the sister of the notorious Earl of Castlehaven referred to in Peter Stallybrass' article Sexuality and Authority. The fierce legal and political dispute engendered by Castlehaven's (extremely nasty) sexual activities - which included persuading his manservant to rape his wife and daughter-in-law - seems particularly interesting in relation to his sister's intervention in another form of masculine genealogy at around the same time.

7. Prophesie of the Last Day ..., E. Davies, London, 1645, pp.3-4.

8. The Benediction from the Almighty Omnipotent, E. Davies, London, 1651.

9. The Blasphemous Charge against her, E. Davies, London, 1649.

10. The Resurrection of the Witnesse, M. Cary, London, 1648, Epistle Dedicatory.

11. John Bunyan, William Tyndall.

12. *The City of Stone*, A. Trapuel, London, 1654, Sig a_2^V.

13. *The City of Stone*, Sig D_3^R.

14. *The City of Stone*, Sig H_4^R.

15. *Travels in Cornwall*, A. Trapuel, London, 1654.

16. *Travels in Cornwall*.

17. For further details see *The World Turned Upside Down*, C. Hill.

18. *Screen*, Vol.19, No.3, p.56.

19. *Freud: Collected Works II*, Hogarth Press, 1955, pp.320-1.

HURRICANES IN THE CARIBBEES: THE CONSTITUTION OF THE DISCOURSE OF ENGLISH COLONIALISM (1)

Peter Hulme

'Tropic ... pl. With the: ... the torrid zone and parts immediately adjacent'. (OED)

'Tropics is the process by which all discourse constitutes the objects which it pretends only to describe realistically and to analyze objectively'. (2)

'language is the perfect instrument of empire'. (Bishop of Avila to Queen Isabella of Castile in 1492) (3)

If you take for granted, as I'm going to do, that an essential part of the task of conceptualising the working of ideology involves study of particular ideologies at work, then the path to the beginning of this paper is not difficult to understand. The colonial experience, for everyone concerned, has obviously been, and still is, of central importance to the modern world. English colonialism made significant advances, in terms of territory controlled and numbers involved in colonial emigration, in the first half of the seventeenth century. One would therefore expect to see at this time the establishment of an ideology appropriate to that enterprise. That moment might well then offer a valuable site for observing the process of constitution of an ideological discourse. What that moment consists of can by no means be taken as given. What I've therefore done is to constitute one aspect of that conjuncture as consisting of a period - from the 25th July 1609 to the 19th December 1686 - and a series of texts written in or about that period which focus on the relationship between coloniser and colonised in a number of islands that later became known as the British West Indies. I'm not claiming that these texts are necessarily more important than other series of colonial texts in the seventeenth century (however those series are constituted), although I would claim that what gives this particular series special relevance is the fact that it includes, and is indeed given its terminal dates by, two texts that have come to play central roles within the canon of English literature.

More baldly, between 25th July 1609, when the Sea-Venture was wrecked off the coast of the Bermudas, and 19th December 1686, when Robinson Crusoe left his island near Trinidad, a discourse was established which enabled England as a colonising power to talk about its relationship with the indigenous population of the islands it only later called the British West Indies. In what follows I'm going to refer to that discourse as the discourse of the Caribbees - the English name for those islands during this period.

The assumptions that I'm making are threefold. That a particular ideological discourse comes into existence through a process of tactical adaptation of earlier discourses.[(4)] That one significant, if crude, indicator of such adaptations is the use of a new vocabulary. And that the available discourses - particularly in the realms of geography and ethnography - at the beginning of the seventeenth century were, broadly speaking, Mediterranean: using that term to cover biblical and classical discourses.

My starting point is the observation that two of the central terms in the discourse of the Caribbees are the words 'cannibal' and 'hurricane', both of these being relatively new words to the English language, not found before the middle of the sixteenth century and not settling to their present forms before the latter half of the seventeenth.

It could therefore be said that what I'm doing is investigating the way in which those two words came to play such central roles in a particular seventeenth century colonial discourse, through a study of certain of the texts pertaining to that discourse. This will clearly involve detailed analysis of the relationship between these 'strange' words and the 'familiar' Mediterranean discourses into which they were eventually inserted; and I'll be paying special attention to the critical textual distortions that result from this process of insertion.

Another - though not different - way of looking at what follows would be to see it as an attempt to create a context for a reading of the figure of Caliban in The Tempest. Although that particular text comes at the beginning of the period in question, I'm going to discuss it last of all, circling round it anti-cyclonically, like the hurricane around its one eye.

When Spain colonised the islands of the West Indies in the late fifteenth and early sixteenth century it distinguished between them on two grounds: the presence or absence of gold and the presence or absence of a powerful and hostile native population. Cuba, Española, Jamaica and Puerto Rico therefore constituted the main settlements: some gold was found there; the natives, initially friendly, were made hostile by Spanish behaviour but were never powerful enough to threaten Spanish presence. On Columbus' first voyage in the winter of 1492-93 he heard accounts of fierce natives living further down the chain of islands in a land called Caribana. The hostility of these Caribs, as they came to be known, persuaded the Spanish to ignore the eastern and southern islands of the chain and concentrate on the western islands and the mainland.(5) It was also the mainland of both north and south America that English colonising expeditions visited at the end of the sixteenth and beginning of the seventeenth century, though this did bring the first incidental English contacts with the islands, among them the sixty-seven passengers from the Olive Branch, which put in at Santa Lucía for food in August 1605, who stayed to begin planting, and of whom forty-eight were killed in a fight with the Caribs, the other nineteen 'escaping' as the history books put it - although it turns out that the Caribs had to build them a boat;(6) and, later, the crew and passengers of the Sea-Venture, which was wrecked off the Bermudas in 1607.

During the seventeenth century England was consistently interested in Guiana and it was only during an enforced hiatus when James I cancelled the patent of the Amazon company that English settlers began to think of the islands as possible sites for plantation. Thomas Warner settled on St. Christopher in 1624 and by the terminus date of 1686 the English had also occupied Barbuda, Nevis, Montserrat, Antigua, Anguilla, Barbados and Jamaica. Other islands were colonised by France - who actually shared St. Christopher with the English - Holland, and Denmark.

The islands had become attractive propositions for the North Europeans because of their distance from what by now had become established spheres of Spanish, Portuguese and Dutch influence, but most of these islands were still inhabited or controlled by the Caribs, a fact implicitly recognised by the term, Caribbee Islands, employed by the English during this period. It's probably only one of the smaller ironies of colonialism that while an important legal argument turned on the point that Barbados couldn't properly be considered a Caribbee Island because it had never been inhabited by Caribs,[7] the English should be involved in removing the Caribs from the other islands as quickly as possible.

The struggle was long and hard. Most of the Caribs on St. Christopher were massacred in a joint night attack by the English and French in 1626; and they were driven off Guadeloupe (1636), Grenada (1650) and Martinique (1658). But the Caribs did succeed in destroying many of the smaller European colonies: four separate attempts to colonise Tobago were wiped out between 1632 and 1642, and likewise four on St. Lucia between 1637 and 1663. And the larger settlements were constantly attacked until in a peace treaty in 1660 the Caribs agreed to accept St. Vincent and Dominica in perpetuity in return for agreeing not to attack the islands already settled by Europeans. The English attitude to the Caribs can be summarised in the words of James Williamson, one of the most distinguished of English colonial historians, writing in 1926:

> 'They were a restless and migratory race, often moving from island to island, and when evicted by Europeans prone to return with their friends in unexpected force. This mobility, coupled with their secret and treacherous mentality, rendered them a formidable obstacle to the early settlers, and the ultimate solution of the problem was provided only by a war of extermination.' (8)

*****

First a few general comments about the words 'hurricane' and 'cannibal'. Both belong to native American languages, and both were quickly adopted into all the major European languages.[9] The term 'cannibal' appears in both the limit texts: in that particular form in Robinson Crusoe and as an anagram of the earlier form 'canibal' in The Tempest.[10] The term 'hurricane' appears in Robinson Crusoe to refer to the storm that wrecks Crusoe's ship in the West Indies; but not - with what significance I'll speak later - in The Tempest, although the meteorological phenomenon itself (according to any of the three definitions it's been given in English from the sixteenth century onwards)[11] was responsible for the wrecking of the Sea-Venture, the accounts of which are accepted as source material for The Tempest.[12]

It's with this source material that I want to start precisely because it lies just outside the discourse of the Caribbees and should therefore allow us to chart that discourse's novelty.

In May 1609 five hundred colonists in nine ships set out from Plymouth for Virginia. On 25th July one of the ships, the Sea-Venture, carrying the two leaders of the expedition, was separated from the others in a tropical hurricane and driven onto the rocks off the coast of the Bermudas, a small group of uninhabited islands, feared for many years by ships that had to work northward to their latitude, close-hauled to the trade wind, in search of the prevailing westerlies that would take them back across the Atlantic. It was presumed in England that the Sea-Venture was lost but in fact the crew and passengers managed to survive comfortably in the Bermudas and built another ship that reached Virginia in May 1610. News of this reached England later in the year and inspired a number of narrative accounts, amongst them two that Shakespeare almost certainly read: Sylvester Jourdain's Discovery of the Bermudas, written and published in 1610, and a letter by William Strachey known as A True Reportorie of the Wrack, not published till 1625 but dated 15th July 1610.[13]

In using the word 'tempest' Shakespeare was following his narrative sources, Strachey and Jourdain, who both avoid 'hurricane' (available in English since 1555) and prefer the Mediterranean 'tempest' to refer to what their accounts leave no doubt was a markedly strange occurrence. The connotations in this case are determinedly biblical. St. Paul's perilous voyage in the Mediterranean was threatened by a tempest

(*Acts*, 27, 18) but one controlled, as Paul knew, by a beneficent deity. The Bermuda pamphleteers and Shakespeare - and of course at a later date Robinson Crusoe (if not necessarily Defoe) - were well aware of the allegorical significance of such occurrences when framed in that particular terminology. Redemption - and the word itself is used by Strachey - was made all the more appropriate a conclusion to Sir Thomas Gates' misadventure by the nature of the islands of the Bermudas. As Strachey puts it:

> 'such tempests, thunders, and other fearfull objects are seene and heard about them, that they be called commonly, The Devils Ilands, and are feared and avoyded of all sea travellers alive, above any other place in the world. Yet it pleased our mercifull God, to make even this hideous and hated place, both the place of our safetie and meanes of our deliverance.' (14)

Not only was the island *not* fearful it was, according to Jourdain, 'in truth the richest, healthfullest, and pleasing land ... and merely natural, as ever man set foot upon'.(15) And the conclusion to be drawn from the allegory was therefore that God had kept those islands secret from everyone else and protected them by their reputation for tempest and thunder so that they could be bestowed upon the people of England.(16)

The other conclusion to be drawn from these narratives is the simple one that novelty of experience has no necessary impingement upon ideological discourse. The terrifyingly novel experience of a tropical hurricane proved perfectly comprehensible within biblical terms: 'tempest' proved to be an ideologically adequate and therefore undisturbed signifier.

After the establishment of the island colonies in the 1620's the term 'hurricane' in its various forms seems to have been quickly adopted into English, which I want to claim as a sign of ideological disturbance. The relevant text here is a pamphlet published in London towards the end of 1638 and entitled 'New and strange News from St. *Christophers*, of a tempestuous Spirit, which is called by the *Indians* a *Hurri Cano*, which hapneth in many of those Islands of *America*, or the *West-Indies*, as it did in August last the 5. 1638'.(17) Written by John Taylor, known as the Water-Poet, one of the first professional English writers, this report was presumably - although there is no firm evidence - based on the account of a sailor recently returned from the Caribbee Islands. Ideologically it's a naive text, an early form of popular journalism, which enables us to see more clearly some of the discursive transformations taking place. The title itself gives various clues. The place occupied in Mediterranean discourse by the word 'tempest' now needs a considerable circumlocution: 'of a tempestuous Spirit, which is called by the Indians a Hurri Cano'. The biblical discourse is fractured by the irruption of a new and alien term which is marked as belonging to someone else's discourse ('called by the Indians') and signalled as novel and strange ('new and strange News'). Why should this have been necessary? What was no longer adequate about the word 'tempest'?

The obvious answer - although I think it's a necessary but not sufficient explanation - is that by 1638 the English colonists had had considerably more experience of the devastating nature of hurricanes which almost every year destroyed houses and crops on at least one of the islands: 1642 was in fact a particularly bad year for hurricanes. But although this extra-discursive experience was a necessary condition, biblical discourse was only really troubled because of the discursive difficulty in allegorising - except with very unfavourable conclusions - the destruction of colonists' property. Taylor's pamphlet demonstrates some of the initial responses to this difficulty.

It opens with conventional biblical terminology: God sometimes chooses to punish or restrain by terrible events obstinate sinners, 'by which meanes He makes his wayes to be knowne upon Earth and his saving health among all Nations'.(18) The problem then is to know how to interpret the message, a problem that the pamphlet, having posed, proceeds to avoid, or at least to answer only in the most oblique fashion. The difficulty begins with that last phrase: it's not clear under what interpretation the devastation wrought by a hurricane could be said to bring 'saving health' to anyone. It continues:

'And it is to be noted, that where God is least knowne and

> honoured, there the Devill hath most power and domination. But hee that drew light out of darknesse, hath often (and can when he wil) draw good out of evil: for through slavery and bondage many people and Nations that were heathens, and barbarous, have beene happily brought to Civility and Christian liberty.' (19)

The argument is considerably less logical than the conjunctions suggest. It becomes clear, in the course of those two sentences (though not at any specifiable point within them) that the hurricane has been caused by the savagery and barbarity of the native inhabitants, dominated as they are, in the absence of knowledge of God, by the devil. But what is by no means clear is to whom the 'message' of the hurricane is addressed. Is it to the natives themselves in retribution for their savagery?; in which case why is it that the bearers of God's word suffer more severely than the savage natives?[20] Or is it a broad hint to the settlers that the civilising process should be speeded up? The moment of slippage seems to be that movement of light out of darkness. The text is gesturing towards the language of tempest and redemption, the light of salvation that follows the darkness of the storm. But darkness here is at the same time the _experience_ of the settlers suffering from the hurricane (or more properly here 'tempest') and from which 'good' can in the end be expected to come; and the _state_ of savagery in which the natives live and from which they can be delivered only via a slavery and bondage that will lead them to true liberty. This colonial topos - common in the seventeenth century - of slavery as the necessary stage between savagery and civility,[21] is the firm ground that the text has been looking for, and it rests there unproblematically expounding the topos for more than a page. Taylor then finally makes explicit what has been underlying his text's hesitations; although only in the course of a rapid movement from the topos back to the actual description of the hurricane:

> 'Yet in the latest Dayes of the World all are not civiliz'd; there are yet many Heathens, _Indians_, and barbarous Nations unconverted: as for the knowne _Examples_ in _America_, and in divers Islands adjacent, where this _Hurri Cano_ is frequent; of which with the manner of the _Description of_ it as followeth.' (22)

So the hurricane is to be located where savagery and barbarity are to be found, and is therefore to be recognised as an alien phenomenon (since we have nothing to do with such savagery) by the use of the native word. So the hurricane seems to be less a message from God than an attribute or manifestation of the native savagery that confronts European civility and that, as Taylor's description makes clear, attacks precisely what he has earlier given as the marks of that civility: the building of towns and the practices of tillage and husbandry, all devastated by hurricanes. This rhetorical move is in part also an attempt to cope with the next piece of information that the pamphlet has to convey: the fact that although it doesn't come at set times, the Indians are able to predict when a hurricane is approaching: '... the Indians are so skilfull, that they doe know two or three or foure dayes before hand of the comming of it'.(23) This serves to cement the special relationship between Carib and hurricane, but as a piece of empirical information it's too problematical for Taylor's text to recover from. What started out as a sign from God can, it appears, be most successfully read by those who are supposed to be living in darkness and ignorance. Not able to proceed beyond this point Taylor gives a long description of the precautions taken, repeats himself about how the Indians foretell the hurricane and then takes refuge in recounting the by now much repeated story of the *Sea-Venture*'s deliverance from Bermuda in order to demonstrate exactly how light can come out of darkness, although the example is, in the sense I've established, relevant only to tempests and not to hurricanes. It's therefore a retreat from an ideological problem to an earlier and less problematic discourse. This part of the pamphlet then ends with a totally unmotivated (or at least only commercially motivated) connection made with 'strange and fearefull Signes and warnings' that 'are Recorded in our Owne Histories, to have happened in our owne Countrey' and of which Taylor has an account at hand in verse of a 'prodigious Tempest and lamentable Accident at Withycombe, neare *Dartmoores* in *Devonshiere*'.(24) So the final recuperation is the hurricane as prodigy, a category that - we might remember - included, in Trinculo's phrases, 'strange beasts' and 'dead Indians' to see which 'not a holiday fool ... but would give a piece of silver' (*T*, II, ii, 29-34).

Taylor's report of a hurricane in the Caribbee Islands inevitably refers to 'cannibalism' as one of the signs of barbarity, referring here to the peoples conquered by Alexander: 'in their Freedomes they did use to kill their aged Parents inhumanely, to eate them with savadge, ravenous, most greedy Gormandizing'.(25) Of all the classical narratives used to interpret the experience of the New World, those concerning the anthropophagites were arguably the most frequently invoked. The question has then again to be posed: if 'anthropophagy' was an adequate Mediterranean term to designate savagery, why should a new and strange word be adopted into the European languages? It could be argued that of the two phenomena designated by the two words I'm discussing the hurricane was in the end a radically novel experience for the European (an experience differing in kind not simply in intensity from the Mediterranean tempest), whereas cannibalism was familiar, was indeed expected to be found where non-Europeans were encountered, and had a perfectly adequate signifier in the classical term 'anthropophagy'. Yet if anything the word 'cannibal' and its cognates was accepted into the European languages even more quickly than the word 'hurricane'.

The explanation for this adoption would appear to depend upon the sense of threat. Anthropophagites were familiar from classical texts, but the defining feature of their savagery was that they ate one another: their parents in Taylor's version, their children in Aristotle's, in a sentence paraphrased in Shakespeare's lines: 'The barbarous Scythian/Or he that makes his generation messes to gorge his appetite' (King Lear, I, i, 118-120).(26) What was new and startling to European colonialism was the presence of a native population that was militarily competent enough to resist an alien invasion: it was that novelty that was inscribed as 'cannibalism', the new word indicating the fear that the savage dietary habits might be practised on the coloniser: with Robinson Crusoe as the most eloquent witness to that fear, which he voices on nine separate occasions.(27)

Perhaps the central point to grasp in all this is that the issue is not the anthropological one of the custom of eating people but rather the connotations that constitute the significations of a particular signifier. What I'm trying to suggest is that terms like 'anthropophagite' and 'cannibal' have no denotative content whatsoever: their signification in discourse consists entirely of their connotations or (if it's not acceptable to use that word in the absence of its normal partner), of the characteristics immediately and inevitably associated with that term. Members of certain agricultural societies may well have eaten the dead bodies of fellow members, although almost certainly for ritual rather than dietary reasons. But in Herodotus, for example, anthropophagy functions solely as a marker of savagery: the Scythians are perceived as savages for political reasons, and therefore must be anthropophagites, since eating one another is one of the attributes of savages.(28)

The point is even clearer with the term 'cannibalism' which cannot without considerable effort be conceived of separately from the notions of aggression and hostility; and this is as true of the supposedly neutral and scientific discourse of anthropology as it is of so-called 'everyday' language.(29) This is a process that considerably predates English colonialism being - not accidentally - one of the most immediate effects of the earliest reports of Columbus' voyages.(30) There's a Columbian moment that exemplifies what I'm saying. Columbus' last anchorage on his first voyage in 1493 was at a harbour on the coast of Española which is still called Las Flechas:

> 'Sunday, January 13th/ ... He sent the boat to land at a beautiful beach, in order that they might take ajes to eat, and they found some men with bows and arrows, with whom they paused to talk, and they bought two bows and many arrows, and asked one of them to go to speak with the admiral in the caravel, and he came. The admiral says that he was more ugly in appearance than any whom he had seen. He had his face all stained with charcoal, although in all other parts they are accustomed to paint themselves with various colours; he wore all his hair very long and drawn back and tied behind, and then gathered in meshes of parrots' feathers, and he was as naked as the others. The admiral judged that he must be one of the Caribs who eat men ...' (31)

Columbus' judgement was actually wrong - the man was a Ciguayo Arawak, a small group separated linguistically and culturally from the Arawak with whom Columbus had had most contact(32) - but what's interesting is that the judgement was made entirely on the grounds of appearance. The native was ugly and looked ferocious, therefore he was a cannibal.(33) Nothing illustrates the appropriate connotations better than the series of sixteenth century woodcuts and engravings depicting cannibal feasts and which invariably show bodies being torn limb from limb, a practice for which there is no ethnographic evidence at all from anywhere in the world.[34] The establishment of this 'meaning' as scientifically true for the early colonial period then became the task of etymologists.

What in fact is particularly striking about the history of the two words 'hurricane' and 'cannibal' in the European languages is that having been adopted as new words to strengthen an ideological discourse they were both subsequently subject, in almost identical ways, to attempts at etymological recuperation. (It might be possible to claim - I just don't know enough about historical linguistics to say - that the words may have been accepted into the European languages because of the possibility of etymological and phonetic connections being made: for instance it seems clear that 'hurricane' came at least to take that particular form in English because of the phonetic link with 'hurry', which is presumably why Taylor separates the two syllables. But I'm not going to discuss these possible predispositions since they wouldn't affect my argument one way or the other).

'Hurricane' existed in English in a bewildering number of forms from the mid sixteenth to the late seventeenth century. Dr. Johnson eventually justified the final form by actually giving it the same etymology as 'hurry': the Gothic _hurra_ meaning to move rapidly or violently. The earlier forms tended to favour 'cano' as an ending, according to the OED on the grounds that Spanish words were frequently assumed to end in -o, but perhaps because that other violent manifestation of nature was already well established in English as 'volcano'. That '-cane' became frequent only after 1650 might suggest the influence of 'sugar cane', which was what hurricanes were chiefly destroying after 1650.

But the most interesting of the early English forms, based on an early Spanish variant, is 'furacan' or 'furicano' - a form found as late as 1632 in English. The connotation here is obviously the appropriate one of 'fury' and 'furious', which I'll explore in a minute. But it's worth pointing out that by 1726 the Spanish _Diccionario de autoridades_ could call the contemporary Spanish form 'huracán' (which is phonetically close to the Mayan original) a corruption of the 'earlier' form 'furacán' which it now gave a Latin root: ventus furens. A good example of authority not only erasing the traces of ideology, but leaving a false trail as well.

There's some doubt about exactly what word Columbus heard in the winter of 1492 from the natives of Española to describe the islands occupied by their neighbours to the east but it's clear enough that it exists in his Journal as the form 'Caniba' at least in part because he took it to refer to the Great Khan (Spanish Can) of Cathay. That particular delusion didn't last long, but it was quickly replaced by another which is usually traced to Geraldini, the Bishop of San Domingo in the 1520's: deriving 'caníbal' from the Latin canis (dog) - a derivation also found, again, in Dr. Johnson's dictionary, and which was current in English until the late nineteenth century. According to Humboldt Geraldini 'recognized in the Cannibals the manners of dogs',(35) although the comparison itself is already explicit in Peter Martyr's first Decade where he calls the Caribs 'manhuntynge woolves'.(36) So by the seventeenth century it had been clearly established by empirical observation and scientific etymology that the cannibals of the West Indies hunted like dogs and treated their victims in the ferocious manner of all predators, tearing them limb from limb in order to consume them.

If I can recap very briefly, what I've been trying to do so far is to trace through a history of two words some moments of ideological crisis in an attempt to get a sight of the establishment and consolidation of a particular discursive formation. With this in mind I've discussed the Bermuda pamphlets (1610) and Taylor's 'New and Strange News' (1638), both texts about hurricanes, and, more briefly, some of the texts that established the figure of the cannibal as so important to colonial discourse.

The Tempest (1611) is a considerably more complex text than any of these but one that I want to look at in the intertextual light cast on it by these other texts about hurricanes and cannibals.(37) The particular relationship that exists between The Tempest and the discourse under discussion is difficult to specify with precision, at least in part because of the play's notoriously complicated geography - which I'll be talking about in a minute. It does however seem possible to make two interlinked claims. That Shakespeare's single major addition to the story told in the Bermuda pamphlets is to make the island inhabited before Prospero's arrival; and that, despite the potential setting of Virginia, an English colony supplied with native inhabitants and which had close links with the Bermudas, the naming of Caliban is a distinctly tropical move, although there were as yet no English settlements in the Caribbee Islands.(38)

In focusing, as I now want to do, on Caliban, there's a sense, although a misleading one, in which I'm in agreement with Shakespearean scholarship: Kermode, for example, says that Caliban is 'the core of the play' (T, p.xxiv); and much effort has been expended trying to decide exactly how Caliban should look: one recent scholar - just to give an example of the sorts of excesses to which this approach can lead - decides that the appearance of Caliban poses such a problem that it can only be explained as a holdover from Shakespeare's source, and therefore provides a not particularly similar description from a book by Jean de Léry which there's no evidence Shakespeare ever read.(39) I certainly want to discuss Caliban as an anomaly, but in a rather different way.

As before I want to start by measuring The Tempest's distance from Mediterranean discourse. There are some well-known Virgilian sources to The Tempest(40) but in this context the most relevant precedent is Odysseus' visit to the country of the Cyclops in Book IX of the Odyssey, though this relevance can be seen as double-edged. On the one hand Polyphemus seems to represent the most potent of threats to a sea-faring trading society: the breaking of the universal law of hospitality - which is what horrifies Odysseus about Polyphemus' behaviour(41) - and this could be seen to be equally applicable to the situation of the sea-faring English at the beginning of the seventeenth century. It's interesting that neither Homer nor Ovid uses the term anthropophagite to refer to Polyphemus as if eating one's own was in its own way a respectable social custom not to be put in the same category as Polyphemus' behaviour.

On the other hand the very relevance of this episode could be seen to lie in its colonial undertones: Odysseus lies about the reason for his visit to Polyphemus and openly covets the beautiful land in terms that recall Jourdain's account of the Bermudas.(42) Seen in this light Polyphemus' lack of hospitality can be read as a myth projected by the guilt of the colonist. It does appear to be the case - judging at least from the American examples - that travellers in precapitalist societies were invariably treated with hospitality, provided of course that they were genuine travellers, not rivals for land and resources.(43) The moment of truth in relationships between Europeans and Americans frequently came when the Americans realised that the Europeans were not travellers but had come to settle their land. Ironically, as we've already seen, a favourite European argument for dispossession was that the Americans had not really settled the land: so in one of those inversions that are nowadays said to be too crude a version of how ideology works, European ideology turned the actual settlers into constant travellers in order for the apparent travellers to have the ideological space in which to settle. So it's always the coloniser who will in the end be the breaker of the rules of hospitality (which etymologically apply without distinction to what we separate as guest and host). Perhaps the best evidence for this suggestion of guilt projection is the impermeability of the idea to any contrary empirical evidence. Some of this I'll be looking at in a minute, but there's a good example again in Robinson Crusoe when the news that sixteen shipwrecked Spaniards are living at peace with cannibals has no effect whatsoever on Crusoe's hysterical fear that he'll be devoured alive.(44)

Caliban is not the only example of the continuing relevance of Polyphemus to seventeenth century colonial discourse. Between 1621 and 1625 George Sandys, treasurer and director of industry at Jamestown, completed his translation of Ovid's Metamorphoses, which contains a commentary from which the following is extracted:

> 'Now the Cyclops (as formerly said) were a salvage people given to spoyle and robbery; unsociable amongst themselves, and inhumane to strangers: And no marvell; when lawlesse, and subject to no government, the bond of society; which gives to every man his owne, suppressing vice, and advancing vertue, the two maine columnes of a Common-wealth, without which it

> can have no supportance. Besides man is a politicall and sociable creature: they therefore are to be numbred among beasts who renounce society, whereby they are destitute of lawes, the ordination of civility. Hence it ensues, that man, in creation the best, when averse to justice, is the worst of all creatures. For injustice, armed with power, is most outragious and bloudy. Such Polyphemus, who feasts himselfe with the flesh of his guests; more salvage then are the West-Indians at this day, who onely eat their enemies, whom they have taken in the warres; whose slighting of death and patient sufferance is remarkable; receiving the deadly blow, without distemper, or appearance of sorrow; their fellowes looking on, and heartily feeding on the meate which is given them; yet know how they are to supply the shambles perhaps the day following. The heads of men they account among their delicates, which are onely to be eaten by the great ones, boyling oft times not so few as a douzen together, as hath beene seene by some of our Countrey-men. Injustice and cruelty, are ever accompanied with Atheisme and a contempt of the Deity ...' (45)

The ironies of Homer and Ovid have been removed to give the classical colonial image of the savage though, interestingly, being written just before the first English colony was established in the Caribbee Islands, it was still possible for the horror of cannibalism to be tempered by the observation of militaristic virtues which until then had been directed chiefly at the Spanish.

Looking at these examples it's possible to recognise in Caliban features of both the Mediterranean and the nascent Caribbee discourses. He's a Mediterranean wild man[46] or classical monster - certainly a Polyphemus, possibly even a Minotaur[47] - with an African mother, whose pedigree leads back to Book X of the Odyssey.[48] And yet at the same time he's a cannibal as I've tried to demonstrate that figure emerging in seventeenth century colonial discourse: ugly, hostile, ignorant, devilish - by birth but also having, through Sycorax, a particular connection with the moon (T, V, i, 270) whose signs the Caribs could read, and which makes especially appropriate Caliban's particular form of monstrosity as 'moon-calf' (T, II, ii, 107).[49] His ferocity is rarely apparent in the play but his name certainly suggests that it's only held in check by the strength of Prospero's magic.[50]

In his introduction to the original Arden edition of The Tempest

Morton Luce, tackling what he called 'this supreme puzzle', saw Caliban as Shakespeare's ambitious but in the end somewhat misguided attempt to create a composite figure, and became exasperated by the resulting incongruities. He says at one point:

> '[I]f all the suggestions as to Caliban's form and feature and endowments that are thrown out in the play are collected, it will be found that the one half renders the other half impossible.' (51)

This is certainly the case: 'a strange fish' says Trinculo (T, II, ii, 27-8) ... 'this is no fish' says Trinculo nine lines later (T, II, ii, 36); a man, according to Miranda in Act One since Ferdinand is the third she's seen (T, I, ii, 148), but not in Act Three where Ferdinand is only the second after her father (T, III, i, 51-2). Hence the universal difficulty, mentioned earlier, of actually visualising Caliban. Against Kermode's unificatory recuperation (T, p.xxxviii-xliii) and Luce's ultimate scepticism I want to argue that Caliban's anomalous nature is in fact the key to the play.

Luce also says that the attempts that have been made to sketch Caliban are reminiscent 'of the equally futile attempts to discover his enchanted island'.(52) This seems to me precisely the point, though not quite in the way Luce intends. The island of The Tempest is unlocatable not because it exists only in the rarefied latitudes of art but for more mundane reasons. Firstly because the sea destroys all evidence of distance - the island could be one mile or a thousand miles from Tunis, and likewise from Bermuda; and there are no clear reference points equivalent to the cliffs of Trinidad that position Robinson Crusoe's island. And secondly, and more importantly, because of what Jan Kott has recently called the play's 'extraordinary topographical dualism',(53) in other words, its double series of connotations that consist, not surprisingly, of a Mediterranean and an Atlantic frame of reference, the former including of course the word 'tempest' itself; the latter including, for example, Gonzalo's use of the specifically colonial term 'plantation', its only occurrence in Shakespeare.(54) To ignore one frame of reference in favour of the other seems to me to miss the point: the task is to specify their relationship. Fiedler is on the right track when he talks about the discovery of America as a new magnetic pole compelling a re-orientation of traditional axes;(55) but I want to suggest rather two planes (one Mediterranean, one Atlantic) superimposed, or even a palimpsest on which there are two texts. What is important is that in either case the two referential systems occupy different spaces except for that area which is the island and its first native, Caliban. What I'm suggesting is that, in the case of the geometrical metaphor, the figure of Caliban functions as a central axis about which both planes swivel free of one another; or, in the case of the textual metaphor, that the original Mediterranean text has superimposed upon it an Atlantic text that is written almost entirely in the spaces between the Mediterranean words, the exception being Caliban, who is therefore doubly inscribed, a state perhaps indicated by the need for the four words used to describe him on the list of characters: Caliban, salvage, deformed, slave;(56) an overdetermination peculiarly at odds with his place of habitation which is described as 'an uninhabited island' (T, p.2). Caliban is literally a monster - as we're told thirty-seven times in the play - not because of his habits but because of his mediating position between two sets of connotations.(57) In ideological terms he's a compromise formation and one achieved, like all such formations, only at the expense of distortion elsewhere. In a way Caliban, like Frankenstein's monster, carries the secret of his own guilty genesis; not however, like a bourgeois monster, in the pocket of his coat, but rather, like a savage, inscribed upon his body as his physical shape, whose absolute incongruities baffle the other characters as much as the play's directors. The difficulty in visualising Caliban is not therefore contingent or a result of Shakespeare attempting too much. Caliban, as a compromise formation, can exist only within discourse: he is fundamentally and essentially beyond the bounds of representation.

Exactly what this implies about the relationship between The Tempest and the other texts that constitute Caribbee discourse would need a full analysis of the play to determine. Having, I hope, established The Tempest's relevance to that discourse, and having read some of its complexities in that context, all I want to do in conclusion is to trace one further trope concerning the terms 'hurricane' and 'cannibal'. But it has to be approached at something of a tangent.

One of the strengths of certain sorts of colonialism is the way they bypass the need for complex forms of hegemonisation by their tendency to exterminate potential sources of counter-ideologies. The discourse of the Caribbees existed undisturbed by the voices of the colonised until a different set of political circumstances led others to attempt a subversive rewriting of that discourse - with The Tempest still providing the cast list.(58) In the absence of such opposition ideology can exist untroubled - usually masquerading under the title of anthropology - and it becomes even more essential to discern and interpret the internal contradictions within an ideological discourse.

One of the internal contradictions arises from what I've been trying to identify as a crucial colonial question: the rules of hospitality. However much the ideological image of the cannibal suggested a barbecue at which the guest would double as main course, it was impossible to suppress the evidence of native hospitality to non-aggressive individuals or groups, and many of these cases involved runaways from the European plantations seeking refuge among the natives. After 1642 these would frequently be black slaves; before 1642 they were often white servants - frequently Irish: the victims of class oppression showing scepticism towards the ideological 'truths' of the ruling class.(59)

The alliance of disaffected white servant and native savage was particularly worrying - and of course provides yet another reason for seeing The Tempest as a key Caribbee text. There had in fact been dissension which can be interpreted as class conflict during the Bermuda adventure itself, conflict which one of the pamphlets refers to as 'the tempest of Dissention'.(60)

Earlier I reached the point where the two American words, 'hurricane' and 'cannibal', having been introduced into the European languages because they were foreign words, were given Latin etymologies, 'hurricane' from furens, 'cannibal' from canis, the result being not simply the erasure of linguistic traces but the reinforcement of certain ideological connotations, in particular (in the context of Caribbee discourse) the creation of an ideological topography that would erase the distinguishing features of what lay outside the stockade (or beyond the pale in the language that most of the English colonists were used to).[61] In other words, seventeenth and eighteenth century lexicology supported the establishment of a discursive formation that had defined its notion of order and civility in such a way that everything outside, particularly everything outside that was threatening, was by definition seen as chaotic and wild. Dogs, like cannibals, are wild and furious, like hurricanes.[62] When Prospero remembers Caliban's plot, the conspirators are set upon by spirits in the forms of dogs, and one of the dogs is called Fury (_T_, IV, i, 257).[63]

At that moment the distinction between hurricane and cannibal hardly exists. Cyclops has taken the negligible orthographic step to cyclone; and yet just as the etymologically furious cyclone was in fact controlled by Prospero, so the etymologically canine Caliban is hunted by Prospero's dogs.[64] The danger has not so much been averted as inverted, but in a manner that can only be seen as excessive given that the conspiracy itself, which takes place with Caliban entirely assimilated to the comic genre inhabited by Trinculo and Stephano, is controlled by Prospero's magic.

What seems to be involved here is a displacement and containment of ideological danger that can only take place (like the formation of Caliban himself) at the price of textual disturbance. To put it another way, the cost of Prospero's magic - itself a Mediterranean term occupying the space really inhabited in colonial history by gunpowder - is the excess of his anger, of which the hunting of the conspirators is witness, but whose articulation comes at that other moment of the play that has troubled scholarship, the sudden ending of the masque towards the end of Act IV, which sees Prospero, as Ferdinand says: 'in some passion/that works him strongly' (_T_, IV, i, 143).[65] What Caliban is being punished for is not his 'conspiracy', which is only an alibi initiated by Prospero himself (hence his 'inexplicable' anger), but his indispensability. It is that original hospitality and continuing enforced and essential service - denied by Prospero's trenchant divisions between the grammatical first and second persons - that is Caliban's real crime.[66]

1642 was a crucial date in the Caribbean. In 1640 the technique of sugar refinement was introduced into Barbados from Brazil. By 1643, 150 tons a year of sugar were being produced. In 1642, five thousand black slaves had been imported.

It's obviously no accident that The Tempest is set on an island, where social relationships are inevitably intensified. Caliban has no thought of running away because there's nowhere to run to: a successful slave revolt on an island like Barbados or St. Christophers could only have meant a complete social revolution. What I'm suggesting is that the blurring of the boundaries between 'hurricane' and 'cannibal' was an aspect of the way in which Caribbee discourse was a preparation for its successor, the discourse of the plantation, which recognised only two locations, inside and outside, white and black, and which was itself to provide a central image for the class struggle of industrial Europe.[67]

It's in the light of that history - of the establishment of only one meaningful division within society - that it's not irrelevant to end by going back to the beginning and quoting, not before time, some of the few recorded words of an actual cannibal, the Tupi questioned at Rouen in 1562 by Montaigne, words that we know Shakespeare read:

> 'Some demanded their advise, and would needs know of them what things of note and admirable they had observed amongst us ... They said ... "they had perceived, there were men amongst us full gorged with all sortes of commodities, and others which hunger-starved, and bare with need and povertie, begged at their gates: and found it strange, these moyties so needy could endure such an injustice, and that they tooke not the others by the throte, or set fire on their houses".' (68)

Footnotes

1. This is a slightly expanded version of the paper given at the Essex conference with, however, no attempt made to expand on the points that need theoretical elaboration: that is part of a larger project. The footnotes attempt only to substantiate some of the historical claims and to provide illustration, quotation and bibliography.

2. Hayden White, Tropics of Discourse (Baltimore, 1978), p.2.

3. Quoted by Lewis Hanke, Aristotle and the American Indians (Bloomington, 1959), p.8. The Bishop had just presented to the Queen,

Antonio de Nebrija's Gramática, the first grammar of a European modern language ever written, and been asked by the Queen 'What is it for?'.

4. Cf. 'Dans toute cette littérature consacrée aux voyages, des documents aux romans, nous trouvons toujours cette opposition fondamentale entre le nouveau langage de l'expérience, qui a une fonction démystifiante, et la rhétorique des Écritures et des auteurs classiques, qui forme finalement la théologie providentielle des voyages à l'ouest. Dans l'expression de "Nouveau Monde", on retrouve cette opposition cruciale entre la réalité et le mythe. Le Nouveau Monde est nouveau puisqu'il est différent et à l'état sauvage; mais, en même temps, c'est un monde ancien retrouvé et à l'état pur. An niveau mythique, la nouveauté n'existe pas; le nouveau n'est qu'une répétition transfigurée. Comme dans la structure de la métamorphose, l'ancien et le Nouveau se transforment à tour de rôle. Le monde est nouveau en tant que transformation purifiée ou corrumpue de l'ancien", Jan Kott, 'La tempête, ou la répétition', Tel Quel 70 (1977), p.136. Kott is interested in the same dialectic as I'm looking at here, although his approach and conclusions are rather different.

5. For Spain in the West Indies till 1519 see Carl Sauer's magisterial The Early Spanish Main (Berkeley, 1969). For what follows see, in general, John H. Parry, The Age of Reconnaissance (London, 1973); Ralph Davis, The Rise of the Atlantic Economies (London, 1973) and A. P. Newton, The European Nations in the West Indies, 1492-1688 (London, 1933); for the best study of the English West Indies at this period, Richard S. Dunn, Sugar and Slaves. The Rise of the Planter Class in the English West Indies 1624-1713 (New York, 1973); and, in addition, Carl and Roberta Bridenbaugh, No Peace Beyond the Line: The English in the Caribbean, 1624-1690 (New York, 1972); Alan C. Burns, History of the British West Indies (New York, 1965); James A. Williamson, The Caribbee Islands under the Proprietary Patents (Oxford, 1926); N. M. Crouse, French Pioneers in the West Indies, 1624-1664 (New York, 1940); H. C. Wilkinson, The Adventurers of Bermuda (London, 1958); the most interesting contemporary account is J-B. du Tertre's Histoire Générale des Antilles, 4 vols (Paris, 1667).

6. For a contemporary account by a survivor see John Nicoll, 'An Houre Glasse of Indian News or A true and tragicall discourse, shewing the most lamentable miseries, and distressed Calamities indured by 67 Englishmen, which were sent for a supply to the planting in Guiana in the yeare 1605. Who not finding the saide place, were for want of victuall, left ashore in Saint Lucia, an Island of Caniballs, or Men-eaters in the West-Indyes' [1605] ed. Rev. C. Jesse, Caribbean Quarterly XII (1966), 46-67.

7. See Calendar of State Papers, Colonial Series, (Volume One) America and the West Indies, 1574-1660, ed. W. Noel Sainsbury (London, 1860), p.104. The document is dated 1629.

8. Williamson, The Caribbee Islands, p.4.

9. The native hurakan passed into Spanish from Arawak but may in origin have been Mayan. R. Lehmann-Nitsche's argument to this effect (Revista del Museo de la Plata, XXVIII (1924), 103-145) seems to survived C. H. de Goeje's scepticism (Journal de la Société des Americanistes de Paris, N.S., XXXI (1939), 12): see J. Corominas, Diccionario critico etimológico de la lengua castellana (Madrid, 1954) (entry for 'huracán'), and, more recently, Eva Hunt, The Transformation of the Hummingbird: Cultural Roots of a Zinacantecan Mythical Poem (Ithaca, 1977), p.242 and note. Hurakan is Tezcatlipoca's name in the Popul Vuh, meaning 'he who has one leg', from hum (one), ra (third person possessive), and kan (leg). 'Cannibal' is a variant of an Arawak word used to designate a rival culture that seems (in 1492) to have been in competition with them for possession of the islands to the east of Hispaniola. It's not known exactly what the original Arawak word was, nor whether it was a word used by that rival culture (now known as Carib) itself, nor what it meant (the best guess appears to be 'eaters of manioc'): see on all these issues, Douglas Taylor, 'Carib, Caliban, Cannibal', International Journal of American Linguistics, 24 (1958), 156-157; and Douglas Taylor, Languages of the West Indies (Baltimore, 1977), p.25 (where he speculates that the original form may have been *kanibna). On adoption into English see the entries in the Oxford English Dictionary. That on 'cannibal' is based on J. H. Trumbull, 'Cannibal', Notes and Queries, 5th series, IV (1875), 171-172.

10. Though Gustav Blanke (Amerika in Englisches Schrifttum des 16. und 17. Jahrhunderts (1962)) has pointed out that one Bodley atlas actually has 'Caliban' instead of the normal 'Cariban': referred to in Philip Brockbank, '"The Tempest": conventions of art and empire', in Later Shakespeare, eds. J. R. Brown and B. Harris (London, 1966), note to p.193.

11. As far as sailing ships were concerned the accepted definition was a wind such that no canvas could withstand: see O. G. Sutton, Understanding Weather (Harmondsworth, 1960), p.56. See also I. R. Tannehill, Hurricanes: their nature and history (Princeton, 1950).

12. The only possible supporting piece of evidence internal to The Tempest is Prospero's use of word 'coil' at I, ii, 207. (All textual references to The Tempest are to the corrected reprint of the sixth Arden edition, ed. Frank Kermode (London, 1962), henceforth abbreviated in the text to (T)).

13. Strachey's letter was first published by Samuel Purchas in 1625. References are to the twenty volume Glasgow edition of Purchas His Pilgrimes (1906): volume XIX, 5-72. Jourdain is quoted from the extracts in L. B. Wright, ed., The Elizabethans' America (London, 1965). For Shakespeare's use of the Bermuda pamphlets, see R. R. Cawley, 'Shakespere's Use of the Voyagers', PMLA, 41 (1926), 688-726, and Kermode's summary of the literature: T, pp.xxvi-xxxiv.

14. Purchas, XIX, 13-14.

15. Wright, p.197.

16. A conclusion spelt out in A Letter Sent Into England from the Summer Islands. Written by Mr. Lewis Hughes, Preacher of God's Word There [1615], also in Wright.

17. This pamphlet was entered on the Stationers' Registers on 4th December 1638 as being by John Taylor. It was bought by William Clarke, secretary to General Monck, on 10th January 1638 (i.e. 1639), and left by his son George Clarke to the Library of Worcester College, Oxford in 1736. Quotations are from a photocopy of this pamphlet, with kind permission of the Provost and Fellows of Worcester College, Oxford. The only reprint is in C. H. Wilkinson, ed., Two Tracts (Oxford, 1946). The only other known copy is in the Huntington Library (S.T.C. No. 21558). On John Taylor, see Robert Southey, The Lives and Works of the Uneducated Poets, ed. J. S. Childers (London, 1925), pp.15-87.

18. Taylor, p.2.

19. Taylor, p.2.

20. Gonzalo Fernández de Oviedo thought that hurricanes were less severe after the arrival of the Europeans: 'And in this case the Christian men ought to consider with good reason that in all places where the holy sacrament is reserved, the sayd tempestes are no more so outragious, or so perelous as they were wonte to bee' (Richard Eden's translation [1555], in Edward Arber, ed., The first three English books on America (Birmingham, 1885), p.216). There's no empirical evidence in favour of this view.

21. Cf., for example, Purchas' marginal comment to Strachey's letter: 'Can a leopard change his spots? Can a Savage be civil? Were not wee our selves made and not borne civill in our Progenitors dayes? and were not Caesar's Britaines as brutish as Virginians? The Romane swords were best teachers of civilitie to this and other Countries neere us' (Purchas, XIX, 62); or, for an earlier example, Thomas Smith's letter of 1572 justifying the colonisation of Ireland: '... this contrey of England ones as uncivill as Ireland now is, was by colonies of the Romaynes brought to understand the lawes and orders of thanncient orders' (quoted by Nicholas P. Canny, 'The ideology of English colonization: from Ireland to America', William and Mary Quarterly 30 (1973), 588-589). With the circular use of evidence favoured by ideology the similarities 'perceived' between 'savages' was proof of genetic descent: Spenser claimed that the Irish were descended from the Scythians (Canny, 587-588; and cf. n.28 below), who were also claimed as ancestors of the native Americans. For the establishment of the topos see John H. Elliott, The Old World and the New, 1492-1650 (Cambridge, 1970), chapter two; and Ronald Meek, Social Science and the Ignoble Savage (Cambridge, 1976), chapter two.

22. Taylor, pp.3-4.

23. Taylor, p.5.

24. Taylor, p.12. The closing of the circle - which Taylor's pamphlet

skirts around - was to explain the success of the Caribs' prognostications by the claim that their knowledge came from council with the devil: a step apparently often taken by the colonists themselves, as a justification for banishment (see 'Concerning hurricanes and their prognosticks - and observations of my owne experience thereupon', Egerton Ms. 2395 (British Library), 619; and cf. Oviedo, in Arber, p.215) - a procedure that meant that the English of St. Christophers had to send to Dominica for their weather forecasts. An important Biblical reading of the New World was the association of the natives either with the progeny of Canaan, cursed to be a servant of servants (Genesis, 9, 25), or with Cain; both of which were amenable to phonetic association with 'cannibal'. There may be a hint of this in Noah Biggs' striking version of 'hurricane', 'Harry Cain' (see his The Vanity of the Craft of Physick. Or, A NEW DISPENSATORY (London, 1651), p.99).

25. Taylor, pp.2-3.

26. 'Certain savage tribes on the coasts of the Black Sea, who are alleged to delight in raw meat or in human flesh, and others upon whom each in turn provides a child for the common banquet' (The Nicomachean Ethics, trans. H. Rackham (London, 1962), VII, v, 2 (p.403)). J. A. K. Thomson anachronistically translates αγθρωπωγ as 'cannibal' (The Ethics of Aristotle (Harmondsworth, 1955), VII, v (p.205)).

27. Daniel Defoe, Robinson Crusoe (Harmondsworth, 1965), pp.62, 122, 136, 143, 163, 171, 186, 200, 243.

28. On the function of the Scythians in Herodotus' discourse, although the concentration is on that other mark of savagery, nomadism (cf. Williamson, quoted above p. 58) see Francois Hartog, 'Les Scythes imaginaires: espace et nomadisme', Annales 34 (1979), 1137-1154.

29. I'm thinking, for example of the way in which in the Handbook of South American Indians, ed. J. H. Steward, 6 volumes (Washington, 1946), the cultural traits of each tribe are discussed under a series of headings, one of which is 'Warfare and Cannibalism', as if these two activities were inevitably associated, a common denominator of 'violence' being assumed. The 'image' is summed up in the Diccionario de autoridades (Madrid, 1726) entry for 'caribe': 'El hombre sangriento y cruel, que se enfurece contra otros, sin tener lástima, ni compassión' (A bloody and cruel man, who becomes furious with others, without pity or compassion).

30. See my 'Columbus and the cannibals: a study of the reports of anthropophagy in the Journal of Christopher Columbus', Ibero-Amerikanisches Archiv, N.F. IV (1978), 115-139.

31. The Journal of Christopher Columbus, translated by Cecil Jane, revised and annotated by L. A. Vigneras, with an appendix by R. A. Skelton (London, 1960), p.146. The journal only exists in Las Casas' summary.

32. See Irving Rouse, 'The Arawak', in Handbook of South American Indians, IV, 539.

33. Even when identified as Ciguayos this group was given a spurious Carib pedigree to explain their appearance: 'se cree que traen su origen de los canibales' (Pedro Mártir de Anglería [Peter Martyr], Décadas del nuevo mundo (1493-1525), trans. A. Millares Carlo, 2 vols. (Mexico, 1964), I, 160). Caliban's deformity is of course a mark of his viciousness, just as Ferdinand's beauty is a mark of his nobility. For remarks on this conventional Neoplatonic doctrine, see T, pp.lv-lvi, and p.39, note to I, 460).

34. The most recent study claims that there is no reliable evidence for anthropophagous practices at all, at any time or place: W. Arens, The Man-Eating Myth (New York, 1979). The term 'cannibalism' therefore forms part of a series of discursive manoeuvres which can be identified generically by the category of 'savage war' (see Francis Jennings, The Invasion of America (New York, 1976), chapter nine). Historically the designation 'cannibal' had functioned as the mark of the 'savage', in the sense that the 'cannibal' could not be considered even a potential citizen and could therefore legally be enslaved: for the essential early documents see Columbus' memorial of 30th January 1494 to Ferdinand and Isabella, in Martín Fernández de Navarrete, Colección de los viajes y descubrimientos que hicieron por mar los españoles desde fines del siglo XV, 3 vols. (Madrid, 1825-29), I, 231-2; and Queen Isabella's order of 30th October 1503, in Navarette, II, 414-16. The prime distinction that the Spanish were concerned to make was between Carib and guatiao, not - as is often thought - an ethnographic distinction, but merely a designation as, respectively, hostile and non-hostile. Legitimisation of enslavement was therefore simply a matter of designation of potential slaves as 'Carib': see Sauer, Early Spanish Main, pp.194-5.

35. Quoted by Trumbull, 'Cannibal', 172. The reference is clearly to dogs as predators and eaters of flesh, in Homeric terms the thos or jackal, rather than the trapezeus or table dog: see the relevant comments in James M. Redfield, Nature and Culture in the Iliad (Chicago, 1975), pp.193-203.

36. In Eden's translation: Arber, The first three English books, p.50.

37. For some related readings of The Tempest see: D. G. James, The Dream of Prospero (Oxford, 1967), chapter four; Leslie Fiedler, 'The New World Savage as Stranger: or "Tis new to thee"', in The Stranger in Shakespeare (London, 1973), pp.199-253; Leo Marx, 'Shakespeare's American Fable', in The Machine in the Garden (New York, 1970), pp.34-72; Kott, 'La tempête'; and Brockbank, 'The Tempest'.

38. The mainland Caribs were familiar from accounts of Raleigh's expeditions, but Shakespeare may have known Nicoll's account of the ill-fated landing on St. Lucia (see n.6 above).

39. See John W. Draper, 'Monster Caliban', Revue de Littérature Comparée, 40 (1966), 599-605. Cf. also J. E. Hankins, 'Caliban the Bestial Man', PMLA, 62 (1947), 793-801.

40. See J. M. Nosworthy, 'The Narrative Sources of The Tempest', Review of English Studies, XXIV (1948), 281-284.

41. Odyssey IX, 478-9. References will be to Richard Lattimore's translation, The Odyssey of Homer (New York, 1967).

42. Respectively, IX, 281-286 and IX, 131-141. Polyphemus' Sicily is a locus of the Golden Age, both in terms of its natural resources (most beautifully evoked in Luis de Góngora's rewriting of Book XII of Ovid's Metamorphoses, Fábula de Polifemo y Galatea [1626]), and in that it is defined by the traditional negatives: no laws, no agriculture, no houses, no institutions. This would then be one of the founding instances of the topos that reappears, via Montaigne, in Gonzalo's speech: T, II, i, 139-163: cf. Harry Levin, The Myth of the Golden Age in the Renaissance (New York, 1972), passim.

43. See Jennings, Invasion, p.149 and note 7.

44. Robinson Crusoe, p.243.

45. George Sandys, Ovids Metamorphosis Englished, Mythologized, And Represented in Figures (London, 1640), p.263.

46. See T, pp.xxxiv-xliii. For the wild man, see Richard Bernheimer, Wild Men in the Middle Ages (Harvard, 1952).

47. See Fiedler, 'The New World Savage', p.233.

48. See T, p.26, note to l. 258.

49. See Taylor, pp.5-6.

50. The canine connotations are possibly suggested by 'puppy-headed' (T, II, ii, 154).

51. Morton Luce, introduction to The Tempest (London, 1938), pp.xxxii and xxxv.

52. Luce, p.xxxv.

53. 'Cette étonnante dualité topographique' (Kott, 'La tempête', 137).

54. For the word 'plantation' see Howard Mumford Jones, O Strange New World (London, 1965), p.164.

55. Fiedler, 'The New World Savage', p.203.

56. 'Slave' is very much a Mediterranean term; 'salvage', although in the Romance languages a term associated with the 'wild man', in English was in the early part of the seventeenth century a colonial term, quite often used by Shakespeare, but not at all, for example, by the translators of the King James Bible (1611); for an interesting discussion of the word, see Jennings, Invasion, pp.72-78. 'Savage' appears - to quote a relevant example not discussed by

Jennings - to describe the native inhabitants of St. Christophers in an official document of the Privy Council concerning Thomas Warner's plantation (quoted in V. T. Harlow, ed., Colonizing Expeditions to the West Indies and Guiana, 1623-1667 (London, 1925), pp.xvi-xvii).

57. Mediation always depends on the existence of a third abnormal (i.e. monstruous) category: see Edmund Leach, Genesis as Myth and Other Essays (London, 1969), p.11. Kott discusses the whole of the play in these terms.

58. See in particular Roberto Fernández Retamar, Caliban: apuntes sobre la cultura en nuestra América (Mexico, 1971), and Aimé Césaire, Une tempête (Paris, 1969).

59. For general Carib hospitality, see John Davies, The History of the Caribby-Islands (London, 1666), pp.183 and 309. After the Spanish destroyed the English colony on St. Christophers in 1629, the four hundred English survivors were succoured in the hills by the Caribs that had not yet been banished from the island: Calendar of State Papers, p.102. For white indentured servants running away to the Caribs, see Crouse, French pioneers, p.49. For hostile and rebellious servants, see Dunn, Sugar and Slaves, p.69. For relevant evidence from Virginia, see Nicholas P. Canny, 'The permissive frontier: the problem of social control in English settlements in Ireland and Virginia 1550-1650' (in The Westward Enterprise. English activities in Ireland, the Atlantic and America 1480-1650, eds. K. R. Andrews, N. P. Canny, P. E. H. Hair (Liverpool, 1978), pp.17-44), who concludes that '... significant numbers of the early settlers were so indifferent to the extension of English civility that they happily integrated themselves into the indigenous society' (p.34). On Caribs and black slaves see, for example, David Barry Gaspar, 'Runaways in seventeenth-century Antigua, West Indies', Boletin de Estudios Latinoamericanos y del Caribe, No.26 (1979), pp.3-13; and for one of the long-term results, Douglas Taylor, The Black Caribs of British Honduras (New York, 1951). Tituba, the first person to be accused of witchcraft in Salem in 1692, seems to have been a Black Carib: see M. L. Starkey, The Devil in Massachusetts (London, 1949), p.23.

60. The True Declaration, quoted by Brockbank, 'The Tempest', p.186. Conversely, Prospero refers to the hurricane (not coincidentally at the moment of Caliban's conspiracy) as 'mutinous winds' (T, V, i, 42). Because no one wind dominated in a hurricane they were seen as 'a general conspiracy of all the winds' (Davis, The History, p.143).

61. A process already discernible in Taylor's pamphlet, and even, it might be argued, in the Odyssey where there is a sense in which Polyphemus is just another hazard, generically similar to Scylla and Charybdis, who are (coincidentally?) canine and cyclonic, respectively.

62. Eden has the phrase 'the furie of the cannibals' in the 'manhunting' section referred to on page 67 above: Arber, The first three English books, p.67. See also n.29 above.

63. The ironies here are complex. The hunting of Caliban is immediately followed by Prospero considering his vengeance on his brother and siding with his 'nobler reason 'gainst my fury' (_T_, V, i, 26). Cf. n.65 below.

64. As, of course, the historical 'canine' Indians were: see, for an example Shakespeare would have had access to, Bartolomé de las Casas, _The Spanish Colonie, or Brief Chronicle of the Acts and gestes of the Spaniardes in the West Indies, called the newe World, for the space of xl. yeeres_, trans. M.M.S. (London, 1583), # c.

65. See _T_, pp.lxxi-lxxvi for the troubled scholarship. The excess is also found at _T_, ii, 370-373 when Prospero responds to the justice of Caliban's claim.

66. The relevant sections of the play for these points are, respectively: I, ii, 338-340; I, ii, 313-315; I, ii, 346-350, 353-364. For the linguistic aspects of the division, see Kott, 'La tempête', p.141; and, more broadly, Stephen J. Greenblatt, 'Learning to curse: aspects of linguistic colonialism in the sixteenth century', in F. Chiapelli, ed., _The First Images of America_, 2 vols. (Los Angeles), I, 561-580.

67. 'Il ne faut rien dissimuler; car à quoi bon les feintes et les réticences? La sédition de Lyon a révélé un grave secret, celui de la lutte intestine qui a lieu dans la société entre la classe qui possède et celle qui ne possède pas ... Cherchez dans chaque ville industrielle quel est le nombre relatif des manufacturiers et des ouvriers, vous serez effrayé de la disproportion: chaque fabricant vit dans sa fabrique comme les planteurs des colonies au milieu de leur esclaves, un contre cent; et la sédition de Lyon est une espèce d'insurrection de Saint-Domingue ...' (Saint-Marc Girardin in the _Journal des Débats_ (8th December 1831) referring to the riot of the Lyons silk-workers: reprinted in his _Souvenirs d'un journaliste_ (Paris, 1859), pp.144-145). Jean-Paul Sartre refers to these riots as marking the beginning of the modern class struggle: 'La conscience de classe chez Flaubert', _Les Tempes Modernes_, XXI (April-June), 1924-26. For the relevance of the discourse I've been discussing to class struggle in England in the Tudor and Stuart periods, see Christopher Hill, 'The Many-Headed Monster in Late Tudor and Early Stuart Political Thinking', in _From the Renaissance to the Counter-Reformation_, ed. C. H. Carter (New York, 1965), pp.296-324; and for the eighteenth and nineteenth centuries, Hayden White, 'The Noble Savage Theme as Fetish', in his _Tropics of Discourse_, pp.183-196). White's argument is especially relevant given _The Tempest_'s concern for the vile and the non-vile (i.e. noble): see _T_, p.xivii, note 2.

68. Michel de Montaigne, 'Of the caniballes', _Essays_, trans. John Florio [1603], 3 vols. (London, 1892), I, 231.

A CONTROVERSIAL GUIDE TO THE LANGUAGE OF AMERICA, 1643

Gordon Brotherston

The date of the 'Key', and its form

From its beginnings in sixteenth century Virginia and seventeenth century New England, intercourse between native and Anglo-America has been a linguistically treacherous affair, especially as far as English representation of Indian discourse is concerned. Unique in its exposure of that treachery, in its early, formative stages, is a work by the founder of Rhode Island, Roger Williams, which bears the notable title A Key into the Language of America. Published in 1643, this work perdures, scantily acknowledged yet quite indispensable as a term of literary reference.(1) That it could have been written at all is explained as much by the fierce rivalry between Puritan interest groups after Charles I's death as by Williams' intriguing role as frank rebel and covert informer, dearest friend and traitor to his Narragansett hosts in New England.

Taking advantage of the political upheavals in London, in 1642 the Massachusetts Bay Company began to annex the neighbouring Providence Plantations, to which it had absolutely no right according to its own official doctrine on territory. Felt first by one Samuel Gorton, the Bay's greed threatened above all the man who had founded Providence in 1636, on being banished from the Bay's territories and forbidden to set foot on them ever again under pain of death, that is, Roger Williams. In 1643 Williams sailed to London to get a charter for the Providence lands, later called Rhode Island, as protection against the Bay Company. During the voyage he wrote his first book, the Key, 'drawing the Materialls in a rude lump at Sea' (to use his phrase), so weighty a lump indeed that he feared a watery grave for it and him. Issued in September by Gregory Dexter (a future disciple), the work served as main evidence in his successful suit for Rhode Island. Chronologically, the whole episode came a score or so years after the Mayflower had landed at Plymouth, the Pilgrim Colony also coveted by the Bay Company (whose hungry career began in 1630 with the arrival of Winthrop and other foes of Charles and his archbishop Laud); and hinging into the future it came just the same length of time before Nieuwe Amsterdam capitulated to the Restoration fleet, and before the New England colonies, their charters freshly secured by Charles II, joined an unbroken coastal empire stretching from Maine to Carolina.

Weigh as it did in his dealings with Cromwell, the Board of Commissioners for the Commonwealth, and Parliament, Williams' Key doesn't look like a legal document. Yet by the mere fact of dealing with the 'language of America' or at least that part of it best known to the English, this work couldn't fail to impress a public at that time vociferously concerned about the paltry success of its missioneering efforts in America compared to those of the French further north. If nothing else, the Key could and did leave no doubt about Williams' linguistic competence, in the field at Providence, as far superior to anything in the Bay, with its lazy Harvard scholars. Indeed it allowed him the finesse of suggesting that only with an expertise at least comparable with his could the instruction of converts be worth much at all, since 'Christenings make not Christians' (his phrase) of natives with religious ideas of their own. When he was awarded his charter, special mention was in fact made of his 'printed Indian labours'.(2) Then, developing the trope in the title of his work, he makes the Algonkin language itself into a key, to 'open a Box, where lies a bunch of Keyes', with which the reader may enter the 'secrets of those Countries'. This has the effect of suggesting that those not equipped with his Key could well fail to appreciate and 'convert' even the material wealth of the land.

First and foremost, Williams' Key is a practical 'help', and stems directly from his experience of living and talking with New England natives in their homes and on their terms. He tells his reader how to pronounce Narragansett words, how they differ from neighbouring Algonkin dialects, and how to distinguish forms of address according to rank and occasion. Indeed, his opening chapters are entirely situational: by stages the reader greets, eats, sleeps and counts, within a veritable atmosphere of native words and phrases, the first of which is nétop - friend. And into these situations Williams drops brief observations, entirely dependent on the associative flow, to give sharper definition, often through his own experience of a term in Indian life and custom. 'Whatever your occasion bee,' Williams tells us, 'either of Travell, Discourse, Trading &c, turne to the Table which will direct you to the Proper Chapter.' Precisely because of this respect for native speech in context, for its 'copious' synonyms and the world view implied in its verbal polysynthesis, does the Key go unrivalled among linguistic studies of the time. In principle the emphasis falls always on the native source from which English terms derive as more or less equivalent, the opposite in arrangement and effect to those contemporary dictionaries and grammars of American languages compiled perforce according to European norms.

Yet such norms can still be felt in the sheer layout of the Key, its division into chapters (explicit) and parts (implicit) which reveals the force of Williams' training as a Puritan scholar. The degree to which the chapter divisions serve to control an otherwise irreducible word-mass or potentially subversive native syntax is brought out in the 'Spirituall Observations' proper to each of them. General and particular, in prose (roman) and verse (italic), these Observations round off and hence insulate each chapter topic in itself, with an appropriate touch of Christian or scriptural piety. The implicit threefold division of the total thirty-two chapters into parts is best seen in the Table (Fig. 1). There we begin like Williams by entering the Narragansett home (salutation, eating, etc., chs. 1 - 10), only to pass into apparently abstract contemplation of sky, earth and sea, to each of which belong distinctly biblical creatures and 'fruits' (chs. 11 - 19), finally to end up with such highly sensitive socio-economic topics as trade, government and law, each of which is grammatically distinguished and disowned as Indian by the pronoun 'their' ('Of their nakednesse', 'religion', etc., chs. 20 - 32).

Discussing the unprecedented 'Forme' of his work, Williams says he had originally thought of casting it as a dialogue (the form of several subsequent works), but didn't for brevity's sake. Yet, as he goes on to say, every chapter is framed as an 'implicit dialogue'. In the circumstances he creates, this dialogue exists between not just Algonkin (Narragansett) and English but two economies and their respective law and philosophy. On an American scale, the Key emerges as the only English work to bear comparison with the Tupi-French theological dialogues recorded by Yves d'Evreux in Brazil, or with the Nahua-Spanish dialogue best exemplified in Frair Bernardino Sahagún's General History of New Spain whose successive drafts reveal a categorical conflict between their Mexican originals and European Renaissance models.

Solidarity with the Algonkin, against the Bay

In London in 1643, much of Williams' native vocabulary along with his explanatory notes could be read only as an indictment of the Bay and its manoeuvres and hence as a defence of its chief victims, the Indians. On the subject of war, for example, a familiar and accurate contrast is drawn between the bestial 'total war' waged by the Bay Europeans (e.g. against the Pequot in 1637) and the elaborate contracts which governed Indian hostilities. An analogous contrast is made between the sexual demeanour of the natives, naked yet unprurient, and the lewd habits of Europeans. Williams' major attack, however, is on Puritan methods of acquiring land. In practice the Bay got hold of land however it could, even condescending to purchase and compensatory payment, to kill Indians who sold to others, and to argue claims (especially to accompanying tribute rights) according to the native history and law of conquest. Yet officially it preached the doctrine of the vacuum domicilium previously used by Purchas and his pilgrims in Virginia (Jennings, 1976: 135-6). According to this doctrine, Indian land couldn't be bought because it had no owner, by virtue of not being properly 'subdued' or cultivated, or of being governed in a way (e.g. tribally) incommensurate with the newcomers' law. Stereotypes dear to this politic, all too recognisable in the literary cant of Europe, are the nomadic savages who traverse but do not inhabit their land and who obey laws written only in some Miltonic 'Book of Nature' (cf. Hunsaker, 1979).

On both counts, Williams energetically vindicates Indian rights.

He takes pains to point out the extent and nature of Indian agriculture (which relied heavily on fish fertilizer, munna whatteaug, in areas of poor soil), the variety of crops, their tastiness and medical virtues, here following unbeknown a philosophy of diet, especially re maize, elaborated in the Toltec books of Mexico (Brotherston, 1979: 189). And he speaks of their communal labour, women and men together, as exemplary of his own Renaissance faith in concord:

> 'Wompiscannémeneash. | White seed-corne.
>
> Obs. There be diverse sorts of this Corne, and of the colours: yet all of it either boild in milke, or buttered, if the use of it were knowne and received in England (it is the opinion of some skillfull in physick) it might save many thousand lives in England, occasioned by the binding nature of English wheat, the Indian Corne keeping the body in a constant moderate loosenesse.
>
> Aukeeteaûmen. | To plant Corne.
> Quttáunemun. | To plant Corne.
> Anakáusu. | A labourer.
> Anakáusichick. | Labourers.
> Aukeeteaûmitch. | Planting time.
> Aukeeteáhettit. | When they set Corne.
> Nummautaukeeteaûmen. | I have done planting.
> Anaskhómmin. | To how or break up.
>
> Obs. The Women set or plant, weede, and hill, and gather and barne all the corne, and Fruites of the field: Yet sometimes the man himselfe, (either out of love to his Wife, or care for his Children, or being an old man) will help the Woman which (by the custome of the Countrey,) they are not bound to.
>
> When a field is to be broken up, they have a very loving sociable speedy way to dispatch it: All the neighbours men and Women forty, fifty, a hundred &c, joyne, and come in to help freely.
>
> With friendly joyning they breake up their fields, build their Forts, hunt the Woods, stop and kill fish in the Rivers, it being true with them as in all the World in the Affaires of Earth or Heaven: By concord little things grow great, by discord the greatest come to nothing *Concordiâ parvae res crescunt, Discordiâ magnae dilabuntur*.' (*CW*, 1: 183)

As for the 'governing' of the land, we learn of laws which remove poverty and make open doors the norm, which cause decisions to be ratified by a parliament, and which foster a population so well-ordered that town follows upon town along every road 'some bigger, some lesser, it may be a dozen in 20 miles of Travell'. The names of these towns appear still in Williams' letters and were only later Anglicised

(Nonantum, Cambridge; Nameaug, New London; Cawcawmscussick, Wickford; Metewemesick, Sturbridge). So far from having no adequate government, the Algonkin are shown to know their land to the last tree and brook. Such were Williams' feelings on the subject that he condemned his fellow Christians of the Bay with the theologically pungent term 'sinful':

> | | |
> |---|---|
> | 'Sepoêse. | A little River. |
> | Sepoêmese. | A little Rivelet. |
> | Takêkum. | A Spring. |
> | Takekummûo? | Is there a Spring? |
> | Sepûo? | Is there a River? |
> | Toyusquanûo? | Is there a Bridge? |
>
> *Obs*. The *Natives* are very exact and punctuall in the bounds of their Lands, belonging to this or that Prince or People, (even to a River, Brooke) &c. And I have knowne them make bargaine and sale amongst themselves for a small piece, or quantity of Ground: notwithstanding a sinfull opinion amongst mauy that Christians have right to *Heathens* Lands:' (*CW*, 1: 179-80)

No doubt Williams' contempt for the vacuum domicilium doctrine professed by the Bay was sharpened by the fact that it invalidated his own claim to the land he had bought from Canonicus and Miantonomu, chief sachems of the Narragansett jurisdiction which became Rhode Island. Nonetheless he held such opinions long before buying land himself; indeed it was because his views on the subject were found 'heretical' that he was expelled from the Bay in the first place. Moreover this 'heresy' was acknowledged at the time as the prime reason for his expulsion, and more significant than the theological offences and disputes later quoted as reasons (cf. *CW*, 7: 7).

With Williams the land doctrine was part of a larger view of Indian society. Like no other author he alludes to it as a working economy, regulated calendrically by seasonal fairs and tribute collections at the Long House (cunnekamuck), an economy coherent from the lowest level of tree and brook to the grand geo-political system of courts (kitteickauick) which linked New England with the Ohio Valley or Southwest, 'Sowianu, the great Subject of their discourse' (*CW*, 1: 84, 257). There the great rulers were buried and from there came the staple crops of maize and beans, like their traditions, from the court of the great Cautantouwit (*CW*, 1: 208-14). This is a perspective more and more vindicated archeologically and by such revolutionary historians as Francis Jennings (1976), for whom indeed Williams serves as a welcome aide in the exposure of 'colonialism and the cant of conquest'. It is a perspective fragmented and denied in the official versions of colonial then US history forged by Parkman and, not least, the novelist Cooper (Clark, 1980). Williams' obscurity may indeed be accounted in part to the fact that his _Key_ doesn't fit easily into that history. By the same token that work stands as the first touchstone for 'Indianist' writing in the US, which in the nineteenth century emerges in that neglected antecedent of _Hiawatha_, Whittier's 'Mogg Megone' (1836) with its direct quotation of the _Key_'s resonant Algonkin, and which in the twentieth century finds by far its most distinguished expression in Ed Dorn's _Gran Apachería_ (1974).

Complicity with the Bay

For all its virtue in representing Algonkin language and reality, in strophes of native words and reminiscence that have no historical parallel, Williams' _Key_ must be deemed yet more loyal to the Puritan ideals which give it its structure. It even betrays complicity with the very party that harassed its author, the Bay. The reason for this paradox can be traced simply and surely to the values Williams and the Bay concurred in holding in highest esteem and honour: pounds sterling. The _Key_'s three chapters on Indian Coyne, Trading, and Debts and Trusting, absolutely confirm that the 'racial' gulf between Indian and Englishman in seventeenth century New England found its origin in economic practice. This was not in any way due to Indian incompetence in money matters. On the contrary, the natives handle and reckon with ease in sterling, expertly detect counterfeit coin, and register the slightest shift in the exchange rate against their own currency, materially based on shell (strung as wampum) rather than metal:

'Quttatashincheck aumscat, _or_, _more commonly used_ Piúckquat.	$5^{s.}$ 10 quttaúatues, _or_, 10 six pences.

Obs. This _Piúckquat_ being sixtie pence, they call _Nquittómpeg_, or _nquitnishcâusu_, that is, one fathom, 5 shillings. This one fathom of this their stringed money, now worth of the English but five shillings (sometimes more) some few

> yeeres since was worth nine, and sometimes ten shillings per Fathome: the fall is occasioned by the fall of Beaver in England: the Natives are very impatient, when for English commodities they pay so much more of their money, and not understanding the cause of it; and many say the English cheat and deceive them, though I have laboured to make them understand the reason of it.
>
> | | |
> |---|---|
> | Neesaumpaúgatuck. | 10 shil. 2 Fathom. |
> | Shwaumpáugatuck. | 15 shil. 3 Fathom. |
> | Yowompaugatuck, &c. | 20 shil. 4 Fathom. |
> | Piuckquampáugatuck. | 50 shil. 10 Fathome.' |
>
> (CW, 1: 234-5)

Rather, the problem arose from the ultimate imbalance between the two economic systems themselves.

Williams' complete collusion with the English or non-Indian system built up over long years as a debt-collector and agent of Winthrop ('I ... so dull a tool', he says) as well as a speculator in his own right. In a famous letter to Major Mason of Connecticut written in 1670 towards the end of his life, his trading activities become a sort of leit-motif (CW, 6: 333-50). Reflecting on his fortune in Rhode Island between the vaster enterprises of the Bay (Massachusetts) and Connecticut, and alluding to the secret understanding between all three vis-à-vis the Indians, Williams here recalls the many services he rendered to the white cause, the most remarkable of which was to betray the last native stronghold at Fort Mystic in the 1637 war to the armies of Underhill and Mason himself.(3) Only against this background of overriding racial and economic interest, beside which even internal disputes over land took second place, can we appreciate the 'true cause' of Williams' grief on being exiled from the Bay:

> 'And surely between those, my friends of the Bay and Plymouth, I was sorely tossed, for one fourteen weeks, in a bitter winter season, not knowing what bread or bed did mean, beside the yearly loss of no small matter in my trading with English and natives, being debarred from Boston, the chief mart and port of New England. God knows that many thousand pounds cannot repay the losses I have sustained. It lies upon the Massachusetts and me, yea, and other colonies joining with them, to examine with fear and trembling, before the eyes of flaming fire, the true cause of all my sorrows and sufferings. It pleased the Father of Spirits to touch many hearts dear to him with some relentings; amongst which that great and pious soul, Mr. Winslow, melted, and kindly visited me, at Providence,

> and put a piece of gold into the hands of my wife for our supply.' (CW, 6: 337-8)

The loss of profits on the Boston market inspires in him the intensely biblical rhetoric of fear and trembling, in a way which anticipates Defoe and could hardly better corroborate Weber's thesis on the Protestant ethic and the spirit of capitalism. For in his Key, in registering the Indians' financial suffering, through the fall of shell against gold, he omits all biblical piety. His refusal to acknowledge that the heart of Indian dispossession is economic in fact leads to a highly partial account of the peltry work cycle in the Key, only fragments of which surface in chapters on Travel, Hunting, and Gaming (here quite dissociated from Puritan 'speculation'). It also leads to the more preposterous of his Spirituall Observations: as compensation for losing out Indians can remember they have actually handled garments that adorn the mighty, a thought so cynical as to appear all but revolutionary:

> 'Generall Observation of Trade.
>
> O the infinite wisedome of the most holy wise God, who hath so advanced Europe above America, that there is not a sorry Howe, Hatchet, Knife, nor a rag of cloth in all America, but what comes over the dreadfull Atlantick Ocean from Europe: and yet that Europe be not proud, nor America discouraged. What treasures are hid in some parts of America, and in our New English parts, how have foule hands (in smoakie houses) the first handling of whose Furres which are after worne upon the hands of Queens and heads of Princes?
>
> More particular:
>
> 1 Oft have I heard these Indians say,
> These English will deceive us.
> Of all that's ours, our lands and lives
> In th' end they will bereave us.' (CW, 1: 185)

For the most part the Spirituall Observations which round off each chapter in the Key draw directly on the Bible for their moral piety, scriptures which as the masking ideology for Puritan capitalism Williams never failed to revere in common with the Bay, whatever their sectarian differences. Hence that capitalism can fairly be said to correspond to the very structure of chapters and Observations imposed on the Indian 'material' in the Key. This is exemplarily true of chapter 16, placed in the second non-economic part of the Key under the biblical title

'Of the Earth and the Fruits thereof', along with the Spirituall Observation quoted below, all of which militates against its implicit defence of Indian land rights on grounds of their agriculture:

> 'Yeeres thousands since, God gaue command
> (as we in Scripture find)
> That Earth and Trees & Plants should bring
> Forth fruits each in his kind.
>
> The Wildernesse remembers this,
> The wild and howling land
> Answers the toyling labour of,
> The wildest Indians hand.
>
> But man forgets his Maker, who,
> Fram'd him in Righteousnesse.
> A paradise in Paradise, now worse
> Then Indian wildernesse.' (*CW*, 1: 186)

Contorted as it is, the ideological structure here imposed by Williams means that human effort in the language of America is somehow to be construed after all as the bounty of the imported god of Genesis. Despite all that he has told us about the wealth of cultivated fields around him, and lapsing into a tone of pure prophecy at once biblical and economically actual, Williams makes Indian land revert to the 'wildernesse' spoken of by Winthrop, Weld and the official theologian-historians of the Bay, and hence invites in that most repugnant of literary inventions, the white American Adam.

God, clothes and books

To justify intrusion into Algonkin life and territory, the *Key*, like all good Puritan tracts, turns to the scriptures, to verses endlessly repeated in the Spirituall Observations that urge increase and the spread of the gospel throughout the world. As a result the *Key* resolutely suppresses the notion that New England possessed anything remotely equivalent to those scriptures before the Mayflower landed. At the most basic level this is done simply by means of the Renaissance trope that presents us with a naked native American innocent who, in Montaigne's words, has yet to learn his ABC. In the chapters 'Of their Nakednesse and Clothing' and 'Of their Paintings' (20 and 30), we learn of Algonkin who neither dress nor write. And such 'paintings' as they have, found in a 'varietie of formes and colours' on their deer-skin cloaks, these they take off in the rain, since they are not proof against the elements. Again despite evidence implied elsewhere in the Key itself and now confirmed by archeology, the language of America is stated to be utterly oral, and quite devoid of any graphic correlative be it tribute accounts, the roll of political succession, or larger-scale history. Williams can therefore pronounce the Indians happy but biblically 'lost', in the very paragraph that tells of their traditional bond with that great millennial centre Sowaniu.

The trope of naked illiterate virtue did not entirely satisfy Williams, however. In his chapter 'Of their Religion, Soule, &c', reporting a conversation overheard between Miantonomu and a Cunnihticut (Connecticut) archpriest, he reveals, perhaps unwittingly, that the Indians thoroughly understood the social and other powers of script, for which a native term proved readily available, wussuck wheke, a cognate of the term for the deer-skin paintings worn as clothes, wussuck hosu. And in the two chapters directly concerned with clothing and painting, his uncertainty and the extreme weight he places on the Bible as the authorised script lead him into self-contradiction. For naked innocence becomes not so much a prelapsarian virtue ('Truth is a Native, naked Beauty') as the blemish on the soul that is not 'cloth'd with Christ'. In other words, for the double Renaissance trope of clothes and script with its sentimental view of innocence, Williams substitutes the triple fundamentalist trope 'God, clothes and bookes', with its highly purposive contrary view. He explains the switch by suggesting that in his naked state the native is the more susceptible to 'Indian paints', while now crediting these with being not so much a childish irrelevance as 'Lying invention', a scriptural truth after all, but of the wrong kind and the core of an opposed heathen intelligence.

Williams' extreme emphasis on biblical script to validate conquest, in his equation of books, clothes and God, cannot but reflect on the Key's own status as a printed text. The very typographical arrangement of its chapters and Spirituall Observations may thus be seen as Puritan prudery, a means of clothing 'with Christ' a heathen and reprehensible nakedness in America's language. Yet at the same time

Williams exposes the cant in such prudery, in his conflicting tropes and not least in his palpable respect not for the nakedness but the propriety of that language. This is especially true of his appreciation of formal and liturgical language, which echoed that of Sowaniu and, further on again, the Nahua poetics of Mexico: the orphan song 'proper' to the onset of night along the road ntouagon nausin nummin; or the verses of funereal grief and consolation mat wonck kunnawmone, kutchimmoke ('you shall see him no more, yet be of good cheer', CW, 1: 160, 276; in turn these reminded him of how on the death of his son Canonicus burnt his own palace and goods regardless of their 'great value'). Through just this truly literary commitment to native discourse was Williams able, uniquely, to trace its roots so deep into native economy and government and to use it as the key that unlocks but does not destroy New England's more ancient secrets.

Footnotes

1. Reprinted in 1827, the Key appeared in the first of the six volumes of the 1866 Narragansett edition of Williams' Complete Writings (= CW); in the 1963 reprint of this edition, a seventh volume is added which includes Christenings make not Christians, contemporary with the Key, and other works previously thought lost, as well as an interpretative essay by Perry Miller.

2. In a letter of 1644 signed by the Earl of Northumberland and others, quote in CW, 1: 73. On the missionary question, one of the Harvard scholars, Thomas Weld, acted as the Bay's agent against Williams; the Bay's seal of 1629 (Fig. 2) had shown a would-be Indian convert simple-mindedly asking for 'help', which the Bay certainly taught him to need (cf. Jennings, 1976: 228-35). Further ideological reasons for Williams' success are suggested below. It is the case that Cromwell's cousin Hampden had strongly invested in Rhode Island, and that Williams' term of governorship of the Colony, 1654-8, exactly coincided with the Protectorate. There is a whole other story in the intrigue between the English investors, notably the above and such figures as Sir Henry Vane (Williams' host in England), Vane's son (Winthrop's rival as governor of the Bay) and Arthur Pym, and between the chief New England colonies of the Bay (Massachusetts and later Plymouth), Rhode Island and Connecticut.

3. This much may be deduced from his letter to John Winthrop from New Providence in 1637, CW, 6: 16-20 (see Fig. 3); Indian auxiliaries were led by Miantonomu and Uncas, Cooper's hero. Still trusted by the Narragansett, Williams again used his influence in the second colonial war of 1675, to prevent them from joining forces with Metacom (King Philip) until it was militarily too late.

A Key into the

LANGUAGE

OF

AMERICA:

OR,

An help to the *Language* of the *Natives* in that part of America, called *NEW-ENGLAND.*

Together, with briefe *Obſervations* of the Cuſtomes, Manners and Worſhips, *&c.* of the aforeſaid *Natives*, in Peace and Warre, in Life and Death.

On all which are added Spirituall *Obſervations*, Generall and Particular by the *Authour*, of chiefe and ſpeciall uſe (upon all occaſions,) to all the *Engliſh* Inhabiting thoſe parts; yet pleaſant and profitable to the view of all men:

By ROGER WILLIAMS
of *Providence* in *New-England.*

LONDON,
Printed by *Gregory Dexter*, 1643.

The Table.

Fig. 1: The title page and table of the Key

Fig. 2: The Bay's seal

(Courtesy of the Archives Division, Office of the Secretary, Commonwealth of Massachusetts, Boston.)

Sir, you may pleafe to take notice of a rude view, how the Pequots lie:

River Connecticut.

O *a fort of the Nayantic men, confederate with the Pequots.*

Mohigadic

River.

Wein **O** ***shauks, where***

Sassacus the chief Sachem is.

Mis O *tick, where is Mamoho, another chief sachim.*

Obom | | | | *owauke, the swamp, three or four miles from*———

River.

Nayantic, **O** *where is Wepiteammock and our friends.*

River.

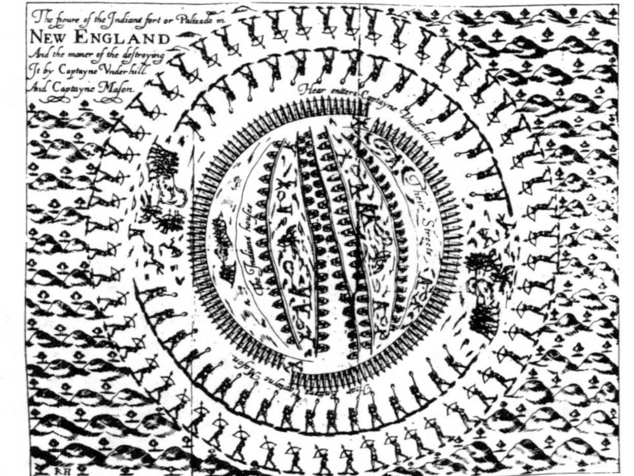

Fig. 3: (a) Extract from Williams' letter to Winthrop about the Pequot at Mystic;
(b) Underhill's diagram of his and Mason's attack on the Pequot at Mystic, 1637

Bibliography

Brockunier, S. H. (1940), The Irrepressible Democrat: Roger Williams. New York.

Brotherston, Gordon (1979), Image of the New World. London and New York.

Clark, Robert (1980), History and Myth in United States Fiction 1823-1852. Unpublished PhD Dissertation, University of Essex.

Franklin, Wayne (1979), Discoverers, Explorers, Settlers. Chicago and London.

Gorton, Samuel (1643), Simplicities Defence against Seven-Headed Policy. In P. Force, Tracts and Other Papers, IV, Washington 1846.

Horowitz, David (1978), The First Frontier. The Indian Wars and America's Origins. New York.

Hunsaker, O. Glade (1979), 'Roger Williams and John Milton: the Calling of the Puritan Writer'. In E. Elliott, Puritan Influences in American Literature, Urbana, Chicago and London.

Jennings, Francis (1976), The Invasion of America. Indians, Colonialism and the Cant of Conquest. New York.

Mason, John (1677), 'A Brief History of the Pequot War'. In Increase Mather, A Relation of the Troubles which have hapned in New-England, by reason of the Indians there, reprinted Boston 1736.

Miller, Perry (1953), Roger Williams, his contribution to the American Tradition. New York.

(1963), 'Roger Williams. An Essay in Interpretation'. In CW, 7: 5-25.

Purchas, Samuel (1625), Hakluytus Posthumus or Purchas His Pilgrimes. London, 4 vols.

Sahagún, Bernardino de (1956), Historia general de las cosas de Nueva España. Mexico, 4 vols.

Underhill, John (1638), Newes from America; or, A New and Experimentall Discoverie of New England. London.

Weber, Max (1904-5), 'Die protestantische Ethik und der Geist des Kapitalismus'. Archiv für Sozialwissenschaft und Sozialpolitik, Tübingen XX and XXI.

Weld, Thomas and Hugh Peter (1643), New England's First Fruits, in respect to the progress of learning, in the Colledge at Cambridge. In Collections of the Massachusetts Historical Society, 1st Series I, 1792.

Williams, Roger (1963), The Complete Writings of Roger Williams. New York, 7 vols.

Winthrop, John (1690), The History of New England from 1630 to 1649. Second edition by J. Savage, Boston, 1853, 2 vols.

Yves d'Evreux (1864), Voyage dans le nord de Brésil fait durant les années 1613-14. Leipzig and Paris.

THE APPROPRIATION OF PASCAL

Ian H. Birchall

'Literary works cannot be taken over like factories'. (Brecht)[1]

'The apologists want to "recuperate" Pascal, just as they have recuperated Joan of Arc'. (Henri Lefebvre) (2)

In this paper I want to attempt an account of Pascal in terms of one of the perennial questions of a Marxist approach to literature - how do we deal with works which are written from an explicitly reactionary standpoint? There have been two main lines of response: one stemming from Marx and Engels' comments on Balzac, and Lenin's on Tolstoy, which plays down the overt intentions of the writer in favour of the lessons of the work; the other - to which I must confess my own gut sympathies go - is crystallised in Mayakovsky's declaration: 'The White Guard is given over to a firing squad: why not Pushkin?'.[3]

Pascal, of course, has been the object of a major work of Marxist analysis, Goldmann's Le Dieu Caché, generally acknowledged even by his critics to be Goldmann's best and most complex endeavour in the field of literary sociology. Goldmann's work is rich and many-sided, and I shall not attempt to challenge the overall analysis, but will merely try to bring out some aspects that seem to me unsatisfactory.

Goldmann's work is complex precisely because it establishes a three-fold relationship to Pascal:

(1) Pascal is the object to which Goldmann's method is applied; his work is to be understood and explained. As such, Pascal could have been replaced by any other 'great' writer, given Goldmann's peculiar reverence for the established literary tradition. The choice of a classic writer such as Pascal fits Goldmann's position that, since for the foreseeable future Marxist theory was detached from revolutionary practice,

the job of Marxist intellectuals was to defend the Marxist method by demonstrating its superiority in competition with bourgeois scholarship on the latter's terrain.[4]

(2) Secondly, the work is an attempt to recruit Pascal as part of a tradition of thought which, running through Kant, Hegel and Marx, leads to Goldmann's mentor Lukács. 'The work of Pascal represents the major turning-point in Western thought moving from rationalist or empiricist atomism towards dialectical thought'.[5] Although Goldmann distinguishes between the 'tragic' vision of Pascal and Kant and the 'dialectical' vision of Marx and Lukács, he puts far more stress on what the two visions have in common than on what divides them, and on occasion he quite simply refers to Pascal as a representative of 'dialectical philosophy'.[6]

(3) Thirdly, Pascal is cited by Goldmann as having understood the correct method required in the study of a text. In expounding his concept of coherence[7] he quotes Pascal's view of the approach to Holy Scripture:

> 'To understand the meaning of an author, we must reconcile all the contradictory passages. So, to understand Scripture, we must have a meaning in which all the contradictory passages are reconciled. It's not enough to have one which fits several passages that agree with each other, we must have one which reconciles even the contradictory passages. Every author has a meaning in which all the contradictory passages are reconciled, or he has no meaning at all. We cannot say that of Scripture and the prophets; their meaning was certainly too good for that. So we must find one that reconciles all the contradictions.' (684) (8)

This last point poses problems. Goldmann, as a materialist, presumably accepted that Pascal's attempt to discover coherence in the Bible could be only a grotesque mystification. Yet the attempt to discover coherence in the *Pensées* is also problematical. Goldmann's attempt to co-opt the *Pensées* comes at the end of a long history of varying interpretations from Catholic, rationalist and Romantic viewpoints. The fragmentary state of the text invites a variety of interpretations. Originally published in 1670, the text, which Pascal had left incomplete at his death, was mutilated by his family and friends in keeping with the needs of contemporary theological controversy. An adequate text was produced only in the nineteenth century, and the question of the order in which the fragments should be arranged is still a question of scholarly debate.

But beyond this Pascal's whole position is riddled with contradictions. Time and again he seems to become aware that the logic of his position is leading him where he doesn't want to go. Thus in a short essay comparing the primitive Christians with the seventeenth century Church, Pascal writes:

> 'When instruction preceded baptism, all were instructed. But now that baptism precedes instruction, the education which was necessary becomes voluntary and hence neglected and finally almost abolished. The true reason for this behaviour is that we are convinced of the necessity for baptism and that we aren't convinced of the necessity for instruction. So that, when instruction preceded baptism, the necessity of the one meant that people necessarily had recourse to the other; whereas today, when baptism precedes instruction, since people become Christians without having been instructed, they think they can remain Christians without getting themselves instructed ...' (9)

With the remorseless logic of which he is capable, Pascal is making the case against infant baptism. That, however, would lead to Anabaptism, and Anabaptism was not only heretical but communistic. So Pascal stops short and concludes with some platitudes about keeping up moral standards.

The contradictions and ambiguities that run through Pascal's work must, of course, be understood in terms of the relations of class forces. Goldmann's celebrated analysis of the relations between Pascal, Jansenism and the <u>noblesse de robe</u> is based on a large bulk of evidence, and I would not attempt to propose a detailed counter-argument. But one point is striking about Goldmann's general presentation. His account of the changing fortunes of the <u>noblesse de robe</u> is presented in terms of conflicts between groups within the privileged <u>bloc</u> which shared a common interest in living off the backs of the peasantry. In so doing Goldmann makes use of the ambiguous and populist concept of the 'third estate'. And symptomatically, in his account of class relations, his only references to popular revolts are to be found within brackets or in a footnote.(10)

The contradictions of the society Pascal grew up into can be seen vividly in the career of Pascal's own father, Etienne Pascal. The years 1630 to 1648 saw a tripling of the tax burden to meet the needs of war expenditure. But different classes were affected differently. Etienne Pascal was the holder of government bonds on the Hôtel de Ville de Paris. These were paid by the government out of taxation, hence ultimately by the peasantry. In 1638 the interest payments had not been made, and Etienne Pascal was one of a group of investors who organised an occupation at the office of the _chancelier_ Séguier. Richelieu had some of the ringleaders arrested and Etienne Pascal fled to Auvergne.

However, the following year he was pardoned, and soon after was sent to Normandy as a tax collector. Now for some time the common people of Normandy had felt the effects of the economic crisis; like Etienne Pascal they had fought for what they believed to be their rights, though in rather more vigorous form. Thus in July 1639, when an official of the Rouen _parlement_ came to Avranches:

> 'An hour and a half later four hundred people, mostly salt makers and wood porters, were kicking and punching Poupinel and beating him with sticks and stones. The wretched man, his flesh in shreds, died about half past twelve noon. The spinning women put out his eyes with their spindles.' (11)

The revolts in Normandy were put down with the utmost brutality; those who had participated were hung and broken on the wheel; their houses were razed to the ground. While we do not know Etienne Pascal's exact role, he certainly participated in the repression. Young Blaise had so few qualms about the whole thing that he invented a calculating machine to help his father add up the money he was screwing out of the peasantry.

It is against this background of double standards and fear of the masses that we can understand the resolutely conservative nature of Pascal's thought.

The _Pensées_ are a systematic polemic against reason and rationalism. Pascal is not, of course, an irrationalist; his scheme carefully assigns a place to reason; but by arguing that reason is subject to strict limits, he in effect seeks to protect whole areas of experience, both theological and political, from critical enquiry. As Henri Lefebvre has pointed out, since Pascal was unable to reconcile science and religion, he solved the problem - at least to his own satisfaction - by establishing the hierarchy of different orders (coeur, raison, charité).(12)

But the undoubted polemic thrust of the Pensées is to attack the claims of reason. 'How I love to see that proud reason humiliated and begging!' (388). He advises unbelievers to go through the motions of holy water, masses, etc.: 'That will make you believe and stupefy you (vous abetira)'. (233)

Now it is undoubtedly true that, both in the Provinciales and the Pensées, Pascal shows himself to be a very competent polemic writer. But it is also the case that in many places he uses some lamentably weak arguments. Thus he undermines his own point about the nature of miracles when he writes: 'Why should a virgin not give birth? Doesn't a hen produce eggs without a cock; and who can tell them from the others from the outside?' (222).

Likewise some of his attempts to reason by analogy are pathetic failures:

> 'We know that there is an infinite and we don't know its nature. Since we know that it is false that numbers are finite, then it is true that there is an infinite in numbers. But we don't know what it is: it's false that it's even, it's false that it's odd; for if we add unity, it doesn't change its nature; none the less, it's a number, and all numbers are even or odd (it's true that that's the case with every finite number). Thus we can indeed know that there is a God without knowing what he is.' (233)

If logic-chopping of that sort qualifies as dialectics, then it must do so on the same level as J. V. Stalin's claim that 'the state will die out, not by the weakening of state authority, but by strengthening it to the utmost necessary'.(13)

Equally Pascal denies any real notion of historical development. He admits the possibility of progress in scientific knowledge, but denies it as far as theology is concerned,[14] already in the Préface sur le Traité du Vide. By the time of the Pensées human history has become nothing but a series of squalid accidents. Cleopatra's nose (162), perhaps because of its sexist overtones, has become proverbial; even more significant, perhaps, is the little grain of sand in Cromwell's ureter which, Pascal notes with satisfaction, prevented him from devastating the whole of Christendom (176). That such small things can lead to counter-revolution is clearly a source of consolation to Pascal.

But the most significant and penetrating of Pascal's comments on history comes in a discussion of the origins of social conventions and institutions:

> 'That's why the wisest of legislators said that, for the good of men, they must be often duped; and another, very shrewd, "As he doesn't know the truth that liberates, it is good for him to be deceived". He must not feel the truth of usurpation; it was introduced long ago without reason; it has become reasonable; it must be made to seem authentic and eternal; its beginning must be hidden, if we don't want it to end soon.' (294)

Here Pascal seizes with great acuteness the subversiveness of the historical method.

The explicitly political comments in the Pensées are equally reactionary. It is indeed possible to find apparently radical passages in Pascal, and some of the other Jansenists, such as Arnauld and Nicole, were alarmed at Pascal's suggestion that social institutions are purely arbitrary. In his Trois Discours sur la Condition des Grands he argues the arbitrary nature of social institutions, only to end up by insisting on the necessity for maintaining the conventions,[15] 'The greatest of evils is civil wars' (313) - a very worldly 'greatest evil' for one so steeped in the transcendent. The image of civil war seems to haunt his work - 'when a private soldier takes the square hat of a premier président and throws it out of the window ...' (310). The sentence trails off into horrified silence.

In particular Pascal is aware of the danger of a meritocratic organisation of society. The minority who had argued for the meritocratic principle had been defeated a generation earlier with the establishment of the sale of offices, though the principle was to revive in 1789 with the 'career open to talents'. For Pascal civil wars 'are certain, if we try to reward merit, for everyone will say they are deserving. The ill to be feared from a fool who succeeds by right of birth is neither so great nor so certain'. (313)

The ultimate theme of the Pensées, then, is one of total passivity, of the futility of human action: 'I have learnt that all human unhappiness comes from one single thing, that people don't know how to remain at rest in one room'. (139)

A view of the world in which human beings are unable to make their own history, indeed in which there is no history to make; it is hard to see in what way this can be part of a tradition leading to Marxism.

Why then was Goldmann so insistent on trying to co-opt so openly conservative a thinker as Pascal to his tradition? One reason may lie in previous treatments of Pascal. Goldmann was deeply hostile to the Marxism of the French Communist Party, saying that much of the work of PCF intellectuals was such as to 'turn young students away from Marxism' because of its lack of 'intellectual integrity'.[(16)] The PCF had always been resolutely Cartesian. In 1937, at a time when the French ruling class was trying to roll back the gains of June 1936, two PCF deputies found time to put down a parliamentary resolution calling on the government to organise a national celebration of the tricentenary of Le Discours de la Méthode.

However, one PCF intellectual did produce a major study of Pascal. Henri Lefebvre's Pascal (1949-54), which has largely been overshadowed by Le Dieu Caché, is in some ways a more interesting work, although uneven and revealing the pressures under which it was produced. There is a five-year gap between the first and second volumes, and the second volume begins with an act of 'self-criticism' in which Lefebvre responds to criticisms he has received, including comments sent to him by Lukács. He had been accused of being too soft on both Jansenism and modern existentialism; in replying he quotes Zhdanov in order to show that works from the past may contain a 'grain of truth'. He insists on the concept of 'reflection' which he says has the gift of 'infuriating idealists and making them grind their teeth'.(17) Lefebvre confronts Pascal as an unambiguously reactionary thinker; he accuses him of holding a 'police conception (conception policière) of history', because he believes small causes can have great effects;(18) and he writes an imaginary dialogue with Pascal confronting the latter's views with his own and concluding 'we're no longer speaking the same language'.(19) However, Lefebvre resolves the problem of how to categorise Pascal by an evasion; he argues that the work is 'displaced from the ideological to the aesthetic level', that we can understand and like it without believing, just as we can respond to medieval cathedrals or Greek temples.(20)

Goldmann and Lefebvre appear to have encountered each other at a debate on Pascal at the Centre d'Etudes Sociologiques in 1951; but while Lefebvre is sharply critical of Goldmann's positions, Goldmann studiously refuses to engage a debate with Lefebvre. In some ways Goldmann's attitude to Stalinism seems analogous to that of Pascal towards the absolute monarchy; he will not compromise with it, but he is unable or unwilling to organise against it. Goldmann had originally intended to follow his first work, on Kant, with studies of Goethe and Marx, showing the emergence of dialectical thought.(21) The decision to abandon this project, and instead to follow the line backwards to Pascal, can be understood only in the context of a political choice to turn his back on the struggle of his own time.

Moreover, Goldmann projects back on to the seventeenth century the fatalism he feels about his own period. He concludes his study of Pascal by declaring: 'But Pascal lived in France in the seventeenth century; there was therefore no question for him of a historical dialectic'.(22) Of course, in a sense this is true; yet by placing himself on the terrain of the literary 'great tradition', and by playing down the possibilities of struggle, Goldmann apologises for Pascal by ignoring those who did push as far as they could go towards a revolutionary dialectic. In 1621, a generation before Pascal wrote his logic-chopping critique of atheism, two Paris atheists had been burnt alive in the Place de la Grève. Louis XIV's regime understood its enemies well enough to ban Cartesianism from the Universities; and it was above all under Cartesian influence that Jean Meslier, born two years after Pascal's death, was able to develop a thought that was so radical in both its atheism and its communism (including the advocacy of the general strike) that Voltaire himself had to suppress substantial sections of his writings.(23)

Goldmann has had much harsh criticism from English commentators over the last decade. Most of the criticism has focused on the alleged 'reductionism' of his method. He is accused of having 'no concept of the relative autonomy of art';(24) of displaying 'no developed notion of the "relative autonomy" of superstructural forms';(25) in his hands 'the text ... is rudely robbed of its materiality, reduced to no more than the microcosm of a mental structure'.(26) Reductionism, of course, is like sin; we are all against it without needing to say why; but it seems to me that what is wrong with Goldmann is not so much reductionism as what is being reduced to what; that it is not so much his method as his whole critical aim and perspective that needs criticism. Many of his critics, however, do not differ from those aims; for example, Eagleton, who argues that 'most of the agreed (agreed by whom? I.H.B.) major writers of the twentieth century ... are political conservatives who each had truck with fascism',(27) seems to stand ultimately on the same ground as Goldmann.

Perhaps a final comparison will help to illuminate this point. Goldmann alleges that the rationalist tradition from Malebranche to Voltaire and Valéry shows a 'radical incomprehension' of the tragic position of Pascal.(28) I am not competent to argue whether Valéry ever understood anything about anything, but I want to argue that Voltaire understood Pascal better than Goldmann did.

Indeed Goldmann himself seems to show a radical incomprehension of the revolutionary nature of Enlightenment thought. To argue that the relations between thought and action in Voltaire are 'desirable and realisable'(29) is to grossly over-simplify Voltaire's complex apprehension of the historical process. Beyond this, Goldmann actually argues that the modern French state is the 'product of a normal organic development of the Third Estate', and that 'even the years 1789-1815 were only a powerful and grandiose episode of this organic development which they neither stopped nor deflected'.[30] Writing revolution out of the present leads to a bizarre rewriting of the past.

Voltaire was never able to read a complete edition of the Pensées, yet he saw enough in what he read to understand the nature of his adversary. Voltaire first criticised Pascal in the Lettres Philosophiques, written in the 1720's; he alluded to him time and time again throughout his life, and returned in 1777, the year before his death, to launch yet another and sharper polemic against Pascal.

Voltaire was no facile optimist, and there are many passages in Voltaire which show an echo of the Pascalian vision: 'All I know is that we are sheep whom the butcher never tells when he is going to kill them'.[31] But if Voltaire could find echoes of Pascal within himself, he understood very clearly the need to fight all that Pascal stood for. In the early years of the eighteenth century Jansenism still had a deep and pervasive influence in layers of the bourgeoisie; Voltaire understood all too well that Jansenist asceticism was not good for trade, that a nascent French capitalism needed consumption and luxury not other-worldliness (cf. Le Mondain). In particular, Voltaire insists on the possibility of human progress without lapsing into the abstraction of a 'Progress' which not only does not need human self-activity but can be directed against it. Voltaire's historical writings, especially his Essai sur les Moeurs, can be seen as the most significant example of an uncomplacent concept of progress before Marx.

Voltaire recognises Pascal's enormous superiority over the theological pedants of his age - he is a 'man of genius, still standing on the ruins of his century'.[32] But that does not lead Voltaire to any false reverence; on the contrary Pascal's abilities serve only to make him the more dangerous. When Pascal writes: 'The infinite distance from bodies to spirits represents the infinitely more infinite distance from spirits to charity' (793), Voltaire simply comments that this is 'gibberish' (galimatias), which Pascal would probably have omitted from the finished work.[33]

Voltaire focuses sharply on the key aspects of Pascal's reactionary doctrine: 'he writes against human nature somewhat as he wrote against the Jesuits ... he utters eloquent insults against the human race. I dare to take the side of humanity against this sublime misanthropist.'[34] 'Man is born for action, as the fire tends upwards and the stone downwards.'[35]

And to Pascal's contention that a society based on merit must lead to civil war, Voltaire responds in concrete terms, albeit within his own reformist absolutist framework:

> 'This needs explanation. Civil war if the Prince de Conti says "I have as much merit as the Prince de Condé"; if Retz says "I'm worth more than Mazarin"; if Beaufort says "I'll get the better of Turenne"; and if there's nobody to put them in their place. But when Louis XIV comes along and says "I shall reward only merit", then there is no more civil war.' (36)

As Goldmann, in a somewhat different context points out, 'in great social and ideological struggles the contending parties are rarely mistaken, and virtually never as far as the essential positions of their adversaries are concerned'.[37] Voltaire understood Pascal better than Goldmann because, bourgeois that he was, he was more class-conscious. Goldmann, despite his erudition, despite his methodological insights from which we can learn much, failed - in Marx's words - to turn 'the criticism of religion into the criticism of right and the criticism of theology into the criticism of politics'.[38]

If Pascal could see the gathering of libertines and atheists that makes up this conference, he would have no hesitation in condemning us all to the eternal flames. I am not even suggesting we should condemn Pascal's works to the flames; but simply that, if we read him, we should do so in order to encounter a lucid spokesperson for the enemy, and not to pretend that he is somehow on our side.

Footnotes

All translations from the French are my own, except where the footnote indicates an English translation (I.H.B.).

1. J. Willett (Ed.), Brecht on Theatre (Eyre Methuen, 1978), p.109.
2. H. Lefebvre, Pascal (Nagel, Vol.I 1949, Vol.II 1954), I, 8.
3. Cited in M. Slonim, Soviet Russian Literature (OUP, 1967), p.21.
4. This point (implicit throughout Goldmann's work) was made explicitly in a lecture given by Goldmann at LSE on 19th May 1969.
5. L. Goldmann, Le Dieu Caché (Gallimard, 1955), p.15.
6. L. Goldmann, Marxisme et Sciences Humaines (Gallimard, 1970), p.274.
7. Goldmann, Le Dieu Caché, p.22.
8. All references to the Pensées are given as numbers in the text, according to the Brunschvicg classification. I have chosen this classification as the one used by Goldmann, and as being easily available in the Classiques Garnier edition (ed. Ch-M. des Granges, Paris, 1964).
9. B. Pascal, Opuscules et Lettres, ed. L. Lafuma (Aubier, 1955), p.113.
10. E.g. Goldmann, Le Dieu Caché, p.120.
11. R. Mousnier, Peasant Uprisings (Allen & Unwin, 1971), p.98.
12. Lefebvre, op cit, I, 112-3.
13. J. V. Stalin, Report to January 1933 Plenum, CPSU(B).
14. Pascal, Opuscules et Lettres, p.50.
15. Ibid, pp.166-9.
16. L. Goldmann, Structures Mentales et Création Culturelle (Anthropos, 1970), p.489.
17. Lefebvre, op cit, II, 13; I, 33.
18. Ibid, II, 204.
19. Ibid, II, 117-9.
20. Ibid, I, 147.
21. S. Naïr and M. Lowy, Lucien Goldmann (Seghers, 1973), p.13.

22. Goldmann, Le Dieu Caché, p.343.

23. Cf. M. Dommanget, Le Curé Meslier (Julliard, 1965).

24. M. Glucksmann, 'Lucien Goldmann: Humanist or Marxist?', New Left Review, 56 (1969), p.57.

25. A. Mellor, 'The Hidden Method: Lucien Goldmann and the Sociology of Literature', Working Papers in Cultural Studies, 4 (Birmingham, 1973), p.99.

26. T. Eagleton, Criticism and Ideology (Verso, 1978), p.97.

27. T. Eagleton, Marxism and Literary Criticism (Methuen, 1976), p.8.

28. Goldmann, Le Dieu Caché, p.35.

29. Goldmann, Structures Mentales et Création Culturelle, p.171.

30. L. Goldmann, Introduction à la Philosophie de Kant (Gallimard, 1967), pp.44-5.

31. Voltaire, Correspondence, ed. T. Besterman (Institut et Musée Voltaire, Geneva, 1953-65), letter 1138.

32. Voltaire, Lettres Philosophiques (Garnier, 1964), p.277. (This edition contains not only the 25th lettre philosophique on Pascal, but also a selection from the Dernières Remarques of 1777, many of which deal with Pascal).

33. Ibid, p.155.

34. Ibid, p.141.

35. Ibid, p.159.

36. Ibid, p.292.

37. Goldmann, Le Dieu Caché, p.182.

38. K. Marx, 'Contribution to the Critique of Hegel's Philosophy of Right', in K. Marx and F. Engels, On Religion (Foreign Languages Publishing House, Moscow, n.d.), p.42.

MERIT AND DESTINY: IDEOLOGY AND NARRATIVE IN FRENCH CLASSICISM

Jerry Palmer

'May the force be with you'
(unintentionally apposite quote from another civilisation)

The aim of this paper is to provide a formalist reading of the French classical theatre, and through it to engage the literary practice of French classicism as ideology. Classical dramaturgy is best known in the form of a limited number of canonical authors (Corneille, Molière, Racine), but at the level of narrative structure it can be shown that canonical authors follow a pattern common to all the writers of the classical school - this pattern is in fact the defining, central feature of French classicism, its 'dominant procedure', to use Tomashevski's term.[(1)] Centrally, dramaturgy is rooted in concepts: the very shape of stories, the matrix of narrative functions in which their 'literary-ness' is rooted, is that which enables them to grasp something outside of themselves and thus to inscribe themselves in the ideological formation.

Like many, if not all, narrative forms, French classical narrative moves from a hypostasised, antecedent order, through a moment of disorder, to resolution. The generality of such a formulation leaves it practically devoid of information content, but specifying the contents, or components of order, disorder and resolution both applies this very general formula to a specific corpus of literature and places its application in history.

In the optimistic version which (quantitatively) dominated the seventeenth century novel and theatre, at the end happiness abounds thanks to the workings of Providence; such is the tension and ecstasy of this moment that the abolition of obstacles to happiness should be felt as - in the literal sense - an epiphany, and should be 'understood' only in the sensation of admiration. In the tragic version the resolution incarnates justice but not happiness, a justice which is also divine in origin and therefore barely comprehensible. This movement was clearly theorised by contemporary aesthetics:

> '... dans le cinquième (acte) le noeud se démêle avec vraisemblance par des voies imprévues, d'où résulte la merveille.'
>
> [... in the fifth act the nodus of the plot is plausibly unravelled, by unforeseen means, which brings about wonder.]
>
> (Chapelain, Discours de la Poésie Représentative, p.131)

Thus the order that is hypostasised as antecedent, and which is refounded in the resolution, is thought as God's order - not, certainly, the order of eternity but the order of the present, appropriate moment in the long progress towards universal redemption and the end of history; in any event, it is an order that is ideal and transcendental as well as incarnated in the secular world:

> '... une céleste flamme
> D'un rayon prophétique illumine mon âme.
> Oyez ce que les dieux vous font savoir par moi;
> De votre heureux destin c'est l'immuable loi.
> Après cette action vous n'avez rien à craindre,
> On portera le joug désormais sans se plaindre;
> Et les plus indomptés, renversant leurs projets,
> Mettront toute leur gloire à mourir vos sujets;
> ...'
>
> [... a heavenly flame
> Lights up my soul with a ray of prophecy.
> Listen to what the gods have me say to you:
> It is the immutable law of your happy destiny.
> After this act you have nothing to fear,
> Bearing the yoke will cause no complaints;
> And the least cowed will cast aside their intentions
> And will find all their glory in dying your subjects.]
>
> (Corneille, Cinna, Act V, Sc. 3, ll.1753-60)

If the order implied in classicism is, finally, sufficiently vague to be capable of rapid summary, the source of disorder and the secular installing of order is far more complex; and it is in these processes that the details of classical dramaturgy have their origin.

The source of disorder has a name, and it is a name which recurs, excessively, in classical texts: destiny (destin or fortune - the fortuna of pagan antiquity). At the beginning of du Rocher's Indienne

Amoureuse Cléraste's fleet is wrecked as he is sailing to help an ally:

'Que le ciel a pour nous des pointes rigoureuses,
Et qu'il se rend contraire aux âmes genereuses!
...
Voyez que la fortune inconstamment se joue
De ceux que le bonheur élève sur sa roue,
...
Avouez que celui s'aveugle en son bonheur
Dont l'esprit attiré d'un appas suborneur
Dessus un élément fonde son espérance,
Qui n'a rien de constant que dans son inconstance.'

[How harsh is Heaven's sting,
And how it crosses noble souls!
...
See how fortune's inconstancy plays
With those whom happiness lifts on its wheel,
...
Admit that he is blind in his happiness
Whose mind is lured and corrupted,
And who founds his hope on an element
Whose only constant is inconstancy.]

(Act 1, Sc. 1, pp.1-2)

But - literally - 'it's an ill wind ...', and Cléraste is providentially/coincidentally thrown ashore at exactly the right place and time to save the Princess of Florida from rape by her would-be lover, the Prince of Mexico; Cléraste thus acquires a new lover and a new enemy simultaneously and is forced to drastically revise his plans for the future.

Even when destiny is not named explicitly, the role of coincidence in forming the noeud of the plot is clear: it is destiny that wills, in Le Cid, that it should be Rodrigue's father who is preferred for royal favour over Chimène's father, thus leading by a rapid and inevitable sequence to the latter's death at Rodrigue's hands.

Destiny, in the form of coincidence, illusion, etc., not only provides the initial impetus for the classical narrative,(2) but also maintains it in motion. In Rotrou's La Céliane Nise, disguised as a man and distracted by the disappearance of her lover Pamphile, is wandering through the countryside; arbitrarily, she stops at the edge of a wood and attempts to commit suicide - by coincidence she has chosen the exact spot where Pamphile is asleep under a tree. He awakens, and -

without recognising her - prevents the attempt. She assumes that he is not recognising her on purpose and provokes him to a duel, in the course of which she is wounded; only then does she reveal her identity. Pamphile, of course, had left because of a misunderstanding, thinking she was tired of him, and the dramatic clarification of the situation is more than enough to resolve all the conflicting emotions aroused by their misunderstandings and misadventures. The plots of such plays are based on a plethora of such incidents: half a dozen per act, with a bewildering variety of scene changes and incidental characters such as pirates, witches, neighbouring tyrants, abducted princesses, identical twins ...

Finally, destiny may play a part in the resolution, though never a determinant role: even where it operates, characters have to deserve its intervention. Traditionally, it took the form of the _deus ex machina_; at the end of the anonymous _Folie de Silène_ (c. 1620), the god Pan literally comes down in a machine and intervenes to prevent catastrophe:

> 'Penserais-tu forcer d'une atteinte faiblette,
> Des arrêts de là-haut la contrainte secrète?'
>
> [Did you think your feeble efforts could force
> The secret strictures of Heaven's decrees?]

After 1630 the _deus ex machina_ was largely discredited - Corneille's condemnation in the _Discours de la Tragédie_ was drastic, and typical(3) - but it was never entirely discarded: even the purest and severest of classical tragedies, such as Racine's _Phèdre_, can finish with the cosmic apparition of a sea-monster so terrifying that 'Le flot qui l'apporta recule épouvanté' [The wave that bore it draws back in horror].(4) But if the _deus ex machina_ became a rarity, destiny in the form of coincidence was still extremely common. To take only a famous example: the ending of _Cinna_ is motivated by the order in which the conspirators appear before Auguste. The treachery of each is a severe blow to the emperor's sense of justice and pride of place, but the truth about Maxime is the cruellest since it reveals just how low the moral climate of his entourage has fallen: the order in which they appear, Maxime last, is entirely providential/coincidental.

If disorder is not produced by destiny, in the form of coincidence, illusion, etc., it is brought about by evil, an evil whose source is non-secular. Ravaillac, in Billard de Courgenay's Tragédie de Henri le Grand, claims in his introductory monologue to be directly inspired by Satan (who makes an appearance to confirm the attribution), and continues to refer to his action in similar terms:

'Démons, corps enfumés des parfums de Cocyte,
Démons, mes seuls tyrans, race fausse et maudite,
Qui sortez de l'enfer pour me perdre en perdant
La fleur des valeureux, l'honneur de l'Occident:
Pourquoi me poussez-vous si souvent, à toute heure,
Sans me tenir la main? Il faut, il faut qu'il meure,
Je le juge au transport qui me met hors de moi:
Il faut que j'aie l'heur d'être meurtrier d'un Roi
Qui ne m'a point meffait: cruel, abominable,
Avorton de Satan: suis-je pas misérable,
Maudit comme Judas, voulant assassiner
Ce Roi doux, et bénin ...'

[Demons, bodies redolent with the smoke of Cocytus,
Demons, my only tyrants, false and cursèd race,
Who come from Hell to lose me by losing
The flower of valour, the honour of the West:
Why do you push me so often, all the time,
Without holding me back? He must die, he must die,
I know it by the transport that carries me out of myself:
I shall have the good fortune to be the murderer of a king
Who has done me no harm: cruel, abominable,
Devil's abortion: am I not miserable,
Accursed like Judas, wishing to murder
This gentle benign king ...] (Act IV)

Emblematic figures such as Ravaillac disappeared in the 1630's to be replaced by villains with a more human face and subsequently - as we shall see - by an ethical conflict in which the attribution of evil in an unproblematic manner is impossible. Nonetheless, behind the humanisation of the villain lies the sense of evil as a transcendental force in the absence of which the world would be trouble free.

This is indicated in various ways. In the first place, by functional equivalence: it is only disruption in some form which is capable of starting the plot, and it is frequently evil in the form of illicit desire that does so. Recurrently, political power is abused to try to force love on an unwilling recipient - usually a male tyrant on a woman (e.g. Baro's Parthénie, Tristan's Marianne), but occasionally the inverse: Tristan's Mort de Chrispe, for instance. Where the abuse is not sexual, it is the illicit desire for power itself that is responsible - du Ryer's Nitocris and Dynamis, for example. In the second place, there is a revealing link between destiny and evil in the commonplace theme of gullibility. If characters are often, and easily, deceived as to each others' intentions by the force of accidental illusion (at its simplest: two identical twins whose spectacularly 'inconsistent' behaviour causes agony to their lovers), it is also the case that illusion is exploited by the villain: in Il Pastor Fido (widely known and imitated in France) Corisque nearly succeeds in having Amarillis condemned to death for adultery by having her own lover lie down beside her when she is asleep under a tree.(5)

If such simple devices met with an easy acceptance unlikely today, it is because illusion - like coincidence - was a manifestation of destiny; and if such devices can easily be used by the villain, it is because they serve the same end: disruption; that is, evil and illusion both seemed to be manifestations of the same underlying force - destiny. Now this is not to deny that illusory devices are also used beneficially, to trick the wrongdoer back to conformity. Examples abound: in Durval's Agarite the king is dissuaded from his illicit love for the heroine by such a device. Believing her dead, he has constructed a memento mori from her clothes and a dummy; while he is asleep she is smuggled in to replace the dummy and speaks to him when he awakes; the shock forces him to recognise the truth of the situation, and to desist. Is this possibility incompatible with the previous assertion? As we shall see shortly, the ethical imperative that is one of the bases of this theatre is founded in an ambiguity: many categories of action can be either good or bad (which makes them ethically neutral) depending on the motive for which they are undertaken. Thus the application of the powers of illusion can be estimated on the grounds of motive. But there is a further, ontological or praxiological, basis for the estimation of actions: do they tend to promote the stability and order that the dramatic resolution demands? For any action that tends to promote disorder - by arousing legitimate resentment against the performer, for instance - is to be condemned, for it extends the arena of destiny; if it is not countered - we shall see how shortly - it will lead ultimately to the secular disorder of tragedy (in the modern sense).

Canonical texts use the same matrix of narrative conventions, but shorn of the more creaking devices. In Corneille's Cinna, for instance, destiny manifests itself in the fact that Auguste is tempted to abandon power, and to favour Cinna, on the very day that Cinna, Maxime and Emilie are plotting to kill him. This in itself would provide no obstacle but for the fact that the conspirators' motives are less noble than they would like to think, and Auguste's decision reduces them to total disarray. However, his abdication is equally ignobly motivated, and the tangle of ethical and psychological complexities that constitute this confrontation dispenses with all but the most discreet versions of coincidence and illusion. Of course, texts like Cinna are in a small minority, and in the great majority of texts the forces of destiny are more obviously visible.

Destiny was a formal concept in the Renaissance: the ontology of Fortune's wheel is well known. But it is somewhat less well known that this concept functioned within a clearly defined matrix of political notions, which considerably restrict the scope of destiny, giving it a precise place in the combinatory.(6) According to traditional political theory, all policy was to be based in custom and usage, which were universal: universal in space because accepted by everyone within the bounds of a particular polity/community; universal in time because dating 'from time immemorial'. Custom thus both legitimated power, and gave practical guidance in policy making: it was both ethical and praxiological. But it had a concomitant disadvantage: any event for which there was no customary prescription could not fit into the order of universals in general, since custom was the only universal; thus any event was either a particular version of a universal, or it was entirely random, and could only be dealt with by personal prudence, which was felt to be a poor substitute for custom. Now the realm of the particular and the random was the realm of destiny, the area where policy and legitimacy were so uncertain and so dependent upon the individual that the forces of destiny roamed free. Thus the ontology of Fortune's wheel is not general, but only applies under specified circumstances: destiny only enters the arena of human actions because things occur for which there is no customary prescription; but, in its turn, this situation only arises because people innovate, and innovation, where politics is concerned, is primarily the result of ambition. It is often assumed that ambition was deprecated by classicism, since attacks on its ill-effects were so common. But in itself ambition was considered a normal, acceptable desire; only when it took the wrong form did it become unacceptable. When Perrot d'Ablancourt wishes to praise Caesar he can think of no higher compliment than to recall his 'dessein de se saisir de l'Empire, qui est le plus grand qui soit jamais tombé dans l'esprit humain; ...' [plan to seize the Empire, which is the greatest that ever entered human mind; ...] (preface to his edition of Caesar's Commentaries). Such judgments were a cliché.

The workings of ambition give play to destiny. So too does love, for love involves an innovation at the level of the family and the ego that has just as destabilising an effect as does ambition at the level of the polity. As Jacques Ehrmann has argued à propos L'Astrée, for classicism love involves the total abolition of the previous personality and the creation of a new self on its ruins, a new self whose subsistence is extremely problematic because of the necessary role of the loved one:(7) hence the neo-Stoic dislike of love, for neo-Stoic apatheia consisted of disregarding everything outside the control of the individual. It is for this reason that love in the classical theatre is almost invariably instantaneous - le coup de foudre; as Jean Starobinski has pointed out, this creates an instability so intense that a prolonged testing of the relationship is essential in order to ensure that their love is capable of founding a stable order both in the ego and the family.(8)

If the disruptive effects of destiny are not countered by a sufficiently potent force, disaster results. The tragédie à fin funeste is far from unknown before Racine, of course, and by the 1630's it was already normal to ensure that those who suffered deserved to do so, in some measure at least: the Aristotelian hamartia was re-interpreted in the exclusively ethical sense that has remained usual. In the early century frequently, and later occasionally, undeserved suffering was nonetheless the focus of dramatic emotion (Rotrou's *Bélisaire* and *Crisante*, du Ryer's *Lucrèce*, Tristan's *Marianne* - though the latter is ambiguous, as the focus is on the tyrant in the manner subsequently perfected by Racine). In the case of martyr plays one can argue that the innocent are amply rewarded by an eternity of bliss, but this is not possible for pagan subjects; here one can only say that destiny has triumphed and disorder rules. Indeed, contemporary writers are explicit that the ethical interpretation of the hamartia is essential to maintain a belief in divine justice: if the innocent are shown to suffer unjustifiably, this is perilously close to blasphemy.(9)

Disaster occurs because the countervailing force to destiny is not there; this force is heroism, a heroism which this entire theatre delineated. Just as destiny is the summary term for the twists and turns of coincidence, evil and ethical conflict, so there is a term for the qualities that the individual - cast into the arena of destiny - deploys in his attempts to deal with these situations: *mérite*:

> 'Le mérite aujourd'hui, contre l'erreur commune,
> Fait voir qu'il est parfois maître de la fortune.'
>
> [Today merit shows, against common misunderstanding,
> That it sometimes masters destiny.]
>
> (Rotrou, *Laure Persécutée*, Act 1, Sc. 2)

Everyone, of course, has *mérite*: it is no more than those qualities (*vertus*) that compose the personality, the force that everyone has at his disposal; but at the core of French classicism is the drive to isolate one particular, superior version of *mérite*, to indicate that it is superior to others because of its social and personal functions, and to think out its contradictions. It is to this version that the name heroism is given.

Within dramaturgy the function of heroism is to provide the resolution. Now frequently the resolution is in fact provided by the direct intervention of providence (classically, a messenger arrives just in time to reveal that all is not what it seems to be), but in order for providence to be able to operate the hero(ine) must have at the very least not given way to despair and sought an easy solution or committed suicide,[10] and more normally have resisted a series of threats, temptations and blandishments which would have led to the ruin of a lesser mortal. For instance: remaining faithful despite 'proof' of one's lover's infidelity and the offer of love from another, the subject of many a pastoral, comedy and tragi-comedy; or resisting threats of the 'marry me, or else' variety, which could be resolved either optimistically (e.g. Baro's Parthénie) or tragically (Tristan's Marianne, Racine's Andromaque and Bajazet).[11] Then providence can tear the veils of illusion and coincidence that brought near-catastrophe, or can bring about a change of heart in the tyrant whose persecutions have had the same result. Providence, that is, can only operate in a world where someone is prepared to make an exceptional effort; to be good is not enough, for exceptional situations demand exceptional solutions; when this exceptional effort is made, disorder is expunged and stability restored.

But the 'exceptional' is a morally neutral category. People undertake exceptional actions for the worst as well as the best of motives, and the exceptionally bad does not promote stability but disorder, the reign of evil. Thus the exceptional, and the type of character prepared to undertake the exceptional, are the ground from which heroism may emerge, but no more:

> 'Cléopâtre, dans Rodogune, est très-méchante; il n'y a point de parricide qui lui fasse horreur, pourvu qu'il la puisse conserver sur un trône qu'elle préfère à toutes choses, tant son attachement à la domination est violente; mais tous ses crimes sont accompagnés d'une grandeur d'âme qui a quelque chose de si haut, qu'en même temps qu'on déteste ses actions, on admire la source dont elles partent.'
>
> [Cleopatra, in Rodogune, is evil; not even parricide horrifies her so long as it keeps her on a throne she prefers to anything else, so violent is her attraction to power; but all her crimes are accompanied by a greatness of soul which has something so sublime that at the same time that one detests her actions one admires their source.]
>
> (Corneille, Trois Discours, p.55)

For a different reason the good alone is not equivalent to heroism either: for the good is universal, whereas the heroic - the exceptional - by definition is not:

> '... la Vertu Héroïque n'est à la bien définir, qu'une Vertu excellente et relevée au-dessus des Vertus communes.'
>
> [... Heroic Virtue, properly defined, is no more than an excellent Virtue raised above common Virtues.]
>
> (Le Moyne, La Gallerie des Femmes Fortes, p.311)

It is in short only the combination of the good and the exceptional that constitutes the heroic, and therefore only a person who is willing to undertake both is capable of being heroic. Now there was no argument in principle about why anyone should do good: it was for its own sake, and the good was defined by the quality of the love of God (the ultimate good) in the will. But observably people undertook the exceptional for lesser reasons, and even the noblest was dubious - to do the good and the exceptional in order to win praise and the reputation for doing what was good and exceptional: for to do good for anything other than its own sake was not to do good, but to seek some other reward. This was the subject of a protracted debate which was 'resolved' in the seventeenth century by recourse to a formula borrowed from Cicero,(12) according to which glory (the praise bestowed upon heroes) is less

> 'une lumière étrangère, qui vient de dehors aux actions héroïques, qu'une réflexion de la propre lumière de ces actions, et un éclat qui leur est renvoyé par les objets qui l'ont reçu d'elles.'
>
> [a foreign light that comes upon heroic actions from without, than the reflection of these actions' own light, and a lustre that is reflected upon them by objects that have received it from them.]
>
> (J. L. Guez de Balzac, 'De la Gloire', Oeuvres II, p.460)

That is to say, glory was not something given by others, but simply the natural result of the great and the good; it was this because it could not be given:

> 'la Gloire n'est pas tant une dette dont s'acquitte le public qu'un aveu de ce qu'il doit, et tout ensemble une protestation qu'il est insolvable: ...'

> [Glory is not so much a debt that the public pays off as an admission of what it owes and at the same time a declaration of insolvency: ...] (Ibid)

The heroic conception of heroic virtue seems at first sight, perhaps, no more than the commonplace 'virtue is its own reward'; in reality its claim was far more radical - heroic virtue was to be thought as unrewardable.

The exceptional was a necessity in the arena of destiny (without it, disaster ensued), for the only alternative to customary praxis was individual prudence, and it was taken for granted that those who undertook the exceptional did so out of a desire for a reward - hence the conventional validation of ambition referred to above. Indeed, it is a logical necessity: the good can be judged (in principle) by the comparison between any given action and a rule, or set of rules, objectively therefore, without reference to the opinions of others; but the exceptional can only be judged by a comparison within a finite empirical set, and has to be judged so by others: the ascription of the exceptional is inseparable from its minimal reward, glory.

But the exceptional is also divisive, for to demand the adhesion of others engaged in the same process and seeking the same reward observably arouses resentment: one is close to Hobbes' state of nature. And this divisiveness extends and perpetuates the arena of destiny. It is the function of the heroic insistence on the unrewardable nature of heroism to avoid this divisiveness, by eliding the role of public opinion. But because it is integral, by definition, the contradictions are insuperable, and the heroic formula can only paper over the cracks.

The formula is also curiously abstract: it is difficult to deduce any concrete advice from it, and it is no doubt for this reason that so much heroic writing takes the form of examples - encomia and other character assessments (among the precursors of biography) and fiction. In exemplary descriptions two crucial aspects of the heroic system are worked out: firstly, a detailed imperative which transforms the 'unrewardability' thesis into a (potentially) workable ethic by demonstrating how the exceptional can overcome divisiveness; secondly, the benefits nonetheless accruing to the individual who attains heroism.

The detailed imperative which becomes, effectively, the basis of the heroic ethic can be simply phrased: 'act without seeking reciprocation'; but, phrased thus, it is nowhere to be found in the seventeenth century - the only possible source of this information is a deduction from the structure of classical dramaturgy. Corneille's Cinna is a perfect example.(13)

In Cinna the destruction of an entire polity is threatened: all of the protagonists are engaged in projects that are mutually contradictory, and that therefore, in conjunction, would rip Rome apart at the seams. The threat is only averted by the emperor Auguste's decision to forego punishment of the conspiracy and to make the offer of friendship and forgiveness whose acceptance restores peace and stability. This much is clear and probably uncontroversial. What is less clear (and certainly more subject to controversy) is why the protagonists' projects are mutually contradictory.

Emilie, Cinna and Maxime are conspiring to murder Auguste: Emilie because he killed her father (many years ago), Maxime because he wishes to restore republican and patrician liberties, Cinna because he loves Emilie (she will only marry him after Auguste's death) and believes in Maxime's politics; all three are well established at the centre of the imperial entourage. Auguste wishes to abdicate - he is sick of politics and tired of the personal strain imposed by exercising power, but Cinna dissuades him, in Maxime's presence; afterwards he explains to Maxime that only while Auguste has power is their assassination justifiable, and he wishes to punish the emperor for his past crimes - usurpation and political murders. However, Auguste has not only accepted Cinna's advice, but offered them both substantial rewards for their services: Maxime the governorship of Sicily, and Cinna marriage with Emilie, who is the emperor's adoptive daughter or ward; it is only at this point that Maxime finds out about Cinna's relationship with Emilie, and her involvement in the conspiracy - he re-interprets the situation and concludes that Cinna is only organising the conspiracy in order to win

Emilie, for this is the only explanation he can find of Cinna's refusal to accept Auguste's abdication. Maxime too loves Emilie; he betrays Cinna to Auguste and tries to persuade Emilie to turn her affections to himself, but fails. In the meantime Cinna too has his doubts, and tries to persuade Emilie to allow him to call off the conspiracy on the grounds that Caesar's offer reveals that he is no longer the tyrant he was, an argument Emilie has no difficulty in refuting; Cinna decides to keep his word to her and to commit suicide afterwards, in expiation of his broken allegiance to the emperor. The evidence of the conspiracy reduces Auguste to despondency: already weary of the nastiness of power, the defection of some of his most trusted advisers is a bitter blow. Nonetheless, he rallies, and in the confrontation with Cinna shows a degree of charismatic authority that makes the latter's lack of conviction pitiable: trying to hide the role of Emilie he pretends to be acting to avenge Pompey and his family (his relatives) since his defence of absolute monarchy in Act II makes the plea of republicanism implausible and Auguste pours scorn on the possibility that he might be seeking the throne for himself. Emilie decides to confess and die with Cinna, and they vie with each other to claim overall responsibility for the conspiracy; finally Maxime is shamed into admitting his real motive for betraying Cinna, and Auguste, at the lowest point of bitterness and despondency, finds the courage to offer forgiveness and friendship: the conspirators are overcome with joy and gratitude, and the golden age of Imperial Rome is announced in the closing lines.

The basic plan of Cinna - a vicious circle of persecution and revenge only broken by an act of heroic générosité - is far from uncommon in French classicism, and the status of the notion of clemency is attested in countless political writings of the period.[(14)] The problem (for any of these texts) is to indicate both why the projects that dominate the play before the heroic offer threaten disaster (and therefore are wrong, in some sense) and how it is that Auguste's offer is able to provide a resolution: what is it that is, in some form, common to both?

The projects of all the protagonists (with the exception of Auguste's final offer) are less than heroic because each is undertaken with a view to a direct return, or reciprocation, and when the return is not forthcoming, due to changing circumstances, the point of reference for action is missing and projects fall apart. Cinna's dilemma, the conflict between his allegiances, given careful and direct expression in his monologue in Act III, is largely due to the debased motivation of his actions: he is intending to kill the emperor because that is the only way he can win Emilie, for if he originally believed in his own political condemnation of Auguste as a tyrant, he certainly no longer does so by the time of his monologue: he has indeed, as Emilie says, been bought off by an unwitting Auguste. In his terms, of course, Auguste has revealed that he is no longer a tyrant, but his changed estimation is due solely to Auguste's increased recognition of him, which reveals clearly enough that his politics is entirely based on the expectation of personal reward. Similarly, his love for Emilie is sub-heroic: he will kill Auguste, knowing it to be wrong, in order to win her; the correct action would be to do what is right and to continue to love her without hope. 'Loving without hope' is a commonplace theme in the immense literature of love of the period (*L'Astrée* is the *locus classicus*): to love without hope is to indicate that one's love is truly worthy for it seeks no reward beyond itself, not even the minimally noble reward of freely given reciprocation. The theme was sufficiently commonplace to give rise to a specialised rhetoric of naturalised metaphors - e.g. *soupirer*, literally 'to sigh', meant 'to love in the approved manner'; *un soupirant*, therefore, meant a lover, in theory an ideologically correct one, often in practice simply a lover.

Emilie is no better. One is easily misled by her opening soliloquy where the synthesis between love and duty (attained with such pain by Chimène, and subsequently to become Corneille's benchmark) is *apparently* a high point of ethical development. In reality she acts solely out of a desire for revenge, and sees Auguste's death as the quantitative equivalent of, and thus an adequate return for, her father's death at the emperor's hands. Thus, she is quite unable to appreciate Cinna's change of attitude towards Auguste because her own evaluation of everything is dominated by her 'returns'-based conception of her situation, in which her sense of her own identity is based in the extraction of the equivalent. In this sense, she loves Cinna in order to use him; or, more accurately, given that they love one another, she forces their love to work for her sense of retribution.

Maxime, of course, is the least heroic. If his betrayal of Cinna was based on a changed political estimation, it would be justified, but his own confession to Auguste in Act V underlines the significance of his debased motives - he betrayed Cinna in order to win Emilie, thus committing two cardinal sins: acting in order to gain a return, and assuming that Emilie would see one lover as a viable substitute, as the equivalent of another, that is, that she would act in the same way as himself.

Auguste's motives are similarly sub-heroic. He wants to abdicate because he failed to find in power what he wanted: personal security and happiness. His inability to decide on a firm policy when confronted with the revelation of Cinna's conspiracy is a corollary of his motives: nothing he can do appears to guarantee him what he wants. It is only with his act of clemency and offer of friendship that he reaches the point of heroism, for it is only here that - for the first time in the play - an action is undertaken without a view to a return: in the purest sense, Auguste's offer is disinterested, for (a) there is no guarantee at all that it will succeed; (b) he foregoes the emotional satisfaction of the revenge he was planning; (c) he is changing himself to such an extent by making this offer that he cannot even be sure what would constitute a return for his action. Lastly, there is a clear contrast between his action and all the actions that precede it: he is clearly intending to break a vicious circle of self-interest calculation. Moreover, the actual effects of his action - the political adhesion of the conspirators and their admiration - are incommensurable with the action taken: there is no way of measuring up his act of faith and self-control against its results and seeing them as quantifiable equivalents, for they are of such different orders.

If Auguste is able to make this offer, it is because he was already minimally noble: whatever injustices he may have committed in the past, his reign is still better than civil strife, and his desire to create a stable monarchy, even if undertaken for the wrong motives, is in itself praiseworthy, according to seventeenth century estimations. Moreover, he has, demonstrably, one of the main qualities of the hero: the energy necessary to couple thought and action; if he vacillates briefly at the end of Act IV, his energy is visibly restored in the confrontation with the conspirators. This is true of the conspirators too: if they are sub-heroic, they are not disastrously so. Even Maxime is sufficiently noble to learn from Emilie's analysis of his actions, and to act accordingly. Both Emilie and Cinna have the minimum nobility of seeking rewards that are acceptable to the heroic mentality: reciprocated love and glory;[(15)] and when betrayed prefer the noble solution of death for what they believe in (each other, primarily) to any easy solution. Thus they are sufficiently noble to benefit from Auguste's decision, and therefore to make it viable; had Auguste chosen less worthy recipients of his _générosité_ the outcome might have been very different.

The ultimate guarantee of the nature of Auguste's act is its place within dramaturgy: it is the secular equivalent of the resolution by coincidence or direct divine intervention. In both versions, tensions mount to snapping point, and stability can only be restored by an act of such striking proportions that it, literally, stops everyone in their tracks: in dramaturgical terms, '_la merveille_'. In this moment, it is the mechanism of admiration that is central: both the theatre audience and the characters onstage must be so 'thunderstruck' that the impact of the action is instantaneous, by-passing any discussion, second thoughts, rational calculation, etc. Hence the rhetoric: 'grandiloquent', in the etymological sense - '_sublime_' was the usual seventeenth century term for the style used in tragedy.

Thus the delineation of exemplary action, especially in fiction, provides the heroic ethic - the unrewardability thesis - with an element of praxiology: do something of such magnanimous[(16)] proportions that men will universally admire you. At that point social stability is ensured:

> 'La puissance est une chose lourde et matérielle, qui traîne après soi un long équipage de moyens humains, sans lesquels elle demeurerait immobile. Elle n'agit qu'avec des armées de terre et de mer. Pour marcher il lui faut mille ressorts, mille roues, mille machines. Elle fait un effort, pour faire un pas. L'authorité, au contraire, qui tient de la noblesse de son origine, et de la vertu des choses divines, opère ses miracles en repos; n'a besoin ni d'instruments ni de matériaux, ni de temps même pour les opérer; est toute recueillie en la personne qui l'exerce, sans chercher d'aide, ni se servir de

second. Elle est forte, toute nue et toute seule: elle combat désarmée.'

[Power is something heavy and material, which drags behind it a long train of human means, without which it would be motionless. Armies and navies are its only means of action. To move, it needs a thousand springs, a thousand wheels, a thousand machines. Its every step is an effort. Authority, on the contrary, which shares in the nobility of its origin and the qualities of the divine, achieves its miracles while at rest; needs neither instruments nor materials, nor even time, to bring them about; is entirely contained in the person who exercises it, without seeking aid or using a second. It is strong, quite naked and alone: it needs no weapons to fight.]

(Guez de Balzac, 'Le Romain', Oeuvres II, p.426)

And individual stability is also assured: the coherence of the ego, threatened by the fissiparity of unworthy projects certain to fail, is restored in the same moment as the stability of the social fabric. It is for this reason that the heroic alternative to the moment of resolution is suicide (in the tragédie à fin funeste), for in suicide the ego affirms its capacity to transcend the inflictions of destiny, to avoid being forced to do something unworthy: even restrictive theorists like d'Aubignac and La Mesnardière refer to suicide as the product of 'noble' despair.

It is at this point that we can start to grasp classicism as an ideological practice: the classical narrative is an argument in favour of charismatic authority, for it presents human praxis in such a way that only charismatic authority is capable of dealing with the twists and turns that characterise the arena of destiny.(17) In plays such as Cinna this is explored in explicitly political terms - although even here not exclusively, for among other implications is the possibility of sexual happiness for Cinna and Emilie, impossible otherwise. In general, at least until 1660, plays called tragédies explored the theme of heroism in a predominantly political setting, but the other, minor, genres were concerned primarily with domestic happiness, albeit often with the domestic happiness of royalty, where dynastic considerations easily turned sexual unhappiness into politics. Now it is easily demonstrable that the central core of heroism - Destiny/Providence, unrewardability, quitting the nexus of reciprocity - is as integral to the minor genres as to tragedy: but it is equally clear that in the minor genres the delineation of charismatic authority cannot be said to have a directly political intention in the sense that Guez de Balzac's distinction between power and authority does, for all that it ensures is purely personal happiness in a domestic context only. Thus to see French classicism as a directly political ideology - perhaps as the ideology of the absolutist state - is questionable, despite the large number of plays (especially before 1660) that deal directly with explicitly political themes:[18] for it is the systematic of heroism that permits the discussion of issues relating to the structure of the absolutist state, in the same moment that it structures them in the way that it does. That is to say, it is the 'principle of dispersion' (to use Foucault's phrase) of classical utterances that permits, that creates the space for, the thematics of both political stability (relationship of hero and state) and of domestic personal happiness.

That principle of dispersion is the nexus of merit and destiny and the recommendation of charismatic authority. In what sense is this an ideology?[19] In the following sense:

(1) This literature was the vehicle for the separation off of 'literature' in the modern sense: texts with (usually) a single author, written in a definitive version and in a national language. It occupied a space defined by the exclusion of popular, regional and professional cultural artefacts - most clearly, its theatrical version excluded popular theatre (farces, clowns, jugglers, mystery plays, bear-baiting, sports, etc.) and its novel version excluded oral narrative and the popular prose versions of the epics.[20]

(2) This literature was one of the vehicles of the creation of a national language, defined by the exclusion of popular, regional and professional 'dialects'. In fact, in the seventeenth century it was probably the main vehicle since the other, the education system, depended very heavily upon literature for its teaching, both in method and content.[21]

Thus this literature was an important element in the creation of a 'national' culture, defined as 'superior to' other indigenous cultures.

(3) The conception both of the hero and of the state promoted in the political version of this literature is an argument against feudalism and for the central monarchy: the feudal insistence was that blood was sufficient reason in itself; the heroic ethic insisted that the hero's privileges and claim to respect were based upon his achievements, not just upon membership of a class.

(4) All action which falls outside the nexus of merit merely serves destiny: it is irrational and random. The limits of worthwhile action become strictly circumscribed. Noteworthy exclusions are play and pleasure (both, admittedly, ill-defined concepts).

(5) Most importantly: the argument for charismatic authority, and the exclusions that it enforces, weld together a continuum: individual-family-state. That is to say, all worthwhile action is that which holds these entities together, binds them one to the other (or is potentially capable of doing so); all other action is defined as (minimally) inferior or (maximally) wrong.

What is the nature of this continuum? In the first place, it has no internal dominant: none of its moments dominates the others, for it is so constructed that each is defined in terms of the others. The heroic individual is such that he is capable of founding the state and the family, and can only find happiness and stability by doing so, and any noble individual is defined by his possession of qualities that enable him to participate in this process, albeit not at its apex. The state is such that it can only be founded by someone with these qualities, and be accepted by people who can appreciate them at their true worth: the mechanism of admiration is intrinsic to the polity. The family is such that it is the condition of sexual happiness for the heroic individual and his followers: only by founding it can he find sexual happiness, and - concomitantly - by finding sexual happiness he necessarily founds a secure social unit. The family is thought in parallel with the state: the heroic individual can find another, non-sexual happiness through the exercise of legitimate authority, and sexual happiness involves a political authority over a smaller unit - the authority of master over servant, husband over wife, father over children, etc. Thus the family in classicism is a distinctly patriarchal unit. Apparently this is not so, for it is often asserted that women's heroism is responsible for the restoration of order. It is only knowledge of legal structures that enables one to assert the feminist interpretation. The heroic wife's relationship to the husband is isomorphic with the political hero's relationship with the king: recognition/admiration from the hierarchical superior is the basis of order and happiness for both. The family is thus an arena whose internal structure is identical to that of the state, and it is a purely contingent question whether any given individual operates within one or the other: the guarantees of order and happiness are the same in both.

Each of these five 'senses' in which the structure of classicism is ideology is, from the internal, immanent point of view, a systematicity, or discursivity: it is that which orders and structures utterances. It is in its insertion into the social formation that it is ideology: by the manner in which it ties praxis to a set of institutions that have an extra-discursive existence: the individual, the family and the state; and in doing so both defines an arena for praxis and ascribes content to the institutions.

Footnotes

1. 'Thématique', pp.302 ff; in Théorie de la Littérature, ed. Todorov.

2. The moment of disruption by destiny conventionally precedes the opening of the narrative: this is the meaning of the universally accepted notion of *in medias res*.

3. In Trois Discours sur le Poème Dramatique (ed. Forestier), p.99; cf. p.50.

4. Phèdre, Act V, Sc. 6. This line, Boileau tells us, was literally a show stopper. The habit of applauding individual lines or short passages of a play was commonplace.

5. In its more sophisticated, but rare, versions - Phèdre's calumny of Hippolyte, for instance - the lie is believed because the gull is predisposed by his own behaviour to believe that such things are likely: Thésée's own sexual past makes Phèdre's allegations plausible. It is sometimes said that something similar is true of Othello and Desdemona, Cassio and the handkerchief.

6. See J. G. A. Pocock, The Machiavellian Moment, ch.1 esp.

7. See Un Paradis Désespèré.

8. See 'Sur Corneille'.

9. La Mesnardière, La Poétique, p.144 e.g. This is part of a very general debate on whether the theatre should always show virtue rewarded and vice punished. As is well known, Corneille was sceptical on this point; elsewhere I have argued that this dissension did not alter a fundamental agreement; see my 'Function of le Vraisemblable in French classical aesthetics'.

10. Despair and suicide were ethically possible in pagan subjects, although of dubious status in the eyes of the Church. Even despair by itself was unacceptable in Christians (except briefly - a human failing), for it involved doubting divine wisdom - the correct attitude was resignation.

11. These instances indicate that the separation of genres advocated by classical aesthetic theory was based on a fundamental unity. Even the apparently still valid distinction between tragedy (in the modern sense) and providential melodrama is subordinate to this unity.

12. Specifically, of a series of debates from Cicero through the troubadours to the seventeenth century; see my Form and Meaning in the Early French Classical Theatre, ch. 3. The resolution was possible in the form that it took in the seventeenth century thanks to a recent shift within theological definitions of the will and its relation to reason. See A. Levi, French Moralists, chs. 6 and 7. Cf. M. R. L. de Malkiel, L'Idée de la Gloire dans la Tradition Occidentale and J. G. Peristiany (ed.), Honour and Shame, especially the essays by Pitt-Rivers and Baroja. This is not to suggest that the debate is trans-historical: as Foucault has it, discourses are 'tactically polyvalent', i.e. subject to changing significance by their closure (La Volonté de Savoir, pp.132 ff).

13. It is central to this thesis that the structure outlined here is universal within French classicism, and basing analysis on a single example will appear dubious. A further six examples, drawn from all genres, may be found in ch. 4 of my Form and Meaning in the Early French Classical Theatre.

14. The sub-title of Cinna is 'La Clémence d'Auguste'.

15. The unacceptable ones are tyrannical power, lust (usually in the form of forced marriage, sometimes rape) and money - the latter for the reasons given by Timon of Athens in his soliloquy in Act IV; the degrading power of money was a commonplace aristocratic theme in the sixteenth and seventeenth centuries.

16. Also to be taken in its etymological sense.

17. The alternative solution, unthinkable in seventeenth century

France but central to Florentine political thought, is republican democracy, which is also thought out in terms of virtù and fortuna; see Pocock, op cit.

18. See for example Jean Rohou's discussion of the politics of heroism elsewhere in this volume. Cinna is untypical, in one respect, of political tragedy at this time: the hero and the state are one and the same person; Jean Rohou argues (rightly) that the relationship between hero and state is conceived as problematic throughout this period. However, even when they are not incarnated in the same individual, either the state has to learn from the hero (and this implies a degree of nobility as in Cinna, Emilie and Maxime), or disaster occurs, as in the tyrant plays and later in Racine. Thus recognition of heroic action is integral, whether hero and monarch are the same persons or not.

19. Assuming ideology to be one instance in the reproduction of the relations of production, which functions by persuading individual subjects that its representation of their imaginary relationships to the real relations of production is in fact correct, as Althusser has it. This formulation does not involve accepting either Althusser's functionalism, or his conception of ideology as a seamless web, or his identification of subjectivity and ideology. However, it still leaves as problems the definition of 'imaginary' and the nature of 'persuasion'.

20. See R. Mandrou, De la Culture Populaire aux 17e et 18e Siècles.

21. See W. J. Ong, Ramus, Method and the Decay of Dialogue.

Bibliography

Ablancourt, Perrot d' (tr. and intr.), Les Commentaires de César (Paris, 1652).

Anon., La Folie de Silène in Théâtre Français (Paris, 1625).

Balzac, J. L. Guez de, Oeuvres (2 vv., Paris, 1665).

Baro, B., La Parthénie (Paris, 1642).

Chapelain, J., Discours sur la Poésie Représentative in Opuscules Critiques, ed. Hunter (Paris, 1936).

Corneille, P., Théâtre Complet, ed. Rat (3 vv., Paris, undated).

______ Trois Discours sur le Poème Dramatique, ed. Forestier (Paris, 1963).

Courgenay, C. Billard de, Tragédies (Paris, 1612).

Durval, Agarite (Paris, 1636).

Ehrmann, J., Un Paradis Désespéré (Paris, 1963).

Foucault, M., La Volonté de Savoir (Paris, 1976).

Guarini, G., Il Pastor Fido (tr. with additions A. de Giraud, Paris, 1609 and 1623).

Levi, A., French Moralists (Oxford, 1964).

Malkiel, M. R. L. de, L'Idée de la Gloire dans la Tradition Occidentale (Paris, 1968).

Mandrou, R., De la Culture Populaire aux 17e et 18e Siècles (Paris, 1964).

La Mesnardière, La Poétique (Paris, 1639).

Le Moyne, P., La Gallerie des Femmes Fortes (Paris, 1647).

Ong, W. J., Ramus, Method and the Decay of Dialogue (Cambridge, Mass., 1958).

Palmer, J., Form and Meaning in the Early French Classical Theatre (Ph.D. thesis, Southampton, 1972).

'The Function of "le Vraisemblable" in French Classical Aesthetics', French Studies 29, 1, 1975.

Peristiany, J. G. (ed.), Honour and Shame (London, 1965).

Pocock, J. G. A., The Machiavellian Moment (Princeton, N.J., 1975).

Racine, J., Théâtre Complet ed. Rat (Paris, undated).

Du Rocher, L'Indienne Amoureuse (Paris, 1636).

Rotrou, J. de, La Céliane (Paris, 1637).

Laure Persécutée (Paris, 1639).

Crisante (Paris, 1640).

Bélisaire (Paris, 1644).

Du Ryer, P., Lucrèce (Paris, 1638).

Nitocris (Paris, 1651).

Dynamis (Paris, 1653).

Starobinski, J., 'Sur Corneille', Les Temps Modernes 10, pp.713-29.

Todorov, T. (ed.), Théorie de la Littérature (Paris, 1965).

Tristan l'Hermite, La Marianne (Paris, 1637).

La Mort de Chrispe (Paris, 1645).

D'Urfé, H., L'Astrée, ed. Vaganay (5 vv., Lyon, 1925-8).

N.B. Dates of French plays refer to publication, not performance: the usual delay in the seventeenth century, imposed by the actors, was two years.

THE ARTICULATION OF SOCIAL, IDEOLOGICAL AND LITERARY PRACTICES IN FRANCE: THE HISTORICAL MOMENT OF 1641-1643

Jean Rohou

Translated by John Coombes

There is a need for Marxist literary history to explain literary practice in its dialectical articulation upon praxis and the class struggle in general, based as they are on a specific stage in the development of the relations of production and of a specific form of social relationships. The operation of this system of concepts (generally lacking in literary studies, even in those emanating from 'Marxist' pens) has need, not only of the general theory of dialectical materialism, but of a theory (as yet only fragmentary) of the practice of literature as a social, psychological, symbolical and linguistic practice. From this emerges the necessity of the following hypotheses - hypotheses which remain of necessity at the stage of conjecture.

We then proceed to test them out through 'concrete analysis of the concrete situation'. Such an analysis must be done in detail, not through love of erudition for its own sake, but in order to set it apart from facile experiments in demonstration which tend to exclude any facts which do not immediately seem to corroborate an initial hypothesis. A situation, then, relocated in a continuing ebb and flow of temporal factors which alone enable us to define a historical turning point and prevent us from allowing it to spin round at random. That, at least, is the theory ...

Theoretical Hypotheses

A. The human condition is lived as the contradiction between material and cultural reality (determined by the state of development of the mode of production and varying according to social environment) and multi-faceted desire (determined by that same process and by its own reaction against it).

B. The function of art is the metaphorical resolution of this contradiction between the subject and the objective world through the production of images which the desire of the subject invests with reality, a process which does not occur in the case of the dream. (This is why woman becomes the supreme aesthetic object: in a male-dominated culture she, as the duplicate of man - at once the replication for him of the real and the principle and object of his desire - constitutes the most satisfying figure of a reality invested with the desire which structures it - from Eve the temptress up to the Virgin Mary.)

C. In literary practice, this function operates through the doubly metaphorical use of language (the objective metaphor which transforms the image of the real, the subjective metaphor which makes possible the representation of desire) and through the production of a structure, a systemic network of a whole range of activated signifiers and of their possible signifieds (from which the plasticity of the work derives).

D. In concrete terms, literary practice is the activation (by a writer formed by his environment - notably by dint of having experienced its founding contradiction - and recognised by it: success alone defines genius _a posteriori_) within a style and a structure, of themes (realities, ideas, feelings, values ...) which are caught by systems of perception (realism, psychology ...). Now, no single one of these materials or forms is available autonomously or in absolute terms. Each exists only in historical modes, in the context of social practices which determine its meaning and its degree of interest (just as in the case of available literary models). Only a historically grounded perspective (engaging with the real in its most insistent or most dynamic manifestation and with desire at its most active, whether directed toward hope or negation), albeit capable of variation when set against a specific conjuncture, can enable us to capture these materials in their most productive manifestation (at a specific point in time), to integrate them into the richest and truest vision (from this particular point of view) and to choose, indeed to invent, in order to invest them with meaning, appropriate structure and style.

A masterpiece is to be distinguished by a process of signification (= conversion into signs) developed (as opposed to simple linguistic transcription) within a coherent system (themes, structures and style deriving from the same social practice, expressive of the same historical vision). It thus maintains its organic coherence and its capacity for meaning throughout the transpositions demanded by readings corresponding to new referential systems and to new perspectives.

E. Literary practices are not to be distinguished (though such a distinction is formally possible) by their differences of appearance, but by their differing functions, a single genre being capable of fulfilling various functions in differing modes of production (exactly as the same sign in two different semiotic systems). We may thus distinguish:

- a lyrical practice, in which the representation of desire is of more significance (through the importance of metaphor and of a process of structuring arbitrariness - metre, verse, rhythm, rhyme ...) than the refusal of reality - especially on the part of a dominant class in crisis or of a dominated class in process of liberation. Imaginative fantasy is here to be seen as a lyricism which is incapable of representing desire otherwise than through a drab idealisation of the real and of improbable reversals.

- a dramatic practice in which reality and desire are confronted, thus directly structuring the work itself (with an extremely variable degree of metaphorisation). It expresses a balanced perspective on the class struggle, whether in comic compensation, dramatic expectation or tragic despair (there being, of course, no necessary correspondence between these terms used here and the genres to whose names they correspond).

In reality, these practices (not always expressed by literary genres of the same name) tend frequently to combine: here as elsewhere 'concrete analysis of the concrete situation' is indispensable; but it cannot be achieved without certain hypotheses concerning the essence of literary works, that is to say the laws governing their production and function.

Historical Hypotheses

After the uncontrolled development, during the Renaissance, of new productive forces, of a new social class, of a new vision of man and the world and before the concerted struggle, during the Enlightenment, of a bourgeoisie by now fully conscious of its interests, the seventeenth century represents a period of superstructural stabilisation in which the new, tendentially determinant from the economy through to philosophy, is formally co-opted by the old, still dominant in the structure of society as well as in the domain of ideology. The development of this contradiction becomes evident in the formation of a kind of historic compromise: monarchic centralism or absolutism (the term defines both its weakness - it is not the organic expression of a dominant class - and its strength - equally necessary to former and future dominant classes, both weakened by mutual attrition, it can be supported by either or can impose its arbitrary will on both).

Infrastructural elements, investments, the protection and policing of a new economic site, extended now to that of the nation as a whole, the extraction of a new surplus value beyond the reach of the apparatus of feudalism; all of these demand the development (starting with the monarchy) of a form of state power hitherto unnecessary in an economy consisting of autarchic units and in a society securely dominated by a single class.

In its first stage, up to the 1640's, the development of absolutism is thus characterised principally:

- by the decline of the feudal order (unable to extract novel surplus value and to dominate or integrate new forces), by the enforced submission of the nobility, by the crisis in vitalist philosophy and in naturalist and spontaneist ideology (products of an economy in which natural processes were of much more significance than human intervention and where superiority derived from birth).

- by the development of the productive and administrative bourgeoisie, of the monarchic order, of mechanist philosophy and humanist, rationalist and voluntarist ideology (since the new economics derives from human action through the domination of physical forces and labour now provides a precondition for rising in society).

Initially, new forces develop principally in the field of real practices whilst metaphorical practice serves mainly as a compensatory factor for the crisis of traditional values. From 1598 to 1626-34 the dominant tendency is a practice desperate in its lyricism, observable in the utopian novel, the pastoral and in baroque poetry, as well as in abstract mysticism or the suicidal frenzy of the duelling tradition. The most considerable work is, however, already that of Malherbe, in which rational stability finally comes to outweigh, both in ideas and in form, pessimistic spontaneity.

Then, from Richelieu to the Fronde, society and thought are structured upon the gigantic struggle around the question of monarchic centralism. For this reason, from 1623-34 to 1643-48 dramatic practice comes to dominate a literature whose intentions are still divided, but whose means of signification (unities, logic, clarity) already constitute an expression of the new order. Herein lies the reason for Corneille's superiority over his feudal competitors, in whose work signs contradict meaning.

*****

But, from the outset, a second function of the state apparatus complements the first one of regulation of the new economy: that of control of the class struggle. So long as this is manifest as the repression of popular revolt and domination of the nobility, the two functions overlap. But they come into contradiction as soon as royal power manages to impose itself upon the traditional order, whose interests it shares through a multiplicity of connections as well as by its very nature as a superstructure threatened by the socially and ideologically subversive effects of the developing infrastructure.

Nonetheless this development is restrained, in France, by a geography of quasi-continental dimensions and by the Catholic church (conservative not only as an ideological force but as an intricated element within the social hierarchy and as the inactive proprietor of a significant proportion of the material and intellectual forces of production): a very different series of conditions from those obtaining in England or Holland.

It is for this reason that absolutism, once having dominated the aristocratic opposition to it, becomes stabilised from the mid-century onwards as a centralised feudalism. We find that henceforth, rather than the control apparatus of the new infrastructure, a parasitic superstructure (although it aims to develop new productive forces in order to extract the maximum surplus value) maintains the social and ideological supremacy of non-productivity, limits the drive towards productive investment, offers to the bourgeoisie the parasitic options of speculation and of purchase of offices leading eventually to integration into the nobility, opposes social and ideological dynamism and reduces a practical and subversive rationalism to a formal and regulatory one.

From this situation emerges (if it is true that man can only find meaning in the relationship to the real and to others made possible by the process of production of his material and spiritual conditions of existence) within a nobility and a bourgeoisie equally disoriented, parasitic and dependent, yet filled with admiration for the absolutist superstructure, that tragic dissatisfaction sublimated into aesthetic perfectionism which constitutes the essence of French classical literature, until the hidden development of the new forces and the paralysis of the superstructure are again capable of activating critical activity.

*****

That is, in theory, the form of development taken; but interferences and accidents were capable of modulating it. In particular, at the very moment at which absolutism had completed its initial function (regulation of the new mode of production and reduction of centrifugal forces) the deaths of Richelieu and of Louis XIII gave rise to a crisis which was to last ten years.

It is in this perspective that the purpose of the present conference - the year 1642 - is to be understood.

The Political and Ideological Turnabout of 1641-43: Spectacular Events and Underlying Causes

It would appear that everything happens at once between the end of November 1642 and the end of August 1643: the death of Richelieu (4th December) and of Louis XIII (14th May); the first debates on Jansenism, from the sermons of Isaac Habert (1st and 3rd Sundays of Advent - November-December 1642) to Arnauld's Fréquente Communion and Théologie morale des jésuites (August 1643).

But, however spectacular, events must not be taken for the causes of a history of which they are, rather, the effect or the accidental illumination. A date of death is always relatively speaking a matter of chance - and this double event all the more so. And, at the level of what was then apparent, it was by no means clear that the nine months in question would be the gestation period for more than eighteen years of rule by Mazarin. To get a clearer view we must look further into the order of causality apparent through a succession of events whose meaning for history they determine, even when they are accidental.

We see, then, two personality types which, as products and producers of their epoch, embody its essence. On the one hand the heroism of the noble in the service of the state against his fellow nobles, equally heroic, from Montmorency to Cinq-Mars: a culminating outburst of aristocratic energy in the final struggle for or against the implantation of the new system. On the other, mercantile skill placed at the disposal of the state and of the Minister himself, against 'Great Ones' and Frondeurs similarly motivated by pecuniary interest, whilst speculators, war profiteers and fixers triumph generally. The political and psychic expression of the new system in all its crude spontaneity, in the absence of any generally recognised authority. On the one hand a market economy sustains the profit motive (easier still to maintain in a war economy); on the other, absolutism, reducing all men to subjects and concentrating authority at a single point, fosters lust for the conquest of this power monopoly (at a time when its official incumbent is weak and those recently defeated are once again able to raise their heads). Suddenly there emerges into the forefront of events the new man of the absolutist and proto-capitalist world: his psychic principle being self-esteem, as a form of ego-insecurity in the crisis of social and ideological structures which have served to define him, and of aspiration to the favours of King-God and Money-God alike.

> 'Glory and virtue are only seen nowadays as stage properties, whose existence is a mere illusion ... people put profit before Glory ... The accursed principle of financial interest, which ought to be restricted to the bankers of Genoa and Amsterdam ... has now become the God of the Court; everything is subjugated to it - wit, courage, virtue, vice, good as well as evil actions ... What is certain by now is that Ambition is only ever directed towards serving Avarice ... and the Ambition which used to carry most weight as a way of securing public admiration, the esteem of one's Prince and the verdict conferred by one's Reputation, is now only concerned with the King's wealth, the profit to be gained from official Office and the money to be made from War'. (1)

This jungle of conflicting interests was well established before the death of Richelieu and Louis XIII. Their deaths in no way brought it on; they only served to relax certain restraints upon it. And the conclusion is unavoidable that the authority maintaining this set of relationships was also, in itself, the expression of a particular interest: reason of state, the higher interest of the site of the national economy, confronted both by aristocratic reaction and by Hapsburg imperialism.

*****

We must now show how the same underlying cause (the new mode of production), through its varying political and psychic modes, induced French society to confer historical importance upon what appeared as another fortuitous event, the publication in August 1640 at Louvain of Augustinius. The reason for the immediate re-publication in Paris (in December 1640 or January 1641) and in Rouen (1643) of its several hundred dense folio pages of abstruse disquisition in Latin, is to be found in the fact that its antihumanism, its refusal of the world, its severely pessimistic religion correspond to the feelings of a large proportion of French intellectuals, reveal those feelings to themselves, confirm them and propagate them but in no sense create them. A catalyst - not a first cause.

The new mode of production no longer had as its principle the qualitative virtue of natural categories, but rather a quantity of primary material, of energy, capital, labour. A quantity on which it was worthwhile economising. The rising class is now making its way either through the accumulation of capital, or through administrative control. As against the nobility (which, guaranteed by birth, seeks to assert itself through lavish expenditure and display), the rising class has to make itself recognised, acceptable: that is, to demonstrate its conformity to an ideal model. It even has to submit in conformity with the demands of the new monarchic and rational order. These preoccupations form the basis of bourgeois moralism, founded on economy and discipline.

This ideology is reinforced and goes into opposition from the end of the 1630's, when it becomes apparent that the state and the majority of the successful bourgeoisie are betraying its ideals. The development of motives of economic self-interest in the conduct of individuals as well as in that of the state was not only shocking to elderly bigots (or indeed to all those whose interests were threatened by it!). It awoke in certain particularly rigorous minds an opposition to the system, indeed a disgust with man and the world, since everything (themselves included) was infected by this concupiscence. In August 1637, one of the rising young stars of the legal profession, Antoine Le Maître, abandoned his career to withdraw from the world. By early 1638 there are already seven recluses at Port-Royal des Champs. Repression follows: on 14th May 1638, Saint-Cyran, the most notable of these men of God, is thrown into prison. So, two or three years before *Augustinius*, initial reactions were already setting in and influences spreading beyond these élite troops, amongst all who found their interests or convictions threatened and who were thus predisposed to seize on the first justification which came to hand. Accordingly, Father Senault (an acute and representative observer, later to become - in

1663 - general superior of the Oratory) published in 1641 his *Traité de l'Usage des passions* - his view of passions tending towards indulgence. But in 1644 he published *L'homme criminel ou la corruption de la nature par le péché selon les sentiments de Saint-Augustin*, which condemns them rigorously.

This is why, from Spring 1641 on, the name of Jansenius 'triumphed among right-thinking people' (Gui Patin): two years later, 'preachers from the pulpit tell their audiences of nothing else' but this dispute,(2) which by now is dividing 'not only the schools, but the salons and the town as well as the Court'.(3)

The deaths of Richelieu and Louis XIII, and the publication of *Augustinius* may be seen thus as revelatory accidents. They created possibilities, but their significance derives from the latent forces which they allowed to surface. No doubt this is a matter of great importance: what, after all, is a cause which, for lack of opportunity, produces no effects? But in most cases, underlying causes manage to create their opportunities. For they at once transform men and reality: their status, their visions, their possibilities, their language and, even, their desires. The study of literary history is well placed to demonstrate this.

1641-43 as a Turning Point in Literary History

- The previous situation

The second phase of seventeenth century literature, from 1626-34 to 1643-48, is dominated by dramatic practice: the conflict between the hero and state power structures the works of Corneille and his main competitors: Mairet (secretary to the Duc de Montmorency, the rebel of 1632), Tristan l'Hermite (secretary to Gaston d'Orléans, the King's main rival and at the centre of every conspiracy), Du Ryer (secretary to the Duc de Vendôme, the King's half-brother and another perennial conspirator) and Rotrou (who also enjoyed the support of the feudal opposition).

The leading literary successes are the works of these men: Sylvie (1626, 1628),[4] Sophonisbe (1634, 1635), Marianne (1636, 1637): traditional ideology, imagination, semiotics, are still fruitful. At this time, Corneille is still only - apart from Médée - an author of comedies, a less noble and even more bourgeois genre (though he strives to adapt it for high society), connected with the need for critical compensation experienced by a dominated class. All of a sudden, however, he puts the opposition in the shade with Le Cid (about 7th January 1637, 23rd March 1637) and Horace (early March 1640, 15th January 1641). How do these masterpieces come about? Because a historically extremely accurate vision enabled him (through a wider understanding and a more total integrative power) to work themes, visions, structures and languages in their most vital contemporary mode. For example, whilst the 'feudal' elements saw the state simply as a tyranny, he alone could understand that, as an embodiment of the interests of the collectivity, it was in the process of becoming the mediator of activities and values. Thus he alone could invest aristocratic heroism with a glorious future, whilst the limited vision of its established defenders condemned it to defeat, contrary to its high vocation and largely sterile, in literary terms, since the language of pathetic tragedy was scarcely available in this period of militancy.

This highly fruitful vision derives not from the chance factor of genius, but primarily from Corneille's status, from his vision of reality and from the social and ideological desire which informs it.

His primary originality, by comparison with other dramatists, consists in his having been born in the French capital of the new mode of production: Rouen, a manufacturing, shipping and financial centre. His income, including that from two administrative offices, gave him a degree of independence. In fact he was, at a time when dramatists were dependent on princely favours or attached to a theatrical troupe, the first bourgeois writer, that is to say the first to administer his own capital (not that he didn't have several noble patrons: they were indispensable at the time). After his second play, he demanded payment from the players on a pro rata basis rather than, as was usual, in a lump sum. On 1st August 1642, in a 'frontal attack on the publishing world',[5] he has Cinna registered in his own name, and not that of a bookseller: he can now resell his works at a profit, having them printed at his own expense, rather than relying on a lump sum payment from the bookseller. In 1643, he asks the King for 'the right to have his plays performed only by companies approved by himself' - i.e. paying him fees, at a time when any published play could be performed freely. He manages to take advantage of the competition between the two (subsequently three) Paris theatres.

On the surface, Corneille's status appears to be one of total independence. In fact, it is deeply integrated into the new order. As a man of private means, as an official, as a theatrical producer, as a man of affairs, he needs the guarantee of the centralised monarchy. And his ideology of loyalty to the legal profession and of commercial viability suggests to him strongly that the only career possible henceforth for the nobility lies in the service of the state, which, for its part, needs this kind of capital in terms of energy and prestige.

1. The overthrow of heroic drama

The first instance of the literary revolution of 1641-43 is the reversal of heroic drama in both senses: both that the 'feudal' dramatists adopt Corneille's centralist point of view and, vice versa, but also that heroic drama is going into decline.

In 1626, within a society vigorously opposed to the recent revival of the process of political and ideological suppression, Mairet had been able to set the metaphor of a masterpiece against the reality of the victory of royal power. Gaston d'Orléans, brother and heir of Louis XIII, had just married, against his will and in spite of support from the aristocratic opposition, the woman imposed on him by the King, Richelieu and reason of state (5th August 1626). Sylvie, performed some weeks later (in October or November) and running into sixteen editions between 1627 and 1635, concludes, by contrast, with the marriage of the princely heir to the shepherdess, against initial veto of King and reason of state: triumphal lyricism overcomes fate's vagaries and culminates in this reversal.

Fourteen years later, the same author returns to the same theme in Sidonie (1640, 16th September 1643); but what demands to be signified has changed, as well as the means of signification; lyric dynamism now functions in a vacuum; love, once the joyous affirmation of liberty and value-participation, has no further object and becomes lost in gallantry; lyricism is supplanted by critical rationalism as a means for the new men to valorise the new reality. Mairet abandons the theatre after the failure of this mediocre production.

But now the conditions for the genesis of Sylvie are renewed. After the death of Louis XIII (14th May 1643), his brother Gaston is at last able to bring his second wife, excluded for eleven years from the kingdom for reasons of state, to Paris. Tristan l'Hermite, secretary to the prince, takes the opportunity of writing his first play since 1637, La Folie du Sage (late 1643 or early 1644, 8th January 1645) which, apart from the fact of its mediocrity, bears strong resemblance to Sylvie.[1]

So, at the very moment when the behaviour of Mazarin and the 'Great Ones', together with the success of Augustinius, testify to the ruin of heroic humanism, literature undergoes the same process, with neither time-lag nor dependency. Better still: its failures testify to the breakdown in every detail of those illusions which still operate on the social scene. They demonstrate that the themes and motives, the visions and structures, the words and the style of the traditional opposition have no further efficacy: the impotence of a practice reveals its historic inadequacy.

*****

There is more than impotence: there is also denial. These failures are paralleled by a surprising change among the dramatists of the feudal opposition. Du Ryer builds up a conversion to monarchic centralism - through Saül (1639-40, 31st May 1642), valiant king, heroic fighter, admirable father, repenting from the third act onwards of his persecutions and piously accepting punishment for them; through the king in Esther (1642, 1644) whose virtue is only momentarily obscured by the sinister Haman, we come to his masterpieces: Scévole (probably performed in 1644) and Thémistocle (performed late 1646 - early 1647). In these, as in Horace, heroism is identified with patriotism, moral value with duty to the state.

For his part, Tristan, in La Mort de Sénéque (late 1643 - early 1644, 10th January 1645) castigates both Nero's tyranny and the ineffectuality of the plotters. He appears to come close to the centralist point of view in La Mort de Chrispe (1644, 1645) in which the Emperor Constantine is much better treated than in his sources.(6) And he adopts it unambiguously in Osman (1646-47?, 1656), the story of a revolt in which the sultan is praised and the rebels denigrated in the extreme.

Why should such a change occur? In imitation of Le Cid and Horace, whose success made them into models? But why a delay of several years, by which time Corneille's perspective had changed? There is another reason, less superficial than that of literary imitation: these authors have managed to free themselves from their former dependency and are beginning to develop a more correct and fruitful vision of the world.

In early 1641 Vendôme, accused of trying to poison Richelieu, flees to England. From now on Du Ryer has to live by his pen. He becomes committed to this tenuous existence: when the duke returns in 1643, his secretary does not resume his employment and his later works carry no dedication. It may be that his experienced seemed to him sufficiently negative(7) to make him turn back to the ideology appropriate to a lawyer and son of a lawyer. At any event, he deepens his moral and political reflections, translating Cicero, Seneca and several historians - elements which help us to understand the moralising patriotism of Scévole and Thémistocle and the conversion to monarchic centralism.

Tristan l'Hermite du Solier, 'too free to take up the occupation of a slave'(8) but too poor not to have to be a subordinate, took his revenge on the great and the rich(9) by cultivating a stoic virtue.

From 1621-22 on, as secretary to Monsieur, the King's brother and (until 1638) his heir and leader of the opposition before becoming lieutenant-general of the kingdom (from May 1643), he only seems to have derived a bitterness which is expressed in La Mort de Sénèque.(10) In 1645, finally disillusioned with Monsieur, the very embodiment of the historic impotence of the feudal element, he gives up his job.

At the same time, Rotrou has become incorporated into the social system, as a legal officer at Dreux (spring or early summer, 1639), married (9th July 1640) and father of six children (born between 6th August 1641 and 17th December 1648). The deaths of the Comte de Soissons (6th July 1641) and the Comte de Belin and his son (29th September 1637 and 7th December 1642) leave him without a patron. He does not look for another. From 1631 to 1639, he had published twenty-three plays, seventeen of which bore a dedication: from 1640 to 1654 he published thirteen, only three bearing one. At this point he is clearly free to deepen his critical reflections and in a position, professionally, to recognise the necessity of the state whilst remaining discontented with the government; in a position, too, to note the conflicts between ideal justice and the demands of social order: contradictions which will emerge in Venceslas and Cosroès.(11)

These transformations, then, do not derive from literary imitation, but from an attitude taken up towards feudal decadence (objectively translated into the decline of aristocratic patronage) and from a change of status which consolidates this change of vision. The success of Scévole and Thémistocle, La Mort de Sénèque, Venceslas and Cosroès is due to the fact that they derive from an authentic experience of France in the 1640's (the first in the idealist transcendence, the others with realism). Their vision is socially and ideologically grounded, and as such signifiable. While the vision of Osman, impossibly centralist, was not capable of being put into operation two years before the Fronde. The result is, in fact, mediocre in the extreme.

*****

Was this the moment to become converted to Corneille's perspective, when he himself was abandoning it?

In bringing critical reflection to bear on the attitude of the monarch as well as on that of the citizen-hero, Cinna (performed between December 1640 and September 1642, probably in July-August 1642) complements Le Cid and Horace for the third time, the individual passion which inspired the feudal element is opposed and then subordinated to the critical duty of monarchic order. But at the same time, Cinna appears to tend towards closing the very possibilities, in Cornelian drama, of heroic conversion, since, after such indulgence, there would be no longer any rebel hero.(12) And above all the collective interest (the homeland threatened), the prime motive of Le Cid and Horace, is now taken over by the monarch's calculation. The need to 'look for what is most useful' (line 1212); 'a head chopped off causes a thousand more to grow' (line 1116). Indeed, it 'is possible, through pardon, to secure one's power' (line 1624). Clemency, in fact, leads to enthusiastic support by the conspirators (lines 1715-1732). And so to the message of the play, in which the relationship between the submission of the aristocratic hero and his praise is reversed by comparison with Le Cid and Horace:

> 'After this action, you have nothing to fear,
> The yoke will now be born without complaint;
> No more assassins, nor more conspirators.'
> (lines 1757-58 and 1763)

Conversely, the image of the oppositional hero is similarly degraded. Cinna, a bashful lover and unconvinced plotter, is weak to the point of hypocrisy (lines 405-438 and 499-504 cf. 649 and Act III, scenes 2 and 3); Maxime's 'jealous rage' pushes him into treason; finally the plot itself is a low deceit as much as a justified vengeance: Auguste treated Emilie as his daughter, Cinna and Maxime as confidants (having bestowed great benefits on them).

In short, we already see in Cinna, written(13) before the political collapse of heroism and perhaps before the considerable spread of antihumanist writings, the writings, the interests and calculations which emerge triumphant in La Mort de Pompée. This contradiction can be found in another form, at the time of the play's publication (18th January 1643). I have already defined Corneille as a bourgeois organically linked to the interests of royal power. But here we see the man of affairs separated from the royal bard. The latter writes Cinna to the glory of the merciful monarch and his loyal princes. But the former dedicates it to the financier Montoron. On the one hand monarchic order, on the other liberal economics. The play celebrates traditional 'generosity': the innate vigour and virtue of the noble-born. But the dedication praises the new 'generosity' of Montoron; in fact, his willingness to give 2,000 livres for a dedication. What Corneille, in comparing him to Auguste, terms 'the soul of your soul' is merely the conceited ostentation of a prominent speculator, who has just begun to make a name for himself as a patron of the arts. One after the other, Tristan dedicates La Lyre to him (November 1641), Mareschal his Mausolée (1642), Chevreau his Lettres nouvelles (1642) and Corneille Cinna. But how can authentic heroism be maintained under the patronage of a parvenu? Even before Richelieu's death, Montoron announces his patronage of Fouquet and the ensuing success of an artificial poetry of trivialisation, intended to please the parvenu. In La Mort de Pompée, written immediately after Richelieu's death (winter 1642) and performed in November-December 1643, Corneille reverses his own heroic drama of self-realisation in the service of collective ends. Now, individual motives, like those of the state, are, apart from a few exceptions, no longer values but cynical or hypocritical interests.(14) Even Caesar is not inspiring: it's easy for him to attack Pompey's killers now that they have got rid of his rival; he avenges him, but at the same time putting down a plot against his own life; he would like to pardon Ptolomée ... in the interests of his love for Cleopatra, that dread passion which will cause his death for having broken Rome's laws (lines 1745-52). The only exception is Cornélie, the widow of the defeated man. But to Caesar, this 'great powerless heart' is reduced to 'vain projects' (lines 1761-62). For the process of history is no longer the triumph of value, the realisation of the order of providence. It is the reign of force, guided by self-interest ...

> '... when matters are sorted out by the sword
> Justice and law are but vain ideas'. (lines 49-50)

> 'When the Gods, astonished, seemed divided
> Pharsale decided on what they dared not judge
> ... the law of the sword,
> Justifying Caesar, has condemned Pompey.' (lines 3-4 and 13-14)

Even Cornélie, whilst affirming that the future will re-establish justice, notes that the Gods themselves have 'deceived' her (line 1737) and that (provisionally?) Providence has broken down - a pessimism to be confirmed in Rodogune (1644-45), Théodore (1645-46) and Héraclius (1646-47).

As Corneille himself puts it in his Examen de Pompée, 'There is something extraordinary in the title of this poem, which bears the name of a hero who has nothing to say in it'. How can heroic drama function if the principle of value which 'carries with it the fate of the world' is to be found neither in words nor deeds? Pompey absent, Cornélie overcome, Caesar ambiguous, all the others pursuing their interests makeshift, with no thought of good or evil: value-conflict no longer dominates plot, feeling or style. These all work in a vacuum of improbability, gallantry,(15) grandiloquence or incoherence.

So heroic drama, which had sought to integrate reality and desire, declines into the fictionality which characterises Corneille's later tragedies as well as Venceslas and Cosroès. Yet these plays still maintain a critical dimension which is the basis of their superior quality. Fictional dislocation is much more marked in Mairet (after 1637) and later in Du Ryer, abandoning the depiction of an all-too-disillusioning reality and returning to tragi-comedy(16) at a time when the ideology, the symbols and the language of this practice are already moribund. The restuls are, not surprisingly, worthless. Fictional practice could only produce great works - insofar as it was capable of this at all - in a freer form and in a style which could integrate the improbable with new demands for verisimilitude and analysis; the result being the heroic-gallant novel whose evolution begins at the same time, 1641-42.

2. The lyric experiment and its slippage into the fictional

So long as the conflict between feudal elements and state power structured social life and expressed essential aspirations, heroic drama remained the best means of aesthetic production, in its confrontation, indeed in Corneille its combination, of reality and desire.

But now the most clear-sighted of the feudal element have lost all hope of realising their aspirations. Then Mazarin, the 'Great Ones' or the speculators, if they represent the interests of reality, are incapable of embodying the ideals of desire. The main contradiction is no longer felt as the confrontation of equivalent forces, but as a hiatus between reality and desire. A lyrical or a critical practice constitutes the only possibility for a metaphorical overcoming of this contradiction.

Lyrical practice, to substitute for the real an image invested with desire, presupposed its transposition into an imaginary realm. Three possible forms: heroic, amorous, religious.

The heroic realm of the imaginary had a rich past, but the new political and ideological problematic emptied it of all substance, deprived it of its operative structures, condemned its language to inflation. Writers now react to the realisation of their impotence by inflating their pretensions. This leads to an infatuation with the epic (with simultaneously heroic and religious subjects) whose products are seen to collapse soon after the failure of the Fronde: Saint-Amant's _Moyse Sauvé_ (1653),(17) Le Moyne's _Saint-Louis_ (1653), Godeau's _Saint-Paul_ (1654), Scudéry's _Alaric ou Rome vaincue_ (1654), Chapelain's _La Pucelle ou la France délivrée_ (1655), Desmarets' _Clovis ou la France Chrétienne_ (1656). Besides the authors' incompetence, these failures are not the product of chance: how could the fantastic succeed in a period of triumphant rationalism?

As for love, so well suited to lyrical expression because, like faith and religious hope, it expresses the direction of the self towards the ideal, it is too engulfed in gallantry to constitute an option. With Voiture officiating at the Hôtel de Rambouillet from 1625 on, not for a generation after the death of Richelieu will Racine, Guilleragues, Mme. de La Fayette show themselves capable, from out of the depths of absolutism's gilded constraints, of making love into the tragic aspiration of the self devoid of any reason for living.

There thus remains religion. And thus a spurt of religious

tragedies. In Mariane, his first play, Tristan went beyond praise of the spiritual superiority of his heroine to show her revenge, through the moral and religious conversion of her executioner: the summary of the play states that he 'suddenly imagines he sees Mariane ascending into Heaven' and he implores the 'beautiful Angel' (line 1782) to pardon his 'blind fury' (line 1787) and his 'horrible crime' (line 1791). The justified success of this play (three editions in three years) is all the more noteworthy since its author was a libertine: the richness of history can sometimes emerge through its actors' insincere metaphors.

Pierre Du Ryer's Saül (1639-40, 31st May 1642) is still a committed work, in which political conflict is much more important than in the Bible or in La Taille and Billard. But there is scarcely any heroic action: rather, the play is a moral and religious tragedy in which the tyrannical king admits his faults and accepts his punishment, with a nobility which induces sympathy, through a conversion not allowed by the biblical God (cf. Book of Samuel I, 15 to 31). This religious alternative to the defeat of the hero by established power can be felt at the same time in Rotrou's Antigone (1637, 1639) and Iphigénie (1640, 1641). Du Ryer asserts it in Esther (1642, 1644).

At the same time Corneille himself is engaging with religious tragedy. Polyeucte (performed before Richelieu between 17th October and 18th November 1642 and in public the following January or February) is not only a work which goes beyond the political form of the order of providence (that of Le Cid, Horace and Cinna) towards its transcendant form. It is, in addition, the denigration of Machiavellianism: the emperor is a sadistic egotist, the governor mediocre and base, financially scheming and calculating. It is yet again a demonstration of the limits of the humanism of secular heroism: as a perfect man, Sévère is nonetheless as 'useless and uncertain' as Descartes for Pascal.

Here again, we should note that all these religious tragedies were written before the spectacular events of 1642-43, whilst the only later religious tragedy is Rotrou's Saint-Genest (1645, 1647). The possibilities of dramatic practice, even when brought into line by the religious alternative, are outworn from the time when Mazarin, the 'Great Ones' and the speculators occupy the domain of reality: all the more so as, at the same time, the themes, visions and language of religion are appropriated by antihumanism, refusal of the world and, at most, aspiration to a by now distant God.

This last possibility had the effect of allowing a degree of fertility in religious poetry. The Oeuvres Chrétiennes of Arnauld d'Andilly, published in 1642, ran into nine editions in three years. In 1646, Tristan published L'Office de la Sainte Vierge, a collection of about 1850 religious verses of reasonably high quality. Later, Racan,(18) Godeau,(19) Corneille,(20) Brébeuf(21) all take to religious lyricism, in spite of the obstacles to it of probability, propriety and respect of the sacred Truth.(22)

*****

Lyrical practice could not be very fertile during these years when ideals, though lost, had not yet been supplanted by despair; the tendency of strong religious commitment was to mistrust literary art as the generator of concupiscence, even when showing the punishment of passion:

> 'The cure is less pleasing than poison would be.' (23)

For this reason lyrical practice, in its loss of nerve, drifts off into fantastic exaltation of delusive fashionable ideals: a heroism and a gallantry as pale and as hollow as they are formally perfect. This inflation has free rein in interminable novels, constrained neither by the real structures of dramatic practice nor by the formal structures of theatre or poetry.

Yet again, this literary revolution precedes the death of Richelieu. In 1641 there appears Ibrahim by Georges and Madeleine de Scudéry: a braggart and a psychologist of gallantry respectively. In 1642 appears the first of ten volumes of Cassandre, by another braggart, La Calprenède. A considerable fashion had been started which was to last twenty years (even longer if we count its survival in the theatre of Thomas Corneille and Quinault). It's worthy of note that La Calprenède and Scudéry, formerly dramatic authors, give up the theatre in 1642 and 1643 respectively.

3. The beginnings of a critical literary practice

After the death of Richelieu, the most evident form of the historical process is no longer the contradiction between centralism and feudalism, but the moral contradiction between the laws of the economical and political market and the ideology of all those unwilling or unable to participate in it. On one side profit, ambition, self-interest and egoism govern the conduct of the state, of ministers and their hangers-on, of the 'Great' and of courtiers, of commerce and finance, of all institutions and individuals aiming to rise in society or to cope with competition. Against this, moralistic ideology is propagated not only by a small minority opposed to such an economy, society and market mentality, but by lawyers who (when they do not become speculators) find their rise in society blocked; and finally by many others, since critical ideology can always serve as a mask of one's own conduct and as a criticism of that of others. From this time on, self-esteem or self-love, terms which had designated the self-idolatry of the sinner as opposed to the love of God, come to mean self-interested egoism as opposed to the social virtues of heroic abnegation or altruistic generosity.[24]

In the context of this new contradiction, the most fruitful literary practice - that most able to work available themes and mentalities in effective structure and language - is represented by critical moralism, which marks all the greatest theatrical works of the period.

In his masterpiece, La Mort de Sénèque (performed in late 1643-early 1644), Tristan attacks royal power as embodied in Nero, and the mediocrity and cowardice of the plotters, whilst the stoic, Seneca, overcomes the tyranny which crushed him by his moral stature, and a woman, a former slave, alone embodies courage in the face of all the cowardly nobility.

To work through all the available elements might have meant going too far in denigration and losing a grip on the problem as a whole. The feudal element might be base, but their spectacular conduct offered aesthetic possibilities not to be found in La Mort de Sénèque, already a classic of its kind. A prince or minister might appear tyrannical: the state, at this time, was nonetheless becoming a fundamental necessity. Rotrou's moralism does not prevent him from being simultaneously baroque and realist. Through lively plots, psychology and style he portrays on the stage both the necessity and the vices of monarchic centralism. Venceslas (1647, 1648) shows the necessity of subordinating morality to the interests of the state as the expression of the general interest and in consequence the only practically possible source of value. Cosroès (1648, 1649) by contrast reaffirms the divorce between value - both source and effect of the resistance to tyranny - and power, whose operation can lead to crime. These tragedies do not limit themselves to denouncing the conduct of self-interest; they make it live for us at the psychological level.

Corneille adopts this critical perspective as well after La Mort de Pompée. But only in Nicomède (winter of 1650-51) does he manage to identify heroism and moralism, and to make them live in a single character. In Rodogune (winter of 1644-45, 31st January 1647), through an astonishing conjunction of old and new perspectives, heroism is maintained, but only by becoming criminal: Corneille himself says of his Cleopatra 'whilst hating her actions, we admire the source from which they derive'.[(25)] Elsewhere, drama becomes lost in complexity of intrigue and analysis: its motives are no longer embodied in living characters. Corneille is caught in the contradiction between heroic drama - where meaning becomes action, character and rhetoric - and critical analysis, which dissolves all of this.

In general, critical practice could only be the product of social and ideological forces which held on to their illusions: which were condemned to ineffectual lyrical or fictional practice. Only the Jansenist tendency was capable of a coherent critical stance. But they rejected the metaphorical devices of literature as the mendacious flattery of concupiscence.

For the time being, only parody, the most spontaneous critical form, can develop. All that was needed was to make caricature evolve a little, from a style into a fashion. In 1643 Scarron published a *Recueil de quelques vers burlesques* and Saint-Amant his *Rome ridicule* (written it is true ten years before). A new literary fashion is under way, developing from the dislocation of signifier from signified but, of course, incapable of bridging the gap. We might say that the new Corneille parodies himself. Ineptly, since his means of signification become ambiguous, obscure, tending to arbitrariness or obscurity: their language simultaneously epic and critical, ironic in the case of the writer but hypocritical or cynical in the character, obscure, complicated, intransitive. Only some time later does critical parody produce the dominant works of the Regency: *Les États et Empires de la Lune*, *L'Histoire comique des États du Soleil*, *Le Roman comique*, *Les Provinciales*, *Les Précieuses Ridicules*; all of these lead to the major abstract criticism of the *Maximes* and the *Pensées*.

Conclusion: The Autonomy and Dependence of Literary Practice

The literary revolution of the years 1641-43 was not, then, the result of the spectacular events of those years: the deaths of Richelieu and of Louis XIII, the conspiracy of the 'Great Ones' and the ministry of Mazarin, the first battle of Jansenism. The survival or death of a King, the publication of a manifesto, significant only as effects or instances revelatory of the mode of production, cannot constitute the foundations of literary history.

Even before the death of Richelieu, at a time when the illusions of heroic ideology have at least ten years still to live, heroic drama has already ceased to be the solution to the relationship between reality and desire and its means of operation, of its *signification*, are already disappearing. Lyrical practice, expressive of the feudal vision at the beginning of its declining years, turns to the fantastic, ten years before the Fronde. Can the future be seen already as lying with critical practice, as yet only producing its first parodies? We know that its development will be held up for twenty years by monarchic sublimation (incorporating Molière but not La Fontaine) and that the same agency will revitalise a tragic dramatic practice, the expression of a sublime and despairing illusion, that of the final cessation of the class struggle.

*****

Far from being the derivative of events, of its sources or of the births of figures of genius, literary practice is directly a <u>function</u> (that is, principally an effect and secondarily a cause) of the development of the mode of production of the human condition. Therein lies its reason for existing, since it seeks to overcome metaphorically the constitutive contradiction of the human condition as men experience it, on the basis of a historical heritage, according to the diversity of their social situation and their ideological position. And again in its workings it is a <u>function</u> not only of its own traditions, but of the general availability of its means of signification (visions, themes, structures, languages) which have no existence outside those social and ideological practices which constantly change their meaning and their intensity. And so, rather than the sovereign free will of genius or of its audience, it is basically in the impossibility of artificial production of such means of signification that we find the autonomy of a literary practice, which can only generate masterpieces out of a historically grounded vision.

<u>Footnotes</u>

1. Balzac, <u>De la gloire</u> in <u>Oeuvres diverses</u> (licensed 10th August 1643, printed 30th April 1644).

2. Sarrau, letter of February 1643.

3. Mme. de Motteville, <u>Mémoires</u> (Collection Petitot, 1819), Vol.37, p.224.

4. The dates I give are - in order - those of the first performance and of the first printing.

5. B. Dort, <u>Pierre Corneille dramaturge</u> (L'Arche, 1957), p.15.

6. Cf. especially lines 608-635. But this tragedy, often compared to <u>Phèdre</u>, is more concerned with passions than politics.

7. 'With this unhappy situation are associated a thousand drudgeries and difficulties which spring from the senseless impulse we see to show affection for the great and to give them proof of total devotion.' (Faret, L'honnête homme).

8. Lettres mêlées 88 (1642).

9. The last straw for him was to be deprived of his small inheritance in 1639 after fourteen years of lawsuits.

10. See below.

11. See below. In Bélisaire (1643, 1644) and Don Bernard de Cabrère (1646, 1647) Rotrou advocates a reconciliation which recalls Cinna: the king is to recognise and honour the hero, to the advantage of both. 'Thus does a grateful king/Become more powerful by giving' (the last words of Don Bernard). If Mairet did not operate this transformation (who could have facilitated new successes for him?) he had good reason. In contrast to Tristan and Du Ryer, he had fond memories of his principal patron, a victim of state tyranny. In the dedication of Solyman (1639) he promised his widow a work in praise of Montmorency. And again, born in Besançon, capital of the relatively autonomous Spanish Franche-Comté, Mairet was hardly favourable to dreams of annexation on the part of French centralism. Representing the Franche-Comté in Paris from 1645 on, he was to be expelled in 1653.

12. In fact Cinna ou la clémence d'Auguste - when written a happy synthesis - since Richelieu was appearing to seek generously the King's clemency for the fugitive Vendôme (17th May 1641) and for accomplices of the dead Soissons (July 1641) - had its first performances between the arrest of Cinq-Mars (13th June 1642) and his execution (12th September).

13. Probably between autumn 1640 and spring 1642.

14. 'Justice is not a virtue of the state' (line 104). 'Timid equity destroys the art of governing' (line 108). 'And so your pride, disguised as zeal/Makes self-interest act under the guise of virtue' (lines 279-80).

15. This is how conquering Caesar becomes a poor lover of Cleopatra:
'And with the hand which drops his sword
Still steaming with the blood of Pompey's friends
He traces sighs and in a plaintive voice
Declares himself my captive on his victor's field.'
(lines 397-400)

16. Mairet had four tragi-comedies and one comedy performed (1625-33), three of them during the period when the 'Great Ones' were holding their own against the royal power; and then three tragedies (1634-37) and, again, four tragi-comedies (1637-40). Du Ryer starts with five tragi-comedies, a pastoral and a comedy (1629-34), then goes on to two tragi-comedies and six tragedies (1636-47) and ends with three tragi-comedies (1648-54) of which the two last are extremely fanciful.

17. A first version had been completed as early as 1642.

18. *Odes sacrées* (1651), *Poésies Chrétiennes* (1660, completed in 1655).

19. *Poésies Chrétiennes* (1654).

20. Translation of *The Imitation of Christ* (1656).

21. *Entretiens solitaires* (1660).

22. Cf. Godeau's Preface to his *Poésies Chrétiennes*.

23. Godeau, *Sur la comédie*, in *Poésies Chrétiennes* (1654).

24. As I have said, the new mode of production was not sufficiently developed in France for moralists to perceive the fruitful dynamism of avid self-interest. They were condemned to see the motives of the new economic man as those of a superceded psychological type. English and Dutch thinkers could see more clearly. 'That rare work, *Of The Citizen*, by the incomparable Monsieur Hobbes' (Mersenne, letter of 25th April 1646) appears in Paris in 1642, where its author had been in exile since 1640.

25. *Discours de l'utilité et des parties du poème dramatique* (1660).

TRAGEDY, JUSTICE AND THE SUBJECT

Catherine Belsey

1

Shirley's tragedy, The Cardinal, was performed by the King's Men in 1641. The Cardinal is the revenge play to end all revenge plays (literally, I want to argue). Most obviously, it combines motifs from Hamlet, The Spanish Tragedy, The Duchess of Malfi and The White Devil. Less obviously, at least to bourgeois criticism in quest of the essential coherence of the text, The Cardinal spectacularly gives way under the pressure of precisely those contradictions which are held in precarious balance in earlier revenge plays.

'Revenge tragedy' is a modern category with no Renaissance authority.(1) It was produced by and has produced a mode of criticism which focused on psychology and motive - the state of mind of the revenger - and the history of ideas - the moral status of revenge in the period. On those counts we have probably got as far as can be expected: revengers are well-intentioned but unbalanced; seventeenth century audiences knew that private revenge was contrary to Christian morality ('Vengeance is mine; I will repay, saith the Lord'),(2) but they probably had a tendency to sympathise with revengers all the same. The banality of those conclusions may suggest the inadequacy of the original classification.

The word which insists most vehemently throughout The Cardinal is 'justice', and it is at the moment when justice is announced, defined and installed that the point of collapse is reached. On the wedding day of the Duchess Rosaura to D'Alvarez, the bridegroom is murdered in a masque by his rival, Columbo. The King, who is present and in control, promises justice and imprisons Columbo. As Act III ends, guards escort Columbo from the stage, and the Duchess declares, 'This shows like justice' (III, ii, 247).(3) Immediately afterwards, at the beginning of Act IV, Columbo is at large and vowing to kill at the altar any future bridegroom of the Duchess. The King is conspicuously absent at this point, and he remains so until the final scene, when he reappears at the climactic moment, authoritatively interrogates all those present, encourages the innocent Duchess to take poison by mistake, expresses amazement at the extraordinary wickedness of the Cardinal (V, iii, 270-71), and concludes that Kings should be more careful (V, iii, 299).

Whether or not the Machiavellian Cardinal himself was identified by contemporary audiences as Archbishop Laud, misleader of Charles I, there is no doubt that this is a royalist play. There is one explicit reference to the extra-textual events of the period: the Duchess urges the Cardinal to reform his ways, 'before the short hair'd men/Do crowd and call for justice' (II, iii, 165-66). But the royalist project is most readily apparent in the displacement of the revenger, Hernando, by the figure of the King. Hernando has a relatively minor role in the play; he is apparently killed by the Cardinal's servants before the final scene (V, iii, 181 S.D.); and although he kills Columbo and wounds the Cardinal, he does not dominate the play at its climax in the manner of Hamlet, Hieronimo or Vindice. On the contrary, the dominant figure at the high points of the action is the King.

The two symmetrically placed scenes of violence, the murder of D'Alvarez and the murder of the Duchess (III, ii and V, iii, 184 ff.), are conducted in the presence of the King and centre in each case on an appeal to him for justice. The King's response each time is prompt, authoritative, confident and entirely ineffectual. It is clear that the sovereign is the only source of justice, that he acts with the authority of heaven, that he must be just 'Or be no king' (III, ii, 205) and that his failure to impose justice is the pivot of the tragedy.

There are several ways of accounting for the radical incoherence of the play (without resorting to the inanity, simply contradicted by the emphatic, authoritative parataxis of his key speeches, that the King is to be seen as a weak character).(4) Reflectionist criticism would find the play a precise mirror of the problems of the period, with Charles I's heroic, confident, stubborn blindness central among them. Alternatively, we can find here a collision between the ideological project of the play - to show that kings, because they are the source of justice, must be vigilant - and the interest of the narrative, which necessitates that justice is withheld so that revenge becomes imperative. If the King's promise of justice had stood uncontradicted, the play would have had to end with Act III. In order to be a play about revenge, The Cardinal has to become a play about a crisis of justice. But because the ideological project foregrounds the figure of the King, the crisis of justice is not merely the context of an act of revenge: on the contrary, it is at the centre of the play.

2

Our commitment to our own classifications tends to suppress the preoccupation with justice in the plays of the Renaissance. Measure for Measure, a problem play interpreted in relation to All's Well and Troilus, is only secondarily seen as posing the problem of the just administration of the law. Measure for Measure is rarely linked with The Merchant of Venice and The Tempest, which quite overtly propose related debates about the nature of justice and the right to inflict punishment. Similar questions reverberate through the political plays of Shakespeare and Ben Jonson, and the so-called revenge plays of Chapman and Marston. But they ring out in the speeches of the earliest revengers: Hieronimo ripping the bowels of the earth with his dagger, and begging for 'Justice, O justice, justice, gentle king' (The Spanish Tragedy, III, xii, 63);[(5)] and Titus Andronicus, urging his kinsmen to dig a passage to Pluto's region, with a petition 'for justice and for aid' (Titus Andronicus, IV, iii, 15).[(6)]

The problems posed in these plays are never fully resolved, and the chronic interrogation of justice in the drama of the period becomes critical in certain of the revenge plays. Hieronimo and Titus, like Vindice in The Revenger's Tragedy, act unjustly in the interests of justice and are justly destroyed in consequence. When 'the world's justice fails' (The Cardinal, V, iii, 78), they act against the will of God, on behalf of an earthly justice which is consistent with the will of God. There is no closure in these plays, no obvious position of final knowingness for the audience, because neither the ordering of the discourses within the texts themselves nor the colliding planes of their intelligibility permit the spectators to know whether Hieronimo, Titus and

Vindice - or Hamlet, or Hernando in The Cardinal - are, simply, right or wrong.

No closure is possible in that that question cannot be resolved, and this in turn is because the terms in which the question is posed prevent the possibility of resolution. It is my hypothesis that there is a radical discontinuity between medieval justice and the form of justice brought into being by the English revolution, and that The Cardinal is the last in a succession of plays which are themselves the site of this discontinuity, instances of a discourse of justice in crisis. I do not want to seem to privilege drama, nor in any way to diminish the well-documented struggles being fought out within and between the institutions of the law, the monarchy and parliament. I want to argue that the discourse of the theatre and these institutional struggles converge in the 'theatricals' of the trial and execution of Charles I, and that this is the moment at which the Renaissance contradictions, crystallised and made visible in the tragedy of the period, finally precipitate a bourgeois justice, guaranteed by and guaranteeing the existence of the bourgeois subject. In consequence, tragedy itself begins to give way to classic realism, the dominant mode of bourgeois fiction. To substantiate this I need to move some way from 1642.

3

Medieval justice is divine and offence against it is sin. Its paradigm is the Last Judgment and its guarantee is the presence of God as judge. At the end of The Castle of Perseverance (c. 1400) the Four Daughters of God participate in the trial of Mankind's soul after his death. Righteousness and Truth as prosecution hold that he is damned for his sins; Mercy and Peace in his defence plead for clemency. God pronounces sentence from his throne above the playing area. Mankind is to be saved because he cast himself on God's mercy, but God utters a solemn warning to the audience:

> 'Lytyl and mekyl, the more and the les,
> All the statys of the werld is at myn renoun; [control]
> To me schal the yeue acompt at my dygne des.
> Whanne Myhel hys horn blowyth at my dred dom ...' (11.3614-17)[7]

Medieval justice haunts the Renaissance. Macbeth's murder of Duncan is performed in the shadow of the Last Judgment:

> 'this Duncan
> Hath borne his faculties so meek, hath been
> So clear in his great office, that his virtues
> Will plead like angels, trumpet-tongu'd, against
> The deep damnation of his taking-off.' (Macbeth, I, vii, 16-20)

The soul of Desdemona will confront Othello in that high court of justice:

> 'When we shall meet at compt,
> This look of thine will hurl my soul from heaven,
> And fiends will snatch at it.' (Othello, V, ii, 276-78)

The will of God is not constrained by any external, abstract measure of justice. On the contrary, the divine will is itself the source and guarantee of justice: 'God must first will a thing before it can be just'.(8) God's justice is absolute, and the divine sovereignty is displayed in the tortures of hell, where each sin has its just penalty:

> 'Where usurers are chok'd with melting gold,
> And wantons are embrac'd with ugly snakes,
> And murderers groan with never-killing wounds,
> And perjur'd wights scalded in boiling lead,
> And all foul sins with torments overwhelm'd.' (The Spanish Tragedy, I, i, 67-71)

This justice descends vertically from heaven to earth. Its order is one and continuous, from God to the individual soul, and its intermediaries, whether these are the church, the sovereign or conscience, are links in a chain of command. In the medieval moralities this vertical order is evident in the ironic mode of the plays, where an uncomprehending protagonist chooses between good and evil at the instigation of counsellors marked as knowing, while the audience, equally knowing, watches the hero stumble towards the inevitable Judgment. Whatever contradictions may be present in the medieval morality plays, they are not here, in the ordering of justice.

The institutional practices of feudal law maintain the vertical system of control. The abandonment of trial by ordeal in 1215 meant that

God no longer exercised his judgment in a direct way. But the medieval judicial system identified justice with power, and progressively centralised both in the hands of the sovereign.(9) By the sixteenth century the sovereign, as God's representative on earth, has become the guardian of earthly justice, in the interest of the common weal, which, as Foucault points out, defines 'a state of affairs where all the subjects without exception obey the laws, accomplish the tasks expected of them, practise the trade to which they are assigned, and respect the established order so far as this order conforms to the laws imposed by God on nature and men.'.(10) This circular justice finds its guarantee in the delegation of power from God to princes 'that sit in the throne of God', and in the analogy between God's will and the will of the sovereign:

> 'It is atheism and blasphemy to dispute what God can do; good Christians content themselves with His Will revealed in His Word: so it is presumption and high contempt in a subject to dispute what a King can do, or say that a King cannot do this or that, but rest with that which is the King's revealed will in his law.' (11)

When in <u>The Cardinal</u> the Duchess appeals to the King for justice, she identifies crime with sin, law with the law of God, and faith in sovereignty with Christian faith:

> 'If you do think there is a Heaven, or pains
> To punish such black crimes i' th' other world,
> Let me have swift and such exemplar justice
> As shall become this great assassinate.
> You will take off our faith else, and if here
> Such innocence must bleed and you look on,
> Poor men that call you gods on earth will doubt
> To obey your laws; may, practise to be devils,
> As fearing, if such monstrous sins go on,
> The saints will not be safe in Heaven.'

The King's reply is emphatic, authoritative and comes from the heart of Stuart ideology: 'You shall,/You shall have justice' (III, ii, 102-12).

By 1641, of course, this ideology is itself in crisis, but the challenge to it begins to emerge much earlier in sixteenth century glimpses of a new and broadly horizontal order of justice. The Protestant reformers could not praise a fugitive and cloistered virtue. The dissolution of the monasteries ensured that the world became the arena of the Protestant struggle for the practice of charity, and sin began to have consequences for the social body as well as for the soul. In The Castle of Perseverance Mankind's avarice is evidence of a misplaced sense of values, but in Enough is as Good as a Feast, a morality of the 1560's, Worldly Man's surrender to the persuasions of Covetous precipitates the appearance on stage of three representative social types, Tenant, Servant and Hireling, with a petition against rack-renting and exploitation.

No redress is available to these pathetic figures except the conviction that God will punish Worldly Man when the time comes:

> 'No more shall it prevail him, the Scripture saith indeed,
> To ask mercy of the Lord when he standeth in need.' (ll.1155-56)(12)

In The Longer Thou Livest, the More Fool Thou Art, also in the 1560's, the complaint of People is similarly pathetic and similarly without relief in the world:

> 'For remedy we wot not whither to go
> To have our calamity redressed.
> Unto God only we refer our cause;
> Humbly we commit all to his judgment.' (ll.1737-40)

Divine justice acts more swiftly in this instance, when God's Judgment, 'with a terrible visure', arrests the offending hero and strikes him with the sword of vengeance (l.1791).(13)

Divine justice here is purely retributive: it does not undertake to cure the ills of the social body. The hero is damned, but God does not intervene to avert the sufferings of People. A gap begins to appear between divine retribution and earthly justice. Once the arena of the struggle for salvation is the world, justice in the world becomes an issue, and so does the question of action to secure it. God wills the world to be just and brands injustice a sin which is to be punished. But God as the only source of justice does not undertake to bring it about in a fallen world. On the contrary, the vertical order of justice withholds authority to act from human beings who are nonetheless required to act in the interests of justice precisely because the divine order does not guarantee it. Vengeance is God's, but God may defer it till doomsday, and in the meantime human beings are committed to an ideal of justice in the world.(14)

This is the problem of Hieronimo, who seeks justice in the earth and cannot find it, and of Titus, who shoots arrows at the gods soliciting them 'to send down Justice for to wreak our wrongs' (IV, iii, 51). But Astraea, goddess of justice, left the earth when the golden age came to an end, and she has ceased to intervene in human affairs (Titus Andronicus, IV, iii, 4; The Spanish Tragedy, III, xiii, 140).(15)

Revenge is not justice. Titus is a man 'so just that he will not revenge' (IV, i, 129). Revenge is an act of will, devoid of grace, contrary to the will of God and the authority of the sovereign. But revengers may act as instruments of God's judgment, in the same way that the devils enact divine justice by tormenting the damned in hell. The bloody masques and Thyestean banquets of the plays originate in hell, but they have the effect in each case of securing divine retribution and purging a corrupt social body. Revenge is an (as yet unauthorised) assertion of the individual in the interests of social justice.

4

In The Longer Thou Livest (c.1560), the instrument of divine retribution was a personified abstraction, God's Judgment. Stage revengers are human beings who are entitled to be instruments but not agents of justice. The discontinuity in the concept of justice is matched by a parallel discontinuity in the concept of the subject, and the same group of plays which show justice in crisis are also instances of a discourse of subjectivity in crisis.

The protagonist of The Castle of Perseverance is a subject-in-fragments. The circular playing area shown on the stage-plan as surrounded by water is the world in which Mankind makes a series of critical choices which will determine his eternal future.(16) It is also the little world of man, the microcosm, peopled by virtues and vices which together constitute Mankind's nature, his being in the world. The play shows the cosmic struggles between God and the Devil duplicated in the conflict within the protagonist. He is perplexed, torn, wavering, confused, invited to co-operate with the fragments of his own being, to _subject_ himself to their promises, arguments, lies. Control is divided between these knowing fragments and the bewildered figure who, nonetheless, is required to choose. He has no power of himself to help himself, and is saved only in consequence of the will of God, the Absolute Subject.

In the tradition of the psychomachia these fragments are abstract spiritual qualities, but the distinction between physical and psychological properties is a modern one. In the 'little world, made cunningly/Of elements', where the blend of humours defines disposition, the physical and the psychological are continuous. The repentant Everyman greets his own Beauty, Strength and Five Senses, as well as Discretion and Knowledge, only to be parted from them all as he crawls into his grave.

In 1637 Prynne and two others had their ears cut off for libel. It is the humanist concept of the subject as a unit to be trained, disciplined, rendered docile, which makes punishment by mutilation a scandal. Titus cuts off his hand and Hieronimo bites out his tongue, reproducing the medieval subject-in-fragments. In Book V of _The Faerie Queene_ Talus, with more obviously allegorical implications, executes justice by cutting off Munera's hands and feet (V, ii, 26).

Lady Macbeth's invocation to cruelty displays the nature of the Renaissance subject:

'Come, you spirits
That tend on mortal thoughts, unsex me here;
And fill me, from the crown to the toe, top-full
Of direst cruelty. Make thick my blood,
Stop up th' access and passage to remorse,
That no compunctious visitings of nature
Shake my fell purpose nor keep peace between
Th' effect and it. Come to my woman's breasts,
And take my milk for gall, you murd'ring ministers,
Wherever in your sightless substances
You wait on nature's mischief. Come, thick night,
And pall thee in the dunnest smoke of hell,

That my keen knife see not the wound it makes,
Nor heaven peep through the blanket of the dark
To cry "Hold, hold".' (<u>Macbeth</u>, I, v, 37-51)

The personified abstractions of the moralities have given way to fictional human beings in the Renaissance theatre, and the speaker, the subject of the enunciation, is visible on the stage, there before us as a unity, performing the invocation. But it is noticeable that the subject of the <u>énoncé</u>, the 'I' of discourse, is barely present in the speech. It is not the grammatical subject of the actions, and the moment it appears (as 'me') in the text, it is divided into crown, toe, cruelty, blood, remorse, nature, breasts, milk. The speech concludes with the opposition between heaven and hell, reproducing the morality pattern of the subject as a battleground between cosmic forces duplicated in its own being, autonomous only to the point of choosing between them.

Hieronimo's 'eyes, no eyes, but fountains fraught with tears' (III, ii, 1) constitutes a modest instance of fragmentation compared with the whole text of <u>Titus Andronicus</u>, where messengers deliver heads and hands with calm mockery (III, i, 234-40) and bones are ground with blood to make pastry (V, ii, 187-8). The discourse of subjectivity in <u>Titus</u> incorporates the mutilation of the narrative to produce a high degree of instability, a series of slides between unity and a fragmentation which borders on disintegration (Titus' madness). Here is an instance:

'Marcus, unknit that sorrow-wreathen knot;
Thy niece and I, poor creatures, want our hands,
And cannot passionate our tenfold grief
With folded arms. This poor right hand of mine
Is left to tyrannize upon my breast;
Who, when my heart, all mad with misery,
Beats in this hollow prison of my flesh,
Then thus I thump it down.' (III, ii, 4-11)

Folded arms are signifiers of grief (11.4-7), but breast-beating becomes the signified of a tangle of signifiers ('This poor right hand ... is left ...) in which the grammatical subject shifts from 'hand' (1.7) to 'I' (1.11) by means of a 'who' (1.9) which has no obvious antecedent.

<u>Titus</u> is an extreme case, but vestiges of the subject-in-fragments

survive even in The Cardinal in the exchanges between the Duchess and Hernando, at the precise moment when Hernando becomes a revenger on her behalf. He urges the Duchess not to keep her heart alive without vengeance; her hand should be guided by honour to Columbo's heart; her hand is too weak alone, and another arm must interpose (IV, ii, 135-60). (If the fragmentation here has begun to sound figurative, a formal and rhetorical use of synecdoche, this is a measure of the imminence in 1641 of the unitary bourgeois subject).

The choice of action once made, however, the fragments must be assembled, brought under control. Macbeth exclaims, 'I ... bend up/Each corporal agent to this terrible feat' (I, vii, 79-80). Hieronimo tells himself,

> 'thou must enjoin
> Thine eyes to observation, and thy tongue
> To milder speeches than thy spirit affords,
> Thy heart to patience, and thy hands to rest,
> Thy cap to courtesy and thy knee to bow,
> Till to revenge thou know, when, where and how.' (III, xiii, 39-44)

Thus unified, in defiance of nature, the subject appropriates an imaginary autonomy, claims a false authority, fails to observe a proper subjection to the will of God which is justice, and acts unjustly, however good the cause.

5

The revenger performs a heroic act of injustice on behalf of justice, inviting the audience to pose (without answering) the question, 'Whether 'tis nobler in the mind to suffer/The slings and arrows of outrageous fortune,/Or to take arms ...'. Hamlet, as always, is a special case, and deserves special treatment. The other plays I have focused on (Titus Andronicus, The Spanish Tragedy, The Revenger's Tragedy) avoid the collapse which occurs in The Cardinal by holding in precarious balance distinct and sometimes contradictory planes of intelligibility.

The clearest case is The Spanish Tragedy, where G. K. Hunter has identified an ironic relationship between divine justice, represented in the framing dialogue between Andrea and Revenge, and the blind human attempts to secure justice which constitute the main plot of the play. Thus, he argues, Hieronimo and the other figures on the stage are not perceived by the audience as autonomous subjects, but as puppets of a divine justice they do not understand.(17) There is in the play a hierarchy of discourses in which only the discourse of Revenge is fully knowing, and the human figures merely _think_ they know, from Andrea himself, who cannot see where the action is leading, down to Pedringano, who _thinks_ on the scaffold that Lorenzo has placed his reprieve in the box which the audience knows to be empty.

The ironic mode here traces a direct descent from the morality plays. The difference, however, is that while the allegorical mode of the moralities insists on the subject-in-fragments, the quasi-realism of Elizabethan drama permits us to perceive the protagonist as a unity. However much the speeches may deal in fragments, they are uttered by a subject of the enunciation who appears autonomous: '_I will_ revenge his death' (_The Spanish Tragedy_, III, xiii, 20; my italics).

The Spanish Tragedy is about divine justice; it is also about a human quest for earthly justice. The murder of Horatio is a sin which incurs divine vengeance. But the murders of Horatio, Serberine and Pedringano, and Lorenzo's deception of the King, the fountainhead of justice on earth, are evidence of corruption in the social body. Hieronimo invokes divine vengeance and royal justice, apparently in vain. When the vertical order of justice fails, he turns to the horizontal (and incipient bourgeois) scheme of human action on behalf of earthly justice, and purges the corruption of the social body. He thus becomes an _instrument_ of divine vengeance - and an _agent_ of hell. Hieronimo is poised at the intersection of the feudal scheme of justice and a newly glimpsed, but not yet authoritative, bourgeois order in which the individual acts on behalf of society. He is poised also at the intersection of two orders of subjectivity: he is both instrument and agent, ironic and heroic, subject-in-fragments and Cartesian unity. These orders are held in balance within the play by the intersection of two modes: the medieval, allegorical, divine comedy of the Andrea-Revenge dialogue; and the quasi-realist tragedy of Hieronimo's revenge.

In Titus Andronicus the relationship between the two modes is differently ordered. Like Hieronimo, Titus as revenger is mad, located in an unauthorised order of subjectivity. In his madness he promises to embrace Tamora, who is disguised as a personification of revenge (V, ii, 67-69). Tamora is a human being: her adoption of the role of Revenge is a device to delude Titus. At the same time, Tamora, barbaric Gothic queen, brings revenge to Rome and initiates the series of acts of vengeance which constitutes the narrative. An emblematic reading of this extremely emblematic play would see Tamora as, precisely, a personification of Revenge. Titus is not really deluded:

> 'I knew them all, though they suppos'd me mad,
> And will o'erreach them in their own devices.' (V, ii, 142-43)

He falls in with Tamora's scheme only with a view to inviting her to dine on her children. At the same time, it is in the moment that he promises to embrace Tamora that he is appropriated by revenge. In this episode the human being of the realist mode momentarily becomes a morality fragment without ceasing to be a human subject.

In The Revenger's Tragedy Vindice is both human figure and fragment simultaneously. The entire action is intelligible on two distinct planes. In his opening speech, Vindice addresses himself direct to vengeance:

> 'Vengeance, thou murder's quit-rent, and whereby
> Thou show'st thyself tenant to Tragedy ...' (I, i, 39-40)[18]

On one plane he is a wronged man, holding the skull of his murdered love and invoking vengeance; on another he is vengeance, as his name implies, addressing himself as abstract participant in the tragic order of divine justice. But it is as human subject that Vindice is required to pay the tragic price of his actions. At the end of the play Antonio summarily despatches the avenger of his wife's death to execution. The new, just ruler, justly installed as sovereign by the unjust actions of the human hero, has the hero justly punished.

'Vengeance is mine; I will repay, saith the Lord'. Vindice as abstraction brings a series of vices (Lussurioso, Spurio, Ambitioso, etc.) to divine retribution; Vindice as human subject takes vengeance on a corrupt court dominated by corrupt human beings (Lussurioso, Spurio, Ambitioso, etc.). In doing so Vindice arrogates the vengeance which belongs to God, and himself merits divine retribution. The play achieves its precarious coherence by signifying on these two planes simultaneously, but the planes are brought into direct collision in the judicial execution of the protagonist.

In The Cardinal the pressure of the tragic contradictions of revenge is such that the play collapses into incoherence. The absolutist project of the text is unable to generate a narrative, and in the gap between the ideological and the formal constraints there insists the continuing crisis of justice which in 1641 remains unresolved.

6

In 1637, when Prynne's ears were cut off 'against all law and justice',[19] he did not flinch 'even to the astonishment of all the beholders'.[20] Prynne's Christian martyrdom promptly became part of the popular mythology of Puritanism.[21] In 1649 Charles I met his death 'with the saint-like behaviour of a blessed martyr'.[22] Divine justice had reached a point of impasse when each side invoked it against the other. The collision precipitated a new form of justice.

Prynne claimed that his illegal sentence was an encroachment on the liberties of the people of England:

> 'Alas! poor England, what will become of thee if thou look not the sooner into thine own privileges, and maintainest not thine own lawful liberty? Christian people, I beseech you all, stand firm, and be zealous for the cause of God and His true Religion, to the shedding of your dearest blood, otherwise you will bring yourselves and all your posterities into perpetual bondage and slavery.' (23)

Charles I at his trial protested against the illegality of the court, in the name of the liberties of the people of England:

> 'and do you pretend what you will, I stand more for their

> liberties, for if power without Law may make laws, may alter the fundamental laws of the Kingdom, I do not know what subject he is in England that can be sure of his life or anything that he calls his own.' (24)

But there is no contradiction. For Charles I the liberty of the people consists in having a government which guarantees law and order. 'It is not for having a share in Government, Sirs; that is nothing pertaining to them. A subject and a sovereign are clean different things ...'.(25)

Meanwhile, in 1642 Henry Parker, a lawyer of Lincoln's Inn, called for the supremacy of the people through their representatives in parliament.(26) In January 1649 the House of Commons declared 'that the People under God are the original of all just Power'.(27) God is included here but the grammatical subject, the presence which is the source and guarantee of just power, is the people. Parliament went on to declare 'that the Commons of England assembled in Parliament, being chosen by and representing the People, have the supreme Authority of this Nation'.(28) A fortnight later, the Lord President addressed the King:

> '... the Commons of England ... according to the debt they did owe to God, to justice, the Kingdom and themselves, and according to that fundamental power that is vested, and trust reposed in them by the people ... have ... constituted this Court of Justice before which you are now brought, where you are to hear your charge, upon which the Court will proceed according to justice.' (29)

Charles I was tried and executed in the name of the People of England, represented by the House of Commons. The real content of these phrases is, of course, male forty-shilling freeholders represented by a severely purged Commons. In 1649 Britain officially became, as it largely remains, a politically managed patriarchal democracy where property is power. Nevertheless, the vertical scheme of authority has been supplanted by a broadly horizontal one in which individuals, including the sovereign, are accountable to the social body. Charles I's assertion that 'a subject and a sovereign are clean different things' takes on a new meaning unknown to him. The people are now sovereign, and the way is open for their subjection to that sovereignty.

Their sovereignty is the natural heritage of the people, 'being originally and naturally in every one of them, and unitedly in them all'.(30) In consequence:

> 'the power of kings and magistrates is nothing else but what is only derivative, transferred, and committed to them in trust from the people to the common good of them all, in whom the power yet remains fundamentally and cannot be taken from them without a violation of their natural birthright.' (31)

Law and order is now firmly grounded in human nature and guaranteed by civil society. The opposition is no longer between heavenly justice and earthly justice, nor between monarch and people, but between the individual and society. Liberal humanism is installed, and with it the autonomous, unified bourgeois subject, subject to and subjected by new and more ruthless mechanisms of power.

The crisis of justice, confronted but not resolved in a series of tragedies, is settled by the production of a new order of justice out of institutional collision. Ironically, this collision itself, a clash between the 'just' Cromwell and the king's 'helpless right', culminated in the dramatic spectacle of the 'royal actor' on the 'tragic scaffold', 'While round the armed bands/Did clap their bloody hands'.(32) Charles I, unlike the revengers, submitted to earthly justice, accepting it without defiance as the will of God. His death was the death of an entire order of justice and of subjectivity.

7

It was also the beginning of the slow death of tragedy. In Otway's Venice Preserved (1682) the driving motive of the hero, Jaffeir, is revenge, but the emphasis of the play is on his individual, psychological instability. There is no serious interest in the problem of justice.

Jaffeir is an impoverished gentleman who holds the Venetian Senate responsible in some undefined way for the loss of his fortunes, and is persuaded under the stress of financial desperation to join a conspiracy to overthrow them. Thus isolated from the social body, Jaffeir is induced by his virtuous wife to confess all to the Senate. In consequence, he is cast out by the conspirators too. The only means by which he is able to reassert his integrity is by killing himself, after stabbing to death his friend, Pierre, to save him from being broken on the wheel as a conspirator. Both Pierre and Jaffeir thus die nobly, unfragmented, as individuals (literally, undivided).

The key concerns of Venice Preserved are psychological error, social obligation and personal integrity. Jaffeir is anti-social:

> 'I hate this Senate, am a foe to Venice;
> A friend to none but men resolved like me,
> To push on mischief.' (II, iii, 141-43) (33)

He is thus a deviant. But social isolation is intolerable to him. He chooses conspiracy under pressure of friendship, and chooses to betray it under pressure of love. His final act of heroism - killing his friend and himself - is both a recognition of the right of the social body to punish deviants and an assertion of the autonomy of the subject. The two are not in contradiction: Jaffeir acts as an individual on behalf of the social interest and this constitutes an act of justice. Venice Preserved points forwards to The Searchers rather than backwards to The Cardinal and The Revenger's Tragedy.

Venice Preserved displays most of the features of classic realism. There are no abstract figures, no distinct planes of the action. The play takes place in a self-contained fictional world and the diegesis is not fractured. The play moves from enigma to closure, offering the audience a clear position from which it is ethically intelligible. Correspondingly, the Restoration theatre which is its setting contains the world of the fiction by a proscenium arch, and stands its characters against a perspective backdrop, offering a single place from which the coherence of its world is visible. From the position of the audience, relations between characters on the stage, and between characters and their context, are seen to be both internally coherent and consistent with relations in the world outside the theatre. The stage itself contains a microcosmic reflection of the social body, becomes a little world of society, resolving the contradictions and simultaneously displacing the grandeur of the little world of man.

Restoration heroes, for all their deference to the classical proprieties of heroic drama, are not grand. The autonomous subject of classic realism is a more subjected being than the subject-in-fragments, because bourgeois ideology provides no space for the microcosm which defies the macrocosm, and does so in the imagery of the macrocosm with which it is continuous and which is duplicated in its own being. The final location of the revenge tradition is the classic western, where the central figure acts justly, conforming to the true interest of a God-fearing society. This mode of heroism calls for skill, judgment, authority and independence - the true bourgeois virtues - but not for grandeur.

Tragedy thrives on grandeur and on contradiction. It is dispelled by the provision for the spectator of a unitary position of transcendent knowingness. Renaissance tragedy is produced by the crises of a period of discontinuity between one social order and another.

In the Restoration period, Renaissance tragedy (particularly Shakespeare) was re-written, smoothed out, rendered coherent and intelligible to the spectator of classic realism. In the nineteenth century, Shakespeare was re-read as analysing erring individual subjectivity. Titus' problem of justice has been dissolved into the psychological problems of his 'character'; Lady Macbeth's fragments have been re-assembled to make her intelligible as perversely feminine. Coleridge, Hazlitt and Bradley between them reduced Renaissance tragedy to the novelistic. Meanwhile, twentieth century criticism systematically dissipates the contradictions of *The Cardinal* in the character of the King, and recuperates the crises of *The Spanish Tragedy* and *The Revenger's Tragedy* as authorial incompetence. In doing so the critical apparatus performs an act of injustice which demonstrates its subjection to an order of justice and of subjectivity which badly needs to be brought into crisis once more.

Footnotes

1. Fredson Bowers, Elizabethan Revenge Tragedy 1587-1642 (Princeton, 1966), pp.62, 259.

2. Romans xii, 19.

3. James Shirley, The Cardinal, in R. G. Lawrence, ed., Jacobean and Caroline Tragedies (London, 1974). References are to this edition.

4. Lawrence, p.187.

5. Thomas Kyd, The Spanish Tragedy, ed. Philip Edwards (London, 1959; The Revels Plays). References are to this edition.

6. Shakespeare references are to the one-volume edition of Peter Alexander (London, 1951).

7. Mark Eccles, ed., The Macro Plays (London, 1969; EETS, O.S. 262).

8. William Perkins, Works (3 vols.), Vol.1 (Cambridge, 1612), p.288.

9. See S. F. C. Milson, Historical Foundations of the Common Law (London, 1969), pp.3-22.

10. Michel Foucault, 'Governmentality', in Ideology and Consciousness, 6, 1979, 5-21, p.12.

11. James I, quoted in Stuart E. Prall, The Agitation for Law Reform during the Puritan Revolution 1640-1660 (The Hague, 1966), p.9.

12. W. Wager, The Longer Thou Livest and Enough is as Good as a Feast, ed. R. Mark Benbow (London, 1968; Regents Renaissance Drama Series). References to both plays are to this edition.

13. These representatives of the oppressed become standard figures on the late morality stage: see George Wapull, The Tide Tarrieth no Man (printed 1576); Thomas Lupton, All for Money (1560's or 70's); Robert Greene and Thomas Lodge, A Looking Glass for London and England (c.1590); anon, A Knack to Know a Knave (1592).

14. For Calvinism the contradiction is finally resolved only with the coming of the Kingdom of God on earth: 'In completing the redemption of man God will restore order to the present confusion of earth ... We are content with the simple doctrine that such measure and order will prevail in the world as will exclude all distortion and destruction.'. Calvin, Commentary on Romans v, 21, quoted in David Little, Religion, Order and Law (Oxford, 1970), p.63. (This did not absolve Calvinists, of course, of the need to be just).

15. For the other instances see Frances Yates, 'Queen Elizabeth I as Astraea', in Astraea, the Imperial Theme in the Sixteenth Century (London, 1975), pp.29-87.

16. See Catherine Belsey, 'The Stage-Plan of _The Castle of Perseverance_', in _Theatre Notebook_, 28, 1974, pp.124-32.

17. G. K. Hunter, 'Ironies of Justice in _The Spanish Tragedy_', in _Dramatic Identities and Cultural Tradition_ (Liverpool, 1978), pp.214-29.

18. Cyril Tourneur, _The Revenger's Tragedy_, ed. R. A. Foakes (London, 1966; The Revels Plays).

19. William Lamont and Sybil Oldfield, _Politics, Religion and Literature in the Seventeenth Century_ (London, 1975), p.51.

20. _Ibid_, p.53.

21. _Ibid_, p.53 ff.

22. _Ibid_, p.142.

23. _Ibid_, p.52.

24. Roger Lockyer, ed., _The Trial of Charles I_ (London, 1974), p.88.

25. _Ibid_, p.135.

26. Prall, p.17.

27. Lockyer, p.76.

28. _Ibid_.

29. _Ibid_, pp.81-2.

30. John Milton, 'The Tenure of Kings and Magistrates' (1649), _Prose Writings_ (London, 1958), p.191.

31. _Ibid_, p.192. Milton cites in his support Christopher Goodman, who fled to Geneva from the Marian persecutions a hundred years earlier. The differences between them are as revealing as the similarities. In the earlier text vengeance belongs to God and it can be executed against a sovereign only when all right to sovereignty has been forfeited: 'When kings or rulers become blasphemers of God, oppressors and murderers of their subjects, they ought _no more to be accounted kings_ or lawful magistrates, but as _private men to be examined, accused_, condemned and punished _by the law of God_, and being convicted and punished by that law, it is _not man's but God's doing_' (my italics). It is God who acts, and the people are his instruments: 'When magistrates cease to do their duty, the people are as it were without magistrates; yea worse, and then God giveth the sword into the people's hand, and he himself is become immediately their head' (p.203).

32. Andrew Marvell, 'An Horatian Ode upon Cromwell's Return from Ireland', in _The Complete Poems_, ed. Elizabeth Story Donno (Harmondsworth, 1972).

33. Thomas Otway, <u>Venice Preserved</u>, ed. Malcolm Kelsall (London, 1969; Regents Restoration Drama Series).

ANGLICANS, PURITANS AND PLAIN STYLE

Roger Pooley

There has been a practice within English literary studies, certainly since the 1930's, of examining non-literary texts, or texts from the hinterland of high literature, with the same 'close reading' techniques that are used for exploring and revealing the works of Shakespeare, Donne and the rest. Characteristically, this has been undertaken to expose the poverty of mass culture in our own times. But there are examples of this strategy applied to other periods. L. C. Knights' Public Voices (1971) is an interesting example; here we have a former Scrutiny editor making a plea for an open, liberal political discourse in our own time largely through an examination of the political languages of the seventeenth century. The following judgment of Milton shows how stylistic analysis leads into a distinction of political value:

> '... in his political writings there is not the tension, the recognition of conflicting claims, that you find in Marvell - who was as capable of decisive choice and effective action as Milton himself.' (1)

That comes at the end of a long analysis of Milton's rhetoric. Clearly, such an exercise cannot be an innocent exercise in 'practical criticism'. Indeed, one of its virtues may be to point to the way in which such critical activity plays cox and box with the contexts, origins and evaluation of texts which were so artfully excluded from I. A. Richards' original experiments. It is practical criticism being unusually explicit, and tentative, about its own practice.

In what follows my aim is to attempt just such an exercise, though, as my title indicates, I shall put party loyalty firmly centre stage in a way that Knights largely rejects. My subject is that crucial episode in the literary history of the seventeenth century, the victory of the plain style. I hope I am not being naïve in my use of the military metaphor: the question is inextricably linked with political, social and ideological victories in the period. The usual date in literary history is 1660, the date of the Restoration of the monarchy and Anglicanism, and the foundation of the Royal Society. Does it make more sense to date the vital change in the 1640's? Is the plain style the property of either side in the Civil War, or parts of those sides? Is the choice of style observably ideological? Or, if it's not just contingent, is there a sociology of style in this period?

My choice of examples for this exploration is limited almost entirely to prose texts on the vexed questions of church polity. This makes party loyalty fairly easy to define, even if it doesn't make for the most exciting choice of texts. The other essential preliminary - my working definition of plain style - is not so straightforward.

Simplicity, directness, restraint; that much is common. But any account of the plain style in the sixteenth and seventeenth centuries must give weight both to the classical origins of the term, in rhetoric, and to the native strain.(2) Classical plain style sounds different from native plainness; it tends to the abstract and is more sparing in imagery. Use of the classical plain style has social implications, too, emphasising differences in education for example. Similarly, the different register which a plain appeal to the colloquial involves is going to vary with the status of the author.

Plain style, then, is not just <u>sermo humilis</u>, the lowest of the three levels of decorum in classical rhetoric, but Englishness. And so, like all appeals to patriotism, it has a certain social ambivalence, an appeal to what unites a country and an appeal to quite specific interests within it. The plain style of the classical tradition still maintains class decorum, and we will see its practitioners particularly interested in images of boundary and enclosure, images which stand out in the plain texture of their writing. I shall argue that the language of the Separatists leans more towards a 'native' plainness, and that this has consequences for the nature of their arguments, and our sense of the people to whom they were appealing.

Let us first consider the importance of the 1630's and 1640's in the history of Anglican plain style in the seventeenth century.

Trevor-Roper was right: Lancelot Andrewes was the great spiritual hero of Laud and his party, but this does not make Laud and the Laudians 'metaphysical' preachers like Andrewes. Now, we are familiar with the contrast between the plain, logical and affectionate preaching of the Puritans and the witty, allusive Arminian preachers of the early part of the century. William Perkins, one of the fathers of Elizabethan Puritanism, advises 'the hiding of human wisdom' in the promulgation of sermons.(3) Donne, on the other hand, makes use of the eloquence and metaphysical wit he ascribes to the Holy Ghost in scripture to effect in his preaching. But it is just as easy to find followers of Perkins' position in Anglican writing far removed from any theological agreement with him. Fraser Mitchell, while arguing that 'the history of English preaching in the seventeenth century is largely concerned with "witty" or "metaphysical" preaching',(4) finds most of the attacks on that form of preaching from outside the Puritan camp. Eachard and Glanvill, his main witnesses, are figures from the Restoration establishment; and there are warnings against witty, learned eloquence in George Herbert's A Priest to the Temple (published 1652, though Herbert died twenty years earlier).

Laud's preaching is plain, blunt, even awkward; this is as near to a rhetorical flourish as he gets:

> 'For to murmur, and make the people believe, there are I know not what cracks and flaws in the "pillars"; to disesteem their strength; to undervalue their bearing; is to trouble the earth and inhabitants of it; to make the people fear a "melting" where there is none. And what office that is, you all know.' (5)

The syntax is simple, paratactic, cumulative in effect; what learning there is is concealed in marginal notes and English translations. If he'd been preaching the right doctrines Perkins would have been proud of him. Had the Anglicans of the mid-century simply learned from the Puritans?

It's not as simple as that. In the first place, the symbolic centre of Anglican worship was shifting from preached word to acted eucharistic drama. The promulgator of those brief, pointed sermons was also introducing hangings, vestments and church furniture which offended another sense of plainness and decorum. Laud's letters constantly refer to decency and order in worship as his motives, and clearly he was worried just as much by those parishes with lazy and poorly educated clergy as he was by the incursions of Puritan lecturers and people using the Lord's Table for writing and leaving their hats on. But through all this runs the thread of putting up, or maintaining, barriers. In the extract above there is the fear of 'melting'. 'A wall-palsy is ever dangerous'.(6) The security of the Church is the security of the state - 'the Church hath the same walls that the state hath'.(7) And if we turn to the Articles of Visitation Laud used when Bishop of London, a similar obsession is found; in sermons, for instance, the main consideration ought to be the teaching of obedience:

> 'you shall carefully and heedefully observe and inquire, whether your Ministers in their sermons preached by them in your publique Churches and Congregations, doe raise and deliver out of the texts chosen by them, such pertinent notes as tend to teach obedience, and edifie the understanding of their auditory, in matters of faith and religion, without intermeddling with any state-matters ...' (8)

Obedience precedes faith, it would appear. Laud is signalling the demotion of the central Reformation doctrine (and metaphor) of justification by faith for a discipline of moral and prayerful endeavour.

A more explicit and detailed version of a Laudian visitation is provided by Bishop Richard Montagu's articles for the Norwich diocese in 1638. He is worried by 'swaggerers' as well as Puritans in the pulpit; though he is also concerned about the ownership of Puritan and Papist books. He also satirises Puritan phraseology when criticising those who attend other churches where 'a more sanctified (in their opinion) Minister preacheth powerfully to their edification'.(9) Here Puritanism is seen to have a private language, with its own codewords for the faithful. But Montagu is interested in other kinds of barrier, too:

> 'Is your Communion Table enclosed and ranged about with a Rayle of Joyners and Turners worke, close enough, to keepe out little Dogs or Cats from going in and prophaning that

> holy place, from pissing against it, or worse: and is there a Doore of the same worke, to open and shut: doe any persons presume to enter thereinto, except such as be in holy orders?' (10)

What seems to be happening in Laudian thinking is the confluence of worries about profanity and that of a threatened social group - a ruling class with an absolute monarch. (I think the 1630's may be judged to be the period of attempted absolutism, even if the parallels with the European practice of absolute monarchy are not complete). Mary Douglas' arguments seem relevant here:

> 'Small competitive communities tend to believe themselves in a dangerous universe, threatened by sinister powers operated by fellow human beings.' (11)

These communities' religious practice is contrasted with that where social classification is relatively secure; here 'these people use the incidence of misfortune to uphold the natural law'. It might be most accurate in using this contrast for the conflicts of the seventeenth century to say that we are witnessing the change from the secure to the threatened sense of social classification; so not only is there the need to define boundaries, but the old appeal to providence (used with confidence for the whole country on the Armada medal, for example - 'God blew and they were scattered') becomes competitive, with rival Puritan and Anglican interpretations of disasters demonstrating God's wrath on each other.

The move to tighten the boundaries of social and religious profanity in Anglican thinking was given a strange twist in the cult of King Charles the Martyr. The arguments from providence - that God is punishing the country with civil war in order to reform it - are expected, and common to both sides. But the identification of Charles' sufferings with Christ's enables his followers to draw the boundaries of secular and sacred power in exactly the same place. The extraordinary emblematic frontispiece to Eikon Basilike (1648) with Charles holding a crown of thorns while looking to a crown of glory, makes the point most succinctly. This symbolisation means that certain things have to be seen as deliberate which probably weren't, like giving up the crown:

> 'That splendid, but yet toilsom Crown
> Regardlessly I trample down.
> With joie I take this Crown of Thorn,
> Though sharp, yet easy to be born.' (12)

The text of the work itself is an interesting mixture; much of it unashamedly rich in imagery and emotional appeal, something which Milton found a little suspect:

> 'The whole Book might perhaps be intended a peece of Poetrie. The words are good, the fiction smooth and cleanly ...' (13)

No plainness there. But, particularly in the prayers at the end of each chapter, there is that appeal to rationality which becomes a key-note in Anglicanism as the century progresses. Rationality is a word that doesn't always mean rational argument; here, I think, it means quietness, the opposite of enthusiasm:

> 'Make us unpassionately to see the light of reason and religion.' (ch. 4)

> 'native, rational, and religious freedom'. (ch. 6)

In the second example we have an appeal to reason, religion and patriotism in one. The text, whoever its author was, is clearly having to work hard to reconcile beliefs with events. This unusually long sentence, full of subordination, cannot contain its constituent parts with any comfort:

> 'O my God, preserve Thy servant in this native, rational, and religious freedom, for this, I believe, is Thy will that we should maintain; who, though Thou does justly require us to submit our understandings and wills to Thine, whose wisdom and goodness can neither err or misguide us, and so far to deny our carnal reason in order to Thy sacred mysteries and commands, that we should believe and obey rather than dispute them; yet dost Thou expect from us only such a reasonable service of Thee, as not to do anything for Thee against our consciences; and as to the desires of men, enjoinest us to try all things by the touchstone of reason and laws, which are the

> rules of civil justice, and to declare our consent to that only which our judgments approve.' (14)

It's not that the content is unclear - it might be paraphrased, unkindly, as 'O God, preserve and approve what I believe'. But from 'yet' onwards, the syntax dangles. Like a good Laudian, the desire to 'believe and obey rather than dispute' is linked to trumping the characteristically Puritan appeal to conscience. But such facing both ways is too much for any sentence, and its plainness crumbles.

There is another strain of Anglicanism in the 1640's, prestigious in itself as well as in its ancestry and progeny, in the Great Tew circle. If we want to build a 'tradition' of plainness in the seventeenth century, Lord Falkland would do nicely as the link between the earlier plain style of Ben Jonson (Falkland was a 'son of Ben') and the new, scientific plainness of the 1660's, as many of the Tew circle became Fellows of the Royal Society. But 'tradition' is covertly exclusive, and one could construct some alternatives to this conservative one, Jonson to Marvell, for example, or Jonson, Richard Bernard, Bunyan and Defoe, which would emphasise that a drive to plainness of a different sort, popular and colloquial, would echo social and religious nonconformity.

There's a nice tension in Falkland's own position. His prose style is aphoristic, even Baconian, and his view of authority in matters of faith is, at first sight, more genuinely rational than that of the author of _Eikon Basilike_, and a good deal more liberal than most of the Puritans:

> 'To all who follow their _reason_ in the _interpretation_ of the Scriptures, and search for _Tradition_, God will either give his _grace_ for assistance to _finde_ the truth, or his _pardon_ if they _misse_ it.' (15)

But Falkland's own family circumstances - his mother and six of her children were Catholics - made him recognise that the appeal of a 'Catholic Umpire' in matters of faith would be too great if there were not an established Church of England to preserve peace and order in this rational search for the truth of Christianity. It's the paradox pointed to by McAdoo:

> 'The perennial paradox of Anglicanism that its theological method should be involved not only with the freedom of reason, but with the inevitability of the visible Church.' (16)

Fortunately for our purposes, we can see a controversy in which Falkland makes the choice. It's an argument with a Catholic, Walter Montague, and it involves a difference over what is plain. (Not strictly a part of the plain style argument, but an important parallel to it). Montague argues that plainness derives from authority:

> 'Natural reason not being able to proportion to a man a course that must certainly bring him to a state of supernaturall happinesse, and that such a course being necessary to mankind, which otherwise would totally fail of the end it was created for, there remayned no other way, but that it must be proposed to us by one whose authoritie wee could not doubt of, and that in so plain a manner, as even the simplest might be capable of it as well as the Learned.' (17)

Anglican arguments about authority are peculiarly vulnerable to Catholic counter-arguments, because tradition and succession are so much a part of both, and Anglican appeals to the first five centuries A.D., like Hooker's, seem _prima facie_ more difficult to sustain than an apparently unbroken succession to the present. Falkland's reply is essentially liberal. Playful in tone, sailing close to Cavalier flippancy at times, he sets the judgment of plain truth in the reasonable individual:

> 'We building our faith onely upon plain places, and all reasonable men being sufficient judges of what is plain.' (18)

We must beware of over-stressing the liberalism of the Tew circle - after all, it contained Clarendon as well as Hales and Chillingworth - but it does demonstrate how the Anglican avant-garde could appeal to reason in a genuine and not simply authoritarian fashion, and in doing so push back the boundaries of plainness in decorum further.

*****

I want now to return to the dominant symbol of the enclosure in writing about the church, to see how it is used in the Presbyterian writing of the 1640's. If, as David Little's book on the period argues, one of the functions of theology is to try to solve the problem of order by the elaboration and development of symbolic categories,[19] the image of the hedge in the middle of the Solemn League and Covenant is of particular theological interest:

> 'The heart of man is backsliding, and a Covenant is like a hedge or wall to stop us from going back.' (20)

'To stop us from going back' indicates a more dynamic, confident community than is implied by the Laudian use of the image. Even so, the Presbyterians shared Laud's view of the relationship between state and religion, like him using Old Testament examples to make the point. 'Toleration', they argued, 'would be the putting of a sword into a mad man's hand.'.[21] Here is another, self-conscious community putting up the walls of Church discipline round the doctrine of the Covenant:

> 'Discipline and Government in the Church being the golden reins (whereunto also this present Parliament hath wel likened it) serving to curb and restrain men, who are by nature like a wilde asses colt, affecting unbridled liberty; it is the rod wherewith to correct petulant and forward children; the shepherds crook which the faithful Pastors cannot want, but to the spiritual prejudice of their flocks; the keyes opening the doors for the admitance in of those whom Christ would have to be admited into his Church, and the shuting out of whom he would have kept out; it is the hedg or wal to keep the ravenous beasts from entering into Gods garden and vineyard.' (22)

But there is a tension between this extraordinary series of embattled images and the metaphoric appropriation of the Biblical idea of Covenant, which is not unlike the Anglican tension between authority and reason. Behind the idea of the Covenant lies the contract model of society, only half explicit, but nonetheless undermining the patriarchal model. The tension is felt more and more keenly as the Puritan movement fissures and begins to fly apart under the pressure of its own authority in the 1640's and 1650's.

The language of the radicals - by that I mean anyone to the left of the Westminster Assembly - exposes this difficulty, and recognises that the debate can be recognised in the language, metaphors and models of the various sides. Within that, the appeal to Englishness, an important sub-set of plainness from the sixteenth century, is crucial to Royalist rhetoric, as we have seen, as well as to the democrats':

> 'We dare not be Classical, Provincial, National; these are no forms of wholsome words to which we are commanded, nor know we any such power; but that of Brethren, and Ministery, and fellowship.' (23)

There are at least two layers of linguistic appeal here, first to the Bible, second to a 'native' sound of English. The first trio, all Presbyterian forms of church government, are Latinate in origin; in the second trio, 'ministery' is, the others are Teutonic. It must be said that Saltmarsh's rhetoric, despite the above, is generally rather vague; and his appeal to 'consultation, debating, counselling, prophesying, voting, etc.' is later qualified by doubts as to whether votes carry the day in spiritual matters.(24) But he is sensitive to the threats hidden in the language of obedience, particularly in the partial use of the biblical metaphor of the church as a building, and thus to the whole complex of hedges and walls already discussed.

His appeal for toleration - 'Let us attain to union, though not to unity' - is echoed and extended by such antinomian radicals as William Dell, who argued 'the variety of forms is the beauty of the world ... unity is Christian, uniformity Antichristian'.(25) It will underline what Dell is saying if we remember that Antichrist was usually a synonym for the Pope in that period.

The most impressive of the radical texts arguing for some kind of toleration is Roger Williams' The Bloudy Tenent of Persecution (1644); in the context of the present argument, impressive because of the plain, dialogue-based method and particularly in his willingness to investigate that dominant metaphor of the hedge. Twice Williams uses the characteristic New England contrast of the garden of the Church with the wilderness of the world to attack those who would use civil power to enforce religious conformity, and thus encourage the reprobate to think that he's in the garden, and saved, when he's not. It might be thought that this view of the church needs a hedge more intrinsically than, say, a Laudian one. In fact, Williams deals with this by insisting on a sharp division between the disciplines of church and state, quite unlike Laudian and Presbyterian practice. He warns of 'The danger and mischiefe of a civill sword in soule matters, which makes the civill Magistrate deeply guilty of all those evils which he aims to suppresse'.[26]

Williams' attack on John Cotton shows clearly his sensitivity to the careless use of biblical images for political ends. He takes exception to Cotton's double interpretation of the sheepfold image in John 10 (the main New Testament source for the hedge metaphor), arguing that he makes the same image do two jobs, breaking the narrative flow of the parable to do so - 'the same dog that assaulteth and teareth the Wolfe, frighteth and forceth in the straggling sheepe'.[27] In other words, Williams is arguing for a plainness of interpretation, that images should have only one level of signification. That sounds like a definition of allegory, but in many ways recalls the early Reformers' position as against the scholastic four levels of interpretation. And he argues from images himself; his case rests on the Parable of the Wheat and the Tares, showing that distinctions cannot be made by men in this world that are reserved for God in the next. His treatment of imagery, then, might be best seen as a desire to retain the liveliness and accessibility of an image-rich discourse while resisting the kind of intellectual smuggling that such a discourse tends to permit.

It's tempting to treat Williams in a Whiggish manner, as if he were a prototype of that liberal tolerance we have come to accept in religious matters. Such a radical, in fact, was less marginal than a Winstanley, because he challenged less. But we see in both of them a willingness to be imaginatively stirred by the old, biblical metaphors, to examine them closely and derive fresh light for social practice from them. So then, the history of the plain style as the history of demystification is clearly seen in the work of Roger Williams; that is not to say that he abandoned metaphor (as the Anglicans did as the century progressed) but that he shows unusual perspicacity as to what it could and couldn't achieve.

Finally, we come to the other strand in the Independent/Separatist version of plain style, its link with a popular, colloquial tradition. Since Elizabethan times Puritan writing had combined logic, rhetoric and image in a conscious imitation of New Testament style, especially St. Paul's, within a Ramist organisation of logic. That in itself was constituted from a desire to help ordinary people understand. As the Puritan movement progressed and began to fragment, the popular voice grew louder, with preaching and praying regiments and mechanic preachers. Bunyan is the classic example, combining the Puritan characteristics of strictness, psychological self-examination and sensitivity to biblical metaphor with the folk tale apparatus of giants, quests and proverbial wisdom. But Bunyan's achievements take us into the Restoration. Before that, the antinomian tradition developed a prophetic, apocalyptic language under the pressure of accelerating events which stands to one side of any history of political style as the history of plainness. The language of mysticism and apocalypse, far from lifting the reader out of history, is characteristic of moments of crisis, at once realising new possibilities, and at the same time a world away from the politic language of the art of the possible. Coppe and Fox, loosely paratactic, emotive, opportunistic in their use of images, use a mystical language of power which requires an unusually large adjustment in our perception of reality. The churches have always had difficulty recuperating their mystics, because their church polity, for one thing, is logically anarchic.

*****

My conclusions can be expressed at a number of levels. I have cut a broad swathe through the styles of the period, and, like Marvell's levelling mowers, have inevitably left bleeding chunks along the way. A concentration on imagery and syntax has also meant a rather impressionistic description of style. But I hope I have demonstrated that the plain style and its cognate theology of obedience that we associate with Restoration Anglicanism is already highly developed before the Civil War, not just in the avant-garde of Great Tew. An increasing tendency towards plainness has the by-product of foregrounding the dominant metaphors, and here I have argued that there is a certain complicity between Royalist and Presbyterian arguments, important as the Presbyterian initiative was. One feature of the more radical writing of the period is that it investigates dominant images as well as suggesting new ones.

At the methodological level I have suggested that the apparatus of 'practical criticism' is by no means bankrupt for a proper historical criticism; not, of course, the dating exercise, with its assumption of a history of discrete 'sensibilities', but one with a proper sensitivity to class and party loyalties as well as an unwillingness to instantly translate Christian material into secular equivalents. It might even have more mileage left in it than some of the hermetic, anti-historical systems that pass for socialist criticism these days, a result which would delight someone whose appreciation of the virtues of an honest, alert plainness has been increased by this study.

Footnotes

1. L. C. Knights, Public Voices (London, 1971: Chatto & Windus), p.70.

2. Standard discussions include Wesley Trimpi, Ben Jonson's Poems (Stanford, 1962: Stanford U.P.); Yvor Winters, Forms of Discovery (Chicago, 1967: Swallow); R. F. Jones, The Seventeenth Century (Stanford, 1951: Stanford U.P.).

3. Ian Breward (ed.), The Work of William Perkins (Abingdon, 1970: Sutton Courtenay Press), p.345.

4. W. Fraser Mitchell, English Pulpit Oratory from Andrewes to Tillotson (London, 1932: SPCK), p.137.

5. William Laud, 'A Sermon preached for King Charles' First Parliament, 19 June 1625', Works (Library of Anglo-Catholic Theology, 1847-60), I, 107.

6. Laud, 'A Sermon preached before his Majesty [i.e. James I] Tuesday 19 June 1621', loc. cit., p.25.

7. Ibid, p.23.

8. 'Articles to be enquired of ...' (1628), sig. [A4], v.

9. Articles of Enquiry and Direction for the Diocese of Norwich (1638), sig. [B4].

10. Ibid, sig. [A4], v.

11. Mary Douglas, *Natural Symbols* (Harmondsworth, 1978: Penguin), p.137. See the whole chapter, 'The Problem of Evil'.

12. *Eikon Basilike*, ed. Edward Scott (1880), frontispiece.

13. John Milton, 'Eikonoklastes', *Complete Prose Works*, III (New Haven, 1962: Yale U.P.), p.406.

14. *Eikon Basilike*, p.32.

15. Lord Viscount Falkland, 'Of the Infallibilitie of the Church of Rome', in Henry Hammond, *A View of Some Exceptions ...* (Oxford, 1646), p.4.

16. H. R. McAdoo, *The Spirit of Anglicanism* (London, 1965: A. & C. Black), p.22.

17. *The Coppy of a Letter* sent from France by Mr. Walter Montagu to his Father the Lord Privie Seale, with his answer thereunto. Also a second answere to the same Letter by the Lord Falkland (1641), p.4.

18. *Ibid*, p.22.

19. David Little, *Religion, Order and Law* (Oxford, 1970: Basil Blackwell), p.23. A Weberian analysis of the conflict between the 'traditional' and 'legal-rational' views of the social order in the sixteenth and seventeenth centuries.

20. *A Solemn League and Covenant* (Dec. 11, 1643), p.3.

21. *The Harmonious Consent* of the Ministers of the Province within the County Palatine of Lancaster ... to our Solemn League and Covenant (1648), p.12.

22. *Ibid*, p.15.

23. John Saltmarsh, *The Smoke in the Temple* (1646), p.2. (This is the second page 2; the pagination begins again half way through the book).

24. *Ibid*, pp.61, 70.

25. *Ibid*, first pagination, p.6. William Dell, *Select Sermons and Discourses* (1652), pp.46, 49.

26. [Roger Williams], *The Bloudy Tenent, of Persecution* (1644), p.65 margin.

27. *Ibid*, p.67.

PSYCHOANALYSIS, THE KABBALA AND THE SEVENTEENTH CENTURY

Terry Eagleton

The drive, for Freudianism, lies somewhere on the border between the somatic and the ideational; psychoanalysis, as Charles Ryecroft has remarked, is a 'biological theory of meaning', precariously poised between the twin dangers of mechanical materialism and idealism. (Jacques Derrida, in an Oxford seminar, has accused Jacques Lacan of avoiding the former error only to fall foul of the latter, producing a psychoanalytic theory which suppresses the biological). One can envisage the strange kind of distracted attention required of the analyst as the patient speaks. Listening to *what* is said, to be sure, but in the light of how it is said, straining to catch the peculiar *composition* of this text, to follow its stresses and syncopations, striving in an almost impossible double-optic to credit and discredit the reality of the discourse, glimpsing 'form' one minute and 'content' the next, veering from 'surface' to 'depth' and back while suspecting that very metaphor. How do you hear and overhear at once, grasp a speech which is at once somehow pre-given script and ceaselessly invented, disclose a ground-plot which precedes the discourse yet is indissociable from it, tackle a concealment which is staring you in the face? Tracking symptoms to their causes, the text turns round to reveal that each was already included in the structure of the other; the 'obvious' is reduced to an esoteric meaning that is even more obvious, signifiers unmasked as substitutions for substitutions, sub-texts momentarily glimpsed as master-codes before they vanish from sight into yet further sub-texts. Do the double-basses come in 'under', 'over', 'behind' or 'above' the violins? How do you hear them 'come in' and listen to the violins simultaneously, and can the violins now sound 'the same'? It is clear, moreover, that utterer and listener can never quite catch up with each other, can never be historically synchronous, since the listener deciphers the utterance through certain common codes which that utterance alters, so that to listen truly we must listen again, equipped with a transformed code which will in turn be transformed by the utterance, and so on *ad infinitum*.

To grasp the chord or statement in its fullness we must wait until the end and then go back to the beginning, re-reading what we heard first in the light of what we heard after; but what we heard first will then no longer be there, since it will be transformed by the new code it has produced to be heard by. The Owl of Minerva takes flight at dusk - understanding is always _post festum_ - but how then can it be understanding, and how alternatively could we understand something 'as it happens'? Only somebody inside a situation can judge it, said Brecht, and he's the last person to judge.

How is the analyst to listen immanently yet symptomatically to the analysand's discourse, to be simultaneously where it happens and where it doesn't? For the discourse speaks of more than itself, but it does not merely repeat some other discourse, which perhaps could have been spoken in its place. Or if something else could have been said, then what that something _is_ is determined precisely by the discursive happening/non-happening we have. Is it that something precise has not been said or that something has precisely not been said? In the first case, the text we have becomes a pre-text, and our attention is diverted to the master-script it muffles; in the second case, we have a text for which we need to construct a sub-text. But if all we know is that something has precisely not been said, we cannot know what sub-text it should be; it is only when we discover that something has been precisely not said, perhaps in the sense of not precisely or too precisely said, that we can begin to write a sub-text which will be the sub-text of _this_ text. But the more that sub-text then assumes a distinct identity - the sub-text of _this_ text - the more it loses it: sub-text _of_ this text, function or further articulation of it rather than ground to its figure or base to its superstructure.

It is not in any case just a matter of what is (im)precisely not said - of seizing this as directly symptomatic. For the not-said is of course a function of the said, which returns us from the symptomatic to the immanent, signals that we cannot step outside this discourse without remaining within it. It is not that we travel the smooth surface of the text until we stumble upon a fissure, through which the hidden depths of some immeasurable 'outside' can be dimly glimpsed. We would rather need some Einsteinian model of this process, whereby every direction leads us at once 'out' and 'in', every point becomes a problematising of 'surface' and 'depth', every extra-discursive dimension is continually in the process of being transformed into an 'intra-textual' one and vice versa. If for Einsteinian physics objects are configurations of force, so, one might say, are signs for psychoanalysis. The enigma of a 'biological theory of meaning' lies precisely in this - that meanings are certainly meanings, not the mere reflexes or impresses of drives, but that once this whole textual process is so to speak flipped over, focused through a different optic, viewed another way up, it can be read as nothing less than a mighty warring of somatic forces, a dispersed semantic field where desire achieves, or fails to achieve, speech. The psyche, to quote Paul Ricoeur, lies at the intersection of meaning and force; and so it is that Ricoeur's great essay on Freud pivots on the conjoining of an economics and a hermeneutics, on that double marking whereby psychical phenomena are for Freud at once power and signification, somatic and semiotic together.(1)

Attending to the speech of the analysand, the analyst must search its most casual crevices for significance, suspending any prejudgements of 'centrality' and 'contingency'. But this in itself involves a sort of paradox. For nobody who observed this dogged, persistent, wide-eyed attention to detail could suspect the immense, iconoclastic scepticism which is its other face. Accompanying this hermeneutic of restoration, to use Ricoeur's terms once more, is a hermeneutic of suspicion, which stubbornly refuses to take anything at face value, denies all self-identity, and reads the most scandalously implausible meanings into the most innocent bits of behaviour. Tenaciously engaged with the materiality of its text, psychoanalysis nevertheless rewrites it with breathtaking boldness; and in this, as in its constant focusing on the 'join' between force and meaning, it resembles nothing quite so much as that tradition of Jewish scriptural critique which is the Kabbala.

The Kabbala, a sacred, esoteric lineage of scriptural interpretation, plays havoc with the hallowed writings of the Torah, reading them against the grain, violating their conceptual schemas and apparent meanings to dredge from them truths sometimes wildly at odds with their construable 'intentions'. A violent, potentially heretical hermeneutic in sporadic conflict with the conservative Rabbinical tradition, the Kabbala is a mode of textual deconstruction which may fasten on the most apparently marginal of signifiers to wrench from it an unexpected meaning, slashing across the settled categories of a text with its esoteric method of 'correspondences', smelting it down in order to rewrite it in terms of an apparently alien logic. Such Kabbalistic deconstruction, however, is more than a merely cavalier manipulation of the object. For to displace scripture so violently demands an intricately immanent reading, one for which the text is nothing less than a great ceremony or subtle web of material hieroglyphs, a field of force to be entered, negotiated, and transmuted in all its material density into another semantic space. You cannot step outside this discourse without remaining within it, permutating its terms, leaving its letters intact but drawing them into new, shocking 'constellations' of significance which break the text beyond itself while disclosing its supposedly immanent logic. And just as the primary constellation for the subject of psychoanalysis is always that of the present, the actual therapeutic situation from and to which his/her discourse of the past is directed, so for the Kabbalists the truths of scripture crystallise only in their unexpected conjunctures with the current historical situation. The esoteric reading is that which refuses antiquarianism.

Within Judaic thought, the materiality of discourse has a central, indeed holy place. What it comes down to is the creativity of the word, intimately linked as it is to the phenomena it brings to significant life. Discourse is power, utterances are forces, the semantic and somatic as complexly conjoined as for Freud. There is a special sense, then, in which the reading and interpreting of scripture is a material practice for the Jews. The bible is the book of life, just as the 'talking cure' may for the analysand be quite literally a matter of survival. To discern the broken letters of one's desire across a cryptic text, whether this be the anagrammatic play of the Kabbala or the patient's struggle for the lost portions of his/her text, is the hinge between script and social practice, reading and redemption, what is _lisible_ and what may be liberated.

This, in turn, is the hinge between all that has been said so far and historical materialism. It is, in a word, the work of Walter Benjamin. Benjamin's great study of the German seventeenth century _Trauerspiel_, _The Origin of German Tragic Drama_, would hardly have been possible without the Kabbalistic knowledge he had gleaned from his friend Gerhard Scholem; and even at that pre-Marxist point he could dimly discern how such a hermeneutic, which read texts against the grain in order to grasp them as constellations of forces, had more in common with Marxist critique than with bourgeois linguistics. The strange, occultist or alchemical materialism of Benjamin's _Passagenarbeit_ or study of Baudelaire is the upshot of all this: there, in a resolutely immanent (indeed, for Adorno, downright positivistic) reading of the Baudelarian context and image, the poems suddenly turn out to be scriptive acts resonant with the great unspoken material forces of urban shocks, cityscapes, petty-bourgeois decay, the movements of the masses, architectural transformations. In Benjamin's violently Marxist-Kabbalistic reading, force and meaning, history and writing, are re-joined, constellated in the _Darstellung_ or psychical representation of the Baudelarian image.

It is not surprising that Benjamin should have begun his critical career with the seventeenth century. For one so deep in the Kabbala, in problems of materiality and meaning, such a period must have held a special fascination. If the traditional medieval forms of 'iconic' signification are increasingly discredited, it is also the case that writing has not yet properly achieved that sealed stability of signifier and signified, that new confidence in representation, which in the English eighteenth century will be the ideological phenomenon of Literature. Signification, in short, is still unstable and awash, all the way from the baroque flailings of the 'Metaphysicals' or 'Jacobeans' to the tortuous constructions of a Milton. Iconic and 'unmotivated' semiotic theories continue to battle it out; _écriture_ and linguistic empiricism, classical and popular modes continue to contend, sometimes within the same bodies of work. Literature is not yet fully hegemonic: and in that sense the seventeenth century must figure as a kind of pre-history to those who, coming after the event of Literature, seek once more to deconstruct it.

Footnotes

1. See Freud and Philosophy: An Essay on Interpretation (New Haven and London, 1970).

THE SIGNIFICANCE OF ALLEGORY IN THE "URSPRUNG DES DEUTSCHEN TRAUERSPIELS"

Howard Caygill

The *Ursprung des deutschen Trauerspiels* has been the locus of the controversy surrounding Benjamin's attempt to develop a Marxian aesthetic. The ostensibly Marxist writings of the 1930's appear enigmatic in the light of the preceding *Trauerspiel* book; indeed, the book has been used to compromise the seriousness of Benjamin's commitment to Marxism. The *Trauerspiel* book appears so distant from the interests of Marxian aesthetics that Steiner felt able to write: 'In later years Benjamin himself said of the *Ursprung* that it was a "dialectical" work though in no way an example of dialectical materialism.'.(1) The relationship between the *Trauerspiel* book and Benjamin's Marxist writings is more complex than Steiner suggests: the passage in the letter to which I assume he is referring continues: 'between my particular philosophy of language and dialectical materialism there is a mediation, however tense and problematic'.(2) The nature of this mediation defines the connection of the *Trauerspiel* book with the later writings: it is a continuity in Benjamin's conception of dialectic. Benjamin's dialectic lies close to the Platonic genesis of dialectic in the search for truth through the questioning of mythical appearance. This dialectic consists in the presenting of the truth in and of appearance whether in the pomp of Absolutism or the equal exchange of commodities.

The significance of allegory in Benjamin's aesthetic cannot be appreciated apart from an understanding of the allegory of significance. Herein lies the relation of the philosophy of language to the critique of myth in dialectic. Allegory is the destruction of myth and in this it is something beyond the sphere of art, which Benjamin regards as allied with myth through its beautiful appearance. The critique of myth extends beyond art to epistemology and law; the three spheres are aspects of myth which is itself grounded in language. I quote from a letter of 1917: 'Above all: for me the question of the essence of knowledge, law and art is connected with that of the origin of all human spiritual expression from the essence of language'.[3] This comment alludes to the close relation, even identity, of aesthetics, epistemology and law which was to be developed in the study of baroque *Trauerspiel*. The synthesis is reflected in the organisation of the *Trauerspiel* book: the 'Epistemo-Critical Prologue', '*Trauerspiel* and Tragedy' and 'Allegory and *Trauerspiel*' are united under the philosophy of language in the attack upon myth.

The *Trauerspiel* book carries the rather idiosyncratic dedication: 'Conceived 1916 Written 1925 Then, as now, dedicated to my Wife'. The writings of 1916 may be read as fragments striving towards the synthesis eventually realised, 'Written', in the *Trauerspiel* book. The first three fragments in a series of six: 'The happiness of the men of Antiquity', 'Socrates' and 'On the Middle Ages' introduce two of the three basic elements of the *Trauerspiel* book: Mythic and Formal community. The former is the mythic community and forms of thought and art characteristic of Antiquity; the latter characterises the supposed rule of the Church in the Middle Ages. According to this fragment, the Middle Ages sustained the form while denying the content of myth, encouraging an excessive formalism in all areas of life. This constitutes the illegitimate use of myth which Benjamin was to characterise and consistently attack as 'theocratic', the category under which Benjamin was subsequently to consider Fascism. The third form of community is described at this stage as 'Asiatic' or 'Oriental'. In a way that will become clearer, the three communities will be characterised as the Mythical, the Formal and the True.

The concept of community includes the aesthetic, linguistic and legal spheres under the expression of community in language. The subsequent two essays in the series: '*Trauerspiel* and Tragedy' and 'The significance of language in *Trauerspiel* and Tragedy', deal with the art forms of the Formal and Mythic communities; comparing them with one another and with a third comprising 'Religion' or 'Truth'. The final essay of the series: 'On Language as such and on the Language of Man', provides an extended discussion of the nature of the linguistic expression of community.

In the essay '*Trauerspiel* and Tragedy' Benjamin distinguishes the dramatic forms by their different positions on historical time. The argument of this fragment is imperfectly elaborated, but it seems possible to extract three categories of time: the 'empirical time' of *Trauerspiel*, the 'individual heroic' time of Tragedy and finally 'historical time'. Empirical time is the insubstantial formal time of *Trauerspiel*; it is merely a measure of mechanical transformation. Action in empirical time assumes a repetitive quality; each action appears as the distorted reflection of every other. Empirical time disqualifies any fulfilment of action and becomes an apparently endless empty space: 'The *Trauerspiel* is in every respect a transitional form. The universality of its time is spectral, not mythic'.(4) The artistic presentation of the idea of repetition in *Trauerspiel* differs profoundly from that of mythic completion in Tragedy.

Unlike *Trauerspiel*, Tragedy may achieve a fulfilment, but only in the individual time of its hero. The tragic hero fulfils his time at the end of his life; death is the seal of fulfilment through which he gains immortality: 'The personal time of the tragic hero ... describes a sort of magical circle around all his actions and complete being.'.(5) The thorough determination of the sphere of action renders tragic death ironic: determination appears surpassed in its fulfilment. Yet this appearance of fulfilment is not necessarily true. Neither *Trauerspiel* nor Tragedy achieve the true fulfilment of 'historical time'. This fulfilled time implies the transformation of space; a time that is empirically undefined. Benjamin variously calls this time the 'idea', the 'historical idea' and 'messianic time'. It is neither the homogeneous empty infinity of empirical time nor the individually determined and therefore spatial time of heroic individuality; it is an empirically undetermined infinity.

The analogies between the position on historical time in the two art forms and the linguistic communities from which they stem become clear in a consideration of the essay 'The significance of language in *Trauerspiel* and Tragedy'. Tragedy is the representation of a linguistic interaction in which the word is of fixed significance. The domain of significance forms the limit of the tragic 'dialogue': the boundary is surpassed in the heroic silence. Trauerspiel differs from tragedy in that it is based not upon language, but upon a 'feeling' of sadness. The fundamental problem of Trauerspiel is 'how does the feeling of sadness make an entrance into the linguistic order of art?'.(6) Benjamin suggests an answer to this question in the notion of the 'word in transition' as the linguistic principle of Trauerspiel. The possibility of conceiving a word in transition is predicated upon the two key concepts of Benjamin's philosophy: expression and signification.

The relation of expression to signification or representation defines the aesthetic, epistemological and legal form. The final essay of the 1916 series presents the importance of this distinction. The essential proposition of this essay is that objects have a language through which they communicate themselves. The communication of objects is the expression of their 'geistige Wesen'.(7) The expression of man, the communication of his 'geistige Wesen', lies in signification or, in other words, the naming of objects. The process of naming entails raising the expression of objects out of their foundation in material community into the less dense medium of spoken language. The language of man is pure when it contains intensive and extensive totalities. The former is the absolutely communicable nature of all language as expression; the latter the possibility of signifying, through name, all other expressions. The synthesis of the two totalities is their fulfilment; all that expresses is signified; language is in truth.

The unity in truth assumes a religious quality; a truth which is distinguished from the symbolic quality of art: 'only the highest geistige Wesen, as it appears in religion, rests solely on man and on the language in him, whereas all art, not excluding poetry, does not rest on the quintessence of linguistic spirit but on material linguistic spirit, even if in consummate beauty'.(8) Art rests upon language that still carries a residue of matter. The hierarchy of art is defined by the distance of artistic languages from matter; rising from sculpture to poésie pure.(9) All art is distinguished from truth. Benjamin resorts to the Bible for clarification. With God the act of naming is creative; with man the name is in a receptive/signifying but not creative relation with objects. According to Benjamin, man 'fell' through the use of naming in a quasi-creative manner; through the naming of something that did not exist: namely 'Good' and 'Evil'. This act introduced Judgement in questioning the adequacy of signifying name to expressive object. Language is reduced from the communion of expression and signification to a mediation between object and mind; between man and man.

The objects of nature are stripped of their expressive language and sink into lament. The language of man violates that of objects; forcing an arbitrary sense upon objects through 'overnaming'. Benjamin regards this operation as forming the origin of abstract thought; of knowledge, which is of subjective validity, as opposed to truth, which as the agreement of expression and signification is objectively valid. Overnaming is the origin of allegory and myth. Although sharing a linguistic origin in overnaming, allegory and myth differ completely through their opposed reflexive attitudes: allegory represents itself as an incomplete ruin; myth as an apparent unity.

The word in transition, the linguistic principle of _Trauerspiel_, is an expression of the rupture between original expression and signification. The sadness of _Trauerspiel_ stems from this lack of agreement. The inability to connect is represented in repetition. Benjamin assumes a hierarchy of repetition and distinguishes between cycle and repetition. The cycle starts in the lament of nature, moves through the dispersed language of _Trauerspiel_, to music; the insignificant expression of lament. In the linguistic mid-point of this cycle lies repetition proper: the repeated play between saying and signifying. This game is _Trauerspiel_; a sad game because the unity after which it seeks constantly eludes it.

In 1916 Benjamin considered that both Tragedy and _Trauerspiel_ failed to achieve 'truth' in the historical idea. Myth was a false reconciliation of expression and signification. Mythical signification insisted upon a totally enclosed system which forbade any expression or signification outside of its bounds. Myth represents itself in the apparently self-contained beautiful symbol. The heroic silence of Tragedy is deceptive: it is purely reactive against mythical significance, actually accepting the bounds which it appears to surpass. _Trauerspiel_ was not as frozen within its determinations as Tragedy in myth. The dynamic of the word in transition allowed allegory to subvert its own significations, but not to gain truth.

Benjamin's writings of 1916 remained fragmentary, for he could not have written the Trauerspiel book in 1916 because he lacked an adequately elaborated legal/political theory. Benjamin's pre-First World War Jugendbewegung writings chart his early search for a cultural-revolutionary synthesis, and the desire for a unity is mentioned in the letter of 1917 cited above. Benjamin achieved the legal/political theory in his political writings of the early 1920's. Of these only the 'Critique of Violence' and the 'Theologico-Political Fragment' have survived. These writings indicate that the division between expression and signification elaborated in aesthetic, epistemological and historical terms in 1916 may also be extended to law and politics.

At one stage in the argument of the 1919 essay 'Fate and Character' Benjamin suggests that law preserved its mythical form after the death of myth through its false identification with justice. This places the object of the 'Critique of Violence' into context: 'The task of a critique of violence can be summarised as that of expounding its relation to law and justice'.(10) The critique of violence is the critique of different types of violence. The law-preserving violence of positive law is seen as the mere inversion of the law-making violence of natural law. Both are separate poles of what should be a unity. Law-preserving violence is executive/representative while law-making violence is expressive/legislative. The two are usually fused in a false unity, cemented by the spectral actions of the Police, who are neither expressive nor representative.

Against the violence of law-making and law preservation Benjamin suggests a third form of violence. This lies in the unity of expression and representation. The bulk of the essay deals with this unity in terms of the Sorelian General Strike; but Benjamin also hints that this unity is also present in the Absolute Monarchy: 'the power of a ruler in which legislative and executive supremacy are united ...'.(11) This renders Benjamin's attitude to Absolutism extremely problematic, with the corollary that it is inaccurate to characterise his attitude to Fascism as an extension of his theory of Absolutism. The General Strike is pure means and end: pure expression. It is neither the law-making nor law-preserving violence of natural and positive law, but rather the total destruction of law. The anarchistic proletarian general strike is neither legislative nor executive: it is sovereign violence. It may be either anarchistic or dictatorial, or perhaps even both. The pattern of these 'alternatives' is familiar: 'The baroque writer felt bound in every particular to the ideal of an absolutist constitution, as was upheld by the Church of both confessions. The attitude of their present-day heirs, if not actually hostile to the state, that is revolutionary, is characterised by the absence of any idea of the state.'.[12]

Benjamin regarded law as being of mythical origin. The heroic silence is the promise of new laws; not the abolition of the old. What survived of law after the demise of its mythical substance was a formalistic framework. Formal law, whether ecclesiastical or bourgeois, contains a 'mythic ambiguity' in the setting of fixed borders which may not be transgressed by either party in dispute. This setting of boundaries pays no attention to substantive differences between disputants, but confines itself to providing a formal framework for interaction. Justice, on the contrary, does account for substantive difference. Law is of mythic origin insofar as it is a rigid self-referring representation. Justice is the unity of expression and representation.

The synthesis of the aesthetic, epistemological and legal/political areas is possible through their common basis in the philosophy of language. The Ursprung des deutschen Trauerspiels is the presentation of this synthesis as it appeared in German baroque drama. The dialectical seriousness of this work lies in its offensive upon all fronts against myth.

The championing of truth over knowledge in the 'Epistemo-Critical Prologue' is an element of the wider critique of myth. The task of philosophy is to present the idea, to be adequate to its expression. This presentation entails the dissolution of beauty, which as appearance is purely subjective. The revelation of truth, the core of Benjamin's philosophical project, demands the consumption of beauty. According to Benjamin,

Goethe's Elective Affinities shows the consanguinity of beauty and myth; so philosophy, whose concern is truth, must turn against beauty. Benjamin regards Socrates as signifying not only the philosophical attack upon myth, but also a parody of Tragedy. The death of Socrates and the death of Christ share the untragic quality of martyrdom. This similarity is emblematic of the shared opposition of philosophy and Christianity to myth. Tragedy was succeeded by Trauerspiel and the symbol, apparent unity of expression and representation, by the ostensive shattering of this unity in allegory.

The second part of the Trauerspiel book is concerned with the differences between Trauerspiel and Tragedy; clearly another component of the critique of myth. Tragedy is paradoxical. The sacrifice of the hero complies with the old statutes whilst creating new ones. The heart of the paradox is located in the heroic silence. In the refusal to use language the hero forsakes any possibility of justification within the old mythic law. Yet the silence appears a judgement of all law from an external point. The hero becomes an absolute; his silence the medium through which new laws may be transmitted. The performance of tragedy is the assessment of the heroic absolute which reflexively diagnoses the state of the spectating linguistic community. The community is bound to judge with and from within law; but as law is powerless in the face of absolute right it must seek conciliation. In so doing the tragic audience judges itself. The tragic chorus is the voice of conciliation between absolute and limited right: 'Choric diction, rather, has the effect of restoring the ruins of the tragic dialogue to a linguistic edifice firmly established - in ethical society and in religious community - both before and after the conflict.' (13) The multiple irony contained in the heroic silence is evident in its ultimate conciliation with myth and law. The assumption of an apparently absolute position has a limited effect: as a symbol the apparent absolute betrays a real limitation.

The limitation within Tragedy constitutes its difference from philosophy and Trauerspiel. The breakdown of the self-defined limitation of myth through philosophy is succeeded by the Trauerspiel. The kernel of the Trauerspiel is the distinction between expression and representation, a split which powered the movement of the Trauerspiel. This dynamic principle was fused with the principle of the chronicles and medieval mystery plays to represent the movement of the church through history to redemption in the day of judgement. The shattering of Western Christendom in the Reformation finally ended this doctrine of progress, replacing it with a doctrine of the quasi-timelessness of the ordinances of the churches. The dramatists of this period had to bring the cycle of Trauerspiel to a halt; history was to be brought to a standstill: 'In philosophical-historical terms its ideal was the acme: a golden age of peace and culture, free from any apocalyptic features, constituted and guaranteed in aeternum by the authority of the Church'.(14)

The attempt to bring history to a standstill conflicted with the desire of the authors for a unity of expression and representation: 'Of all the profoundly disturbed and divided periods of European history, the baroque is the only one which occurred at a time when the authority of Christianity was unshaken. Heresy, the mediaeval road of revolt, was barred; in part precisely because the ardour of the new secular will could not come anywhere near to expressing itself in the heterodox nuances of doctrine and conduct. Since therefore neither rebellion nor submission was practicable in religious terms, all the energy of the age was concentrated on a complete revolution of the content of life, while orthodox ecclesiastical forms were preserved. The only consequence could be that men were denied all real means of direct expression.'.(15) The pressures led to tensions within the form and subject matter of the drama.

The Trauerspiel revolved around the character of the king, who was regarded as the representative of humanity; the crown of nature. The king was often placed within an oriental court as the epitome of Absolutism; but the flaw in the ideal emerged through the sovereign's propensity to madness. The fascination of the writers with the character of Herod is indicative of the tensions which the ecclesiastical form placed upon the desire for a secular settlement. The pressures of the form led to distortion and false reconciliations which were expressed in the ambiguous character of the king as tyrant and martyr. The attempt to bring the cycle of Trauerspiel to a standstill was stimulated by the desire for a 'restoration' of the lost unity, which contained as its inverse the fear of 'catastrophe'. Stasis was sought in the 'state of emergency' and was achieved through tyranny or martyrdom: 'The function of the tyrant is the restoration of order in the state of emergency: a dictatorship whose utopian goal will always be to replace the unpredictability of historical accident with the iron constitution of the laws of nature. But the stoic technique also aims to establish a corresponding fortification against a state of emergency in the soul, the rule of the emotions.' (16) The innocence of the king and the consequent vacillations in policy are distant from the knowledge of the tragic hero. The hero opposed law with silence; the king responded to the state of emergency with bombast.

The king in Trauerspiel does not achieve fulfilment, but merely the stasis desired by the church. Another important character of the Trauerspiel dissolves the appearance of a standstill: the intriguer. The intriguer thrives in the state of emergency, playing off diabolic knowledge against the innocence of the king. The Trauerspiel becomes more sinister. The intriguer operates in the space between expression and signification; he represents their division. It is his action in this capacity that makes him a personification of the spirit of allegory.

Allegory appears to represent the desired timelessness through representing history in a spatial configuration: events assume a visual quality which renders them self-enclosed and static. The shared origin of allegory and myth becomes evident in this quasi-mythological use of allegory, especially the spatialisation of time, revealed by the architecture of the Trauerspiel: constituent acts do not follow one another but are built up 'in the manner of terraces', each co-existing in time; chronological layers correspond to the frozen unity of word and significance, of the events of history; the stage design reflects the attempt to spatialise time, to reduce dialogue of expression and signification to configuration and commentary: thus the use of drop scene and the simultaneous action fore and full stage. The action of Trauerspiel assumed a visual quality: the speech, a mere commentary upon images.

The duty of allegory is the representation of history at a standstill. Allegory betrays this duty in a manner analogous to the betrayal of the sovereign by the intriguer. Intrigue and allegory conspire in the space imposed upon them by the church; the result of their activity is the destruction of the formal prison of quasi-mythical stasis. 'It is not eternity that is opposed to the disconsolate chronicle of world-history, but the restoration of the timelessness of paradise.' (17) But allegory wants eternity and not mere timelessness. Allegory piles up fragments in the hope of a miracle born of repetition; but the miracle comes from elsewhere.

Allegories are the spirit of artifice and continuously reveal themselves as such; as a product of subjectivity. The spatialisation of time is revealed as a subjective construction; the appearance of myth is mere appearance and not the substantial truth to which it pretends. Allegory betrays the appearance which it sets out to represent; but as that appearance was untrue allegory opens the possibility of gaining truth. This is the source of the miracle: allegory's heap of fragmented detail, a collection of inscrutable objects, reveals itself as the product of subjectivity. Good and Evil are products of subjectivity, of not heeding the expression of objects. Allegory reveals knowledge to be an allegory. Through the subversion of its own project allegory gives the true name to the attempt of subjectivity to signify objects according to its own will. This name is 'folly'. In revealing the truth of itself allegory opens the possibility of the contemplation of truth proper.

Allegory joins philosophy in its dedication to truth. The representative aesthetic form of _Trauerspiel_ is ugly and obscure as opposed to the specious clarity of beauty. Allegory destroys all arbitrary signification; like philosophy it is the enemy of myth. This is the connection between Benjamin's philosophy of language and dialectics. The attack upon mythic signification contained in the _Trauerspiel_ is continued in the 'Arcades project': 'Sundering truth from falsehood is the goal of the materialist method, not its point of departure. In other words, its point of departure is the object riddled with error, with δοξα (conjecture).' (18) To sum up: the significance of allegory lies in the destruction of the allegory of significance.

Footnotes

1. George Steiner, Introduction to The Origin of German Tragic Drama, translated by John Osborne (London, 1977), p.15.

2. Walter Benjamin, Briefe, Herausgegeben und mit Anmerkungen versehen von Gershom Scholem und Theodor W. Adorno (Frankfurt am Main, 1966), p.523. The passage reads: 'Nun war dieses Buch gewiss nicht materialistisch, wenn auch bereits dialektisch. Was ich aber zur seiner Abfassung nicht wusste, das ist mir bald nachher klarer und klarer geworden: dass von meinem sehr besonderen sprachphilosophischen Standort aus es zur Betrachtungsweise des dialektischen Materialismus eine-wenn auch noch so gespannte und problematische-Vermittlung gibt. Zur Saturiertheit der bürgerlichen Wissenschaft aber gar keine.'.

3. Ibid, p.165.

4. Walter Benjamin, Gesammelte Schriften II.I, Herausgeben von Rolf Tiedemann und Hermann Schweppenhäuser (Frankfurt am Main, 1977), p.136.

5. Ibid, p.165.

6. Ibid, p.138.

7. The translation of Über Sprache überhaupt und über die Sprache des Menschen in One-Way Street and Other Writings (London, 1979), renders 'geistige Wesen' as 'mental being'. This obscures the place of the concept in Benjamin's argument. I have used 'spiritual' instead of 'mental' for 'geistige' and 'essence' for 'Wesen'; 'spiritual essence' being more appropriate to the tone of the essay.

8. GS II, p.147. For a more 'secular' translation consult One-Way Street, p.115.

9. Benjamin has already added the implicit proviso that 'even poetry' and, by implication, even that of Mallarmé, does not partake of truth. This qualification is important for Benjamin's theory of Kritik as 'philosophical presentation' which lies in the translation of the partially signified idea of art in the material content (Sachgehalt) to the realm of ideas (Wahrheitsgehalt).

10. One-Way Street, p.132.

11. Ibid, p.142.

12. Origin of German Tragic Drama, p.56.

13. Ibid, p.121.

14. Ibid, p.80.

15. Ibid, p.79.

16. *Ibid*, p.74.

17. *Ibid*, p.92.

18. Conjecture, but also opinion or semblance, Walter Benjamin, *Charles Baudelaire: A Lyric Poet in the Era of High Capitalism*, translated by Harry Zohn (London, 1973), p.103.

REVOLUTION, THE LEVELLERS AND C. B. MACPHERSON

Anthony Arblaster

Professor C. B. Macpherson's The Political Theory of Possessive Individualism(1) appeared as long ago now as 1962, but it has held its place ever since as the most impressive Marxist interpretation of English seventeenth century political thought. Certainly no other study in that field has generated so much discussion.

At first that discussion was predominantly hostile, as was to be expected. The book's appearance antedated by some years the grudging, but nevertheless quite widespread, recognition within British education that Marxism was not simply another name for the Kremlin's foreign policy, but at the very least a formidable and extensive intellectual tradition which had to be taken seriously. Consequently Macpherson's book, like Ralph Miliband's Parliamentary Socialism, which had appeared a year earlier, was generally greeted with jeering patronage, of which the title of a review article by Alan Ryan, 'Locke and the Dictatorship of the Bourgeoisie',(2) may be taken as typical. It was implied that Macpherson, like Marx himself, could easily be made to look ridiculous. But the book has outlived criticism in that vein.

Macpherson's study concentrated essentially on Hobbes, the Levellers, James Harrington and Locke. His central argument was that the roots of liberal individualism were to be found in the seventeenth century, and that this individualism was from the beginning 'possessive': that is to say, it had a 'conception of the individual as essentially the proprietor of his own person or capacities, owing nothing to society for them' (p.3). He argued that 'possessive assumptions' are present not only in Hobbes and Locke, but also in the Levellers and Harrington (pp.3-4). Another way of putting this might be to say that Macpherson is arguing that from the beginning the liberal individualist way of thinking was tied to the concept of property, and that private property was not merely an institution which liberals contingently defended, but provided a style of thought and a range of metaphors which were integral to the ontology, the ethics and politics of individualism. If a man (or even, on occasions, a woman) is seen as owner of his self, of his own body and its potential labour, this ontology clearly provides a conceptual basis for arguments in favour of personal freedom and individual rights. My life belongs to me, not to God or to the community, or to the state: there is then a prima facie case for my being free to do what I like with it.

The fundamental position is stated by no one better than the Leveller Richard Overton, in An Arrow against all Tyrants (1646), which Macpherson quotes at some length:

> 'To every Individuall in nature is given an individual property by nature, not to be invaded or usurped by any: for every one as he is himselfe, so he hath a selfe propriety, else could he not be himselfe, and on this no second may presume to deprive any of, without manifest violation and affront to the very principles of nature, and of the Rules of equity and justice between man and man; ... Every man by nature being a King, Priest and Prophet in his owne naturall circuite and compasse, whereof no second may partake, but by deputation, commission, and free consent from him whose naturall right and freedome it is.' (qu. pp.140-1)

This general case made by Macpherson seems to me absolutely convincing. It has been part of the ideological success of liberalism that it has been able to impose on us, or secure acceptance of, its own self-image. We have tended to accept the liberal account of liberalism as a creed committed above all to such admirable ideals as freedom, tolerance, individual rights and legal equity. 'Property' is not a principle with quite the same moral glamour, and for at least two hundred years the liberals themselves have sensed this, ever since Jefferson, drafting the Declaration of Independence, replaced the traditional Lockean description of rights of man as 'life, liberty and property' with the more generous 'life, liberty and the pursuit of happiness'. Nevertheless, it is hardly possible to study the history of liberalism for very long without becoming aware of the central position which the commitment to property occupies in that history. Concern for property, for example, was one source of many nineteenth century liberals' fear of democracy -

something which Macpherson has discussed in his more recent writings on liberal democracy.

But what is more debatable is the extent to which Macpherson has succeeded in re-interpreting his chosen seventeenth century thinkers as belonging to the nascent tradition of bourgeois individualist liberalism. This, I think, is where some of his critics have been able to make valid points against him. As far as Locke is concerned, Macpherson's interpretation seems wholly appropriate. Not only does Locke clearly contradict his own radical premises in his determination to protect the existing distribution of property; it is also clear that the metaphor of property permeates his thinking about the individual and individual rights. The notorious ambiguity with which he uses the term property - to mean sometimes material possessions, and at others life and liberty as well as possessions - is in fact an illustration of this.

I must leave aside Macpherson's treatment of Harrington, on which I am not competent to comment, but it is relevant to look briefly at his interpretation of Hobbes before we turn to the Levellers.

What 'everyone' knows about Hobbes, and what traditional political theory has tended to concentrate on, are his quasi-absolutist conclusions, and the remorseless logic of his argument. What was less noticed before Macpherson was that the whole structure of his case in Leviathan is founded on thoroughly individualist premises. The sovereign is set up by a contract made between individuals, each of whom is entirely self-interested and is seeking only to protect himself and to preserve his own life. The contract does not imply any sense of community, any degree of self-abnegation, nor yet anything social in human nature. On the basis of an extreme individualistic conception of human beings, Hobbes constructs his model state of extreme authoritarianism.

Macpherson was, I think, the first political theorist to focus attention on the individualist and bourgeois elements in Hobbes' thinking, although Christopher Hill's essay of 1949, re-published in Puritanism and Revolution (1958), adopts much the same approach. By virtue of these elements, which are essential to Hobbes' world-view,

Hobbes deserves his prominent place in the history of liberal thought. It was, as they say, 'no accident' that he was re-discovered and much admired by the Utilitarians.

Having said that, however, I think it must also be said that Macpherson overplays his hand. He over-stresses the bourgeois character of Hobbes' thought, as when, in his 1968 Introduction to the Pelican edition of Leviathan, he writes:

> 'His scientific method required him to build up a model of man and of society, and the models he constructed were bourgeois models.' (3)

In support of this he quotes such passages as the following:

> 'The Value, or WORTH of a man, is as of all other things, his Price; that is to say, so much as would be given for the use of his Power: and therefore is not absolute; but a thing dependant on the need and judgement of another. ... And as in other things, so in men, not the seller, but the buyer determines the Price.' (4)

Yet although the logic of his own arguments brought him to such conclusions, he did not like them. Even Macpherson admits that Hobbes had a 'dislike of bourgeois morality'.[(5)] Like Adam Smith more than one hundred years later, Hobbes was not an admirer of businessmen or merchants. He thought their typical conduct was morally contemptible, as Macpherson acknowledges. Moreover, as Keith Thomas has argued,[(6)] the concepts of honour and glory, which loom large among human aspirations in Leviathan, are properly associated with feudal codes of behaviour rather than bourgeois ones.

There is nothing implausible in suggesting that Hobbes hovered ambiguously and uneasily between the feudal and bourgeois ways of seeing the world, that he was, in Christopher Hill's phrase, 'suspended between two worlds'.[(7)] This is more or less what one would expect of someone who was born in 1588, and was therefore over fifty when the Civil War broke out. It is also what one would expect of a man whose chief employment was as tutor to the Cavendish family, the Dukes of

Devonshire, who remain to this day among England's largest and richest landowners. What is significant for the argument of this essay is that Macpherson should be reluctant to accept this ambiguity, but chooses instead to present Hobbes as an essentially bourgeois thinker.

Turning now to the Levellers, we find Macpherson engaging in the same process of re-interpretation, but with the opposite implications: the Levellers also turn out to be more bourgeois than had previously been supposed, but whereas this makes Hobbes appear less conservative, or feudal, than usual, it makes the Levellers appear less radical and less democratic than has generally been believed.

The traditional view has been that the Levellers were ultimately advocates of something like manhood suffrage, and that the disagreement which dominated the debates at Putney in the autumn of 1647 between their spokesmen and the Army leaders, Cromwell and Ireton, is between the demand for a franchise which would include all men (but not women) except for servants and beggars or alms-takers, and the Army leaders' defence of a restricted, property-based franchise.(8) Macpherson challenges this, first by arguing that most Leveller documents and statements do specifically exclude servants and either beggars or alms-takers, and that these were both quite sizable groups, however narrowly defined. Secondly, he contends that the term 'servants' did not generally in the seventeenth century have the restricted meaning we attach to it, but included all those who worked for wages. I say contended, rather than argued, since he simply asserts as a fact that

> 'the term servant in seventeenth-century England meant anyone who worked for an employer for wages, whether the wages were by piece-rates or time-rates, and whether hired by the day or week or by the year' (p.282)

and, rather surprisingly, this assertion appears only in a footnote (p.105) and in an appendix devoted to calculating the size of the various possible franchises under discussion in the 1640's. This assertion was challenged by, among others, Peter Laslett,(9) and replied to by Macpherson in an essay, 'Servants and Labourers in Seventeenth-Century England', published in <u>Democratic Theory</u> (1973). In fact Macpherson in this essay does qualify his earlier confident assertion. The assertion of fact now becomes a 'presumption that as a general rule "servants" meant all wage-earners'.(10)

Certainly there is some evidence in favour of Macpherson's 'presumption'. Christopher Hill, in his essay 'Pottage for Freeborn Englishmen', quotes Sir Thomas Smith writing in 1565: 'Those who be hired for wages ... be called servants', as well as an anonymous pamphlet of nearly a century later which declared, less explicitly, that 'Servants and labourers are in the nature of vassals'.(11) Macpherson also produces evidence to show that the term servant was not always restricted to household servants living in, but was applied also to wage-earners and labourers not employed in the household.(12)

But this is not really enough for his case against the Levellers. Macpherson has to give reasons for presuming that the Levellers, although radicals, would naturally have used the term servant with its wider meaning, thus making themselves advocates of a franchise which, while, according to Macpherson's calculations, it would have doubled the existing Freeholder franchise of around 200,000, would nevertheless amount to less than forty per cent of the male adult population estimated at 1,170,000.

Macpherson bases his case for so interpreting the Leveller position at Putney on two statements by Maximilian Petty. In the first, Petty declared that 'We judge that all inhabitants that have not lost their birthright should have an equal voice in elections'.(13) Who were these who had lost their birthright - apart from women, who had none to lose? In a later reply, Petty clarifies this:

> 'I conceive the reason why we should exclude apprentices, or servants, or those that take alms, is because they depend upon the will of other men and should be afraid to displease [them]. For servants and apprentices, they are included in their masters, ...'. (p.83)

Of course, this does not explain whom Petty included under the category of servants; so these statements do not prove Macpherson's case about the use of the wider definition of the term, in particular by the Levellers.

But there are further objections to resting the case on these two particular statements made at Putney. One is that it is simply eccentric to single out Petty as the Leveller voice in the debates. He played a far less important part in them than Thomas Rainborough or John Wildman, and he was not one of the acknowledged leaders of the Leveller party.(14) And he subsequently turned out to be one of the less radical Levellers.

Macpherson suggests that 'the only consistent construction of the debate as a whole suggests that the Levellers (and their opponents) assumed that servants and alms-takers, as well as criminals and delinquents, had lost their birthright' (p.122). It may be a fundamental mistake to attempt to produce a consistent construction of what was undoubtedly a somewhat confused and rambling debate; but in any case, as A. L. Morton has pointed out,(15) it is equally plausible to interpret much of the argument as being about manhood suffrage, or about the general principle, famously stated by Rainborough immediately after the first of the two quoted statements by Petty:

> 'For really I think that the poorest he that is in England hath a life to live, as the greatest he; and therefore truly, sir, I think it's clear, that every man that is to live under a government ought first by his own consent to put himself under that government; and I do think that the poorest man in England is not at all bound in a strict sense to that government that he hath not had a voice to put himself under; ...'. (p.53)

It is this claim that, in Ireton's words, 'by a man's being born here he shall have a share in that power that shall dispose of the lands here, and of all things here' (p.54), which Ireton and the army grandees are concerned to reject, asserting that the right to political participation belonged only to property holders, and that if such a right were conceded to non-property holders, then property itself as an institution would be in danger (see pp.62-3). As Ireton succinctly puts it: 'All the main thing that I speak for, is because I would have an eye to property' (p.57).

The Leveller spokesmen challenge this view, and repeatedly assert that men as men, or at least as free-born men (though this qualification is by no means always spelt out) have certain political rights. Wildman asserts:

> 'Every person in England hath as clear a right to elect his representative as the greatest person in England. I conceive that's the undeniable maxim of government: that all government is in the free consent of the people.' (p.66)

William Rainborough asserts 'that the chief end of this government is to preserve persons as well as estates' (p.67), while both Edward Sexby and Thomas Rainborough exclaim bitterly against the idea that the whole war had been fought simply to make the world safe for property owners:

> 'There are many thousands of us soldiers that have ventured our lives; we have had little propriety in the kingdom as to our estates, yet we have had a birthright. But it seems now, except a man hath a fixed estate in this kingdom, he hath no right in this kingdom. I wonder we were so much deceived. If we had not a right in this kingdom, we were mere mercenary soldiers.' (p.69)

Macpherson's interpretation of the Leveller position, so far from offering a 'consistent construction' of the debate, makes all this extremely puzzling. If the Levellers were not disputing the fundamental principle that the franchise should be restricted to property owners, then what was all the heated argument about? If the actual differences between the two sides, the Army leaders and the Agitators and Levellers, were as small as Macpherson implies, why was the debate so fierce and acrimonious? Why did not the Levellers hasten to reassure Ireton and Cromwell that they were not contemplating anything so radical and extreme as manhood suffrage?

These are the questions which Macpherson's 'construction' of the debate must inevitably raise. But the situation is further complicated by the fact that Macpherson wants to claim that the exclusion of servants (meaning wage-earners) and alms-takers was not simply the position adopted by the Levellers at the time of the Putney debates, but was their consistent overall position on the widening of the franchise. Here too I think that critics have shown that he is on weak ground.

First, he works on the assumption that all the various Leveller statements on the issue of the franchise ought to be consistent with each other. This, as has been pointed out,(16) over-estimates both the homogeneity of the Levellers as a group, and their consistency over time. There is much evidence that they were more flexible, more conscious of the tactical need for concessions and compromises, than Macpherson allows, and that the idea of a restricted franchise may have been just such a compromise, involving a retreat from a normally more radical position.(17)

Secondly, there were occasions when they appear, at the very least, not to be excepting the two categories of servants and alms-takers from the franchise. For example, John Wildman, in The Case of the Army Truly Stated, published only a fortnight before the debates at Putney, defined the electorate as follows:

> 'that all the free-born at the age of 21 yeares and upwards, be the electors, excepting those that have, or shall deprive themselves of that their freedome, either for some yeares, or wholly by delinquency, ...'. (18)

Much hangs here upon a comma. Macpherson takes 'either for some years' as an entirely separate category from those who have deprived themselves 'wholly by delinquency', and interprets it as referring by implication to servants and alms-takers (pp.130-1). But it is at least possible that Wildman was referring to delinquents as the only category of exclusions, some of them being temporary and others permanent. As Morton has commented:

> 'It is on the face of it improbable that a document of this sort, having specified delinquency as a reason for disfranchisement, would have included these other grounds in so unspecific and ambiguous a way.' (19)

It is by no means an open and shut case. Macpherson is quite right to stress that, whatever their opponents at Putney might have supposed or imputed to them, the Levellers were not hostile to the institution of private property as such. The allegation that they wished to destroy all property was, like the very label of Leveller, one of those familiar attempts to discredit radicals by making them out to be far more extreme than they actually were. In fact, as Macpherson points out, their later manifestoes urged that Parliament should bind itself, or be bound by the constitution, not to 'levell mens Estates, destroy Propriety, or make all things common' (quoted p.138). It was this relative conservatism which enabled the Diggers to claim that they were the 'True Levellers'.

The real strength of Macpherson's case lies in his historical method of reading. He knows that words change their meanings, and he knows, too, that we always have to probe behind universal-sounding rhetoric to discover what are the unspoken, agreed assumptions which limit the actual implications of that rhetoric. The most obvious of such assumptions, seldom if ever spelt out, was that when you wrote of individuals, or of the individual or the person, you meant only male persons or individuals. This is one of the central hypocrisies or, more politely, contradictions, of liberalism - and not only of liberalism, of course.

The convulsions of the 1640's led to some women asserting their right to equality of respect and consideration. Thus a group of London women submitted their own petition in support of and addition to the Leveller petition of September 11th 1648. They argued that

> 'since we are assured of our creation in the image of God, and of an interest in Christ equal unto men, as also of a proportionable share in the freedoms of this commonwealth ... Have we not an equal interest with the men of this nation in those liberties and securities contained in the Petition of Right, and other the good laws of the land? ... And must we keep at home in our houses, as if our lives and liberties and all were not concerned?'

Woodhouse states that 'It is improbable that this petition was actually composed by the women', but he offers no evidence in support of this patronising supposition.[(20)] Be that as it may, there is no evidence, so far as I know, that the Levellers themselves responded to this plea, or made any explicit demands on behalf of women.

So even as terms like 'the individual' meant not any human being, but only male ones, so other apparently all-embracing terms cannot without investigation be taken at their face value. Most notorious among such terms is that ringing phrase 'the people'. At least until the nineteenth century we find that writers and orators have decidedly exclusive notions of who 'the people' are, and who they are not. We know this because every now and then someone feels obliged to define what he or she means by 'the people', to say explicitly who is being referred to. Here, for example, is James Tyrell, friend and follower of Locke, elaborating on Locke's definition of the right of rebellion:

> 'I do by no means allow the rabble or mob of any nation to take arms against a civil government, but only the whole community of the people of all degrees and orders, commanded by the nobility and gentry thereof.'

And here is Henry Fox, father of Charles James:

> 'When we talk of the people with regard to elections, we ought to think only of those of the better sort, without comprehending the mob or mere dregs of the people.' (21)

We do not have to conclude that the Levellers would have gone along with these haughty definitions of who 'the people' were, politically speaking. But when Wildman says that 'Every person in England hath as clear a right to elect his representative ...', or that 'all government is in the free consent of the people', we know that he was tacitly referring only to men, and we cannot assume *a priori* that he was not making other tacit and generally agreed exceptions.

Thus Macpherson's method - of examining language closely, and searching for the unspoken assumptions which limit the apparently unqualified spoken assertion - is one well designed to avoid the traps of anachronism, of reading the present back into the past. This has been a recurring feature in the interpretation of English history, particularly when general themes like freedom and democracy have been invoked.[(22)] Those who at various times in this century have been concerned to discover, or construct, traditions or pedigrees in support of contemporary liberal, radical or democratic positions, have often turned gratefully to the Levellers as seventeenth century champions of individual rights and political democracy. Tony Benn is only the most recent example. The Levellers can be assimilated only too easily into one or another version of the Whig interpretation of English history. Undoubtedly part of the appeal of Macpherson's re-interpretation of the Levellers is that it challenges Whiggish anachronisms and appears to place them firmly back in their proper seventeenth century context.

Nevertheless, as far as the Levellers are concerned I do not find Macpherson convincing. He is not simply arguing about their policy on an extension of the franchise. He is taking his conclusions in that respect - that is, that they were not advocates of manhood suffrage, but, in his words, 'consistently excluded from their franchise proposals ... servants or wage-earners, and those in receipt of alms or beggars' (p.107) - as the ground for putting forward a general re-interpretation of the Levellers, which he summarises as follows:

> 'The Levellers have generally been regarded as radical democrats, the first democrats in English political theory. We may now suggest that they ought rather to be considered radical liberals than radical democrats. For they put freedom first, and made freedom a function of proprietorship. The Levellers ought to be remembered as much for their assertion of a natural right to property in goods and estates as for anything else ... The Levellers paved the way, unwittingly, for Locke and the Whig tradition ...'. (p.158)

Neither in relation to the Putney debates nor more generally does this seem to me acceptable. It is one thing to say that they were not hostile to the institution of property as such; it is one thing to point to the possessive element in their thinking about the individual (as exemplified in the passage from Richard Overton's pamphlet). It is quite another to suggest that they were spokesmen for, or concerned only with, those who had property, and that they 'made freedom a function of proprietorship'. Their statements at Putney simply do not bear this out. At that moment it was not the 'natural right to property' which was foremost in their arguments, but the rights of those without property, of persons as persons (or at least men as men), the rights of 'persons as well as estates', as William Rainborough quite explicitly put it. As for their not being democrats, or 'radical democrats', I find this contention perverse in the light of the evidence. Even on Macpherson's interpretation they were demanding a doubling of the size of the electorate (see p.114). They also demanded that parliamentary seats be distributed in relation to population; they wanted elections every two years; and they demanded that the sovereignty of the people, and hence the subordination of parliament to the people, be clearly established and acknowledged. (Since even today in Britain sovereignty is not conceded to the people, that at least must qualify as a radical democratic demand). They wanted a written constitution, and asserted the principle of equality before the law:

> 'They proclaimed that men were born equal and that government could be founded only on consent. They stood for religious toleration and equality before the law. Their concern for civil liberties led them into making the first known attempt at writing down a law paramount which not even the legislature could alter.' (23)

All in all, then, the traditional view of the Levellers as radical democrats has more to recommend it than Macpherson's 'revisionist' attempt to incorporate them into the more orthodox tradition of bourgeois liberalism. But can we then be sure of avoiding the traps of anachronism? In fact I do not think that we have to relapse into some updated version of Whig history. There is another way of interpreting the extraordinary radicalism of the Levellers and of those groups who were even more radical than the Levellers, among whom the Diggers are the best known. I want to suggest that such outbreaks of radical and visionary proposals, however much they may seem to antedate their 'proper' time, are in fact entirely characteristic of moments of revolutionary upheaval. It is this which Macpherson fails to take account of.

For if at one level Macpherson's methodology is sophisticated, at another it is all too crude. The reason why he is so determined to incorporate the Levellers (and Hobbes) into the liberal mainstream is because he is working with a simple and strongly polarised two-class model of English history in the seventeenth century. That is to say, having accepted the basic Marxist interpretation of this period as constituting the revolutionary moment of transition from feudalism to capitalism, or from feudalism to bourgeois society, he is then over-anxious to place all the leading figures in the conflict on one side or the other. There is too little room for confusion, mix and ambiguity in Macpherson's schema - hence his one-sided view of Hobbes. As for the Levellers, it is clearly neater if they too can be assimilated into the framework of the bourgeois challenge to feudalism. The result is that the clash between them and the army leaders, this momentous conflict - which led, let us not forget, in the end to their being bloodily suppressed at Burford and elsewhere in the spring of 1649 - is reduced to a minor dispute, even perhaps a difference of emphasis, within the bourgeois liberal tradition, rather than anything more fundamental.

But when we look at revolutionary moments, of which the 1790's and, to a lesser extent, the period around 1917-22 are classic examples, what do we find? We do not find simply a conflict between the two principal classes in society, with everyone aligning themselves on one side or the other. We find a confusion and a profusion of ideas, agitations, movements, manifestoes, pamphlets, demands, demonstrations and debates, many of which open up perspectives reaching far beyond what may, in retrospect, be seen as objectively attainable at that point in history. And I think that this is what we should _expect_ to find. For the revolutionary _moment_, as opposed to an achieved revolution, is not necessarily a point of transition from one social order to another. That transition may or may not occur. The revolutionary moment is the point at which the old order collapses, perhaps permanently, perhaps only temporarily, under adverse pressures, leaving a vacuum which cannot, in the nature of things, be immediately filled. The vacuum is not only a vacuum of power, but also of ideas and beliefs, of ideology. Old ideas are discredited along with the old order. There is the opportunity to put forward new ones. For to describe this situation only as a vacuum is too negative. It is experienced by the great masses of the oppressed and exploited as a time of liberation. This, I think, is part of what Lenin meant when he described revolutions as 'the festivals of the oppressed and the exploited'.

So we find that at these moments of revolution it is not only the new ascendant class which asserts its presence. Groups and classes which appear through so much of history to be silent, or even absent from the record altogether, find a voice at these moments, because these are the points in history at which it really does seem possible that their position and condition can be changed - a possibility which in the context of any stable and enduring social order it is harder to believe in, or to sense as real.

The largest of these oppressed groups has always been women, and it is obviously not coincidental that at each revolutionary moment, the 1640's, the 1790's, the 1920's, the issue of women's role and status is raised. I take it that this is part of what Engels meant when he observed that what he rather quaintly termed the 'free love question' was brought up in every revolution.

A revolutionary moment, as I have indicated above, does not necessarily issue in a fully fledged revolution. Recent examples of such moments which ultimately failed were France in May-June 1968, Czechoslovakia in the same year, and Portugal in 1974-5. So, in many countries, was the 'year of revolutions', 1848. The significance of this distinction between revolutionary moments and revolutions is that it is not essential to the argument of this essay to establish that a full-scale revolution, the crucial transition from feudal to bourgeois society, took place in England in the mid-seventeenth century. Whether or not that was so, what _is_ clear is that the 1640's and early '50's do constitute an authentic revolutionary moment in the sense just sketched out.

One indication of this was the prodigious number of pamphlets published during these years: 2,000 in the year 1642 alone, 20,000 at least between 1640 and 1660. And one Royalist pamphleteer, writing in 1648, provides an indication of what this ferment of debate was about:

> 'All sorts of people dreamed of an utopian and infinite liberty, especially in matters of religion.' (24)

The whole range of traditional and established beliefs and customs was challenged, whether by Milton broaching the possibility of divorce by consent, by the Levellers asserting the sovereignty of the people or opposing Cromwell's colonial war against the Irish, by the Diggers' primitive communism, or by religious radicals who challenged traditional conceptions of hierarchy and authority, and even the traditional sexual ethics which stressed the virtues of chastity and monogamy.

In this situation it would not prima facie be surprising if the Levellers, whatever their social basis and composition as a party may have been, were to have moved beyond the limits of conventional bourgeois and liberal thought, because it is precisely a characteristic of such situations that people are driven and inspired to transcend the limits of what is normally considered to be realistic and practical. And if I am right in following A. L. Morton and those other critics who have argued that Macpherson underplays, or disregards, the extent of the Levellers' radicalism, then there is nothing anachronistic, nothing historically suspect about that radicalism. It is exactly the kind of response and the kind of movement that you regularly find in an open, potentially revolutionary situation.

Commenting on the followers of Robert Owen in The Making of the English Working Class, Edward Thompson remarks:

> 'One feels that, in the 1830's, many English people felt that the structure of industrial capitalism had been only partly built, and the roof not yet set upon the structure. Owenism was only one of the gigantic, but ephemeral, impulses which caught the enthusiasm of the masses, presenting the vision of a quite different structure which might be built in a matter of years or months if only people were united and determined enough.' (25)

That is the sense of openness, of indeterminacy, which stimulates utopian projects; it exists even more strongly, if also more ephemerally, in the brief years of revolutionary tumult. Looking back, the historian sees the revolutionary process as determined, as having an inevitable outcome, or at least as offering only a limited range of real possibilities. But that is not how it seems at the time. Even if it is partly an illusion, the participants experience the moment as a sudden opening up of the future, a time of choice rich with normally undreamt-of possibilities. And so in that moment they make a leap in time, making demands, plans and proposals which it is only too easy to see, in retrospect, were unrealisable then, and often are still. I believe that the Levellers made that kind of leap, even if their demands and their vision were modest compared to those of a thorough-going radical like Gerrard Winstanley. This, I think, offers the basis for a fairer assessment of their position and outlook than Macpherson's attempt to squeeze them into the straitjacket of bourgeois liberalism.

Footnotes

1. The Political Theory of Possessive Individualism (Oxford, 1962). Further references are indicated simply by bracketed page references in the text.

2. Political Studies, 1965.

3. Thomas Hobbes, Leviathan (Harmondsworth, 1968), Introduction, p.12.

4. Ibid, pp.151-2.

5. Ibid, p.51.

6. Keith Thomas, 'The Social Origins of Hobbes' Political Thought', in Hobbes Studies, ed. K. C. Brown (Oxford, 1965).

7. Christopher Hill, 'Thomas Hobbes and the Revolution in Political Thought', in Puritanism and Revolution (London, 1958), p.277.

8. Macpherson quotes some examples of this view in op cit, pp.294-5.

9. Peter Laslett, 'Market Society and Political Theory', Historical Journal (1964).

10. Democratic Theory (Oxford, 1973), p.219.

11. Christopher Hill, 'Pottage for Freeborn Englishmen', in Continuity and Change in 17th-Century England (London, 1975), pp.224 and 227.

12. Democratic Theory, pp.211-13.

13. Puritanism and Liberty, ed. A. S. P. Woodhouse (second edition, London, 1974), p.53. Further direct quotations from the Putney debates are taken from this edition and indicated by bracketed page references in the text.

14. See J. C. Davis, 'The Levellers and Democracy', Past and Present (1968), reprinted in The Intellectual Revolution of the 17th Century, ed. Charles Webster (London, 1974).

15. A. L. Morton, The World of the Ranters (London, 1970), pp.202-6.

And see also Iain Hampsher-Monk, 'The Political Theory of the Levellers: Putney, Property and Professor Macpherson', *Political Studies* (1976), esp. pp.398-406.

16. See J. C. Davis, *op cit*.

17. See Keith Thomas, 'The Levellers and the Franchise', in *The Interregnum*, ed. G. E. Aylmer (London, 1972), pp.66-7.

18. Quoted by Hampsher-Monk, *op cit*, p.419.

19. *Op cit*, p.199.

20. Woodhouse, *op cit*, pp.367-8.

21. Both quotations from H. T. Dickinson, *Liberty and Property* (London, 1977), pp.78 and 128.

22. See Herbert Butterfield, *The Whig Interpretation of History* (1931: Pelican, 1973), *passim*.

23. Keith Thomas, 'The Levellers and the Franchise', *op cit*, p.57.

24. Quoted by Christopher Hill, *The World Turned Upside Down* (London, 1972), p.28.

25. E. P. Thompson, *The Making of the English Working Class* (Harmondsworth, 1968), p.883.

BEYOND THE SEX-ECONOMY OF MYSTICISM: SOME OBSERVATIONS ON THE COMMUNISM OF THE IMAGINATION WITH REFERENCE TO WINSTANLEY AND TRAHERNE

John Hoyles

This essay has three starting points leading into three areas of debate. Firstly, mysticism has to be theorised if its relationship to literature is to be investigated. Take Traherne. According to the editors of The Oxford Book of English Mystical Verse, nearly all Traherne's poems 'are definitely mystical', and on a page count he turns up joint equal with Swinburne (after Browning, Crashaw and Blake) as a leading mystical poet.(1) But his critics are divided. For one, he is 'a mystic of the first order;(2) for another, he 'cannot be put with the great mystics'.(3) It is not surprising that Evelyn Underhill describes mysticism as 'one of the most abused words in the English language'.(4) Secondly, pace Otto's discussion of mysticism's analogies, it is necessary to delineate as relative autonomies (amongst others) the fields of religion, socio-economics and literature.(5) Christopher Hill's hints of connections between Winstanley and Traherne take us into the area where links between mysticism, imagination and communism can be examined.(6) Thirdly, mysticism may provide material for analysis within the framework of recent developments in the Marxist theory of the subject. An example of this can be seen in Tel Quel's defence of Georges Bataille against Sartre's attack on him as 'a new mystic'.(7) A critique of the mechanical materialism of vulgar Marxism cannot bypass the problematic raised by the theory and practice of mysticism.

To pursue these starting points and give flesh to these areas of debate, we shall theorise mysticism dialectically. As thesis, there is the still dominant (but increasingly ignored) notion that orthodox mysticism can be identified and protected from its heretical potentialities. As antithesis, there is the notion that mysticism has no legs to stand on and on analysis resolves itself into a sublimated function of sex-economy. And as synthesis, there is the notion of an alternative tradition and with it an alternative interpretation whereby a materialist (but not mechanical) theory avoids reductionism and gives a local habitation, both psycho-sexual and socio-economic, to the practices and experiences of mysticism. In this connection the relationship between Winstanley and Traherne may be instructive, for here we have, in the space of a generation, a communism with its origins in mysticism, followed by literary work in verse and prose which is clearly on the edges of mysticism and could be interpreted as a communism of the imagination.

A. Theory I - For Mysticism

> 'The greatest mystics have not been heretics but Catholic Saints'. (Evelyn Underhill, Mysticism, 1911, p.126)

> 'Catholic mysticism is protected from such delusions, because we know that the union of the Divine and the Human in our Lord was a hypostatic union'. (Ronald Knox, Enthusiasm, 1950, p.159)

> 'By a fatal instinct, Madame Guyon crosses the line between mysticism and pantheism, between theocentricity and deiformity'. (Ibid, p.333)

What is remarkable about the classical studies of Western mysticism is the unanimity of their dualism. Curiously enough the five authorities consulted to document this section, although they represent five different persuasions (Catholic, Anglican, Lutheran, Quaker and Jewish), are as one in their conviction that orthodox mysticism can be identified, defined and protected from contamination. They are agreed, though with varying emphases, that there is a mysticism which is a good thing, feeding (and fed by) the normative development of Judaeo-Christian-Platonic civilisation, a mysticism which can be distinguished, and recuperated for the good of the human race, from its own aberrant forms which are self-evidently abnormal and evil. Let us examine this unanimous dualism, for it smacks of a plot to monopolise mysticism on behalf of the set orthodoxies of institutionalised religion, including perhaps the religion of humanity.

Underhill (1911; Anglican) defines mysticism as the 'science or art of spiritual life', not to be confused with 'occultism, dilute transcendentalism, vapid symbolism, religious and aesthetic sentimentality and bad metaphysics'.(8) So pervasive is Underhill's dualism that it verges on the Manichean. Thus 'the mono-ideism of the mystic is rational, whilst that of the hysteric patient is invariably irrational';(9) 'magic wants to get, mysticism wants to give';(10) 'the ecstasies of the saints' and 'the science of union with the Absolute' are not to be confused with 'the performances of mediums', 'the tepid speculations of the Cambridge Platonists' and 'the higher branches of intoxication'.(11) For the mystic, 'symbol is not literal but suggestive, though the artist who uses it may sometimes lose sight of this distinction'.(12) 'Catholic saints' are not to be confused with 'spiritual anarchists' and 'heretics' (a point our Quaker authority will of course want to qualify), and, as Madame Guyon has it, 'ecstasies, raptures and visions are far inferior to pure orison' and 'dumb absorption in God' (a point our Catholic authority is not too happy with).(13) Underhill concludes with a pious wish that mysticism might be related to the 'normal world of sense' and the 'general history of man', rather than to the 'remote' and the 'academic'.(14)

Jones (1919; Quaker) reproduces Underhill's dualism, though as one would expect from a Quaker he presents a liberal front. Thus he can actually ask 'whether mysticism is something normal or abnormal',(15) but when it comes to the crunch he is with the founder of his sect Fox against the Naylers of this world. Thus 'Nicholas Storch was decidedly psychopathic, given to visions and conscious of immediate inspiration. Like Munzer he had a passion for the emancipation of the people.'.(16) (Curious, how the apparently liberal sentiments of the second sentence are eaten away by the dogmatic acid of the first!) For Jones, the Ranters were 'the dregs of the Seeker movement'.(17) We remember how Fox was troubled by Ranters, and that, in Christopher Hill's words, 'the whole early Quaker movement was far closer to the Ranters in spirit than its leaders later liked to recall'.(18) Hill's point hits Jones as accurately as it hits Fox, Barclay and Penn, for Jones is even more violent than Underhill in the language with which he attempts to separate good and bad mysticism. Ranterism is a 'contagion', 'a serious outbreak of mental and moral disorder', and he quotes with sympathetic understanding the New England United Colonies Statute which attempted to legislate for 'tender consciences seeking light' and against 'carnal liberty under a deceitful colour of liberty of conscience'.[20] No wonder he asks whether mysticism is normal or abnormal; unfortunately his answer takes us no further than Underhill's arbitrary and partisan dualism. For although Underhill represents Jones as a dangerous fellow ('at present the most eminent upholder of the view which regards the mystic as a spiritual anarchist'),[21] it is clear that for Jones (as for Fox) a line has to be drawn and the enemy is still to the left.

Otto (1917, trs. 1923; Lutheran) comes to us packaged with a translator's warning lest the innocent reader overlook the essential dualism of the text and fall into all manner of contagious errors and enormities. Otto's whisky must be watered to suit the English palate: 'I have sought to mitigate the unfortunate suggestion of the key-word "irrational" in the original by rendering it "non-rational"'.[22] Struggling not only with the idea of the holy but also with the German language, our translator attempts to clarify Otto's theme: 'There is an overplus of meaning which is non-rational, but neither in the sense of being counter to reason on the one hand nor above reason on the other'.[23] No wonder mysticism has got itself a bad name. And yet more well-intentioned blundering awaits us on the next page, where our solicitous translator tackles 'another phrase' which 'is perhaps more misleading', namely, 'the wholly other': 'But Otto (unlike Barth and Brunner) is not open to the criticism of exaggerating and isolating the divine transcendent Otherness. God for him is not, so to speak, <u>wholly</u> "wholly other"'.[24] Thus forewarned, we are now allowed to sip Otto's strong concoction, which turns out to be of the Underhill/Jones milk and water variety, though with less moral rhetoric and more exact philosophy. For Otto, the 'feeling of the numinous' is 'unevolvable';[25] genetic and historical factors are neither here nor there: 'No mere inquiry into the genesis of a thing can throw any light upon its essential nature, and it is hence immaterial to us how mysticism historically arose'.[26] As in Underhill and Jones, the essence of mysticism is preserved intact from the contaminating embrace of historical contingency. And this dualism is compounded when Otto compares the numinous with the sexual (the other two analogies he allows to come within a chapter of the numinous are the sublime and music). Although he is the only one of our orthodox authorities to point out in passing that 'the erotic is analogous to the holy in having in the main no means of linguistic expression but terms drawn from other fields of mental life', his central argument is safely dualistic: 'It goes without saying that the sex instinct lies just on the opposite side of reason to the numinous consciousness; for while this is above all reason, the sex impulse is below it. ... The numinous infuses the rational from above, the sexual presses up from beneath.'.[27]

Knox (1950; Catholic) reproduces Underhill's categories, but with wit rather than solemnity, and with a dash of papal infallibility which the critical reader forgives but does not forget. On the one hand we have Catholic mysticism, protected from delusion by formal theology and the distinctions of the schoolmen (including of course the famous 'hypostatic union');[28] on the other, a whole procession of misguided groups and individuals, often psychopathic or hysterical, and including pious females and noisy quietists, whose behaviour and opinions make Knox's book so readable.[29] There is a considerable amount of historical flesh on Knox's account, which at times modifies his basic dualism. (One could also argue, of course, that, like Swift in <u>A Tale of a Tub</u>, or Milton in <u>Paradise Lost</u>, Knox's actual fascination with what he formally condemns is profoundly subversive). Thus, where Jones the Quaker dismisses Nayler along with the Ranters, Knox the Catholic suggests that in the Nayler case 'what the House of Commons was really debating was the supreme crux of mysticism - whether the contemplative becomes wholly and literally identified with the Object of his contemplation, or whether ... he can say without hesitation, No, I am not Christ'.[30] So Knox acknowledges the crux, but he does solve it in a dualistic fashion (though with some analytical subtlety). Thus: 'Quietism is a morbid growth on the healthy body of mysticism, and mystics of recognised orthodoxy may carry the germs of the disease without developing its symptoms'.[31] With a biological analogy wrapped up in Jesuitical casuistry the carrier is pronounced immune. It follows that there is on the one hand 'formal meditation', on the other 'supernatural paralysis', and that where Eckhart, St. Catherine of Genoa, even Fénelon ('when he is writing in a cool hour') can take mysticism in their stride, 'a psychopath like Molinos' and 'a hysterical subject like Madame Guyon' will go berserk.[32] Knox does however admit that on the face of it there is nothing to distinguish the second of Molinos' condemned propositions, 'that the contemplative ought to be like a lifeless corpse', from St. Ignatius' central tenet 'tamquam cadaver'[33] (is the line then to be drawn merely according to the passing whim of ecclesiastical dictate?). And this ambiguity, though Knox answers it to his own satisfaction by referring with distaste to the general atmosphere of Molinos' personality, is compounded (as we shall see in the next section) by passing references to the sexual, socio-economic and political dimensions of mysticism.

Cohn (1957; Jewish) follows Underhill and Knox in distinguishing the Catholic mystics who 'lived their experiences within a tradition sanctioned and perpetuated by a great institutionalised church', and those, like the 'adepts of the Free Spirit' who 'were intensely subjective' and can be regarded as 'an aberrant form of mysticism'.[34] He adds two further points. Firstly, and 'from the standpoint of depth-psychology', orthodox mystics emerge from their 'psychic adventure' 'with a widened range of sympathy' and 'freer from illusions', whereas the heretical mystics emerge as 'aggressive, wanton ... nihilistic megalomaniacs'.[35] In this fashion psychology is used to reinforce the dualism already foisted on humanity by the defenders of organised religion. Secondly, Cohn suggests that a reading of Marguerite Porete's Mirouer des simples ames reveals that a sixth and seventh stage (each heretical) in the ascent of the soul have been added to the first five (orthodox) stages. In the sixth stage, the 'soul is annihilated in the Deity' and this 'lies quite outside the experience of Catholic mystics'. The seventh stage is heretical in that the 'soul rejoices permanently, while still on this earth, in the glory and blessedness which orthodox theology reserves for heaven'.[36] Like Knox, Cohn is fascinated by his heterodox material, and this in itself allows him (as we shall see in the next section) to adumbrate social and psychological dimensions where the dualist grip begins to slip.

B. Theory II - Against Mysticism

> 'At the back of Bossuet's mind is the idea that mysticism itself is a nuisance'. (Ronald Knox, Enthusiasm, 1950, p.240)

> 'The truth is, to the end of his life, Wesley was only prepared to tolerate mysticisn if he were given leave to edit it'. (Ibid, p.482)

> 'Mysticism is nothing other than unconscious longing for orgasm. ... Adolescents who are sexually sick have an unhealthy appreciation of the legend of Jesus ... Sexual consciousness is the end of mysticism'. (Wilhelm Reich, The Mass Psychology of Fascism, 1933, pp.167, 168, 179)

Knox is more than half in love with his heterodox mystics, but in his mind he sympathises with the Bossuets and Wesleys of this world, for whom all mysticism is a nuisance, at best tolerable, and then only when edited or bowdlerised. Bossuet and Wesley are children of their age, the age of Enlightenment, and were it not that they had a religion to defend they would have shared the absolute hostility to mysticism in all its forms which is the hallmark of the Enlightenment's work of force-marching Europe out of the Dark Ages. Nineteenth century positivism and scientism compounded that hostility into a new orthodoxy, and it was left to the post-Marxist, post-Freudian twentieth century, in the voice of Wilhelm Reich, an erstwhile communist and psychoanalyst, to pronounce the demise of mysticism, in critical theory if not in social practice. Our antithesis is clear and familiar. True, Reich's own formulæ appear more heterodox and problematic than the legacy of Enlightenment thinking which underpins most contemporary conventional wisdom on the subject; but by and large there is little more that needs to be said under this heading. We will confine ourselves to a brief comment on Reich's reductionist theory and some observations on hints in Cohn and Knox which tie up with it.

Reich's concept of sex-economy seeks to combine in a single materialist tool the insights of Marx and Freud. For Reich 'every form of mysticism is reactionary and the reactionary man is mystical'.(37) As his American editor explains, 'sex-economy means the manner in which an individual handles his biological energy; how much of it he dams up and how much of it he discharges orgastically. The factors that influence this manner of regulation are of a sociological, psychological and biological nature.'.(38) Mysticism then is an irrational sublimation of psychological and social energy which must be demystified by subjecting its idealist substance to sexual and economic analysis. The heirs of the Enlightenment, including vulgar Marxists, have, according to Reich, turned their backs on the work of analysing 'irrational ideas that are not to be explained on a purely socio-economic basis';[39] 'the sex-political nature of every form of mysticism ... was as completely overlooked by the freethinkers as the equally evident sexuality of children had been overlooked by the most famous educators.'.[40] To support his argument, Reich holds patriarchy responsible for breaking up an original unity of sexual and religious cults; mysticism and pornography are the dissociated and etiolated fragments of the original unity. Mysticism is thus a 'substitute' for 'the socially affirmed sensuality' of the Golden Age; it cannot result in release, only in fatigue.[41]

Reich's antithesis may not be sufficient, but it is certainly necessary, given the oblivion to such considerations which characterises traditional studies of Western mysticism. What is necessary is the opening up of lines of communication between religious, sexual and socio-economic factors; what is insufficient is the substitution/reduction theory, as if the only realities were sexual and economic.

Both Knox and Cohn would have been more telling in their arguments if they had incorporated elements of Reich's sex-economy theory. On sexuality Knox is unnecessarily dark and prurient when he tells us that Molinos supported the idea of 'going naked for a sign' and 'had 20,000 letters from pious females in his possession at the time of his arrest'.[42] And on the socio-economic side, he doesn't follow up the logic of his distinction between mysticism within convent walls and mysticism as a popular cult.[43] He is, however, honest enough to reveal his own political position when he opts for a mysticism analogous to a 'constitutional monarchy' as opposed to a mysticism where 'a sudden coup d'état has dethroned the speculative intellect altogether'.[44] Similarly Cohn misses an opportunity of discussing the sex-economy of mysticism when he mentions on succeeding pages (a) an item in a mid-fourteenth century Beguine Catechism according to which 'all things that exist belong to the perfect man who is both God and man' and 'all that God ever created is the property of such a man',[45] and (b) the fact that the Thuringian Blood Friends of 1550 regarded the sexual act as a sacrament, which they called 'Christerie'.(46) But in raising these phenomena we are not only suggesting that mysticism can benefit from sexual and economic analysis; we are also suggesting that there may be another kind of mysticism.

C. Theory III - Another Kind of Mysticism

> 'Certain practices of the mystics may succeed in upsetting the normal relations between the different regions of the mind so that the perceptual system becomes able to grasp relations in the deeper layers of the ego and in the id which would otherwise be inaccessible to it.' (Sigmund Freud, New Introductory Lectures on Psychoanalysis, 1933, p.112)

> 'But there is in the Western tradition another kind of mysticism, which can be called Dionysian or body mysticism, which stays with life, which is the body, and seeks to transform and perfect it.' (Norman O. Brown, Life Against Death, 1959, p.271)

> 'Matter is the Urgrund, an indeterminate universum out of which anything may come; it is indistinguishable from the God of pantheism ... The inspiration of the final goal is an inseparable part of Marxist philosophy, which inherits the apocalyptic outlook of radical Anabaptism.' (Leszek Kolakowski, paraphrasing Ernst Bloch, in Main Currents of Marxism, 1978, III, 440-1)

What emerges from the forcible conjunction of Underhill and Reich if mysticism is neither a self-contained absolute nor a demystifiable chimera? In order to eliminate Underhill's dualism and Reich's mechanical reductionism, an alternative theory is required which will do justice to both the underlying unity and the relative autonomy of the mystical, the sexual and the economic. There exists such a theory which claims to transcend both traditional dualism and heterodox sex-economy: we may call it 'dynamic monism'. It can be picked up by reading the 'mystical' Marxist Ernst Bloch, and it is consciously advanced by the left-Freudian Norman O. Brown. But let us first attend to Freud's views on the subject.

Freud was too much a nineteenth century positivist to waste much time on mysticism. Having speculated on the therapeutic value of 'certain mystical practices' (unfortunately unspecified), he remarks drily that 'it may safely be doubted whether this road will lead us to the ultimate truths from which salvation is to be expected'. Nevertheless, Freud does claim that 'the therapeutic efforts of psychoanalysis have chosen a similar line of approach'. What psychoanalysis and mysticism have in common is the project 'to strengthen the ego, to make it more independent of the super-ego, ... so that it can appropriate fresh portions of the id'; and with a pregnant image Freud opens up lines of communication between his own science and the 'science of spiritual life': 'Where id was, there ego shall be. It is a work of culture - not unlike the draining of the Zuider Zee.'.[47] Freud does not, however, say whether this reclamation work is confined to Underhill's <u>bona fide</u> orthodox mystics, and it is the left-Freudians who open up relations with heterodox mysticism. Indeed a hostile critic might suppose that Norman O. Brown's version of the project common to psychoanalysis and mysticism is not so much to drain the Zuider Zee as to drown in it.

Brown may be described as a mystical materialist on his way to becoming (e.g. in <u>Love's Body</u>) a materialistic mystic. In any case he does make an interesting attempt to dissolve the dualism of these terms. He is not far from Reich when he claims that 'having the world within the self' is a sublimated substitute for 'bodily erotic union ... with other bodies',[48] but his key concept is the distinction between the 'Apollonian ego of genital organisation' (together with the 'Apollonian scholasticism of orthodox psychoanalysis') and the 'Dionysian ego' which would be 'freed from genital organisation' (together with a heterodox psychoanalysis which would open up frontiers with mystics, Romantic poets and philosophers).[49] It sounds as if Brown's 'Dionysian or body mysticism' has something in common with the coenaesthesis of Traherne and his ilk. 'Boehme and Freud have too much in common to be able to dispense with each other', and 'Boehme's concept of the spiritual body of Adam before the Fall recognises the latent demand in our unconscious both for an androgynous mode of being and for a narcissistic mode of self-expression, as well as the corruption in our current use of the oral, anal and genital functions.'.[50] For Reich (let alone Bossuet and Wesley), Brown has by now sunk to the bottom of the Zuider Zee, but, for the dynamic monists, another kind of mysticism is well and truly launched.

Susan Sontag, who follows up Brown's hints about Romantic poets and philosophers, has suggested that 'the radical critique of consciousness' which was 'first delineated by the mystical tradition' is 'now administered by unorthodox psychotherapy and high modernist art'. These artists and psychotherapists have taken over from 'the timid legatees of the religious traditions'.(51) This takes us into an important area of relationship between mysticism and literature which this new journal may wish to investigate. But, to keep within the bounds of our present argument, Sontag also pursues an investigation into 'atheist spirituality',(52) and it is in this field that Ernst Bloch may be seen to establish for mysticism and Marxism connections analogous to those which Brown sets up between mysticism and psychoanalysis.

Bloch is interested in relating Marxism (considered insufficiently Utopian) with 'the tradition of chiliastic popular movements and especially German revolutionary Anabaptism'.(53) In his theory of matter we hear echoes of Bruno, Paracelsus and Boehme; 'God's coming into existence involves no threat to materialism since by definition he will be "material" also'. According to Kolakowski, Bloch's doctrine is monist rather than materialist in the strict sense; it relates Marxism to 'the theogony of Plotinus and Erigena', rescues Marxism from its vulgar mechanical tendencies, reinstates a theory of the subject and provides a bulwark against Bernstein and revisionism by arguing that 'metaphysics and social activity must alike be aimed at the *eschaton*'.(54) With Brown and Bloch as our guides and dynamic monism as our motto, the waters of Underhill and Reich seem shallow indeed.

D. Winstanley and Traherne

> 'The public mind was prepared to suspect illuminism wherever the mystical tradition spread beyond convent walls and took on the form of a popular cult'. (Ronald Knox, *Enthusiasm*, 1950, p.242)

> 'Like Winstanley, Traherne believed that men were born innocent, and that they fell because of the covetousness prevalent in the society in which they grew up. But Traherne's communism, unlike Winstanley's, was in the imagination only.' (Christopher Hill, *The World Turned Upside Down*, 1972, p.414)

Given the scope of our theoretical prolegomena, this is not the place for a full formal analysis of the writings of Winstanley and Traherne. What emerges from a juxtaposition of their work in the light of our theory is a sense of mysticism's connections with both socio-economic struggle and psychological well-being. It is not only that the mystic (to adapt Lunacharsky's definition of the prophet) 'is one who demands a re-examination of the agreement with God, and this always becomes also a re-examination of social relations',(55) but also that mysticism is often the expression of the jouissance (bliss) of the subject which may take the form of a drive towards communism, either in the social order or in the imagination.(56) Characteristic of both metaphysics and social activity 'aimed at the eschaton' is a dynamic monism, signs of which are to be found in both Winstanley and Traherne.

Winstanley's critics are not blind to the significance of the mystical origins of his communism. For Sabine, 'Winstanley was a mystic and his communism was revealed to him in a trance', and, more generally, 'every revolution gets its drive from ideas that, psychologically speaking, are religious in their effects on human motivation'. It follows that what makes Winstanley advance beyond the limits of a Puritan Revolution is 'not the loss of religion, but another kind of religious experience'.(57) We should not see his mysticism as a 'compensation for the failure of his political and social projects', but should rather recognise that 'the thirsting soul seeking joy and fulfilment is the first principle behind his reflection on the religious and social problems of his day, which eventuated in his communism'.(58) Even Petegorsky, who is something of an orthodox Marxist, does not write off Winstanley's mysticism along substitutionist/reductionist lines. 'The common people of England ... expressed themselves in the only terms in which they had been trained to think, in the language and forms of religion, spirituality and mysticism.'. It is the mystical tradition, and not 'the prevailing Puritan concepts ... fashioned to fulfil the purposes of a rising middle class', which takes the form of a popular cult to serve 'the needs of the oppressed'. 'The widespread growth of mystical enthusiasm' is not a substitute for, or retreat from, class-consciousness, but an authentic expression of its development.(59) And this applies not only to the 1640's, but also to the 'mystical enthusiasm of the 1650's' when the political expression of class-consciousness 'was inhibited by the repressive policy of the government'.[60] And, we might add, if this is true of the 1650's, then why not also of the 1660's and 70's, when Traherne's mysticism is so strongly coloured with a communism of the imagination?

The point can be illustrated by juxtaposing passages which reveal the mysticism of the communist and the communism of the mystic:

> 'He that looks for a God without himself is led away and deceived by the imagination of his own heart, but he that looks for a God within himself, this man knows whom he worships for he is made subject to and hath community with that spirit that made all flesh in every creature within the globe.' (Winstanley, The Saints Paradise, 1648) (61)

> 'Cursed and devised proprieties ... fled from the splendour of mine eyes. And so did hedges, ditches, limits, bounds, I dreamed not ought of those, but wandered over all men's grounds, and found repose. Proprieties themselves were mine, and hedges ornaments.' (Traherne, Poems, c.1670) (62)

We know that Traherne was an Anglican mystic with no hint of revolutionary social activity to his credit; we know that Winstanley practised his communism with the Diggers (1649-50) and 'shed his mysticism ... to become the most advanced radical of the century'.[63] It is not our purpose to blur this crucial distinction, but rather to set alongside it the notion of a common eschaton, against which to measure the relationship between metaphysics and social activity, mysticism and communism. Traherne, in his vision, is digging over the same ground that Winstanley and his comrades literally dug. And Winstanley's own mature position retains the Christian mysticism of his earlier tracts:

> 'Freedom is the man that will turn the world upside down, therefore no wonder he hath enemies ... True freedom ... lies in the community in spirit and community in the earthly treasury; and this is Christ the true man-child spread abroad in the creation, restoring all things unto himself.' (A Watchword to the City of London and the Army, 1649) (64)

It is this topsy-turvy world which metamorphosed into Traherne's gnomic formula: 'Under our feet, there is as o'er our heads, a place of bliss.'.[65] The mention of bliss reminds us that Traherne's theory of _jouissance_ has received less attention than has Winstanley's mystical communism. We shall examine it briefly, and by way of transition recall the associated phenomenon of Ranterism.

It might be argued that the Ranters constitute a missing link between Winstanley and Traherne. They may have been the 'dregs of the Seekers', but they did have a coherent theory which sought to combine mysticism and materialism in a Dionysian monism which would do away with the distinctions between God and man, soul and body. Like Cohn's Thuringians, they lend themselves to a Reichian sex-economy analysis, and their libertinism has socio-economic as well as psycho-sexual dimensions. They infiltrated Winstanley's Diggers, and we have records of the mutual suspicions and antagonisms the two groups aroused in each other. The Dionysian _jouissance_ of the Ranters is closely related to the origins of Quakerism, but in the Quakers, as in Traherne, this _jouissance_ is internalised and rendered socially and morally innocuous. The Ranters' practices appeared to their contemporaries to be gratuitously libertine, but they were based on a mysticism of the body and an antinomian tradition which has clear links with Winstanley's theory of community and Traherne's theory of bliss. One of their rituals is a practical group demonstration that sin does not exist ('Mistress E. B. offers to unbutton his cod-piece, who demanding of her what she sought for, she answereth, For sin: whereupon he blows out her candle, leads her to bed, where in the sight of all the rest they commit fornication. ... He looked for his sins but they were not there, he could not find them');[66] and the leading Ranter Coppe declares that 'by base impudent kisses my plaguy holiness hath been confounded'.[67] According to A. L. Morton, the Ranters combined a mysticism which found God in everyone and a materialism which abolished God, since if God exists everywhere in general he can be said to exist nowhere in particular.[68]

In Traherne the erotic principle is metamorphosed into a coenaesthetic bliss, and the class-consciousness of the Diggers becomes a communism of the imagination. Ellrodt has noticed that in Traherne there is no struggle against sensuality; the senses are spiritualised; there is no need for voluptuous sensations since existence itself is voluptuous[69] ('I felt a vigour in my sense that was all Spirit').[70] Bliss is associated with silence ('I then my bliss did, when my silence, break. My non-intelligence of human words ten thousand pleasures unto me affords.').[71] Distrust of words is, as Sontag points out, common to both the mystical tradition and high modernism.[72] Winstanley was constantly attacking talkers and verbal professors, hearsay preachers and 'parrot-like speaking from the universities'.[73] For Traherne, 'metaphors conceal', 'all tropes are clouds', universities study alienated knowledge, and felicity consists in 'being dumb'.[74] Nevertheless Traherne does try to communicate his sense of jouissance: 'everything that I did see did with me talk'; 'then was my soul my only all to me, a living endless eye'; 'all or most that silence break discover nothing but their throat'.[75] He distinguishes bliss from mere contentment and, like Barthes, claims it is a sovereign power:

> 'Contentment is a sleepy thing ... A quiet mind is worse than poverty ... Content alone's a dead and silent stone: the real life of Bliss is glory reigning in a throne, where all enjoyment is.' (76)

As in Blake, 'excess is its true moderation'.[77] Ellrodt suggests that Traherne's theory of felicity 'presupposes a set of conditions rarely brought together: a low degree of sensuality, a high degree of aesthetic sense and an inclination towards euphoria'; that 'this strange idealism opens the door to sensualism'; and that 'this tendency is of historic importance, marking a turning point in European consciousness'.[78] If he had had the Diggers and Ranters in mind, Ellrodt might have seen Traherne's work as a sublimated retreat from the economic (things) and the sexual (feelings), via a spiritualisation and interiorisation, towards the establishment of a narcissistic and solipsist freedom in the imagination, in the absence of psycho-economic freedom in society. The hyper-activity of the Diggers and Ranters becomes the super-quietism of the Quakers for, as Ellrodt points out, 'by a singular paradox, to seek to maintain the spirit in perpetual activity, is to condemn it to passivity'.[79]

Hill's The World Turned Upside Down ends curiously enough with a reference to Traherne, who 'does not seem to have shared the Digger hope that all mankind might have equal rights, nor even the Ranter claim that "all is ours"', but who was nevertheless a communist in the imagination.(80) There is some justice in this assessment. Traherne's 'state of innocence and bliss' presupposes a world where 'trades and poverties' no longer exist, and where 'Joy and Beauty' are accompanied by 'Welfare'.(81) When he writes that 'all we see is ours, and everyone possessor of the whole', and that 'every man is like a God incarnate',(82) he is following the mystical communism of the Beguine Catechism as quoted by Cohn. The 'constant holiday' of his New Jerusalem is Felicity incarnate in the here and now ('The Tree of Life in Paradise may grow among us now', and, more prosaically, 'Those Christians that can defer their felicity may be contented with their ignorance').(83) Traherne espouses a Rousseauistic critique of Christian civilisation ('by this you may see who are the rude and barbarous Indians'), and argues the primacy of environment over heredity ('it is not our parents' loins, so much as our parents' lives that enthralls and blinds us').(84) He places 'the common air and light' above the scarce commodities valued by the world,(85) and hints that a reformist ideology based on charity is no substitute for a more radical critique of the world:

> 'Sometimes it may so happen, that to contemn the world in the whole lump, was as acceptable to God, as first to get it with solicitude and care, and then to retail it out in particular charities.' (86)

In his own way, the Anglican mystic who fulminates so sweetly against 'cursed and devised proprieties'(87) reminds us that there is more to mysticism than meets the eye in the pages of Underhill, or Reich.

*****

To conclude, if it is clear that traditional studies of Christian mysticism leave much to be desired, it is in this day and age also necessary to advance beyond the ultra-mechanical analyses of sex-economy. Mysticism must be theorised in a manner that does justice to its relative autonomy, and if materialist criticism is to slough off its crudities, then it must produce a theory of the subject as well as of the object. A <u>sine qua non</u> of such a project might be to pay some attention to Cudworth's response to Hobbes, published in 1678, four years after Traherne's death. To the 'modern atheistic pretender to wit, who satisfies himself worshipfully ... that fancy is but fancy, but the reality of cogitation nothing but local motion', Cudworth modestly exclaims: 'as if there were not as much reality in fancy and consciousness as there is in local motion'.[88]

Footnotes

1. D. H. S. Nicholson and A. H. E. Lee, eds., The Oxford Book of English Mystical Verse (1924), p.viii.
2. Gladys I. Wade, Thomas Traherne (1944), p.168.
3. K. W. Salter, Thomas Traherne, Mystic and Poet (1964), p.46.
4. Evelyn Underhill, Mysticism (1911) p.x.
5. Rudolph Otto, The Idea of the Holy (1917), ch.vii, 'Analogies and Associated Feelings'.
6. Christopher Hill, The World Turned Upside Down (1972), pp.140, 186-7, 413-4.
7. See Sartre, Situations I (1947), and Philippe Sollers, ed., Bataille (1973).
8. Underhill, p.x.
9. Ibid, p.72.
10. Ibid, p.84.
11. Ibid, p.86.
12. Ibid, p.95.
13. Ibid, pp.126, 337.
14. Ibid, p.531.
15. Rufus M. Jones, Studies in Mystical Religion (1919), p.xvi.
16. Ibid, p.389.
17. Ibid, p.467.
18. Hill, p.232.
19. Jones, p.469.
20. Ibid, p.479.

21. Underhill, p.115.

22. John W. Harvey, 1949 Preface, in Otto, pp.xvii-xviii.

23. *Ibid*, p.xvii.

24. *Ibid*, p.xviii.

25. Otto, p.44.

26. *Ibid*, p.22.

27. *Ibid*, pp.46-7.

28. Ronald Knox, *Enthusiasm* (1950), p.159.

29. See esp. *ibid*, p.262.

30. *Ibid*, p.164.

31. *Ibid*, p.240.

32. *Ibid*, pp.246, 351.

33. *Ibid*, p.262.

34. Norman Cohn, *The Pursuit of the Millenium* (1957), p.150.

35. *Ibid*, p.176.

36. *Ibid*, p.184.

37. Wilhelm Reich, *The Mass Psychology of Fascism* (1933), p.24.

38. *Ibid*, p.xxx.

39. *Ibid*, p.24.

40. *Ibid*, pp.143-4.

41. *Ibid*, pp.146-7, 150. Reich's articulation of this theory is worth quoting at length: 'The basic religious idea of all patriarchal religions is the negation of sexual need. There are no exceptions, if we disregard the sexually affirmative primordial religions, in which the religious and the sexual experience were still a unity. In the transition of society from a matriarchal organisation based on natural law to a patriarchal organisation based on the division of classes, the unity of the religious and sexual cult was split. The religious cult became the antithesis of the sexual cult. At this juncture the sexual cult ceases to exist and is replaced by the barbarism of brothels, pornography and clandestine sexuality. No additional proof is required to show that at that moment when sexual experience ceased to constitute a unity with the religious cult and indeed became its antithesis, religious excitation also had to become a substitute for the socially affirmed sensuality

that was lost. It is only on the basis of this contradiction in religious excitation, which is anti-sexual and a substitution for sexuality at one and the same time, that the strength and tenacity of religions can be comprehended.'.

42. Knox, pp.317, 262.

43. Ibid, p.242.

44. Ibid, pp.585-6.

45. Cohn, p.179.

46. Ibid, p.180.

47. Sigmund Freud, New Introductory Lectures on Psychoanalysis (1933), p.112.

48. Norman O. Brown, Life Against Death (1959), p.147.

49. Ibid, pp.158-9, 272.

50. Ibid, p.272.

51. Susan Sontag, Styles of Radical Will (1969), pp.21-3.

52. Ibid, p.87.

53. Leszek Kolakowski, Main Currents of Marxism, III, 423. Bloch's relevant works are Thomas Münzer als Theologe der Revolution (1921) and Geist der Utopie (1918).

54. Kolakowski, III, 440-1.

55. Anatoly Lunacharsky, Religion and Socialism (1908).

56. On jouissance, see Roland Barthes, Le plaisir du texte (1973) and Image, Music, Text (1977), translator's note.

57. George H. Sabine, ed., The Works of Gerrard Winstanley (1941), p.3.

58. Ibid, pp.11, 43.

59. David W. Petegorsky, Left-Wing Democracy in the English Civil War (1940), pp.63-4.

60. Ibid, p.235.

61. Winstanley, The Law of Freedom and Other Writings, ed. C. Hill (1973), pp.18-9. Cf. Petegorsky, p.132.

62. Thomas Traherne, Poems, Centuries and Three Thanksgivings, ed. Anne Ridler (1966), p.8.

63. Petegorsky, p.124.

64. Winstanley (ed. Hill), pp.128, 129.

65. Traherne, p.120.

66. Anon, The Ranters Last Sermon, quoted in A. L. Morton, The World of the Ranters (1970), pp.81, 105.

67. Abiezer Coppe, A Fiery Flying Roll (1650), (Exeter University, 1973), Part II, p.13. See also Hill, ch.15.

68. Morton, p.74.

69. Ellrodt, Les poètes métaphysiques anglais (1960), I, ii, 324. Quotes from Ellrodt are my translations.

70. Traherne, p.7.

71. Ibid, p.23.

72. Sontag, pp.21-3, 31.

73. See Sabine, pp.170, 213, 238; Winstanley (ed. Hill), p.102.

74. Traherne, pp.40, 383, 282-3, 24.

75. Ibid, pp.6, 12, 95.

76. Ibid, p.146. See Barthes, Le plaisir du texte (1973).

77. Ibid, p.239.

78. Ellrodt, p.327.

79. Ibid, p.329.

80. Hill, p.414.

81. Traherne, p.7.

82. Ibid, p.35.

83. Ibid, pp.98-9, 111, 320.

84. Ibid, pp.269, 268.

85. Ibid, pp.109, 291.

86. Ibid, p.330.

87. Ibid, p.8.

88. Ralph Cudworth, The True Intellectual System of the Universe (1678), III, 418, quoted in Basil Willey, Seventeenth Century Background (1934), p.143.

LAW AND THE IDEOLOGY OF ORDER: THE PROBLEM OF KNOWLEDGE IN TH. HOBBES' "LEVIATHAN"*

Jon Stratton

It is a commonplace to say that Leviathan is based on a recognition of the importance of power and its fundamental place in all human relationships. What is not so often noted is that power is not an ahistorical constant which just happened to be recognised and theorised into a philosophy of the nature of man and the organisation of society by Hobbes. The concept of power, in a political context, arises out of the manner of existence of a society. It is not enough to say that all human relationships are mediated by power. It may be that we might wish to translate interaction accounted for, and therefore we might reasonably assume 'generated', by other terms such as obligation, into power relationships. However, this translation is only possible through the reification of power into a generalisable concept. It will be the contention of this paper that seventeenth century English society was a society undergoing radical and fundamental changes both to its political ordering and to the mode of practice of its social order, and that changes in the mode of practice of its social order reflect directly onto problems such as the socially constructed concept of knowledge and the practice of government. In the context of these changes Leviathan represents the most developed understanding of the complexities surrounding the new construction of knowledge gained through the individualising of the concept of 'method' and the developing practices of a social order based on the idea of the individual who must be held in check by the exercise of force. Hobbes' conception of what power was and how it related to the structure of society was a conception generated to try and help make sense of changes which appeared to him to be fundamental in the practice of order in early seventeenth century society.

---

* In this paper the pronoun 'he' is used throughout. The reason for this is that Hobbes uses 'he' throughout Leviathan and in following his thought I did not want to become involved in the important, but here not fundamentally relevant, issue of Hobbes' view of women. It should not be necessary for me to add that no sexism is intended.

The practical expression of shifts in what is experienced as being 'knowledge' and in the practice of order may be found in, among other places, a new understanding and practice of what we call law. Leviathan gives us a new view of law as being fundamental to the structure of social order rather than being a reflection of a God-given social order which it exists to preserve. This new view of law and its function is grounded by Hobbes in his elaboration of the way in which the individual lives the world. Near the end of the second part of Leviathan, which is, in effect, the end of the secular outline of the constitution of Hobbes' Commonwealth, Hobbes writes:

> 'Hitherto I have set forth the nature of Man (whose Pride and other Passions have compelled him to submit himselfe to Government); together with the great power of his Governour ...' (1)

Here, as Strauss(2) points out, Hobbes is not suggesting that it is in the nature of social relationships that they must be controlled by the imposition of power. Hobbes is saying, rather, that it is in nature of man, and the most significant aspect of this nature is singled out as Pride. Strauss pursues this point in the context of the moral basis of Hobbes' view of man but there is another side to the problem which may be ascertained by asking what is the existential grounding which allows the individual such pride that he must be kept in check. The answer to this problem comes some two chapters earlier; vain-glory which appears to lead to pride is based on valuing oneself by one's great wealth or by one's large number of kin or friends or it resides in those that:

> '... have a great and false opinion of their own Wisdome, |and| take upon them to reprehend the actions, and call in question the Authority of them that govern, and so to unsettle the lawes with their publique discourse, as that nothing shall be a Crime, but what their own designes require should be so.' (3)

So vain-glory, when not based on material things such as wealth or popularity,is based on a wrong attitude to one's own 'Wisdome'. Significantly whereas a multitude of friends give one the courage to 'violate the lawes' a person's great and false opinion of their own Wisdome 'unsettles the lawes'. Moreover the end result of this unsettling of the laws is that crime, which as we shall see Hobbes defines as transgression of the Law, comes to be individualised in the sense that it becomes defined with reference to individual opinion. In other words, other things that generate vain-glory only enable one to transgress the pre-existing laws: that is to say they generate activities which, taking the laws for granted, then overstep them. By contrast the use of 'Wisdome' strikes at the very root of the laws by criticising them publicly.

The problem, however, is not located for Hobbes in the social situation of criticism. It lies one step removed in the very possibility of criticism. This possibility exists, according to Hobbes, because each individual has his own 'Wisdome'. This would appear to be implicit in the above quotation. Hobbes is here talking about one's own 'false' (note the categoricalness here) opinion of one's personal 'Wisdome'. The implication would appear to be that each individual has formulated, somehow, his own 'Wisdome'. Hobbes' problem here is not what happens when one person's Wisdome is not in congruence with another's, but one's attitude towards one's own Wisdome, which is fundamentally distinct from the Wisdome of other individuals. The problem for Hobbes here is that of how one individual's personal 'Wisdome' may be related to that of other individuals. This, as we shall see, leads Hobbes to consider the relationship between an individual's 'Wisdome' - we, perhaps, might think of this as an opinion or a personal belief - and the problem of knowledge as a belief system which establishes the social order.

Let us turn to the problem of crime in Leviathan:

> 'The source of every Crime, is some defect of the Understanding or some error in Reasoning, or some sudden force of the Passions.' (4)

Crime is here defined by Hobbes in such a way that it exists in its own right quite unambiguously in relation to some absolute moral order. Moreover it exists in relation to that Law which is the practical manifestation of the controlling 'power' which exists because men have submitted themselves to it:

> 'A Crime, is a sinne, consisting in the Committing (by Deed or Word) of that which the law forbiddeth, or the omission of what it hath commanded.' (5)

Now what Hobbes is concerned with is not the practice of crime but where crime as a practice comes from; in other words what it is that gives individuals the ability to commit crimes. We may note here that Hobbes' conception of Crime is dependent upon a view of the Law as being 'right' not merely because it is exercisable but because it is Right in some absolute sense. I would suggest that much of Leviathan is concerned not only with articulating a theory of law as being based on power but with then bringing that law into harmony with Hobbes' belief in Divine Order (or Law) which society reflects. It is this isomorphism which gives transgression its absolute quality. The differentiation between these two forms of law in relation to human beings is well brought out in Hobbes' discussion of how a 'defect of Understanding' may be a source of Crime. Hobbes suggests that '... ignorance of the Civill Law, shall excuse a man in a strange Country, till it be declared to him'.(6) However, if an individual in a strange country attempts to teach a new Religion or teaches anything that might lead people to disobey the civil law then this transgresses the Law of Nature. Thus it is individual 'Wisdome' which mediates between civil law and absolute order.

Here we have our first intimation of how individual Wisdome may be a threat. It is a threat when it is able to transgress the Law of Nature by teaching a new Religion - I shall return to this point later - and it is a threat when it enables an individual to challenge the civil law as being 'right'. The problem of knowing what is 'right' brings us to Hobbes' discussion of reason and the question of the possibility of erroneous Reasoning. Hobbes breaks this category down into three possibilities: first the presumption of false principles; second the impact of false teachers, that is to say people who spread teaching 'which either is a misinterpretation of the Law of Nature' or is 'inconsistent with the duty of a Subject'; third the effect of 'Erroneous Inferences from True Principles'.(7) The question now is what does the individual think he has when he orders his life in the light of the conclusions he has gained from any of these three possible modes of erroneous Reasoning?

The answer inevitably must be that the individual considers himself to have 'Wisdome'. Wisdome which is inherently his because, whilst possibly based on other people's information, such as that given by teachers, it is made the individual's own by the personal use of Reason. Reason, for Hobbes, is not a faculty of the mind; it is an activity the possibility for which is dependent upon the individual's interaction with 'society':

> '... it appears that Reason is not as Sense, and Memory, borne with us; nor gotten by Experience onely; as Prudence is; but attayned by Industry; first in the apt imposing of Names; and secondly by getting a good and orderly Method in proceeding from the Elements, which are Names, to Assertions made by connexion of one of them to another.' (8)

Reason becomes the pivotal practice which allows the individual to engage with other individuals in society. It is reason which generates individual 'Wisdome' but the practice of reason is only possible once the world is labelled by language. Now, leaving aside the problem of language, it is possible to see that Hobbes' view of science as giving 'knowledge' is dependent not only, as he says, on Reasoning[(9)] but is also dependent on the generation of correct Reason, through interaction with society, in the first place. Indeed, for Hobbes, there could not be incorrect Reason; there could only be mistakes made in the use of Reason or Reason based on false principles. Reason in the abstract must be, by definition, correct. Thus, for Hobbes, an argument could not be 'reasonable' in the sense of being convincing; it would either be right because it was based on right principles and used the method of Reason, or it would be wrong because it was based on incorrect principles or because a mistake had been made in the use of reason as a method. However, whilst '... Reason itselfe is always Right Reason ...'[(10)] which is to say that the correctness of Reason in the abstract is an inherent part of the conceptualisation of Reason, '... no one mans Reason, nor the Reason of any number of men, makes the certaintie'.[(11)] Thus, no matter how right Reason may be in the abstract, the individual is liable to make mistakes in using it. It is because of this that all conclusions reached by individuals are questionable.

In his discussion of the ordering of society Hobbes takes this understanding of what reason is and goes on to draw this conclusion:

> 'And therefore, as when there is a controversy in an account, the parties must by their own accord, set up for right Reason, the Reason of some Arbitrator or Judge, to whose sentence they will both stand or (their) controversie must either come to blows, or be undecided, for want of a right Reason constituted by Nature.' (12)

Reason, then, is not only inherently right but it is also directly related to Nature - the implication being, as we shall see when we come to talk about Natural Law, that Nature itself is 'right'. But Hobbesian man is a man who does not have direct access to Reason. The problem then becomes one of elucidating where the knowledge lies that 'Reason' is being used correctly. If all men reasoned correctly using correct principles then all men would be in fundamental agreement; it is because men do not all agree that we know that either they are not using the right principles or they are not using reason with proper methodological rigour. If this interpretation of Hobbes' thought is correct, it might be suggested that Hobbes' premise is not that in the natural state all men are for some reason essentially separated from one another and in continual war with each other[(13)] but, rather, quite the reverse. Hobbes' basic image of society is of a harmonious society where man, using his reason, is on amicable terms with his neighbours and where this is occasioned because reason is 'right' and is also 'natural'. However, in the day-to-day life of Hobbesian individuated man, where correct Reason is not always practised, disputes do arise and when they do what is required is an 'Arbitrator or Judge'. The mere fact of arbitration, it would seem, brings the individuals, and therefore perhaps 'the social order', closer to observance of the right Reason constituted by Nature. In other words, there is an implication here that arbitration itself is an essentially <u>reasonable</u> activity, reasonable in the sense that its practice is an act of 'Reason'. It is significant also that arbitration is here linked with legal terminology: 'Judge' and 'sentence'. Yet Hobbes is apparently here talking about disputes which do not involve the civil law as he defines the term with reference to imposed power. I would suggest that here, in his discussion of arbitration, Hobbes comes close to conflating his two views of society; his ideal of a harmonious society in which shared (correct) assumptions order the polity and his understanding of the society in which he was living where knowledge, the shared assumptions of the (correct) belief system, was obscured by bad use of Reason and the mistaken use of false principles from which to start the process of Reasoning. I will now attempt to explain this.

In order to understand what is going on here we must leave Leviathan for a moment and turn to the reality of seventeenth century society. Wrightson, writing of village society at this time, says:

> 'Some way removed from the notion of order espoused by the moralists and legislators ... lay the complex of attitudes which surrounded the maintenance of harmony not so much between God and man, or even prince and people, as between neighbours in the face to face and day to day relationships of the village community. Order, as it was conceived at this most intimate local level, was less a positive aspiration towards a national condition of disciplined social harmony than a negative absence of disruption conflict locally.' (14)

The focus at village level, then, is on an avoidance of disruption, but an avoidance which in its very articulation assumes that an order exists which can be disrupted. It is this assumption which is crucially important for it gives us the reverse of the conventional Hobbesian view of man in society. Rather than rules or laws having to be generated and then enforced in order to create and perpetuate a society which by virtue of these regulations may subsequently be said to be ordered, here we have a society which takes for granted its existence and organises itself on this premise to ensure its continuity. This situation is one well understood by anthropologists; it is one in which all the members of a society take for granted the same fundamental belief system which means that, as Gluckman notes in The Ideas of Barotse Jurisprudence:

> '... all ... members adhere to the same standards of right-doing and wrong-doing as the judges ...'. (15)

There is no question here of the possibility of moral objections to the law, no question that the law or any part of it might be 'wrong' in any way. Law in the sense of a consciously articulated set of regulations does not exist in this context. Indeed, 'law' does not order such a society in the sense of articulating and proscribing certain activities; law is solely the re-ordering of that society where the day-to-day interaction breaks down. It must be emphasised, as Wrighton does in the context of seventeenth century village society, that I am not here suggesting any romanticised view of the harmonious village or conflict-less society. These societies have innumerable conflicts; the point is that they are experienced and understood differently and as a result they are dealt with differently. The emphasis is not placed on punishment for transgression - apart from anything else it is very difficult to know exactly when a taken for granted order has been transgressed - it is placed on mediation and reconciliation when disputes occur or the order is threatened in some other way. Here we may refer back to Hobbes' use of arbitration and see more clearly how it would operate in Hobbes' ideal society. Societies such as those discussed above presuppose an ideal of harmony and work continually to preserve it. Illusion though it might be, its existence is embedded in, indeed is, the collective belief system and its assumption is necessary to the on-going existence of these societies.

Turning to the problem of disorder once more, Wrighton again notes:

> 'Wherever possible mediation was preferred, though it was not always successful'. (16)

By way of example he goes on to cite the case of one Adam Martindale who, in spite of having been badly beaten up, refused to take the matter to the courts - to the imposed law - because he 'took all such courses for pure revenge ...'.(17) Assuming we can take this as Martindale's own view, it is a particularly interesting statement. In societies which make use of an imposed law that law is understood as being for the purposes of social regulation. Martindale, living his life in a situation where 'law' was conceived in terms of the re-ordering and continued articulation of reciprocity, can only conceive of imposed law in those terms. As such he considers that the courts deal in 'pure revenge', which might be said to be the outer limit of reciprocity. It is experienced as the most base form of reciprocity, reciprocity which takes no cognisance of the socio-cultural context within which it operates, where it is the end of the individual action which is perceived as important not the harmony of the society. For Martindale, then, the court is outside his concept of the ordered society in which the problem is not so much to establish guilt or innocence but to preserve the reciprocal ordering of the society. It is, I would suggest, an understanding of mediation in a manner somewhat similar to this which informs Hobbes' discussion of its importance and manner of use. This conflict between the understandings of the practice of social order may be illustrated from Wrighton again, when he talks of a case where the constable - it was occupiers of this post who had the invidious task of mediating between the two forms of law and order - of Worsley, Lancashire attempted to discriminate different degrees of culpability after a purge of unlicensed ale-houses. The clerk of the peace simply dismissed this attempt at gradation based on the social context and exercised the imposed law.(18)

Now it may be demonstrated that Hobbes' understanding of social order and of the law is very similar to the outline I have just given. For example, Hobbes writes:

> '... the same Law which dictateth to men that have no Civil Government, what they ought to do, and what to avoyd in regard of another, dictateth the same in common-wealths that is to the Consciences of Sovereign Princes, and to Sovereign Assemblies; there being no Court of Natural Justice but in the conscience only; where not Man but God reigneth; whose Lawes ... in respect of God, as he is the Author of Nature are Natural.' (19)

The first thing to notice here is the relation between the Sovereign's conscience and natural justice, in 'Common-wealths' it is in the Sovereign that natural justice resides. It is also, for Hobbes, in the Sovereign that the power to make civil law resides. Thus civil law becomes a reflection of the Law of Nature and, I would suggest, the conscience of the Sovereign is given practical expression in his use of his Wisdome. For Hobbes, then, the Sovereign inevitably uses Reason and uses it correctly. The Sovereign, then, is the ultimate link between the ordering of society and the divine order. Hobbes, however, goes one step further and suggests that in societies which have no Civil

Government society is ordered directly by Natural Law, that is to say the Law of God which orders creation. In these societies there is no need for an imposed power to regulate and control the society because all live in accordance with the Law of Nature. Indeed, from Hobbes' perspective how·else could such a society exist? Natural Justice here, I would suggest, must be present in all individuals; Wisdome is not differentiated, it is the single belief system which informs all social interaction.

In the context of Natural Justice we may note here the historical development of the concept of equity in parallel with the development of imposed law, for this is what the Worsley constable,mentioned above, wished exercised. Equity refers to the situation where a court takes into account more than the matter immediately before it. It is, therefore, a concept not relevant to societies where the starting point for the 'law' is the social context. It is only of significance in those societies where the principle and practice of imposed law is so strongly adhered to that it is necessary to recognise institutionally the possibility that the law should at times be tempered. In England the concept and practice of equity in this context originated in the late sixteenth and early seventeenth centuries when:

> '... reports of equity cases began to make their appearance and then ... the doctrine of judicial precedent turned the principles of fair dealing into a settled system as technical as the common law'. (20)

Hobbes, of course, given what I have just said about his understanding of natural justice, saw the place of equity - which must be implicit in civil law as it reflects Natural Law - as being the reason of the Sovereign.

The developing articulation and institutionalisation of equity is a reflection of the development and exercise of a concept of law where that law is perceived as existing <u>outside</u> of the community and is imposed upon it. It is to this change that we must now turn our attention. Outside here refers to a conception of law where what is regarded as the law is not perceived as in any way pre-given to the society in which it operates. When Edward Phelps, speaker of the House of Commons in 1604, said:

> 'The common law [is] grounded or drawn from the law of God, the Law of Reason, and the Law of Nations' (21)

he was not only justifying the legally actionable law of the land in terms of a higher law but he was also reasserting the common law as a manifestation of the order, the Law of God, within which society structured itself. The assumption behind the common law at this time was that, as a body of rules and regulations which structured society, it existed only to aid the ordering of society set out in the Law of God. Here is George Saltern on this problem:

> 'Now I take in hand to speak of our ancient Lawes, and God is the beginning and end of my worke ...'. (22)

God created the world: as an aspect of this creation he created man; logically then society owes its existence to God and, as a consequence, its order must be the order that reflects the order immanent in God. As a result, 'knowledge' is construed as being within the belief system rather than as something alienated, which must be discovered. Judson sums up the problem from the point of view of Law when she says:

> 'Law was normally regarded as more than human, as the reflection of eternal principles of justice' (23)

and here we have in a nutshell what is the most intriguing problem that surrounds the civil war. Both parliament and king not only thought that God was on their side, but that the law was as well. From one point of view this problem may be traced back to Henry VIII. When in 1534 Henry enacted the Act of Supremacy, he gave legal recognition in the most drastic manner to this conception of the relation between divine law and common law; from this moment on heresy was no longer merely a church offence, it became treason.[(24)] Simultaneously the link between the enacted law of the land and the law of God was recognised as being focused in the growing power of the ruler - thus paving the way for the developing theory of Absolutism and Divine Right.[(25)]

This, however, is only one illustration of the dramatic shift which was occurring in the practice of law throughout the late sixteenth century. Plunkett, for example, notes that in mere bulk:

> '... the thirty-eight years of Henry VIII's reign ... produced a volume of statutes equal to the combined output of the previous two and a half centuries ...'. (26)

Moreover, the statutes became more detailed and tended to include long preambles explaining their purpose. At the same time older legal forms were falling into desuetude. For example, Year Books were not printed after 1532, and the Register of Writs was used less and less. Perhaps the most interesting point, however, is that from the sixteenth century onwards, indeed from 1483, collections of statutes began to be printed. By the early seventeenth century this movement had culminated in the completely revised version of the complete Statutes edited by Pulton and published from 1611 onwards. Increasingly the common law was perceived as being closely related to the Statutes and the law was perceived not as practice but as a historical and imposed body of legislation to which reference had constantly to be made. This new historical awareness was matched by the courts' increasing concern with the use of precedents. In practical terms, this was manifested in the shift of emphasis in the late medieval Year Books from a concern with procedure and discussion - where, as with Gluckman's Barotse, lay what we understand as equity - to a concern with the presentation of the case and, most importantly, the decision on it.

Even from this brief outline, it is obvious that the late sixteenth and early seventeenth centuries saw a radical shift in the practice of law which, it may be added, was reflected in a greater degree of institutional training for lawyers.(27) The common law came more and more to be seen as a historically continuous body which, by the nature of its organisation, was instituted and exercised in a hierarchical manner. Conceptually the problem increasingly came to be one of legitimation. More and more the ideology of the common law shifted from it being an institutional reflection and re-ordering of the pre-established order of the lived society to being the manifestation in terms of an imposed ordering of the Divine Law as understood by those in power.(28)

But this latter ,taken for granted understanding which acted to legitimate the common law could only continue to exist if the law itself as legislation was not challenged. The debate between King and Parliament challenged it. Both sides held their position to be legitimated by the extant body of law; both sides attempted to use the divinely legitimated law to back what we could call 'points of view' or ideological positions. The unified, because taken for granted, base of the law began to crack; each side searched to find 'fundamental' laws which would make their arguments unassailable. Judson notes that Englishmen in the early seventeenth century '... drew no clear distinctions between laws which were fundamental and laws which were not ...'.(29) This was because,for people of this period,all laws and no laws were fundamental, because all were reflections of the fundamental law of God. As soon as the attempt was made to discriminate some laws as fundamental from others which were not the end was in sight, for the same ontological arguments used to justify some laws could be used for others and the same critical positions invoked. The only solution, as Hobbes understood, was to view the Law of Nature as a set of moral precepts of which laws in society were a reflection.

The result of the dissension was that it became harder and harder for men to believe that the law existed as one constituted body of knowledge which somehow or other reflected the one Order established by God. Increasingly the philosophical debate came to be concerned with the nature and legitimacy of sovereignty; this is reflected in the etymological shift of the meaning of status. From its original meaning (as in the Ciceronian status reipublicae) of order, understood as the pre-existing order, which enabled it to be applied also to one's position in that order, it gained through the medieval linkage with Divine Law(30) a meaning of 'good' order and was, by the time of Hobbes, coming to be used as 'state' with its modern connotation of a limited, sovereign, order within which hierarchised law/power is exercised. Thus the shift in meaning of law and the shift in meaning of status are both allied to a change in the understanding of order from something which was pre-given and which should be preserved to something which was based on power and hierarchically enforced on individuals who together constitute a society. The limits of the state now become the limits of its ability to enforce its laws. This, in turn, is related to the idea that competing fundamental beliefs are possible provided they do not threaten the stability of the order in which they are allowed to exist.

Here then is our clue to Hobbes' understanding of Reason and Wisdome. Hobbes' genius lay not so much in his recognition of the importance of power in a society of individuals where there is no single unified belief system, but one step further back. It exists in his struggle to understand that people could hold fundamentally different beliefs and his attempt to understand what would be the implications of this for social order; it is this that lies at the root of his discussions of reason as a constructed method rather than as pre-given,and of knowledge as something which would order the previously unknown. It should be noted that it is Reason used as a method which allows Hobbes to identify correctly the inherently Reasonable Laws of Nature which then become an object of knowledge to which reference may be made. Logically, for Hobbes, societies without the mediation of civil law between individual and society must live the Laws of Nature. In other words, this fundamental knowledge is a practice for such societies, not something which is alienated and which must be 'discovered'. The significance of Hobbes' State of Nature, then, is not that it represents Man but that it represents fallen Man, man where knowledge as the practice of personal wisdom has been lost. The essence of correct knowledge for Hobbes lay in its alliance with true Religion which, together with the Law of Nature, exists in that which was created by God. This is why the teaching of a new religion transgresses the Law of Nature. This point has been well demonstrated by Hood in The Divine Politics of Th. Hobbes.

Those who have foreseen in Leviathan the image of totalitarianism are right to an extent, for in this book Hobbes is attempting to outline a society based on power where knowledge is controlled. However, it is a society where that power is so used in conjunction with the method of Reason that social harmony might be reinstated through the repairing of a single (correct) belief system. In such a society the hierarchical articulation and practice of law by means of exercised power would not be necessary. Dare I suggest that Hobbes wished to see the withering away of the State?

Footnotes

1. *Leviathan*, p.362. All references are to the Penguin edition, ed. C. McPherson, Harmondsworth, 1968.

2. L. Strauss, *The Political Philosophy of Hobbes*, trans. E. Sinclair, Chicago, 1952, p.13.

3. *Leviathan*, p.341.

4. *Op cit*, p.338.

5. *Op cit*, p.336.

6. *Op cit*, p.338.

7. *Op cit*, pp.339-341.

8. *Op cit*, p.115.

9. See *op cit*, Chapter IX 'Of the Severall Subjects of Knowledge', *passim.*

10. *Op cit*, p.111.

11. *Op cit*, p.111.

12. *Loc sit*.

13. The common understanding of Hobbes' idea of the situation of man in his 'natural' state is drawn from *Leviathan*, Chapter XIII. See also C. McPherson, *The Philosophy of Possessive Individualism*, Cambridge, 1962.

14. Wrightson, 'Two Concepts of Order', in J. Brewer and J. Styles, *An Ungovernable People*, London, 1980, pp.23-24.

15. M. Gluckman, *The Ideas in Barotse Jurisprudence*, London, repr. 1972, p.10.

16. Wrightson, *op cit*, p.30.

17. Quoted in *loc sit*.

18. Wrightson, *op cit*, p.32.

19. *Leviathan*, p.394.

20. G. Keeton and L. Sheriden, *Equity*, London, 2nd ed. 1976, p.4.

21. Quoted in M. Judson, The Crisis of the Constitution, New Brunswick, 1949, p.53.

22. Quoted in op cit.

23. Op cit, p.44.

24. It may be noted that the Statute of Treason passed by Edward I threatened the whole basis of the old order by making everybody responsible to the Crown, in contrast to the feudal system of reciprocal oaths and responsibilities. Henry VIII rationalised the problem by making the monarch responsible for both the idea of order as it emanated from God through Christianity as well as for the secular order. This formulation of the monarch's role is very similar to Hobbes' view of the role of the Sovereign.

25. See J. N. Figgis, Divine Right of Kings, Cambridge, 1914.

26. T. Plucknett, A Concise History of the Common Law, London, 1956, p.324.

27. See Holdsworth, History of English Law II, London, 1936, pp.267-71.

28. In practice cf e.g. Wrightson, p.35, on increase in regulative prosecutions. Also C. Bridenbaugh, Vexed and Troubled Englishmen, Oxford, 1968.

29. Judson, p.55.

30. M. Wilks, The Problem of Sovereignty in the later Middle Ages, Cambridge, 1963, p.158.

LAW AND CONSCIOUSNESS IN EARLY SEVENTEENTH CENTURY ENGLAND

Michael Lane

In many respects we have an exceptionally detailed and elaborate picture of England in the first half of the seventeenth century. Certainly since Dr. Johnson - and to a high degree in the present century - the writing of the period has been given pride of place in the English literary canon, and with that has gone a commensurate degree of critical attention and exegesis. Equally, since Clarendon, the epochal character of the Civil War has fascinated historians and laypersons alike. In their pursuit of the causes of this traumatically uncharacteristic event the period preceding it has been exhaustively studied: in the last century generally from the point of view emphasising religious and constitutional conflict; in the present generally from one where material forces have been given special weight. I suspect that the sequence from Elizabeth I to Charles II is easily the best known chronology of the Kings and Queens of England, whilst the two generations leading up to and including the struggles of Cavaliers and Roundheads contains the densest patch of common historical myth in our culture.

At the same time we have available a much broader context in which to place the specific cultural-historical picture of Jacobean and Caroline England. Thus we can set religious conflicts in England in the broader matrix of both European and North American patterns, whilst the researches of Frances Yates and others has further elaborated our picture by revealing the significance of hermetic philosophy. The growth of scientific ideologies in the period has similarly received considerable attention, as has the persistence of traditional and magical beliefs.

I am going to argue here that there is a third component in the trinity of forces which shaped the consciousness of the generation preceding the Civil War that has received less attention than it deserves. Alongside religion and science we must set the law.

differently about them. They had none of that aura of mystery or distance which commonly surrounds not just courts but legal processes in general today. If courts were disliked and feared it was not because they were unknown: absolutely the reverse was true.

Through litigation and prosecution, then, all classes of the population were affected by legal processes and interventions. In itself this must have produced at the very least a veneer of legal knowledge. People knew how courts worked and what happened in them. There is, in addition, evidence which strongly suggests that legal knowledge of a more substantive and substantial kind was part of the common culture. Legal texts were a significant element in private libraries, for instance. Again, we don't just find them in the private libraries of the rich and powerful (though we should not underestimate *their* importance); we also frequently find law books listed in the wills of persons of low to middling status - small merchants, shopkeepers, small yeoman farmers, and so on. Law books come second only to religious texts in the libraries of Kentish townspeople (excluding professionals such as lawyers themselves) studied by Peter Clark. As he remarks, the picture revealed by a study of the books people owned is very different from the one familiar to us through the work of Wright and Bennett, where the emphasis lies on literary texts. Littleton's *New Tenures* (which first appeared in 1481 and was the basis for Coke's famous *Commentaries*) was in the sixteenth century reprinted more frequently than even the Bible.

But perhaps the best evidence of the general cultural significance of the law is to be found in the educational role which the Inns of Court played. Lawrence Stone has drawn our attention to the educational explosion of the late sixteenth century. In the thirty years after 1550 admissions to Oxford and Cambridge trebled, to reach around 450 each a year. After a hiccough in the 1590's, they rose again to hover around the 500 mark throughout the first forty years of the seventeenth century. Stone estimates that of the 1,240 graduates in the peak decade, the 1630's, 430 (35%) went into the church whilst 190 (15%) went into law and medicine. However, what is remarkable about the late sixteenth century and early seventeenth century is that Oxford and

One of the most striking features of the late sixteenth century and the first half of the seventeenth century is the extraordinary pervasiveness and penetration both of legal thought and legal action. As W. J. Jones has pointed out in Politics and the Bench: The Judges and the Origins of the English Civil War, it was an outstandingly litigious age. (Why this was so is a question to which I shall return). 'It is impossible to give comparative figures, but it would seem that practically everyone over the rank of yeoman was likely during the course of his life to be involved at law in suits before the major courts, which were single or multitudinous.' There was a tenfold increase in writs issued by the Court of Common Pleas. During the reign of Elizabeth one nobleman was reputed to be engaged in twenty-four pieces of litigation simultaneously. According to Carey (The Present State of England, 1627), a lawsuit between two men over a hive of bees cost each over £500 in legal expenses. In the Court of Chancery, for which we have reasonably accurate figures, at least 16,000 cases were outstanding in 1621 (Coke said 35,000 but this was an exaggeration). By 1653 the figure had risen to 23,000. Nor were the ordinary people spared. Whilst they were unlikely to imitate their social superiors in appearing before the higher courts, we must not forget the persistence of a dense fabric of lower level tribunals - quarter and petty sessions, borough, manorial and ecclesiastical courts. Alan Macfarlane's Witchcraft in Tudor and Stuart England gives, in passing, some illuminating indications of how ordinary villagers might find themselves in court, either accused of or giving evidence of offences such as Sabbath-breaking, non-attendance at church, misbehaving in the churchyard, quarrelling and scolding, refusing to pay tithes, and so on. It would be a mistake, however, to regard the ordinary people as coming to courts only in connection with the prosecution of offences. Minor courts mediated in a variety of disputes, disagreements and simple uncertainties that we now regard as either inappropriate or too trivial to warrant seeking legal intervention. In short, litigation and the courts were for everyone, the common people included, a normal part of everyday life, not - as they are today - distant and exceptional phenomena to which one is drawn only by aberration or catastrophe. It is not simply that the courts then exercised a range of functions far wider than they do today, though that of course is true. Rather it is that people felt and thought very

Cambridge were not alone as elite educational institutions. In addition to providing a professional training in law for graduates (we must remember that the common law, unlike the civil and canon, was not taught at all in the universities), the Inns of Court themselves played very much the same broad socialising role as the universities and enjoyed as much if not more social esteem.

'At this period there were in practice not two universities but three in the kingdom. The third was the Inns of Court whither increasing numbers of young noblemen and gentry resported in order to study the law and at the same time pick up the airs and graces of the nearby Court ' (Stone, Crisis of the Aristocracy). In his study of the Inns of Court in the fifty years before 1680, Professor Prest estimates an annual entry of 264 students to the Inns throughout the 1630's, which is proportionately a far higher ratio in relation to Oxbridge admissions than ever before or since. The mark upon the culture and consciousness of the ruling class can be imagined. As Stone puts it: 'In the late sixteenth century and early seventeenth century more nobles and landed gentlemen acquired a smattering of a legal education than at any time before or possibly since. Indeed although the popularity of the Universities and the Inns of Court rose together, the Inns were at all times more frequented by the gentry than both the older Universities put together.' In the Inns themselves educational functions developed until brought to a halt by the Civil War, from which they never recovered. The status of Readers, who lectured upon statutes, was formalised and in addition students were regularly called on to perform in the moots, which gave them experience of and practice in legal analysis and argument.

Our final indication of the centrality of legal understanding in the culture and consciousness of early seventeenth century England can be seen in the very high proportion of legally educated men in political and high administrative office. The Bench, the Attorney General and above all the office of Lord Chancellor grew steadily in power and prominence. The dominance of lawyers in Elizabethan and Jacobean Houses of Commons is an historian's commonplace, but one well worthy of note. A little more than two-fifths of the Members of the 1593 Parliament had received some legal education. By the Parliament of 1621, the proportion had risen to about a half, whilst at the beginning of the Long Parliament in the autumn of 1640 more than six out of ten members had attended an Inn (though far fewer had actually been called as barristers).

The real question, though, which we must ask has less to do with these external characteristics of the law and much more to do with the extent and nature of the penetration of law into culture and consciousness. How did it affect the way in which people felt, thought and understood their world? I propose to attempt to answer this question rather obliquely by looking at those particular aspects of common law thinking which have, I hope, relevance beyond the narrow confines of the courts and litigation.

The first - and for me easily the most important of these aspects - is the adversary character of the typical English judicial process. English courts do not, save rather trivially and incidentally, purport to be tribunals designed for the elucidation of truth. They are, rather, arenas where two opponents battle for victory. The judge is no privileged creature winnowing ultimate verities from the chaff of events. He (or very occasionally, nowadays, she) is simply a referee who knows the rules of the game and stops the opponents delivering foul blows against one another. 'The principal duty of a judge is to suppress force and fraud, where force is the more pernicious when it is open, and fraud when it is close and disguised. Add thereto contentious suits, which ought to be spewed out as the surfeit of courts ' (Bacon, 'Of Judicature'). Juries are neither omniscient nor do they dispense justice. They keep tally of the points and decide who has won. This is a schematic and over-simplified picture, but essentially faithful to reality. It is, moreover, a model of the process of law that emerged in the course of the sixteenth century and began to dominate thinking - though it was still far from clear-cut - in the seventeenth. Until that time the model of law that had dominated feudal society with its explicit and implicit invocations of divine intervention and its original conception of a jury not so much of peers as of community fellows, prevailed. It clearly continued to resonate in the mind of seventeenth century people, contradicting and counter-pointing newly emergent practices and conceptions.

The adversary model rests on or implies a number of assumptions. To say that it rejects truth as a category is clearly too strong. Nonetheless the growing recognition that, in practice, certain components of the true might be unknowable seems to me as much a solvent of traditional bonds in the field of consciousness as Marx argued money was in the material field. This is apparent in several ways, for instance in the development of the 'fiction' as a legal device. It can also be seen in one of the domains in which the law changed most conspicuously in the early seventeenth century, that of contract. Whilst the emergence in contract of the doctrine of consideration is a complex matter, it has to do (at least in part) with the external and objective nature of a bargain as opposed to the metaphysics of a promise. By the early seventeenth century, courts were in little doubt that their task was to enforce the former, not the latter. Next, the adversary model fits most readily with a conception of society as composed of relatively atomised persons. It is individualistic rather than collectivistic, egalitarian rather than hierarchical. Indeed, it is hard to imagine how an adversary system could function, at the level of consciousness, in a social order composed of radically different statuses. Third, the adversary model presupposes that fights or struggles are socially and cognitively acceptable. It legitimates conflict and implies the antagonism between people is so inescapable that the legal system can do no more than take them as its very basis. I am inclined to regard this as quite critical in the formation of Civil War consciousness. The image and ethic of a struggle for victory that had become essential and integral to English law provided a striking alternative to all those fundamentally consensual models of the social order that typify feudalism - and indeed persist to provide the most striking images of society in the work of Shakespeare.

The second aspect of English law in the early seventeenth century on which I want to focus attention could be described either as the decisive rejection of codification or, indifferently, as the decisive acceptance of the common law. Until the Reformation the common law had co-existed with the codes of the civilians and particularly the highly codified Canon law that emerged with Gratian's Decretals. Renaissance classicism, moreover, had served to remind scholars of the central role played by codes in Roman law. From the 1530's to the era of Bacon and Coke, the replacement of common law by codified law was an intermittently pursued chimera, but it is significant that among the many movements for law reform in the Commonwealth such aspirations were marginal. Indeed, in his account of law reform movements between 1640 and 1660 Veall treats the parliamentary triumph as synonymous with the victory of the common law. Not until Bentham was the issue of a code to be seriously raised again. Two related components of English common law strike me as of particular interest to the student of general culture and consciousness: they are the concept of precedent and the salience of case law. Both these present issues of great complexity so my discussion here must of necessity be selective. (In particular the concept of precedent during the early seventeenth century was confounded with the question of judicial politics and authority). 'Judges', said Francis Bacon, 'ought to remember that their office is *jus dicere*, and not *jus dare*; to interpret law, and not to make law or give law ' ('Of Judicature'). With the virtual elimination of the transcendental as *fons et origo* of law, precedents came to be seen as a kind of expression or distillation of pure human reason: what Coke spoke of as 'that which hath been refined and perfected by all the wisest men in former succession of ages, and proved and approved by continual experience to be good and profitable for the common wealth ' (*Le Quart Part des Reportes*, 1604). Few may have been so eulogistic as Whyte when he wrote (*For the Sacred Law of the Land*, 1652): 'Our laws are sacred, pious, good, merciful and just ... and he must forfeit the whole reason of man who desires a change', but most who thought about the matter would have agreed with his assertion that common law and human reason were very close to one another. Nor did this conception deny the possibility of change; merely, to use Coke's words, that 'Out of the old fields must come the new corn.'

Precedents were articulated through individual cases and it is to case law which I now want to turn. Before I consider the substantive issue though, some remarks on law reporting are germane. For the period from the reign of Edward I to that of Henry VIII the Year Books are the nearest thing we have to law reporting in the modern sense, though it is precisely the details of specific cases we expect to find in modern reports that are missing. Law reporting in the modern sense is basically an invention of the sixteenth century when, in addition, it could be disseminated via the medium of print. If we include the reports which draw on or abstract the Year Books, eight series of reports cover the whole period to 1560. I can find at least sixteen report series dealing with the years 1561-1600, and no fewer than twenty-seven for the years 1601-1642. They characteristically record the essential facts of the case and the legal arguments of the judges, though their reliability varies and some - notoriously those of the great Coke himself - contain a great deal of the reporter's own views and comments. When we examine the substance or content of the case-law tradition the most striking attribute is its anecdotal character. There is a continual tension or contradiction between narrative specificity on the one hand and the untangling of abstract legal principles on the other. In the reports of cases and, almost inevitably, in the jurisprudence of which they are an integral part, we can see the rabid empiricism of English culture whose twentieth century counterpart Perry Anderson so vigorously attacked in 'Components of the national culture'. The practice of both learning by way of the cases and arguing by means of the cases was an early indication of the absent centre, the atheoretical void and the denial of totality that Anderson has argued typifies twentieth century British bourgeois culture.

To sum up, then, I have argued that the generation which preceded the Civil War was one singularly marked by the law. All levels of society had, through prosecution and litigation, an intimate acquaintance with legal processes and legal knowledge. All sorts of people owned law books and the upper strata saw legal education in the Inns of Court as in every respect comparable to and in certain respects more desirable than an education at the ancient universities. Legal language and imagery based on the law permeate writing of all kinds. Social, political and economic conflicts in the reign of James I and Charles I are typically articulated as legal disagreements whilst Parliament was dominated by lawyers and the legally trained.

I have suggested that aspects of legal experience and legal thinking permeated general culture and left an ineradicable mark on the consciousness of the age. In particular the adversary model of the legal process which had crystallised towards the end of the sixteenth century legitimated the very idea of social conflict and made the expression of antagonistic relations between people intellectually acceptable. In conjunction with the explosion of legal actions, it served to diffuse the notion that the social fabric was seamed with disagreements and open struggles, whilst the revolutionary changes in law that had marked the Tudor period and continued into the early Stuart years served to confirm the view that the state and direction of the whole social structure were profoundly uncertain. Finally, the doctrine of precedent and the emphasis on case law, in contrast to the codified Canon and Roman law, served to assert the primacy of the empirical and specific, as against the abstract and theoretical.

HISTORICAL PROCESS, INDIVIDUAL AND COMMUNITIES IN MILTON'S EARLY PROSE

David Aers and Gunther Kress

For the historian of past forms of consciousness texts are the chief source of knowledge, the record of how men thought and felt. Language itself is a social activity expressing forms of life and consciousness evolved by specific social groups. It is a truism that different forms of language articulate different forms of life and perception. In the minute particulars of language writers express their attitudes towards inherited ideology. Linguistic structures carry important meanings which may be so habitual as to remain beneath the level of the writer's (or speaker's) explicit reflection. Words and sentences work at different levels of meaning, allowing subtle contradictions to co-exist in seemingly smooth surface forms. Language is used to present meaning and to evade it. Language can also constrain an individual's or group's consciousness of self and world. A study of writings based on summary or paraphrases misses a vital source of insight into contemporary forms and processes of thought and being.

We are aware of the problems we encounter and the approach we follow could have bearings on certain arguments within contemporary marxism centred on E. P. Thompson's critique of Althusser in *The Poverty of Theory* (Merlin, 1978) and Perry Anderson's *Arguments within English Marxism* (New Left Books, 1980), especially chapter two, 'Agency'. But ours is not an attempt at 'Theory', nor intended as an explicit intervention in the debate we have just referred to. Our methods of analysis, the specific evidence in this paper and the study of which it is part (to be published by Gill-Macmillan) may perhaps offer some contributions to the current marxist debate, but our purpose is the examination of specific discourses, their ideological and linguistic procedures. We wish to explore the complex ways in which received ideology and the challenges to received ideology function in texts. In this paper we concentrate on Milton's version of historical process and communities in *Areopagitica*, hoping to shed light on Milton's world-view and to sketch a form of inquiry which could be extended fruitfully to his other writings and those of his contemporaries, both the more radical and the conservative ones.

We will begin our discussion with a famous passage from *Areopagitica* (1644). It has often been quoted to illustrate Milton's strenuously active version of individual virtue and responsibility, to show his alleged emphasis on the individual's continually active struggle in a world shaped by constant acts of rational choice through which the individual and his community develop in knowledge and virtue:

> 'Good and evill we know in the field of this World grow up together almost inseparably; and the knowledge of good is so involved and interwoven with the knowledge of evill, and in so many cunning resemblances hardly to be discern'd, that those confused seeds which were impos'd on *Psyche* as an incessant labour to cull out, and sort asunder, were not more intermixt. It was from out the rinde of one apple tasted, that the knowledge of good and evill as two twins cleaving together leapt forth into the World. And perhaps this is that doom which *Adam* fell into of knowing good and evill, that is to say of knowing good by evill. As therefore the state of man now is; what wisdome can there be to choose what continence to forebeare without the knowledge of evill? He that can apprehend and consider vice with all her baits and seeming pleasures, and yet abstain, and yet distinguish, and yet prefer that which is truly better, he is the true warfaring Christian. I cannot praise a fugitive and cloister'd vertue, unexercis'd and unbreath'd, that never sallies out and sees her adversary, but slinks out of the race, where that immortall garland is to be run for, not without dust and heat. Assuredly we bring not innocence into the world, we bring impurity much rather: that which purifies us is triall, and triall is by what is contrary. That vertue therefore which is but a youngling in the contemplation of evill, and knows not the utmost that vice promises to her followers, and rejects it, is but a blank vertue, not a pure; her whitenesse is but an excrementall whitenesse; Which was the reason why our sage and serious Poet *Spencer*, whom I dare be known to think a better teacher than *Scotus* or *Aquinas*, describing true temperance under the person of *Guion*, brings him in with his palmer through the cave of Mammon, and the bowr of earthly blisse that he might see and know, and yet abstain. Since therefore the knowledge and survay of vice is in this world so necessary to the constituting of human vertue, and the scanning of error to the confirmation of truth,

> how can we more safely, and with lesse danger scout into the regions of sin and falsity then by reading all manner of tractats, and hearing all manner of reason?' (1)

The argument here is central to Milton's overall defence of the liberty to publish and debate freely. Since human purity, virtue and the discovery of 'truth' in the fallen world can only come through each individual's strenuous and fully conscious combat with 'evil', any suppression of this vital struggle will endanger virtue more than vice. For vice, in Milton's view, has all the advantage of being sanctioned by the weight of inertia, dominant traditions, unexamined customs and human sloth.[2] This represents the traditional reading of the passage. The linguistic particulars of the argument, however, actually suggest a far more complex, tortuous and confused stance than commentators have suggested.

In grasping the substance and implications of Milton's position here, we need to explore the meaning expressed through the organisation of language at the syntactic level. As Halliday's work so often illustrates, patterns of syntax may realise the writer's 'vision' and his underlying themes as they weave together 'different threads of meaning'.[3] Some important linguistic features certainly characterise this passage. Milton selects a number of abstract nouns and creates a discourse in which determinate human agents are conspicuously absent from the sequence he depicts. The passage opens with the claim that we know the abstractions 'good' and 'evil' as distinct entities which grow up as objects of human knowledge. It is noteworthy that they are not treated as attributes or adjectives describing aspects of human <u>activity</u>. Although Milton's claim overtly refers to a process involving growth it is striking that he presents this in a manner which precludes all reference to specific human agency in time. He does so by freely using the passive voice of verbs to delete agents, and by employing abstract rather than concrete and animate nouns as subjects (lines 1-6 in the passage quoted above). As commentators do not normally draw attention to these important characteristics we will outline the main linguistic features and their meaning. The first point to clarify is the basic relationship between an abstract noun such as 'knowledge', and a core sentence, in this case 'A knows B'. The writer can present his perception in either of two linguistic forms: he can select an abstract noun, or he can choose to develop the core sentence, stating the agent (A), the action (knows), and the affected participant (Y). Following general linguistic usage, we call the abstract noun forms nominalizations, thus indicating that they may be derived from the full sentence form. Now the sentence form commits the writer to expressing the 'knower' and the 'known'. It also demands the use of a specific tense, thus presenting the process in time. But these two requirements can be avoided by the use of abstract nouns, such as 'knowledge'. Such abstract nominalizations remove the possibility, or at least the need, to express tense. Where a writer finds problems with the naming of specific human agents or of specific objects, the abstract nominal form enables him to eliminate these from the surface of the text. Where a writer does not wish to, or cannot place an event in a specific time, indeed, where he may wish to present it as outside history, avoiding the use of tense may prove desirable. Furthermore, the use of nominalization enables the writer to treat events and historical processes involving human agents as entities which can function as agents in their own right, initiating action in sentences which purport to describe the real historical world where humans live and die. So in Milton's text 'good' and 'evil' at first seem to be autonomous agents, 'growing up', 'two twins' who 'leapt forth' from the apple rind Adam had tasted. This would be striking enough, but Milton has actually written that it is 'the knowledge ... [which] leapt forth' from the prohibited tree. This indicates how processes of human discovery may become thoroughly reified. For in the chosen linguistic form, these processes are transformed into an abstraction which has a bizarre life of its own, independent of the world of social being and human consciousness from which it has, in fact, been abstracted. If this is a common trait in the discourse it would suggest a writer who tended to forget that men immersed in specific situations make history, to forget that while abstract concepts are essential to our attempts to understand our world, they are not the reality being explored and can, indeed must, be subjected to a genuine dialogue with empirical evidence concerning the past and present. It would suggest a writer who, like Bacon's spider, spins out a self-generating conceptual universe which he wishes to substitute for the phenomena of the material world and social life on which he purports to comment.

We shall now move on to consider the sentences in which Milton gives his account of the procedures through which humans become virtuous and discover 'truth' (lines 15 ff. in the quoted passage). The most obvious impression is of the worthy man's strenuous activity and engagement in the social world. Milton condemns monkish withdrawal into the cloister, and praises running the race in the world's dust and heat with full apprehension of 'vice' and 'error'. Yet the strikingly active verbs mask important features which, as far as we know, commentators have ignored. Milton defines the Christian warrior he admires in the following sequence of verbs: 'He that <u>can apprehend</u> and <u>consider</u> vice ... and yet <u>abstain</u>, and yet <u>distinguish</u>, and yet <u>prefer</u> that which is truly better'. Struck by the overall impression of activity and the energy in the passage, readers have overlooked an extremely curious feature about these verbs. Although these verbs have a <u>transitive surface form</u> (that is, they appear in subject-verb-object structures), in fact the processes they depict are <u>not</u>, syntactically, transitive. That is, they are not actions done by someone/thing to someone/thing. Nothing is 'transacted' from X to Y. Indeed X alone is engaged in an activity, in which Y coincidentally and marginally also appears. We use the term non-transitive for such forms(4) to characterise their real semantic nature. The distinction allows us to draw attention to the seeming active engagement on the surface, and the underlying self-contained reflexive nature of the processes. The verbs in question involve mental processes with no particular consequences for 'virtuous' <u>practice</u>, and they all take the tense which eschews temporal dimensions and distinctions. Similarly with the verbs in the sentences which immediately follow. They describe the kind of contemplative 'virtue' Milton claims he 'cannot praise'. But they are presented in a form which also gives the 'virtue' he <u>can</u> praise. The syntactic agent is, again, a nominal abstraction, 'virtue'. This praiseworthy virtue, we gather, <u>sallies out</u> and <u>sees</u> the adversary. She never <u>slinks out</u> of the race 'where the immortal garland is <u>to be run for</u>'. Once again the verbs are <u>non-transactive</u> and the agent (already an abstract noun) simply does not engage with the world in any concrete <u>practice</u>. She may <u>sally out</u>, <u>see</u> and <u>run a race</u>, but effects nothing, engages in changing or preserving nothing. There is much activity, an atmosphere of immense energy, but an apparent lack of effectual action in this model. Given this, it is natural enough to take the verbs of apparent physical activity as figurative ones representing mental processes alone. If we do this, however, it ceases to be at all clear just how the 'virtue' Milton admires differs from the 'fugitive and cloistered virtue' he so contemptuously dismisses. After all, those favouring and teaching the cloistered life which culminates in the contemplative virtues have hardly seen monastic spirituality, labour and the 'war within' as an 'unexercised and unbreathed' slinking out of the spiritual race for salvation, with its dust, heat and all too potent 'adversary'. Milton's linguistic choices here actually reveal a striking similarity between what he thinks he '*cannot praise*' and what he thinks he *can* praise. Such similarity he quite failed to notice. This is not surprising, for our analysis has begun to disclose how Milton's language is more fit for dissolving social practices and historical processes than for engaging with these. There is much in the rest of this passage that yields similar conclusions, but here we must pass on, though in the longer version of this study, to be published in the book mentioned earlier, we will have more to say on this.

There we will also present an analysis of the various incompatible models of human knowledge which Milton deploys in *Areopagitica*. We now, however, have space only to consider one of the models with which Milton thinks about current revolutionary pursuits of religious knowledge and new ecclesiastic organisation. It comes after he has been celebrating the London of the early 1640's as the 'mansion house of liberty', home of 'beleaguered Truth' (*CPW*, II, 554-55). Milton is pleading to Parliament for toleration towards radical *protestant* activities and reminds the readers of the way the Jews built the temple, an episode he offers as a model for the present rulers of England in the present radical reformation:

> 'Yet these are the men cry'd out against for schismaticks and sectaries; as if, while the Temple of the Lord was building, some cutting, some squaring the marble, others hewing the cedars, there should be a sort of irrationall men who could not consider there must be many schisms and many dissections made in the quarry and in the timber, ere

> the house of God can be built. And when every stone is laid artfully together, it cannot be united into a continuity, it can but be contiguous in this world; neither can every peece of the building be of one form; nay rather the perfection consists in this, that out of many moderat varieties and brotherly dissimilitudes that are not vastly disproportionall arises the goodly and the gracefull symmetry that commends the whole pile and structure. Let us therefore be more considerat builders, more wise in spirituall architecture, when great reformation is expected.

Milton's boundless delight and faith in the exuberant energy of God's 'Englishmen', apparently elected by God himself 'to the reforming of Reformation' (p.553) runs through the long paragraph of which this is a very small portion (pp.551-55). But he is also offering a version of individual and collective action to Parliament as a guide in the present. As such it has some revealing features. To highlight these we will take the Old Testament source first (1 Kings, 5 and 6), then Milton's model and finally its implied application to the 'mansion house of liberty' in 1644. In the Biblical text King Solomon explicitly *commanded* the Jews to prepare stone before they brought it to the building-site, so that there was not any tool of iron heard in the house 'while it was in building' (1 Kings, 6.7, see *CPW*, II, 555, n.244). He himself *organised* the whole process. Indeed, as so often in texts written by and for members of the ruling classes, the men who actually did the work are continuously deleted, and in their place the single hero, the one royal architect and commander stars. For instance: 'So he built the house, and finished it; and covered the house with beams and boards of cedar. And then he built chambers against all the house ... And he built the walls of the house within with boards of cedar ... And he built twenty cubits on the sides of the house ... So Solomon overlaid the house within with pure gold: and he made a partition ...'. The authoritarian and conservative possibilities of the text, as the Yale editors note, were very well known in the seventeenth century. Given the explicitness about the absolute, unquestioned rule and control of the King, this fact is hardly surprising. The Old Testament text also makes it clear that it is *only* the King whom God addresses in connection with building the temple, not any of those involved in doing the actual work. Fairly obviously this does not suit Milton's radical purposes. So in *his* rendering of the story he simply deletes Solomon, deletes the

King and the controller. But who then, if anyone, does he present as governor(s), architect(s) and executive agent(s)? Attempting to answer the question we can look at the way he uses the verb 'build' in the first sentence. It appears in the phrase, 'while the Temple of the Lord was building', and we note that this is non-transactive; and it appears in the final phrase, 'ere the house of God can be built', where it is passive. This contrasts plainly enough with the source. Milton has selected a linguistic form which allows the use of a verb of physical process without specifying any physical agents. The Old Testament made it clear that the workers were unquestioningly under the King's command, and then banished them from the text, attributing all the practical activity of construction to Solomon. Milton does, like the book of Kings, refer to the manual workers, some cutting, some squaring the marble, others hewing the cedars. But in their brief appearance in his text they are not perceived in any chain of command and power. In terms of traditional attitudes to social work this is certainly rare and has thoroughly subversive implications. But Milton does not think about these. Nor does he even glance at the manifest problems which the majority of his readers would have raised. Instead, as he thinks of the activity of construction, he again returns to the passive voice and deletes the crucial agents ('when every stone is laid artfully together, it cannot be united ...'). He does say that the building will never be completed 'in this world'. Yet in the same sentence he asserts that there 'arises the goodly and the graceful symmetry' of 'the whole pile and structure'. The choice of 'arises' once again makes the constructors as invisible as any overall architect(s). How the 'pile and structure' can stand gracefully and symmetrically, its design fully comprehended, while the workers have not yet united the parts 'into a continuity' is hard to envisage. As a model for thinking about collective human activity, physical and intellectual, it has grave defects, all of these very characteristic of the author's outlook. When he applies his model to the contemporary 'mansion house of liberty' and his admirable wish to defend free discussion of ideas, the problems he faces are considerable. But he himself seems rather oblivious of this fact. He asserts that only 'irrational men' could fail to see that processes of construction mean there 'must be many schisms and many dissections made in the quarry and in the timber'. The workers cut marble and hewed wood: Milton turns this activity into 'schisms' and 'dissections', that is, into religious and political decisions made by diverse contemporaries to separate from the dominant traditions of Christian doctrine and ecclesiastical order. Yet he also keeps some of the literal first terms of the model from which he is extrapolating, so that these 'schisms' are 'made in the quarry and in the timber'. But by whom are the present schisms 'made'? What exactly does Milton mean by schisms 'made in the quarry and in the timber'? And precisely what is the distinction between quarry and temple-site in 1644? Furthermore, where does he place his Presbyterian colleagues of 1641? Then he saw them as the Lord's builders; now presumably, they are lumped with prelates and the vaguely defined group of 'irrational men'.

Yet the problems go much deeper than this. For the form of discourse actually precludes any specific answer to these questions. It discourages readers from even asking them, although they are central to the issues with which Milton is supposedly dealing - namely, the necessity of the liberty of publishing in the progressive enhancement of 'reformation, liberty and order'. His text does indeed express his personal values and his faith in the happy outcome of 'schisms' and 'brotherly dissimilitudes' in a 'goodly and graceful symmetry'. He branded as 'irrational' all those who argued that the increasing diversity and dedicatedly partisan commitment of competing religious groups would lead to more and more destructive conflicts, further misery and merely different kinds of tyranny under new tyrants. In doing so he was claiming the role of rational critic engaged with the realities of the situation in the 1640's. 'Let us', he invited the nobles, gentry and substantial citizens gathered in Parliament, 'be more considerate builders, more wise in spiritual architecture, when great reformation is expected'. Yet while this particular rational architect has developed a model which seems concerned with the changing phenomena of the present world, it actually excludes all engagement and dialogue with the empirical realities of changing social relationships, action and conflict. Even his serious (albeit highly abstract) commitment to 'free conscience and Christian liberties' is put in a manner which surely demands an important question we have not yet asked and which we believe he himself failed to put. In Milton's mind who or what is represented by the utterly passive substances cut up, squared, hewed and 'laid artfully together'? Are they people, people's lives, ideas and religious convictions? It is difficult to see what else they could represent, and the implications of this are disturbing. While Milton pleads for toleration for the expression of all _Protestant_ viewpoints (see p.565), he seems to envisage the activists so briefly glimpsed as able, and entitled, to work on an inert mass of human materials in the cause of 'spiritual architecture', of 'great reformation'. Who, on what grounds, and by whom, is to be assessed as inert matter in need of being cut up, squared, hewed and passively placed in a structure over which they have absolutely no control? Milton's model and his basic approach is far too idealist to face such major, highly concrete issues, even though they concern human relations and historical practice in which he believes himself well suited to intervene.

So, for all the energy and apparent orientation to historical change and revolutionary practice in _Areopagitica_, our analysis shows that Milton's discourse employs a range of linguistic strategies which resist engagement with the phenomena of social existence, including those central to his own address. He dissolves the processes of reality in a discourse which lacks any means of treating the _interaction_ between individual consciousness and social being. A discourse which lacks any way of subjecting its abstractions and assertions to the test of engagement with past or present events. A discourse which is closed to the specific and diverse interests of the contemporary social groups making their country's history in specific circumstances.

The second part of this paper is necessarily much briefer, a mere sketch. In it we focus on a real problem for Milton. In fact it is a real problem for any intellectual who discovers that the way things are is not the best of all possible ways, who lives in a period of open, violent conflicts, and notices contemporaries producing diverse religious, social and political programmes. What community does he address? Who precisely does Milton perceive as the audience for his radical utterances in 1642-1644 and where does he see his own social basis? Defining the community to which one belongs and exactly whom one is addressing is peculiarly problematic in periods of accelerated changes when received groupings and ideas come to seem inadequate and anomalous. Furthermore, alignments, and any individual's perceptions of his affiliations, are likely to change in such a period, as the overall circumstances and relationships change. Here we simply want to suggest a way of investigating such problems.

One way of exploring a writer's sense of community and competing groups is to look at his use of pronouns. In Areopagitica Milton presents himself as one of those responsible 'private persons' (his phrase) concerned with that increasingly important concept in political ideology, 'the public good' (see pp.486-88). He explicitly addresses 'the Parliament of England' and the 'I' which features so prominently in the opening pages (486-91) encourages us to expect a text along the basic structure of 'I' (individual champion of 'liberty', p.487): 'You' (Parliament, corporate patron of 'liberty'). This itself is an example of address in a period when conflict was being articulated in consciously ideological forms, when status, tradition and customary authority were losing much of their force in argument. Indeed, Milton presents himself as the responsible private individual, without any specific social status or class other than what he can convey by his control of words and ideas, by his ideological discourse. He is, in a characteristic phrase, 'the voice of reason' (p.490), and it is as such that he demands his audience's attention. When he speaks in this vein he anticipates the illusions of later intellectuals who have seen their own political discourse as a classless 'voice of reason'.(5) But this is certainly not the only stance Milton adopts. He soon uses the pronoun 'we' (p.487). For example:

> 'we are already in good part arrived [i.e. at "the utmost bound of civil liberty"], and yet from such a steep disadvantage of tyranny and superstition grounded into our principles as was beyond the manhood of a Roman recovery ...' (our underlining)

He attributes this happy arrival to God and 'your faithful guidance and undaunted Wisdom, Lords and Commons of England' (p.487). Here the word 'we' seems to stand for all the people of England, the elect 'Nation' about which Milton expressed such exalted views in Of Reformation and the work of the early 1640's. With this nation he currently identified himself - so here 'us' is God's 'Englishmen'. The only group apparently precluded from this us, is 'our obdurat Clergy', (p.533). So the many people in opposition to the dominant group in Parliament, or those desperately attempting to be 'neuters', have no existence in this scheme at all. However, Milton again shifts the referents of the pronoun we. A few pages on, he writes, 'we should be wary therefore what persecution we raise against the living labours of public men' (p.493; similarly p.521, lines 5-8). This use of we identifies him with the current rulers who are actually applying the censorship over the elect nation. This is, of course, partly a sensible tactical move. It implies that Milton understands the practices of the group he addresses and is one of them, sharing their values, aspirations and difficulties, therefore unlikely to be advocating anything against their (our!) real interests. It also implies that we rulers really have interests identical with God and his nation. Yet it is also definitely more than an opportunistic tactic. Milton was himself a leisured intellectual who never in his life had to work for a living, never had to sell his labour-power and never had to join in a degrading scramble for patronage. He did have genuine class and cultural affinities with many men in the revolutionary parliament however far removed his religious and political ideology was from most of its members even by 1644. When he mentions 'the common people' he mentions them as a group of whom he is definitely not a member:

> 'Nor is it to the common people less than a reproach; for if we be so jealous over them, as that we dare not trust them with an English pamphlet, what do we but censure them for a giddy, vicious, and ungrounded people ... That this is care or love of them, we cannot pretend ...'

In this passage 'we' is Parliament and Milton; 'they' are the common people. What becomes of the 'we' who are, in his words, 'the whole Nation' (pp.535, 536, 553), is not clear.(6) It seems to disappear under the real pressure of class divisions which are not openly acknowledged in the text. That this 'we' should vanish is hardly surprising, for the cry of 'one Nation' in a social formation composed of antagonistic classes is hardly well founded.

Perhaps Milton's most interesting representation of his own position is another one which emerges just two paragraphs further on. He describes his tour of Italy, his visit to Galileo and other 'learned men' and their complaints against the Inquisition. He then observes that he has now heard similar arguments in England among 'as learned men' against traditional and parliamentary censorship of publication. What is more, these 'learned men', he reassures Parliament, are ones who 'honour you and are known and respected by you'. These are the men who importune me, John Milton, to write a tract against 'an undeserved thraldom upon learning'. He thus proclaims that there is a community to which he belongs and one which Parliament should respect. This is the opening of the passage in question:

> 'That this is not therefore the disburdening of a particular fancy, but the common grievance of all those who had prepared their minds and studies above the vulgar pitch to advance truth in others, and from others to entertain it, thus much may satisfy. And in their name I shall for neither friend nor foe conceal what the general murmur is ...' (p.539)

Milton plainly claims to represent an intellectual elite, 'above the vulgar pitch', propagators of 'truth' in lesser mortals. Unlike Winstanley, he does not show any signs of having reflected on the social basis of this self-proclaimed elite and on its relationship to the powerful commercial and landed classes in England. Instead he proceeds to merge it into what seems a far more inclusive grouping, as we see in the claims that these learned men murmur

> 'that if it comes to inquisitioning again, and licencing and that we are so timorous of our selves, and so suspicious of all men, as to fear each book, and the shaking of every leaf, before we know what the contents are, if some who but of late were little better then silenced from preaching, shall come now to silence us from reading, except what they please, it cannot be guessed what is intended by some but a second tyranny over learning: and will soon put it out of controversy that Bishops and Presbyters are the same to us both name and thing.' (p.539)

By referring to the complaints of the 'learned' elite as 'the general murmur' Milton implies that such complaints are not, after all, limited to a small group of ideologues, the exalted and classless 'voice of reason'. The pronoun 'we' now includes not only Parliament (whose anxiety Milton signals) but, once again, 'the whole Nation' (pp.535, 536). Wonderful to say, it even includes the 'common people' (pp.536, 539). However this fantasising unification is not maintained; hardly surprising. Milton's text introduces a division between 'some' (who recently suffered censorship) and 'us' (whom those 'some' are now threatening to silence, through the agency of Parliament). Here 'us' unites all those who see themselves threatened by Presbyterian ideologues. Those ideologues are a threat to Milton because they had acquired significant political support among many county gentry who disliked both Laudian church and toleration of local sectarian congregations. They were no disembodied 'voice of reason', to Milton. Yet at the same time he reveals that the 'us' under attack are, after all, a minority of English men. For he picks out the Presbyterian wish to 'silence us from reading'. This implies a group in which the most important liberty and tyranny in the 1640's is that of reading. Maybe such a group is not 'cloistered' or 'fugitive', but it is certainly massively narrower than the 'Nation' which Milton claimed to represent. Milton has not overtly indicated his awareness of the significance in the pronomial shifts and their reference. It would be pleasant to argue that the shifts, and the lack of acknowledgement that these shifts have serious implications for his own case, are just examples of the writer's tactical cunning and famous rhetorical craft. No-one who introduces himself as serving grand abstractions like 'the public good' and 'the Country's liberty' (pp.486-7) is going to admit that he is actually preoccupied with sectional interests, especially when these conflict with other interests which are being branded as sectional and divisive (as the Presbyterian ones are in the above passage). Yet the shifts in the groupings indicated by Milton's use of pronouns suggests a reluctance or inability to focus on the implications of these difficulties which is much more than tactical cunning and rhetorical skill. That we are, in fact, encountering an ideological failure here is probably confirmed by Milton's surprised and outraged reaction to the lack of popular support for the revolution he desired and worked for.(7)

Reflecting on the passage about 'learned men' it is pertinent to take a later statement where Milton threatens Parliament while seemingly praising it. He tells its members that their own 'free, and human government' has sponsored 'liberty ... enfranchised, enlarged and lifted up our apprehensions', before offering a threat: 'You cannot make us now less capable, less knowing, less eagerly pursuing of the truth, unless you first make yourselves, that made us so, less the lovers, less the founders of our true liberty ... you cannot suppress that ...' (p.559). Here Milton reverts to the pronouns 'we', 'us', 'you' in which 'we' are the mass of 'the whole Nation' (pp.535, 536, 551-559 passim) and 'you' the liberating leaders who 'enlarged and lifted up our apprehensions'. (Like other 'learned men' Milton would in fact hardly have felt indebted to an English Parliament for having his intellectual powers improved, so we should emphasise the tactical role of the 'we' here in which the 'learned' writer gracefully submerges his distinction in the putative unity of the elect nation). The next threat is more overt. He warns that if the members of Parliament suppress the 'liberty' which they have introduced they will lose all support which, Milton insists, was not primarily in defence of material and political interests ('for cote and conduct ...') against the encroachments of Charles' rule. However, he does hastily, and wisely, add, 'I dispraise not the defence of just immunities', a concession to one of the chief motives in arousing the country gentry against the monarch.(8)

But after this pragmatic concession he makes a brief statement which is central to his overall outlook: 'Give me the liberty to know, to utter, and to argue freely according to conscience, above all liberties' (p.560). Wage labourers in the hardships of the 1640's, subsistence farmers with copyhold tenures subjected to rack renting as well as traditional feudal impositions, the mass of servants or, at the other end of the society, well-to-do country gentry defending their political, social, economic and religious power in their localities, none would think that the liberty of learning was 'above all liberties'. As we have already suggested, Milton's freedom from ever having had to work as a hired labourer (whether manual or intellectual), his freedom from the labour market, his freedom from the pressures and commitments affecting those in the commercial sector of society or the landed gentry, this social and economic freedom is a shaping factor in his statement about the most valuable liberty, in his whole experience and language. It is, however, one he seems largely unable to bring into self-reflexive consciousness, and this inability was to prove a grave impediment to his understanding of the contemporary conflicts in which he engaged so courageously. We believe that this is as much a matter of imaginative failure and intellectual closure as of any inevitable product of class background, and here it is worth considering the letter his friend Moses Wall wrote to him in 1660:

> 'You complain of the non-progression of the nation, and of its retrograde motion of late, in Liberty and spiritual Truths. It is much to be bewailed; but yet let us pity human frailty when those who had made deep protestations of their zeal for our liberty both spiritual and civil, and made the fairest offers to be asserters thereof, and whom we thereupon trusted; when those being enstated in power, shall betray the good thing committed to them, and lead us back to Egypt, and by that force which we gave them, to win us Liberty, hold us fast in chains what can poor people do? You know who they were that watched our Saviours sepulcher to keep him from rising. Besides, whilst people are not free but straitened in accommodations for life, their spirits will be dejected and servile. And conducing to that end [of liberty] there should be an improving of our native commodities, as our manufacturers, our fisheries, our fens, forests and commons, and our trade at sea which would give the body of the nation a comfortable subsistence, and the breaking that cursed yoak of tithes would help much thereto. Also another thing I cannot but mention, which is that the Norman Conquest and tyranny is continued upon the nation without any thought of removing it: I mean the tenure of land by copyhold, and holding for life under a lord (or rather Tyrant) of a manor, whereby people care not to improve their land by cost upon it, not knowing how soon themselves or theirs may be outed it [ejected], nor what the house is in which they live for the same reason. And they are far more enslaved to the lord of the manor than the rest of the nation is to a King or supreme magistrate!'

Much of this is in close accord with the powerful social criticism and analysis developed by Winstanley, but we thought it of particular interest to quote from a letter actually received by Milton himself, and written by a friend replying to one of his own letters.(9) Wall's attention to the realities of domination in England and to the actual life-processes and daily circumstances of a wide range of people highlights features in his friend's approach with which we have been dealing. For, unlike Wall's, Milton's orientation involves the dissolution of concrete social reality in particular human communities where, and where alone, the individual develops his specific identity and lives his life.

This dissolution is rather indicative of his inability to make the advantages and limitations of his own social and economic position a topic for serious examination. Even Wall's impressively intelligent letter seems not to have persuaded him to do this or reconsider his approach, for his diagnosis of the defeat of the 'good old cause' (in The Ready and Easy Way, for example) shows no signs that he learnt from Wall.

Both Wall's brief letter and especially the sustained commentary and analysis in Winstanley's extensive writings, argue that 'liberty' (including the kinds of religious and intellectual liberties Milton proclaimed so bravely) had to have some basis in the daily lives of all people; that individual freedoms and fulfilments need political and social dimensions which include the sphere of work and a certain level of overall material security. The way Milton dissolved the dialectical relations between individual and social circumstances and discounted the extremely diverse actualities of life confronting God's Englishmen, is an important aspect of his version of liberty, individual and community. It is also very much part of those static, anti-historical, anti-empirical tendencies of his outlook on which we focused in the first part of this paper. Studying his prose we need to remember the issues raised by Areopagitica and discussed in the present paper as we meet the admirable, challenging phrases about liberty throughout his works. Phrases such as the one in The Defence of the People of England maintaining that Christ 'has won for us all proper freedom ... not of religious liberty alone, but also of political' (CPW, IV, 1, 374). The 'us' may seem to be 'the whole Nation', or rather all Christians, but in the same work he shows how easily 'us all' becomes the 'few': 'those who long for liberty or can enjoy it are but few' (CPW, IV, 1, 343). Perhaps so, and circumstances in 1651 were different to 1644. But, recalling Wall's letter, one would like to know more (something at least!) about the empirical content of this 'liberty', the quality of relationships being offered, who is doing the offering and why all but the 'few' should have withdrawn active support from the 'good old cause'. Yet Milton's approach, in Areopagitica, to historical processes, individual and community is one which, as we have attempted to show, systematically screens such considerations; and although his later work is beyond the scope of the present paper, we do not believe that Milton ever fully penetrated this particular and highly complex screen.

Footnotes

1. We quote Milton from the Complete Prose Works of John Milton, Yale University Press, still in process: we cite the edition as CPW and refer to page in text, Areopagitica being in volume two. Of the substantial literature of this text, see especially D. M. Wolfe, Milton in the Puritan Revolution (Cohn and West, 1941), chapter 3; K. W. Stavely, The Politics of Milton's Prose Style (Yale U.P., 1975), chapter 3; C. Hill, Milton and the English Revolution (Faber, 1977), chapter 10. For the linguistic analysis applied here, see G. Kress and R. Hodge, Language as Ideology (Routledge & Kegan Paul, 1979) and R. Fowler et al, Language and Control (Routledge & Kegan Paul, 1979).

2. As he continually makes clear in Doctrine and Discipline of Divorce, Tetrachordon, Christian Doctrine, and indeed throughout his work.

3. For example, M. Halliday, Explorations in the Functions of Language (Oxford U.P., 1976), chapter 5.

4. See Kress and Hodge, Language as Ideology, and Kress, ed., Halliday: System and Function in Language (Oxford U.P., 1976), chapter 2.

5. See especially M. Walzer, Revolution of the Saints (Weidenfeld, 1966); C. Hill, Society and Puritanism (Panther, 1969), pp.215-6, 479-80; D. Hanson, From Kingdom to Commonwealth (Harvard U.P., 1972).

6. On Milton's attitude to 'the people' see Hill, Milton, pp.160-2, 168-70; see Milton's own comments in 1649, CPW, III, 337-49.

7. Besides the references in the previous note, see his Ready and Easy Way and the final acknowledgement of isolation.

8. See Milton's own very pertinent comments in Of Reformation, CPW, I, 592 and his appeal to the big gentry in Ready and Easy Way.

9. Wall's letter is reprinted in Life Records of John Milton, ed. J. M. French (Rutgers U.P., 1949-1958), May 1659, pp.267-8, modernised here. For Winstanley here see especially the following: The Works of Gerard Winstanley, ed. G. Sabine (Russell & Russell, 1965), pp. 506-7, 538, 158-9, 190-1, 316, 389 ff.

TOWARDS THE AUTONOMOUS SUBJECT IN POETRY: MILTON 'ON HIS BLINDNESS'

Antony Easthope

It is convenient to begin with a recent essay on 'The Continuity of Milton's Sonnets'. William McCarthy argues that the twenty-three sonnets (he sets aside the caudate one 'On the new forcers') published in 1645, 1673 and 1694 'are a sequence',(1) numbers 1 to 6 representing young love, 8 to 18 maturity and 20 to 23 retirement, with number 7 ('How soon hath Time') and number 19 ('On his Blindness') as turning points in the series. The argument is convincing, and given that these are Renaissance sonnets it is hard to see how they could not be read as a sequence. Nevertheless McCarthy's argument gives him some anxiety. The sonnets were clearly written and published at different times over forty years; McCarthy cannot feel secure in reading them in sequence unless this is guaranteed by a conscious intention in an individual mind, John Milton, the 'real man' behind the 'implied author' of the poems. In default of this intention he fears collapse into absolute relativism, reading the sonnets 'only as I construe them'. As he recognises, the difficulty is that 'we lack access to Milton's consciousness' - apart from the texts - and so he imputes intention to the fact that many (not all) of the sonnets were published together in 1673 and thus 'brought by Milton deliberately to our attention'. He also admits (in a footnote) that 'Milton ordered his sonnets chiefly in the process of writing them'.(2)

The unnecessary and impossible search for a transcendental subject - the 'real man' 'behind' the text - is familiar in literary criticism. As is its necessary consequence: that the reader in the present should be alienated from his or her own productive energies while the text is expropriated as private property of its supposed metasubject, the Author. Serious literary analysis has recently made advances on the basis that the subject is constituted as an effect of discourse; there is no space, no 'John Milton' behind the discourse in which the sonnets take place; subject position is effected across the text and its readings.

The sonnets are texts whose materiality resists, cannot be exhausted in any reading. Further they are historical texts which work to inscribe a subject position determined historically and not just psycho-analytically, a subject-in-history. While deriving from the basic conception, some modes of analysis, as in a recent book on genre, lead to an abstracted and de-historicised version of discourse and subject position:

> 'As Jacques Lacan stressed, "Repetition demands the new". Moreover, repetition and difference ... function as a relation. There is hence not repetition _and_ difference, but repetition _in_ difference.' (3)

There is a necessary economy of the subject in which difference is always expressed and contained in repetition. But the forms of this process and structure are historically determinate and historically variable, an expression and containment that is simultaneously ideological. And so it is not

> 'that there is first of all the construction of a subject for social/ideological formations and then the placing of that constructed subject-support in those formations, it is that the two processes are one, in a kind of necessary simultaneity - like the recto and verso of a piece of paper.' (4)

The specific problem is to provide terms for the subject of discourse in its historical constitution, the historical text and _its_ subject.

'Modern poetry is _capitalist_ poetry',(5) meaning by 'modern' the poetic tradition since the Renaissance. Possibly, then, it will offer an epochal position, the bourgeois conception of the subject as autonomous, self-present, self-originating, hard-edged, defensively phallocratic, 'As if a man were author of himself' (_Coriolanus_). Yet concern with 1642 poses questions of conjuncture and the need to discriminate within a general poetic development. The distinctions between _discours_ and _histoire_, between enunciation and enounced may permit appropriate discriminations to be made between typical and representative texts of Shakespeare, Milton and Dryden.

Enunciation/Enounced

We have inherited a grammatical notion that there are three persons: first, second and third. Pointing for example to Arabic grammarians who emphasise the first person ('the one who speaks') as coupled to the second ('the one who is addressed') and contrasted with the third ('the one who is absent'), Benveniste in 1946 argues that

> 'very generally, person is inherent only in the positions "I" and "you". The third person, by virtue of its very structure is the non-personal form of verbal inflection ... They contrast as members of a correlation, the correlation of personality: "I-you" possesses the sign of person; "he" lacks it.' (6)

Developing from this (1959) he differentiates two kinds of discourse, *discours* and *histoire*: briefly, *discours* is marked by signs of person while in *histoire* they are absent:

> 'We shall define historical narration as the mode of utterance that excludes every "autobiographical" linguistic form. The historian will never say *je* or *tu* or *maintenant* ... we shall find only the forms of the "third person" in a historical narrative strictly followed.' (7)

In a further development Benveniste goes on to relate 'I-you', the mark of *discours*, with enunciation, and Todorov (1972) defines enunciation as 'the imprint of the process of uttering on the utterance'.(8) As forms of enunciation Todorov lists: personal pronouns (I/you), demonstratives (this/that), relative adverbs and adjectives (here/there), tense of verb, performative verbs ('I swear that'), evaluative and emotive meaning, modifying terms such as 'perhaps', 'certainly'.

At this point in its development the theoretical account risks a technicist error - that is, it risks identifying enunciation with the linguistic *marks* of enunciation. That the equation would be mistaken can be demonstrated in two ways. Firstly on linguistic grounds. Taking up the term 'shifters' from Jespersen (1923) and looking back to both Voloshinov and Benveniste on 'The Nature of Pronouns' (1956) Roman Jakobson (in 1957) distinguished between 'the speech act (*procés de* l'énonciation)' and 'the narrated event (procés de l'énoncé)' dependent upon it:

> '... four terms are to be distinguished: a narrated event (E^n), a speech event (E^s), a participant of the narrated event (P^n), and a participant of the speech event (P^2), whether addresser or addressee.' (9)

As there cannot be a signified without a signifier, so there cannot be an enounced without enunciation. It follows that Benveniste's distinction must be reworked: discours and histoire

> 'are both forms of enunciation, the difference between them lying in the fact that in the discursive form the source of enunciation is present, whereas in the historical it is suppressed.' (10)

The distinction is not in the enunciation but in the enounced: whether marks of person are present or absent there. Secondly, on grounds of subjectivity. Unless the subject is imagined as metaphysically prior to language,(11) all discourse - including histoire - presupposes the subject: 'a signifier is that which represents the subject for another signifier'.(12) Enunciation precedes enounced; there is always the speaker/listener/reader/writer of the discourse, that is, the subject of enunciation in a determinate position. Histoire lacks signs of the subject, discours is marked by them - both are forms of the enounced. The difference is that discours contains shifters and so a subject of the enounced. Further, even when someone is talking about themselves, the subject of enunciation remains disjunct from the subject of the enounced:

> '... the I of the enunciation is not the same as the I of the enounced, that is to say, the shifter, which in the statement, designates him.' (13)

Since enounced takes place on the grounds of enunciation the subject of enunciation can never fully occupy the place of subject of enounced. It is as fixity and closure in the enounced that the subject finds a possibility of presence endlessly displaced along the syntagmatic chain in the process of enunciation - a repetition in difference which is the structuring of desire.

These terms relate directly to the analysis of poetry. For the bourgeois tradition - 'Modern poetry' - can be defined precisely as a regime of representation aiming to disavow enunciation and its subject in favour of the subject of the enounced.[14] Ideologically predicated on the bourgeois tradition, literary criticism would deny the active productivity of readers in the present. Its central term, the notion of 'Imagination', is designed precisely to elide disjunction between subjects of enunciation and enounced. The reader is always the enunciative subject, producing the poem in the continuous present of enunciation, just as from a script actors and technicians produce a play. Milton speaks about his blindness only because I make him. His ghost, however, is not an illusion ('false consciousness') but a material effect of discourse. A full voice, a coherent presence as subject of the enounced is represented through poetic artifice. Its fixity is contrived in various ways, of which four will be emphasised here: the attempt to control sliding of the signifier, to hold signifier onto signified in a sustained syntagmatic order, to contain materiality of language in verse form, to suppress marks of enunciation in the enounced by moving from *discours* to *histoire*.

Shakespeare

Shakespeare's sonnet 136 was written before 1609. It is not easy to speak and follow, perhaps because it is about female desire and this disturbs the habitual control of male propositional discourse. Its sexual reference is only just kept inexplicit and at a level of innuendo. Modern editors refuse to elucidate it[15] - 'will' means sexual desire, 'treasure' and 'thing' mean vagina ('thing' also later means penis), 'prove' means ejaculate:

'If thy soul check thee that I come so near,
Swear to thy blind soul that I was thy "Will",
And will thy soul knows is admitted there,
Thus far for love, my love-suit sweet fulfil.
"Will", will fulfil the treasure of thy love,
Ay, fill it full with wills, and my will one,

In things of great receipt with ease we prove,
Among a number one is reckoned none.
Then in the number let me pass untold,
Though in thy store's account I one must be,
For nothing hold me, so it please thee hold,
That nothing me, a something sweet to thee.
    Make but my name thy love, and love that still.
    And then thou lov'st me for my name is Will.'

Sliding of the signifier is most dramatically illustrated here by the seven instances of 'will' which variously and simultaneously suggest: wish (both noun and verb), sexual desire, sexual organ, last will and testament, a name (William), part of the future tense. The materiality of the signifier - its active work/play - is thus insisted upon in 'fill it full with wills, and my will one', and '"Will", will fulfil' (a play avoided by say, '"Will" may fulfil'). There is also instability in 'come so near' (= 1. conscience; 2. bed), 'treasure', 'one', 'none', 'thing', 'nothing' (or 'no-thing' in Elizabethan pronunciation), 'something'; and sustained ambiguity with 'In things of great receipt with ease we prove' (= 1. 'It is easy to deal with large numbers of items'; 2. 'It is nice to ejaculate in large vaginas').

The sliding, the play of will/fill, sounds like the childish pleasure in 'treating words as things' analysed by Freud:

'I'm Dirty Bill from Vinegar Hill,
Never had a bath and never will.'(16)

Strictly this children's rhyme is not nonsense but jest, since language play is already contained in a meaningful sentence, though not one that is 'valuable or new or even good'.(17) In contrast, to persist with Freud's taxonomy, the play will/fill, is a joke and in fact a tendentious one: will fulfils the treasure of her love, both as Will the man becoming her lover and when sperm fills her vagina.

Overall the floating of the signifier in 136 is marginal. Unlike the children's jest it remains a disturbance rather than a disorder of the planes of enunciation and enounced. It is held firmly but not completely onto the signified by closure in the syntagmatic chain. The briefest way to make this point is from a syntactic outline of the sonnet, particularly its conjunctions: 'If ... And ... Thus ...', followed by general proposition ('Among a number one is reckoned none' is a mathematical proverb, 'one is no number') leading to 'Then ... Though' and a conclusion 'Make ... and then ...'. It's possible that the very disturbance of the signifier corresponds to the idea of female desire and requires compensation in ideas of number and calculation. Certainly there is syntagmatic closure, the form of a logical argument. The speaker of the enounced (named as Will) is sustained in a general coherence, and the sonnet partakes fully of the tradition by foregrounding enounced over enunciation.

Milton

Milton's sonnet 'On his Blindness' (the title added by Newton) is usually dated 1652 or 1655. It refers to a number of passages in the Bible. Whereas the Parable of the Talents (Matthew xxv) promises that the servant who hides his one talent (others get five and two) instead of trading with it shall be cast into 'outer darkness', the sonnet asserts that the labourer 'standing idle in the marketplace' (Matthew xx) is performing adequate service. It is in fact 'a flat rejection of the whole point of the parable of the talents':(18)

'When I consider how my light is spent,
Ere half my days, in this dark world and wide,
And that one Talent which is death to hide,
Lodg'd with me useless, though my Soul more bent
To serve therewith my Maker, and present
My true account, least he returning chide,
Doth God exact day labour, light deny'd,
I fondly ask; But patience to prevent
That murmur, soon replies, God doth not need
Either man's work or his own gifts, who best
Bear his milde yoak, they serve him best, his State
Is Kingly. Thousands at his bidding speed
And post o're Land and Ocean without rest:
They also serve who only stand and waite.'

At no point does the signifier insist upon itself, as do will/fill in Shakespeare's sonnet. Rather there is a repeated and controlled oscillation of the signifier over a delimited circle of signifieds. 'Light' means sight and inward illumination, 'dark' means blindness and fallen human nature, 'talent' means a coin and ability, 'useless' means not used and not producing interest through usury, 'yoak' means wooden cross-piece and the obligation of service, 'waite' means attend as a servant and stay in expectation. This consistent movement between concrete and moral abstract as well as the plain diction ('work', 'gifts', 'bent') rejoins the text to seventeenth century theological and particularly Puritan discourses. Accumulation of consistent connotation helps to give the language of the sonnet the effect of transparency.

It is now familiar wisdom that in Milton's poetry the reader is to be surprised by syntax:

> 'That the syntax of the octave here seems almost out of control gives the poem a perilous suspense, which the straightforward structure of the sestet then disperses and transcends.' (19)

But syntactic inversions and delays cause surprise in relation to the extraordinary high expectation of coherence established. For example, after line 7 ('lest he returning chide')

> 'it seems as if the syntax has collapsed ... we expect the quotation marks will tell the chiding of "He", but instead they tell the complaint of "I".' (20)

Any dislocation is temporary, is fully resolved, and only confirms the decisive and unequivocal closure of the syntagmatic chain strung across these fourteen lines and two sentences.

Contrast between the syntax of this text and the Elizabethan sonnet has been remarked elsewhere:

> 'For all its involutions, sonnet xix (When I consider) turns effortlessly on the simplest axis ("I ask: Patience replies") and is at once intelligible: it differs in its fluency from the typical Elizabethan sonnet, which moves forward from point to point, in that it possesses a controlling centre.' (21)

Whereas Shakespeare's sonnet 136 develops progressively in a cumulative linearity, Milton's sonnet exhibits only superficial coruscations over a structure rigidly determinate at a deeper level. Through this attempted closure, signifier nailed onto signified in univocal syntax, the sonnet produces the effect of a coherent centre, a fixed subject of the enounced, a voice represented speaking, a presence. Wordsworth's response to Milton's sonnets is significant; he thinks of each as 'an orbicular body - a sphere - or dew-drop'.(22)

Poetry is written in lines; as discursive form it is specified by 'parallelism of the signifier'.(23) The economy of poetry is to express enunciative difference by containing it in repetition of the signifier. Verse form in Modern English is determined by line length and rhyme, and it is in rhyme particularly that the materiality of the signifier may open up. The usual contrast between two uses of the sonnet form - respectively Shakespearean and Miltonic - can be understood on this basis. Sonnet 136 is built from three quatrains (each with different rhyme sounds) and a concluding couplet while Milton's sonnet rhymes across an octave (abba abba) and sestet (cde cde), so avoiding the couplet conclusion (only XVI 'To Cromwell' so concludes). Milton has less rhyme variation and more phonetic recurrence than Shakespeare, and so one might suppose comes closer to 'treating words as things' as in the children's jest rhyme ('Dirty Bill'). The opposite is the case.

Each of Shakespeare's four rhyme divisions (three quatrains and a couplet) coincides with a syntactic unit and semantic development (except perhaps in the already dislocated first two lines of the second quatrain). Milton's monolinear syntactic development rides straight across the rhyme scheme with seven run-on lines and with syntactic junctures in the middle (not the end) of lines 8 and 12 and further terminal junctures in lines 9 and 11 ('replies, God', 'best, his'). Milton's practice derives from Italian models, from Tasso and particularly Giovanni della Casa,(24) its aim being - as in Paradise Lost - 'the sense variously drawn out from one Verse into another'. The attempt, then, in Shakespeare's sonnet is to contain the enunciative activity of the signifier by holding it onto syntax and meaning; relatively the Milton sonnet would efface the signifier through syntagmatic closure and so offers a position of closer identification with the subject of the enounced.

Nevertheless the poem remains a sonnet. Although its usage in

1652 is appropriately idiosyncratic and Milton almost alone cultivated the sonnet in the middle of the seventeenth century, through its verse form the text partakes of the elaborated courtly mode of its Elizabethan precedents. This was recognised by Milton (another Milton?) who mocked Charles I for ascribing 'all vertue to his Wife, in straines that come almost to Sonnetting'.[25]

Dryden

Whatever local commitments it is engaged with during the revolutionary period after 1660 'the plain style wins the day'.[26] Transparency becomes an explicit ideal, to be effected as signified is carefully fixed under signifier (in Sprat's formulation of 1667, 'so many things, almost in equal number of words') in a carefully sustained syntagmatic chain (in Hobbes' recommendation of 1673, an 'order of words ... whereby a man may foresee the length of his period', that is, the sentence).

The sonnet becomes completely marginal and 'even including translation only thirteen persons are known to have used the form between 1660 and 1740'.[27] Instead there is the reified use of the couplet uniformly across texts and within. In the couplet the phonetic, syntactic and semantic levels coincide simultaneously in a single closure constantly repeated throughout the poem. It could be argued that Shakespeare's use of the quatrain and indeed the couplet itself anticipates the Augustan couplet (which of course it does) more than the scrupulous avoidance of quatrain and couplet in Milton's sonnet. But the overriding consideration is that Shakespeare's thematic progression is relatively enclosed and acts in correspondence with the rhyme scheme while Milton's transcends rhyme and line length to form its own coherence. In this Milton's sonnet comes very close to the Augustan ideal in which sense is developed ever onwards from one couplet to the next. An apt illustration is the famous opening of *Absalom and Achitophel* (1681):

'In pious times, e're Priest-craft did begin,
Before *Polygamy* was made a sin;

When man, on many, multiply'd his kind,
E'r one to one was, cursedly, confin'd:
When Nature prompted, and no law deny'd
Promiscuous use of Concubine and Bride;
Then, *Israel*'s Monarch, after Heaven's own heart,
His vigorous warmth did, variously, impart
To Wives and Slaves: And, wide as his Command,
Scatter'd his Maker's Image through the Land.
Michal, of Royal blood, the Crown did wear,
A Soyl ungratefull to the Tiller's care:
Not so the rest: for several Mothers bore
To Godlike David, several sons before.'

And so on.

There is hardly need to recall in detail how both sonnets are forms of *discours* and bear the marks of enunciation, with twenty-two instances of 'I-thou' in Shakespeare and eight of the first person in Milton; nor to demonstrate fully that the Dryden passage is an example of the dominance in Augustan poetry of *histoire*. Only 'cursedly' (line 4) is manifestly a mark of enunciation. To cite Benveniste: 'No one speaks here; the events seem to narrate themselves'.[28] With marks of enunciation suppressed the text offers itself as fully transparent medium, the enounced disavows its enunciation.

In relation back to Shakespeare and forward to this, Milton's sonnet can be read as a transitional text. While in verse form it rejoins the now residual courtly mode of the sonnet in sonnet sequence, in its syntagmatic closure it intervenes to make possible the Augustan aim of discursive transparency returning the subject to itself as a unity. Transition is also exemplified within the sonnet where there is a shift from the *discours* of the octave to *histoire* in the sestet. As a result the sestet may be reworked with ease into Augustan couplets, however limping:

'God needs nor His own gifts nor yet man's work.
For those who learn to bear His easy yoke,
Continue those who serve their Maker best.
God's state is regal, and at His request,
Some speed o're land and sea without abate,
While others serve who only stand and wait.'

To insist: discours/histoire is a distinction within the enounced. It only operates to provide subject position as part, possibly a minor aspect, of a whole regime of representation, the relation of enunciation and enounced. Instance of this is the easy transposition between the two modes; a passage in one can be re-written in the other with only minor alteration.(29) Yet within the represented discours/histoire need to be discriminated, possibly as demand and desire. Sonnet 136 clearly represents the would-be closed circle of 'a request for love'.(30) The male 'I' supposes the female 'thou' as 'already possessing the privilege of satisfying needs', even though the circuit is already broken by her 'will' which the speaker would rejoin by closing her desire onto his name ('Make but my name thy love'). Only through major alteration could this sonnet be re-written into histoire.

Milton's sonnet could easily be transposed ('When he considers how his light is spent', or 'considered'). In it desire is represented beginning 'to take shape in the margin in which demand becomes separated from need'. The first person is repeated eight times in the octave unreciprocated by the second. The sonnet articulates both energetic rebellion against loss (classically blindness is a metaphor for castration) and a controlled assertion that the loss be accepted. Progress across these two is enabled as the speaker's 'I' becomes the voice of the Father ('patience ... soon replies') - 'God is satisfied' and by identification '"I" is satisfied'.(31) Theologically the poem is unorthodox since there is still 'this deep strength of ego'(32) deliberately asserting submission to superego; George Herbert is more orthodox in The Holdfast:

> '"... to have nought is ours, not to confess
> That we have nought."'

Progress from egoistic rebellion to identification with the Father develops from octave to sestet, turning on a paternalist self-recognition in 'fondly' (line 8) and the personification of patience which speaks the unquestionable authority of the Father. The turn is also from forms of enunciation to third person discourse, from discours to histoire (a shift recurrent in Paradise Lost and Samson Agonistes). In contrast, histoire is exemplified in the beginning of Absalom and Achitophel by a passage of confident phallocentrism in which His Majesty the Father almost transparently reiterates sons in his own image.

Footnotes

1. W. McCarthy, 'The Continuity of Milton's Sonnets', in PMLA, Vol.92 (January 1977), pp.96-109, p.96.

2. Ibid, pp.97, 96, 107, 98, 108 (footnote 7).

3. S. Neale, Genre (BFI, London, 1980), p.50.

4. S. Heath, 'Anata mo' in Screen, Vol.17 (Winter 1976/7), p.62.

5. C. Caudwell, Illusion and Reality (London, 1946), p.55.

6. E. Benveniste, Problems in General Linguistics (Miami, 1971), p.199.

7. Ibid, p.206.

8. See entry on Énonciation in O. Ducrot and T. Todorov, Dictionnaire encyclopédique des sciences du langage (Paris, 1972).

9. R. Jakobson, 'Shifters, Verbal Categories, and the Russian Verb', in Word and Language (Mouton, The Hague and Paris, 1971), pp.134, 133.

10. G. Nowell-Smith, 'A Note on History/Discourse', in Edinburgh '76 Magazine (BFI), p.27. See also C. MacCabe, 'On Discourse', in Economy and Society, Vol.8 (August 1979), esp. pp.280-88.

11. For which Benveniste has been traduced by Greimas (see A. J. Greimas and J. Courtés, Sémiotique: Dictionnaire Raisonné de la Théorie du Langage (Paris, 1979), entry under Énonciation) - wrongly as it happens (see Benveniste, cited MacCabe, op cit, p.286).

12. J. Lacan, Écrits (London, 1977), p.316.

13. J. Lacan, Four Fundamental Concepts of Psychoanalysis (London, 1977), p.139 ('énoncé' is translated as 'statement' and here retranslated as 'enounced').

14. See my 'Problematising the Pentameter' (New Literary History, forthcoming).

15. W. G. Ingram and T. Redpath (in Shakespeare's Sonnets (London, 1964)) 'feel no obligation to elucidate' and A. L. Rowse (in Shakespeare's Sonnets, also London, 1964) finds it hard to discuss the sonnet 'with any decency'. For a clear account, see Shakespeare's Sonnets, ed. S. Booth (Yale, 1977).

16. Cited in I. and P. Opie, The Lore and Language of Schoolchildren (Oxford, 1967), p.20.

17. S. Freud, Jokes (Penguin, London, 1976), pp.168, 179.

18. W. R. Parker, Milton, A Biography (Oxford, 1968), p.471.

19. T. Stoehr, 'Syntax and Poetic Form in Milton's Sonnets', in English Studies, Vol.45 (1964), p.293.

20. P. Goodman, The Structure of Literature (Chicago, 1954), pp.206, 209-10.

21. E. A. J. Honigman (ed.), Milton's Sonnets (London, 1966), p.41.

22. See Wordsworth's letter to A. Dyce in Poetical Works, ed. E. de Selincourt and H. Darbishire, Vol.8 (Oxford, 1954), p.417.

23. Écrits, p.155.

24. See J. S. Smart, The Sonnets of Milton (Glasgow, 1921) which established the derivation from Della Casa (1503-56); also F. T. Prince, The Italian Element in Milton's Verse (Oxford, 1954). Smart shows that the volta (meaning by this a break between octave and sestet) is not in any way a rigorous requirement of the Italian sonnet.

25. Eikonoklastes in Works, ed. F. A. Patterson et al (New York, 1931-40), Vol.5, p.139.

26. S. E. Fish, 'Epilogue: The Plain Style Question', in Self-Consuming Artifacts (University of California, 1972), p.379.

27. R. D. Havens, The Influence of Milton on English Poetry (Cambridge, Mass., 1922), p.488.

28. Problems in General Linguistics, p.208.

29. As was demonstrated by M. Barrett and J. Radford in 'Modernism in the 1930's', 1936: The Sociology of Literature (Essex, 1979), Vol. 1, pp.267-69.

30. This and the next two quotations are from Écrits, pp.311, 286, 311 respectively.

31. Goodman, op cit, p.206.

32. Stoehr, op cit, p.294.

RELIGION AND IDEOLOGY

Fredric Jameson

Nothing is more appropriate, in the second year of the Iranian revolution and the first year of the Islamic Republic, than a return to 1642 and a meditation on the work of the greatest English political poet. The renewed vitality of a religious politics - and in particular the will to abolish the split between the public and the private, between state and church - can be expected to impose new ways of reading Milton; while the theological coding of the first great bourgeois revolution in the West - an experience which may be called a properly English cultural revolution - ought to place the Iranian situation in a more comprehensible, or at least less alien, light. It should at any rate be clear that Marxists can no longer afford the luxury of assigning the problem of religion to the ashcan of history. An impulse that turned out the largest urban demonstrations ever recorded in the history of the human race,(1) and that overturned a regime that was the model and showcase for high technological repression in the Third World, certainly has something to teach us about how theory 'grips the masses'. Nor should the vital role played by radical religion in the American anti-war movement of the 1960's be forgotten, nor the crucial and strategic one currently being played by the theology of liberation in revolutionary struggles in Central and Latin America.

I would not want to be understood as claiming that religion is not also often reactionary: indeed, I'm afraid that at a certain moment in the revolutionary process it must always become that, and Milton will be no exception, as we'll see. Nor am I suggesting even a primary role for religion in the initiation of revolutions: indeed, it would be the worst kind of historical error, and an affront to the dead, to attribute to the Iranian mullahs a revolution which was in fact begun by armed Left guerrillas in winter 1971, and in which the Left played a major role.(2)

What I would like to do in the following remarks is two-fold: to make at least a beginning in the historically actual and indispensable task of understanding the relations between religion and politics; and to do this by way of a more specifically literary or interpretive problem, namely that of proposing a political reading of Paradise Lost, or better still, of deconcealing the political content of Paradise Lost. The difficulties of this second project should not be underestimated: not merely must such an interpretation impose itself as unavoidable, so that anti-political readers and interpreters are forced to waste precious energies in conjuring it away; it must also open up a perspective on something like a line-by-line or paragraph-by-paragraph rereading or rewriting of the poem.

This means that the political focus generally proposed for Milton is insufficient: to be sure, in a general way, there is no great problem in understanding the relationship between the global impulse of Paradise Lost and the political situation itself: the moment of the failure of revolution, the dissipation of the revolutionary ethos, the reappearance of the old institutions and business as usual (or in other words, in the language of the time, of sin). And one can well imagine that the disintegration of a successful revolution, its ignominious bottoming out in restoration, is a more bitterly disillusioning experience than the triumph of counter-revolution in bloody repression, as in June 1848 or in Chile. Arguably, the English revolution also knew its June 1848: Christopher Hill fixes it in the Battle of Burford in May 1649, when the Levellers in the army are definitively crushed.(3) Still, the stronger analogy would probably be the sense of frustration and bitterness, the self-criticisms and guilty introspection, the fatigue and depolitisation, that followed May '68. This inward turn - a displacement from politics to psychology and ethics - is marked not merely by the revival of the Calvinist meditation on original sin and the Fall, but very explicitly by the emphasis on personal, private salvation and the repudiation of millenarianism in Paradise Regained and the last two books of Paradise Lost.

All this strikes me as self-evident, as I've said, but at best it offers us a perspective in which we are tempted to substitute those old slogans of optimism or pessimism for some concrete reading of the text. In that sense, one cannot even propose an analysis of Paradise Lost in the tradition of the repentant ex- or post-revolutionary narrative, such as Mary Shelley's Frankenstein, which explicitly frames an allegory of Jacobin hybris and the dangers of summoning up that very Adamic and Miltonic monster, the mob or the people.[(4)] The political allegory of Frankenstein, however, is constructed within the now individualistic categories of the essentially expressive literature of the new bourgeois subject: it may well be possible to read Samson Agonistes in this fashion (but then, paradoxically, this reading play emits a far more militant and politicised signal than Paradise Regained!), but Paradise Lost is not yet a narrative of that later type, as we will see, and is unavailable or inaccessible to this kind of expressive or allegorical reading.

I propose then that we retrace our steps, and begin again with the seemingly more abstract problem of religion. But first an initial qualification: if you believe in the theory of modes of production, that is, if you are committed to the idea that capitalism is a qualitatively and structurally distinct type of social formation from the various other kinds that have preceded it upon the earth, then you will want to make room for the possibility that religion in its strong form in precapitalist societies is functionally and substantively distinct from what it is today, which is to say a mere private hobby and one ideological subcode among many others. In a presecular and prescientific world, one in which commerce is itself a limited and interstitial phenomenon, religion is the cultural dominant; it is the master-code in which issues are conceived and debated; it is then - religion, the sacred, the centred body of the despot, the centred space of the Forbidden City and the four cardinal points - the form taken by ideology in precapitalist societies, except that since ideology is a modern term and a modern phenomenon, there is something anachronistic and misleading about putting it this way.

But perhaps this point should also be made in existential terms. We are accustomed, whatever our own positions on the matter, to think of religion in terms of belief. But belief is a very privatised and subjective phenomenon. Rodney Needham once wrote an interesting little book[(5)] to show that the category of belief, as used by anthropologists in relationship to so-called primitive or culturally alien societies, was itself a category of Otherness: belief is always what somebody else 'believes', it is that peculiar and superstitious, quite incomprehensible thing that takes place inside an alien head. In our own society, it seems clear that belief in this privatised sense is an accompaniment of social fragmentation and atomisation, of anomie, of the construction of equivalent monads within the market system, each one of which is endowed with freedom to sell its labour power. Belief in that sense is thus a by-product of that very dissolution and destruction of the older organic social groups of which religion, in the older strong sense, was precisely the organising ideology and the cement. So we will find ourselves pursuing a mirage if we conceive of an earlier religious position, an object of theological debate, such as Milton's Arianism, in terms of a belief, a ghost in the machine, with which you could expect to empathise, much as you feel your way back into Proust's notion of temporality from the inside, or come at least to a suspension of disbelief about Yeats' 'vision'.

To conceive of a social formation for which subjectivity in this modern sense does not exist means, however, to attempt to grasp religion not as a private language or a unique incommunicable form of consciousness, but rather as the sign of group praxis and group membership, as a badge of collective adherence, as something like a set of pseudo-concepts whose concrete function is to organise this or that form of communal relationship and structure. I'm sorry to say so, but I'm afraid that here we still must come to terms with Durkheim's fundamental insight(6) into religion as the privileged mode in which a precapitalist collectivity comes to consciousness of itself and affirms its unity as a group. What follows however is a consequence that Durkheim did not draw, namely that religious and theological debate is the form, in precapitalist societies, in which groups become aware of their political differences and fight them out.

So we must learn to read theological discourse and discursive productions related to it, such as Milton's Christian epic, in terms of class struggle. But now I want to go further than this, and to draw another, perhaps more scandalous or at least paradoxical consequence from this view of religion: namely that if it is the master-code of precapitalist society, we ought to be able to read its major themes as mystified or distorted anticipations of secular and even scientific preoccupations which are ours today. Indeed, I want to see whether one can make a case for reading the terms and conceptual categories of Calvinism and heroic, militant protestantism, as distorted anticipations of the dialectic itself.

Such a thesis would be the reverse of Norman Cohn's notorious conclusion to The Pursuit of the Millenium when, speaking of the radical movements of the 1960's, he observes, 'The old religious idiom has been replaced by a secular one, and this tends to obscure what otherwise would be obvious. For it is the simple truth that, stripped of their original supernatural sanction, revolutionary millenarianism and mystical anarchism are still with us.'.(7) Cohn's operation here is to reduce the struggles and values of living people to so many forms of that culturally and psychologically pathological impulse his book purports to document: his strategy is thus ultimately of a piece with the old argument - generally produced as the final nail in the coffin - that Marxism is essentially just a religion.

But this is a two-edged sword, whose thrust it is important to reverse. To disclose the materialist and political kernel within the mystified forms of a protestant theology is surely to affirm our solidarity with the heroic and militant struggles of the past. These dead belong to us, as Ernst Bloch taught us about Thomas Munzter, as Christopher Hill and others have shown us about the Diggers and the Ranters. Indeed, if Bloch sought to convey one thing throughout his long career, it was that socialism and political action today will be a poor and impoverished thing if it is unwilling to affirm its deeper kinship with millenarianism, with radical Utopianism, with what Norman Cohn describes contemptuously as those 'fantasies of a final, exterminatory struggle against "the great ones" and of a perfect world from which self-seeking would be forever banished'.(8)

On the other hand, let's remember that we have spoken of distorted anticipations of historical materialism; and I stress this now to distance the approach I have in mind from the rather facile way in which a Lucien Goldmann found traces and anticipations of the dialectic in all the great writers and thinkers in history. Religion is not a cognitive but a figural mode, and any attempt to reappropriate it must include a meditation on the nature of figuration itself. 'Through a glass darkly', allegory, types, figures, iconoclasm, the letter rather than the spirit - all these expressions alert us to the essential ambiguity of a plane of expression that risks fixing the mind in external trappings, thereby generating the institutional necessity of a priesthood, of the guardians of interpretation, with their monopoly of meaning and of exegesis, who have alone the right to tell us what a given figure really means. That radical protestantism, however, was only too keenly aware of the dialectic of figuration it is perhaps superfluous to observe.

Figuration - the ambiguous situation in which a figural expression of a cognitive truth is still little more than a picture-thought or hieroglyphic degradation of that same truth - is thus the source of the limits and distortions which the religious or theological master-code imposes on its political content. Yet we must add that the political strength of religion is also intimately related to this very ambiguity. Max Weber thought of the charismatic and militant moment of heroic protestantism as something like a vanishing mediator between the older traditional societies in the process of ruthless disintegration, and the newer secular or desacralised world of capitalism and the market system. This mediatory role is enabled by figuration, on the one hand, in which an unstable suppression of the gap between base and superstructure becomes possible, as well as by the diachronic situation of the moment of radical religion, in which an older hegemonic theological code can provisionally be appropriated for an expression of far-reaching new social possibilities, like new wine poured in old bottles. The instability of this moment of religious activism is of course over and over dramatised by its cooling off into the apolitical quietism of movements like that of Quakerism. Yet this is the price paid for the momentary and transitional power of a religious figural politics to 'grip the masses' and to produce a vision in which praxis and social analysis, the possible future and the structure of the present conjuncture, lived experience and the class structure, are not yet disjoined.

But we have not yet specified the essential, namely how the religious categories of Calvinism can be said to overlap in any way with those of Marxism. Providence - as the absolute foreknowledge of history - is the most obvious place to begin, with its twin certainties of the secret justification of the most senseless events (generally those involving wanton or gratuitous human suffering) and of teleology. We are today, I think, much more keenly aware of everything that is unsatisfactory in the religious or providential attempt to justify the ways of God to men, than we are of what we must still share in this general view of history, and tend to be surprised when the more aggressive Christians continue to claim History as their own particular invention. We are for one thing deeply marked by the existential view of suffering, which Dostoyevsky dramatised in his cry that an eternity of bliss could never redeem an instant of suffering and pain inflicted on a small child. Nor does anyone today feel very comfortable with the old idea that suffering ennobles and is ultimately good for you. Yet the theologians were themselves keenly aware of such contradictions, which were registered virtually from the beginnings of Christian theory in the problem of whether God himself can be said to have willed evil.

Milton seems to have solved this problem to his own intellectual satisfaction in a disarming way: by separating God's will from God's foreknowledge. Knowing how a thing is going to turn out is quite a different matter from wanting it to turn out that way; God knows in advance what Adam will decide, what Eve will do, but that doesn't mean he likes it, nor does it mean that they were not free to do otherwise. Three observations need to be made about this solution, and the first has to do with the relations between freedom, temporal perspective and explanation. We don't seem to have any great difficulty in reconciling the two temporal perspectives on an act: the freedom of choice that precedes it, and the possibility of explanation that now weighs the completed act (including the reasons and the freedom of choice that went into its execution). Yet perhaps that is only because we don't pose the problem sharply enough to the point where it becomes revealed as an antimony, as an unthinkable paradox or aporia. Consider for instance Gide's little fable, Lafcadio's Adventures, which is about a man exasperated by the humiliation of having his acts judged and explained, most immediately by the behaviourists and the positivists, who see everything you do as being determined, but more generally in any kind of character judgement, in which other people say, Well of course he would have done that: he's that kind of person (spiteful, generous, indecisive, etc. - all judgements which reify you by making your character into a kind of determinism in its own right). So Lafcadio, in order to evade this reifying judgement and to remain free, invents a new kind of ethics, that of the famous gratuitous act or acte gratuit, the act that absolutely evades all ex post facto explanation. In the final irony of the novel, a stray button provides evidence that the murder which Lafcadio designed to embody this absolute gratuitousness is on the contrary susceptible of the most banal explanation and motivation possible, namely that of simple jealousy. Meanwhile, in the later Sartrean versions of this dilemma, the screw is given yet another turn by yet a final reifying judgement by other people: if such and such a character does this gratuitous and absolutely unmotivated thing, then the reason is obvious: it's to keep us guessing; in fact, it's quite in character and quite motivated, since the person in question is very precisely defined as capricious. These ethical fables to suggest that there may be something absolutely incommensurable between the temporal perspective of action, the choice and the project; and that of explanation, of meaning, of inevitability.

My other two observations will be briefer: on the one hand, it is clear that even Milton's category of foreknowledge still presupposes the organisational framework of an individual subject. We will return to this point in a moment. And the other point is related to this one, but is too complex for me to develop here at any length: it is this, that the ethical categories, the ethical binary of good and evil, to which the Providential vision is irredeemably shackled, are to my mind the ultimate form of all ideological closure, far more damaging and influential in the long run than either metaphysics or idealism, which have traditionally been the ways in which ideological false consciousness has been characterised. Nietzsche taught us, however, not merely that ethics is absolutely a projection of the positioning of the individual subject (what's good is what's related to my self, to the centre; what's evil is what is other, eccentric, marginalised), but also that all genuine historical and political thought must somehow do the impossible and invent an intellectual space for itself 'beyond good and evil', that is to say, beyond the categories of ethics.

Now I will say that, with these qualifications, the idea of Providence is the distorted anticipation, within the religious and figural master-code, of the idea of historical necessity and historical necessity in historical materialism. Yet this idea is fully as widely misconstrued and misunderstood as the other, and demands some explanation in its own right. The doctrine of historical inevitability is not, as Popper thought, a 'belief' of any kind, and certainly not a belief in the predictability of future events: to put it another way, it is not a teleology and has nothing to do with an eschatological certainty about the end of history. The function of this concept is a far more disappointingly modest and descriptive one, which we may characterise by saying that the notion of historical inevitability or historical necessity is simply the enabling presupposition of the historian herself, and governs the form with which historiography endows the events of the past, the things that have already happened once and for all. The concept of historical necessity is simply the assumption that things happened the way they did because they had to happen that way and no other, and that the business of the historian is to show why they had to happen that way. If you like, then, this is a pseudo-idea: it could have real meaning only if you were able somehow to repeat the past or replay the tape under controlled experimental or laboratory conditions. But of course the latter are themselves a fiction - the enabling presupposition of the natural sciences - and even this counter-factual alternative is therefore incoherent and rigorously meaningless. It may thus be preferable to describe the pseudo-idea of historical necessity or inevitability as something like a meaning-effect: the formal emotion, as the neo-Aristotelians might say, produced by great historiography, the generic satisfaction achieved by historical discourse as a form when it restructures the empirical randomness and chronicle-like sequence of apparently atomic facts, learned by rote out of history manuals, into a sequence that suddenly strikes us as being rigorous and inevitable. But those words are merely synonyms for meaningful; and vice versa: when we talk about meaning in history, we mean little more than inevitability and necessity.

But of course the problem with this secular version of historical necessity is the same problem - that of action - that arises with its religious variant: namely, what happens to human activity when people come to 'believe in' ideas like Providence or historical necessity. This is for one thing the dilemma of predestination: if God knows from all eternity that I am one of the elect, does that mean I can do anything I want to, no matter how unimaginably sinful? This is for another the dilemma of the antithesis between voluntarism and fatalism: if history is inevitable, if revolution depends on the ripening of objective conditions, then my own political praxis or lack of it would not seem to have much bearing on things.

But the Calvinist and the Leninist solutions to these dilemmas are perfectly sensible, provided you understand how profoundly Hegelian both of them are. For Hegel's is the only consequent way of formulating the problem, and for better or for worse we have got no further than his slogan: the owl of Minerva flies at dusk, historical necessity is visible only after the fact, the historical understanding - what Hegel calls Absolute Spirit - is only called into play on the Sunday of life, after action and praxis are over, when history for however brief a moment has come to a stop. Hegel's 'solution' is thus a thoroughgoing double standard, in which the past is necessary and its chain of events as inevitable as in any Providential scheme, but where this understanding of necessity has nothing whatsoever to do with the possibilities of action in the present. The Kairos is then Lenin in April: you can't know whether a thing was possible until it is tried; only after the fact does it transpire that what finally happened had to happen that way and no other.

All of which - these anticipatory relationships between Marxism's notion of historical inevitability and providential religion - may be taken as a gloss and commentary on Walter Benjamin's enigmatic opening image, in the Theses on the Philosophy of History, of the chess-playing automaton with the dwarf hidden inside it to guide its moves: 'The puppet called "historical materialism" is to win all the time. It can easily be a match for anyone if it enlists the services of theology, which today, as we know, is wizened and has to keep out of sight'.(9) The paradox here evidently turns on the sense of the expression 'to win'. Meanwhile, the Hegelian and retrospective character of historical knowledge is underscored in another image from this same text, perhaps the most famous of all, on Klee's Angelus Novus:

> 'His face is turned toward the past. Where we perceive a chain of events, he sees one single catastrophe which keeps piling wreckage upon wreckage and hurls it in front of his feet. The angel would like to stay, awaken the dead, and make whole what has been smashed. But a storm is blowing from Paradise; it has got caught in his wings with such violence that the angel can no longer close them. This storm irresistibly propels him into the future to which his back is turned, while the pile of debris before him grows skyward. This storm is what we call progress.' (10)

Such an image may serve to demonstrate a final proposition about the Hegelian/Marxist notion of historical inevitability which is perhaps less widely understood than anything else; namely that it is not a teleology (unless one could conceive of a teleology after the fact). Nobody today surely believes that anything is inevitable in that teleological sense, certainly not socialism or world revolution. This angel, or Absolute Spirit, cannot look over its shoulder into the future.

It is perhaps fitting to dramatise the paradoxes and the antinomies of such historical concepts by way of Benjamin's images: for this process brings us back to the second feature of our discussion of religion, namely the figural character of the theological master-code and the relationship between the latter's structural limits and cognitive distortions and the process of figuration itself, a term I happen to prefer to the current one of representation which is, I suppose, a general synonym for it. We've begun to suggest that it is in the precognitive aspects of the theological code, and the requirement for its contents to be expressed in essentially narrative categories, that the ultimate structural limits and distortions of the political consciousness of a religious and precapitalist period are to be sought. When we turn to the artistic and cultural expressions of such religious impulses, however, we confront the figural mode again, as it were to the second power. Is it possible that this second-degree process of figural articulation - the process of cultural production generally - may do more than simply replicate the first; indeed, that it may in some central way serve to foreground and to bring out the contradictions and structural limits of its primary theological raw material?

This is at least the theory proposed by Louis Althusser in his

Letter on Art and methodologically developed by Pierre Macherey in his now well-known book Towards a Theory of Literary Production: which it will now be useful to test against the case of Milton. The idea is that the act of figuration or representation does not merely illustrate, exemplify, or replicate its ideological - we may even say its ideational - content; rather it decisively transforms the latter, so that what looked initially like an idea or a concept, when taken in its purely ideological form (Macherey's central example is Jules Verne's 'idea' of progress), is unmasked as ideology when the artist attempts to give it full representation. The ideological, all the while claiming to project a coherent vision, is always contradictory, always structurally incoherent and ultimately unsusceptible of formal intelligibility. Thus, when ideology is taken at its word and endowed with the beginnings of a visionary, figural or representational form, the impossibility of that representation and the essential incoherence of the ideological itself becomes foregrounded and visible in its own right. This is indeed the very vocation of culture itself for Althusser and Macherey: not to transmit ideology, but rather to make ideology visible as an object, to demystify the ideological, not through conceptual analysis, but through the process of its production as figure and representation. Whatever the absolute value of this theory as a transhistorical description of culture generally, it would certainly seem to have some relevance for a text which explicitly sets out to celebrate, dramatise and justify a pre-existing ideology, namely that of Providence.

We should add, however, for those who may be uneasy about the projection of such sophisticated post-contemporary methods into the pre-capitalist past, that something analogous is surely known to the text itself; for the militant Protestants and radical reformers, indeed, representation is fully as suspect a process as it is for the Tel quel group or the Judaic and Islamic traditions. Still, the demands of representation and the epic require Milton to render God anthropomorphically as a character; or in other words, in our previous terminology, to articulate Providence and the whole theme of foreknowledge of the historical totality, within the confines of the individual subject, thus turning history back into a representation offered to that supreme individual consciousness, God; much as, quite against the spirit of his own system, the demands of Hegelian representation ending up forcing the latter towards that weaker anthropomorphic personification which is Absolute Spirit.

Parts of De Doctrina document Milton's sense of the way in which anthropomorphic representation distorts and reifies the theological content of the notions of God and Providence, which we have identified with History; but his Arianism will let us make this point in a more tangible way, and in the process illustrate what was meant earlier by the proposition that such theological issues are not matters of personal 'belief' but rather something quite different. In this case, I will suggest that Milton's Arianism - the repudiation of the Trinity and the emphasis on the created, secondary nature of Christ - is less a matter of opinion, heretical or not, but rather first and foremost a result of the requirements and dialectic of figuration. Milton senses that in endowing the place of historical necessity with something like an individual subjectivity, an anthropomorphic appearance, some fundamental ideological incoherence is betrayed: thus, the radical dissociation of the figure of Christ from God, the insistence on Christ's proper status as an actant, a narrative character - as distinct from this other seeming 'character' who is really not one at all, or should not be one - becomes an attempt to recontain the contradiction, to limit the ravages of demystification released by the representational process.

This reading now allows us to reformulate the positions of William Empson's splendid and passionate book, Milton's God, in a more theoretically adequate way. Leaving aside Empson's admirable eighteenth century Enlightenment hatred of religion and superstition - which, as I observed initially, is probably not the most productive position for people on the Left to take today - what is unsatisfactory about Milton's God is the retention of a framework in which the organising perspective remains the biographical Milton, as author and individual subject, with his opinions, flaws, weaknesses and strengths and the like. Surely Empson's detailed account of the tricks and stratagems whereby Milton's God arranges both for Satan and for his human creations to fall, in order to fulfill his original plan; and his characterisation of the inhuman and sacrificial bloodthirstiness of this deity - these things are quite unanswerable: only we would now prefer to take them, less as testimony about Milton's theological beliefs, than as a demonstration of the way in which the requirement to give anthropomorphic figuration to the ideology of Providence ends up denouncing itself, and undermining the very ideology it set out to embody. Yet this is an objective and impersonal, what would today be called a textual, process: by a kind of ruse of reason, Milton's symbolic act is alienated from itself, turns against itself, ends up producing the opposite of what it originally intended. But if this is an accurate description of what happens to ideology in the text, then it may well be a source of embarrassment to the older strategies for political interpretation, whose aim was to enlist the great writer on your side as an individual subject, and to stress the progressive or humanistic characteristics of Shakespeare, Balzac, and most recently of Milton himself, in Christopher Hill's great biography.

On the other hand, it must be admitted that the comments we have made so far on Milton's ideology are not terribly political yet either. Perhaps turning our attention from God to Satan will help us make some further progress along these lines. On the face of it, indeed, it would seem a priori quite unavoidable, in the revolutionary situation in which Milton wrote, for Satan's rebellion against God not to give off at least faint overtones of the great Rebellion itself, of the militant revolt against a king by divine right; and this, even if we exclude that other predictable psychological reaction which would involve collective guilt and trauma at that historically unique act which is the public execution of a monarch.

Oddly enough, none of this seems to be present in the text, and the current view of Satan as a great feudal baron seems to stand up well to careful reading: the revolt of a peer has in fact little enough in common with the dynamics of middle class revolution but a great deal with the convulsions of medieval feudalism or with that anachronistic contemporary event, the Fronde. Thus, the War in Heaven, the prehistory of the Creation before Eden, oddly inscribes a peculiar and anachronistic diachrony within the first great monument of bourgeois literature - a reminiscence of the distant feudal past that would seem to have little enough relevance to war aims of the New Model Army or the visions of the radical reformation.

Still, I think we can locate the place in which the contemporary reference is repressed: and its structural absence, the irritatingly protestant self-righteousness and complacency of that repression, is not unrelated to the figure of Satan, yet in a rather different way than we might have expected. Milton's party need feel no guilt about the revolt against the king for a simple reason, that he is not really a king at all, but something quite different, namely a tyrant: and the latter is defined as himself being a rebel against God's law. Thus, not the regicides, but the king himself is the rebel, occupies the place of Satan: the thrust of the accusation is structurally reversed - I banish you! you are the only guilty party here!

But note that the structural displacement achieved by the political unconscious at this crucial point succeeds in eliding something significant: there is henceforth, in this particular narrative apparatus, no longer any place for the army of the saints themselves, for that particular emergent subject of history which is the very protagonist of the bourgeois revolution. There are now two separate strategies for overcoming the tyrant, for triumphing over Satan-Charles, but neither makes a place for a collective actor, and only the first is properly political at all. That is of course secured by God himself before the creation of humankind: and the fall of Satan-Charles - the end of the feudal age - with that archaic reminiscence of feudal warfare on which we have already commented - thus comes before us less as class praxis than as what we might today call a systemic transformation, a break between two modes of production, a virtually structural _coupure_: one should perhaps summon up a little of E. P. Thompson's indignation with Althusserian structural history in order to deplore this elision of collective praxis and action from the Miltonic narrative.

As for the second method of routing Satan - of exorcising what Winstanley will call 'kingly power', the sinfulness on which Tyranny breeds - that belongs of course to the quietistic and anti-political turn of the post-revolutionary period, to the business of a merely personal and private salvation. 'Dream not of their fight/As of a duel' (XII, 386-387), Michael warns Adam about the struggle between Christ and Satan in the course of purely earthly history: millenarianism is over and bankrupt;

after the end of ideology and the end of Utopia, all political, properly revolutionary aims are suspect - and the last two books of Paradise Lost open up that privatised and post-political world, to whose disillusionments the mediocrity of Paradise Regained is immediately attributable, with its characteristic failure of hope following upon the failure of revolution, as most recently in the aftermath of May '68.

Still, in between these two moments we have the Garden, and here, if anywhere surely, the political content of Paradise Lost is to be sought. It is no secret, if still mildly paradoxical and unaccountable in a Puritan writer, that Milton is the great poet of sex of the English language. We may today reread with a certain pity, if not contempt, T. S. Eliot's once influential remarks about the Miltonic 'Garden of Eden, where I for one can get pleasure from the verse only by the deliberate effort not to visualize Adam and Eve in their surroundings':(11) an effort, one would have thought, a good deal more puritanical than anything in Milton himself. Still, the ideological signal emitted by this prelapsarian Eden is structurally and strategically ambiguous. That great estrangement effect, which by the unimaginable fiction of emergence

> 'As new awaked from soundest sleep
> Soft on the flowery herb I found me laid
> In balmy sweat' (VIII, 253-255)

causes us to perceive the now fallen world again as for the first time, transfigured - this estrangement effect will also serve to reinforce the very opposite of a revolutionary and millenarian materialism, and will at one and the same time be evoked to document the classic anti-millenarian position that goes back to Saint Augustine, where it is very precisely the fact of the Garden and the fact of the Fall that preclude the re-establishment on Earth of paradise in anything but an internal, allegorical sense. The vision of the Garden of Eden thus in one of the classic semiotic functions of ideology emits two distinct and contradictory messages all at once: that a carnal heaven on earth is imaginable and thus to be sought for here and now by means which in Milton's time have become irredeemably political ones (the Hussites, the Anabaptists, the Diggers), but also that it is impossible in this life and that only renunciation and personal repentance and self-discipline remain for us.

Yet there is another aspect of the representation of Adam that has, if not political, then at least historical resonance in another sense and that deserves brief attention. We've shown how the moment of feudalism is inscribed in this text; but we have not yet determined whether the latter is open enough to history in some way to register the momentous systemic transformation with which Milton's own society is convulsed; and if so, how and in what fashion this diachronic Novum is seismographically recorded. For myself, I cannot help feeling that nothing in Paradise Lost is quite so electrifying as that instant in which Satan, struggling laboriously against the downdrafts of Chaos, suddenly glimpses a modification in the order of Creation as he knew it before his fall, a minute yet perceptible shift in the very spatial relations of that older universe he took to be eternal. 'Strange alteration!' Meanwhile, the very impact of the new itself and the inhabitual has been prepared and underscored in this passage by an otherwise gratuitous foreshadowing of yet another miraculous emergence, which will not find its official representation until Book 10: the construction by Sin and Death of their great causeway from hell gate. Why anticipate that here, except to link the force of these two instants in which, ex nihilo, something quite inconceivable in the previous system suddenly springs into being, modifying the latter beyond all recognition and creating a wholly unforeseeable system of new relationships that never existed before?

'But now at last the sacred influence
Of light appears, and from the walls of Heaven
Shoots far into the bosom of dim Night
A glimmering dawn; here Nature first begins
Her farthest verge, and Chaos to retire
As from her outmost works a broken foe,
With tumult less and with less hostile din,
That Satan with less toil, and now with ease
Wafts on the calmer wave by dubious light,
And like a weather-beaten vessel holds
Gladly the port, though shrouds and tackle torn;
Or in the emptier waste, resembling air,
Weighs his spread wings, at leasure to behold
Far off the empyreal Heaven, extended wide
In circuit, undetermined square or round,
With opal towers, and battlements adorned
Of living sapphire, once his native seat;
And fast by hanging in a golden chain
This pendent world, in bigness as a star

> Of smallest magnitude close by the moon.
> Thither, full fraught with mischievous revenge,
> Accurst, and in a cursed hour, he hies.' (II, 1034-1055)

Alongside the feudal world of God and his court, of Satan and his host, Adam is clearly of another species - the commoner, the first bourgeois, that extraordinary mutation which is middle-class man, destined as we know today to be fruitful and multiply, and to inherit the earth. In that case, that unexpectedly new space of our 'pendent world' and Eden itself, resembling heaven, yet unique and utterly unlike anything that has hitherto existed, springing up 'in the interstices' of that older Creation 'like the Gods of Epicurus in the intermundia or the Jews in the pores of Polish society', marks out the structural place for that equally unforeseen historical emergence which is the market system and capitalism itself. (And if we had time, we might gloss the dual perspective on Nature - before/after, unfallen/fallen - as a reflection of the way in which each closed system, each new mode of production, comes into being complete with its own spurious temporality, its own nostalgic projection of an idyllic past proper to it).

The result is that - thus registering the diachronic event of this great transformation, or transition from one mode of production to another - Milton's poem is historical, even though as we have just seen it fails to be political: let's see if by way of concluding we can find anything to account for this uneven development in the poem's levels. It seems appropriate to approach the problem by way of Milton's own theory of levels or instances, as he outlines it in the <u>Second Defense of the English People</u>: 'I perceived that there are three main kinds of liberty essential to a satisfying mode of life: religious, domestic or private, and civil'.(12) Social life is then here mapped as a concentricity of the three instances of the political or state power; the religious or church organisation; and the domestic or the family. We must first observe that in the secular world in which we live today, we recognise only two of these levels: the public and the private, the political and the personal, the objective and the subjective - that great and incommensurable fissure that cuts across everything in our experience and maims the lives of modern people. It is appropriate, then, to observe that this experiential double standard in modern life presupposes the eclipse of precisely that 'vanishing mediator' which is the religious instance; and this may well lead us to some final thoughts on the relationship between religion and politics. For Milton's formula shows that in his society the religious community serves as a concrete mediation between the public and the private and as a space in which problems of institutions and power meet problems of personal relationships and ethics or private life.

Indeed, we have omitted something from our evocation of the kinship between Marxism and religion which must be rectified at this point: it is the way in which all the issues that turn around church organisation and the community of the faithful constitute a point-by-point anticipation of all the most vital problems of political organisation in our own time: problems of the party, of class solidarity, of the soviets, of communes, of democratic centralism, of council communism, of small group politics, of the relations of intellectuals to the people, of discipline, of bureaucracy - all these crucial issues which are still so very much with us are those most centrally at stake in the great debates of the reformation and of the English cultural revolution. The problem of community - bound for us, for better or for worse, to its concrete expression in the institution of the political party - was for them linked to its concrete or allegorical expression in the notion of a church or congregation or community of the faithful; and the excitement and actuality of the English cultural revolution as it unfolds from 1642 to 1660 is surely at one with this burning preoccupation with the nature of collective life.

So what is astonishing about Paradise Lost is the utter silence and absence of all these great themes of church and collectivity. The narrative moves at once from the family - with its great evocation of married love and sexuality - to the fallen privatised world of individual belief and individual salvation; nor are the other collectives glimpsed in its course - Satan's host or God's - 'gathered' communities of this type, but rather as we've said feudal castes. Milton's text thus anticipates the social impoverishment of the modern world, and as a narrative confronts the formal dilemma of relating the henceforth sundered and distant levels of the political and the domestic.

These meet on the occasion of the fall and of the temptation: only we know that for Milton the content of the occasion is absolutely insignificant - the tree itself, the apple, are little more than pretexts about which Satan himself will make a contemptuous joke. The real issue as we know is obedience itself, the other face of hierarchy, the only theme which permits a homology to be established between Satan's fall and that of Adam and Eve. Indeed, our historical reading suggested that from the perspective of modes of production, these two narratives - the one a feudal revolt, the other the privatisation and monadisation inherent in the development of a capitalist market system - are quite heterogeneous and unrelated. It therefore becomes interesting and strategic to examine the motif of disobedience, and, following our earlier method, to see what the process of figuration or representation foregrounds about this particular component of the ideology of social hierarchy.

As far as Eve's disobedience is concerned, the poem is formal, and her motivation has nothing in common with that feminine vanity which C. S. Lewis complacently attributed to Adam's 'lesser half':

> 'so to add what wants
> In female sex, the more to draw his love,
> And render me more equal, and perhaps,
> A thing not undesirable, sometime
> Superior: for inferior who is free?' (IX, 821-825)

This final touch - the 'sometime superior' - is surely the classic inscription of Milton's own sexual anxiety: the devouring woman, Mary Powell, the Delilah from whom all masculine miseries spring. But when one recalls the more amusing features of the narrative's sexism - and in particular the bourgeois interior scene of Books V-VIII, where Eve, having served the men, Adam and the angel Raphael, leaves them alone to pursue their scientific discussion,

> 'not as not with such discourse
> Delighted, or not capable her ear
> Of what was high: such pleasure she reserved,
> Adam relating, she sole auditress -' (VIII, 48-51)

the amphetamine-type stimulation of the apple suggests a chance for Eve to speak and to converse with Adam as an equal. At any rate the marks of Milton's sexism here and throughout are too obvious and too embarrassing ('for well I understand in the prime end/Of Nature her the inferior', etc., VIII, 540-541) to document at any great length. Meanwhile, the poet's courageous defence of divorce has often been celebrated as a progressive position and a contribution to the struggle for social freedom; is it ungrateful to suggest something Islamic in this conception of a democratic community of males who are free to repudiate their wives? In any case, the limits of Milton's politics - that protestant conservatism and commitment to hierarchy and elite authority which cuts him off from the greater radicalism of his time - is surely profoundly at one with his sexual politics and his belief in the inequality of the sexes. I would only want to resist establishing causal priorities between these two dimensions of the personal and the political, and reconfirming their separation by encouraging the temptation to show that class attitudes condition Milton's sexual politics, or on the other hand that patriarchal values end up programming his public positions in the political field.

Yet as I argued earlier, these personal biases and ideological opinions of the biographical individual John Milton are not really what is at stake here; the point was rather to show that the poem itself inscribes this insight, and faithfully demystifies its own initial raw material (among the latter Milton's private attitudes), designating the latter as ideology and reversing its messages. The official ideological message, the conscious intent, of the poem was the defence and justification of the position that sin, the fallen world, the failure of revolutionary politics, all result ultimately from disobedience, from lack of discipline, from insufficient respect for hierarchy. Yet in the second-degree constructivist reading we have proposed this sequence is reversed, and the poetic narrative rather offers testimony of the constitutive relationship between this image of sin and of the fall and the failure to imagine genuine human equality. Eve has to fall, not because she is sinful or disobedient, but because Milton cannot find it in himself to imagine and to give figuration to an equality between the sexes that would open up into a concrete vision of the community of free people. The poem thus illustrates and documents, not a proposition about human nature, not a type of philosophical or theological content, but rather the operation of ideological closure: in this way, a poem in which as we have said the political is repressed nonetheless ends up producing a political reading of itself.

Footnotes

1. Fred Halliday, 'Theses on the Iranian Revolution', Race and Class, XXI, 1 (Summer, 1979), p.90.

2. Ervand Abrahamian, 'The Guerrilla Movement in Iran, 1963-1977', MERIP Reports, No.86 (March-April, 1980), p.3.

3. Christopher Hill, The World Turned Upside Down (Harmondsworth: Penguin, 1975), pp.345, 360.

4. 'But Paradise Lost excited different and far deeper emotions. I read it, as I had read the other volumes which had fallen into my hands, as a true history. It moved every feeling of wonder and awe, that the picture of an omnipotent God warring with his creatures was capable of exciting. I often referred the several situations, as their similarity struck me, to my own. Like Adam, I was created apparently united by no link to any other being in existence; but his state was far different from mine in every other respect ... Many times I considered Satan as the fitter emblem of my condition ...'. Mary Shelley, Frankenstein (Indianapolis: Bobbs-Merrill, 1974), p.125.

5. Belief, Language and Experience (Chicago: University of Chicago Press, 1972).

6. In The Elementary Forms of Religious Life.

7. Norman Cohn, The Pursuit of the Millenium (New York: Oxford, 1970), p.286.

8. Ibid, p.286.

9. Walter Benjamin, Illuminations (New York: Schocken, 1969), p.253.

10. Ibid, pp.257-258.

11. 'A Note on the Verse of John Milton', in Louis Martz, ed., Milton (Englewood Cliffs: Prentice-Hall, 1966), p.16.

12. John Milton, Complete Poems and Major Prose, ed. M. Y. Hughes (Indianapolis: Bobbs-Merrill, 1957), pp.830-831.

The British Pirandello Society (founded 1980)

PATRON: HAROLD PINTER

Announcement of Publication

THE YEARBOOK OF THE BRITISH PIRANDELLO SOCIETY no.1 (1981)

Editor: Jennifer Stone (Essex University); Editorial Committee: Felicity Firth (Bristol University), Jennifer Lorch and Susan Bassnett-McGuire (Warwick University); Editorial Consultants: Richard Cave and Anna Laura Lepschy (London University).

CONTENTS of YBPS 1 include: A.L. LEPSCHY on the actor in Pirandello/ Clive BARKER on English productions/ J. LORCH: an interview with Philip STONE, Pirandellian actor/ J. STONE on Susan SONTAG's feminist production of *As You Desire Me*/ Paolo PUPPA: a marxist analysis of *Sagra del Signore della Nave*/ Bruce MERRY: a structuralist analysis of two novelle/ Gray STANDEN on the transformation of a novella into a play;

PLUS
REVIEWS of new books on Pirandello by DOMBROSKI/LAURETTA & RAGUSA;

PLUS
PHOTOGRAPHS from recent productions/ INFORMATION of recent publications and productions/ REPORTS on the conferences at AGRIGENTO and BRISTOL.

ORDER YOUR COPY from F. Firth, Dept. of Italian, University of Bristol, Bristol BS8 1US. (Cheques should be made payable to The British Pirandello Society.)

COST: £2.95 plus 20p postage 115 pp. + illus.
ISBN 0-907564-00-3 ISSN 0260-9215

FEATURES planned for future issues include: F. FIRTH on *L'esclusa*/ E. JERONIMIDIS on Pirandello, 'L'umorismo', and FREUD/ Barbara REYNOLDS on Pirandello and THORNTON WILDER/ Peter RINK on Pirandello and GOLDONI/ An interview with Pirandello by OURANIS in 1934, translated from Greek/ An interview with John LINSTRUM/ BBC productions of Pirandello.

PLUS
REVIEWS of new books by BORSELLINO/ DEL MINISTRO/ BASSNETT-McGUIRE/ PUPPA/ plus REPORTS and a BIBLIOGRAPHICAL ENTRY.

The YEARBOOK is published by The BRITISH PIRANDELLO SOCIETY which was founded in Bristol in 1980, with two objects: the documentation of all Pirandello activity in Britain, both academic and theatrical, and the provision of an opportunity to those interested in Pirandello to meet for talks, plays and discussion. (A scheme is also in progress to produce new English translations of Pirandello's works.) The Society's intention is to attract people working in different spheres: theatregoers, actors, translators, students, scholars and critics.

SUBSCRIPTIONS & MEMBERSHIP: membership entitles you to an invitation to attend the yearly British conference, to receive news items and details of the Agrigento conference, and to consult the resources of the Society. (The Yearbook is included.)

£5.00 (£3.00 for students) Overseas incl. postage: $10.00 (U.S.)

SUBSCRIPTIONS & MANUSCRIPTS: send to F. Firth, Dept. of Italian, University of Bristol, Bristol BS8 1US. (Cheques should be made payable to the British Pirandello Society.)